Winners in Peace

Winners in Peace

*MacArthur, Yoshida, and
Postwar Japan*

Richard B. Finn

UNIVERSITY OF CALIFORNIA PRESS
Berkeley · Los Angeles · London

Calligraphy by Cecil Uyehara.

University of California Press
Berkeley and Los Angeles, California

University of California Press, Ltd.
London, England

© 1992 by
The Regents of the University of California

Library of Congress Cataloging-in-Publication Data

Finn, Richard B.
    Winners in peace : MacArthur, Yoshida, and postwar Japan / Richard
B. Finn.
        p.   cm.
    Includes bibliographical references (p.   ) and index.
    ISBN 0-520-06909 (cloth: alk. paper). – ISBN 0-520-20213-9 (pbk.: alk. paper)
    1. Japan—History—Allied occupation, 1945–1952.
2. MacArthur, Douglas, 1880–1964.   3. Yoshida, Shigeru,
1878–1967.   I. Title.
DS889.16.F56   1991
952.04—dc20 .   90-11275
                                                                   CIP

Printed in the United States of America
1 2 3 4 5 6 7 8 9

The paper used in this publication meets the minimum requirements of American
National Standard for Information Sciences—Permanence of Paper for Printed Library
Materials, ANSI Z39.48-1984. ♾

" . . . peace hath her victories
no less renownd than warr"

John Milton
Sonnet to the
Lord Generall Cromwell
May 1652

Contents

List of Illustrations   xi
List of Abbreviations   xiii
Introduction   xvii

Part I. Enemies Face to Face   1

1. Tense Beginnings   5
2. First Encounters   14
3. Planning and Organizing the Occupation   28

Part II. MacArthur's Two Hundred Days   43

4. The First Wave of Reform   47
5. The Allies: Their Role and Reparations   66
6. War Crimes and Punishment by Purge   75
7. The New Constitution   89

Part III. Japan's Search for Stability   105

8. The Emergence of Yoshida Shigeru   107
9. The Second Reform Wave   123

10. The 1947 Labor Crisis and the Defeat of
    Yoshida   136
11. MacArthur, the Allies, and Washington   151
12. The Failure of Coalition Politics   163
13. The End of the War Crimes Trials: The
    Emperor Decides Not to Abdicate   179

Part IV. New Policies and New Directions   191

14. Washington Intervenes: Draper and Kennan   195
15. New Life in Tokyo: Yoshida and Dodge   210
16. Unrest and Violence on the Left   228

Part V. Peace Settlement   241

17. The Search for Peace   245
18. The Korean War   258
19. Shaping the Peace Settlement   270
20. The Firing of MacArthur   286
21. Signing the Treaties and Ending the
    Occupation   293

Part VI. Aftermath   313

Appendixes

  A. Chronology of Main Events   317
  B. List of Principal Actors   322

Notes   325
Bibliography   375
List of Interviews   397
Index   401

To Dallas

Illustrations

(Illustrations follow page 209)
1. Autographed photograph of General Douglas MacArthur and Emperor Hirohito at their first meeting
2. Aerial photograph of Hiroshima, December 22, 1945
3. MacArthur relaxing
4. MacArthur greeting John Foster Dulles on his first trip to Japan
5. Dulles, Ambassador W. J. Sebald, and Prime Minister Yoshida
6. Yoshida signing the peace treaty, as his Japanese co-signers look on
7. Yoshida signing the security treaty
8. Yoshida's calligraphy
9. MacArthur and Yoshida—two old friends
10. Yoshida in retirement

Abbreviations

ACJ	Allied Council for Japan (Allies)
ANZUS	Australia–New Zealand–United States
BCOF	British Commonwealth Occupation Force
CIA	Central Intelligence Agency
CIE	Civil Information and Education Section (SCAP)
CINC	commander in chief
CINCAFPAC	commander in chief, Army Force Pacific
CINCFE	commander in chief, Far East
CIS	Civil Intelligence Section (SCAP)
CIU	Congress of Industrial Unions (Sambetsu Kaigi)
CLKL	Kades letter of Jan. 18, 1987, to author
CLM	Canadian Liaison Mission (Tokyo)
CLO	Central Liaison Office (Japan)
COS	chief of staff (SCAP and FEC)
DA	Department of the Army
desp.	despatch
DCOS	deputy chief of staff

DOS	Department of State
DOSB	*Department of State Bulletin*
DS	Diplomatic Section (SCAP)
EROA	Economic Rehabilitation of Occupied Areas (United States)
ESB	Economic Stabilization Board (Japan)
ESP	economic stabilization program
ESS	Economic and Scientific Section (SCAP)
FDR	Franklin D. Roosevelt
FEAC	Far Eastern Advisory Commission (Allies)
FEC	Far Eastern Commission (Allies)
FEC	Far East Command (U.S. military)
FO	Foreign Office
FRUS	*Foreign Relations of the United States*
FY	fiscal year
G-2	Intelligence Section (GHQ)
GARIOA	Government and Relief in Occupied Areas (United States)
GHQ	General Headquarters
GPO	Government Printing Office, Washington, D. C. (United States)
GS	Government Section (SCAP)
HCLC	Holding Company Liquidation Commission (Japan)
HSTL	Harry S Truman Library, Independence, Missouri
ICFTU	International Confederation of Free Trade Unions
IMTFE	International Military Tribunal for the Far East
Int.	interview
IRAA	Imperial Rule Assistance Association
JCP	Japan Communist Party
JCS	Joint Chiefs of Staff (U.S. military)

JERC	Japanese Educational Reform Council
JFL	Japan Federation of Labor (Nihon Rōdō Kumiai Sōdōmei)
JNR	Japan National Railways
JSP	Japan Socialist Party
JWC	Justin Williams Collection, McKeldin Library, University of Maryland, College Park, Maryland
KJ	*Kaisō jūnen* (Memories of ten years), by Yoshida Shigeru
ltr(s).	letter(s)
MITI	Ministry of International Trade and Industry
MMA	MacArthur Memorial Archives, Norfolk, Virginia
MP	military police (U.S. military)
NAC	National Advisory Council (United States)
NATO	North Atlantic Treaty Organization
NDLT	National Diet Library, Tokyo
NL	Nimitz Library, U.S. Naval Academy, Annapolis, Maryland
NPR	National Police Reserve (Japan)
NPSL	National Public Service Law (Japan)
NRAS	National Records/Archives, Suitland, Maryland
NRAW	National Records/Archives, Washington, D.C.
NSC	National Security Council (United States)
NYT	*New York Times*
POLAD	political adviser (SCAP)
PPS	policy planning staff (United States)
PRC	People's Republic of China
PRJ	*The Political Reorientation of Japan* (United States)
RFB	Reconstruction Finance Bank
RG	Record Group

RLED	Robert L. Eichelberger Diary, Perkins Library, Duke University, Durham, North Carolina
ROC	Republic of China (Taiwan)
ROK	Republic of Korea (South Korea)
SANACC	State-Army-Navy-Air Coordinating Committee (United States)
SCAP	supreme commander for the Allied powers
SCAPIN	SCAP instruction
SD	*Sebald Diary*, U.S. Naval Academy, Nimitz Library, Annapolis, Maryland
Shōden	Shōwa Denkō Company
SWNCC	State-War-Navy Coordinating Committee (United States)
tel(s).	telegram(s)
TIAS	*U.S. Treaties and Other International Agreements*
UKLM	United Kingdom Liaison Mission
USMCR	United States Marine Corps Reserve
YM	*Yoshida Memoirs*

Introduction

I spent five years in Japan during the American occupation. I went there first in October 1945, one month after Japan's surrender, as a naval officer specializing in the Japanese language and spent three months with a team investigating war damage. I returned in 1947 as a fledgling diplomat in the U.S. Foreign Service. My role was modest, handling legal and diplomatic matters in what we called "MacArthur's State Department," the Diplomatic Section of SCAP, the headquarters of the supreme commander for the Allied powers. I had the opportunity to see much of the country and take part in some of the discussions and planning that led to the San Francisco peace settlement of 1951.

By the time I returned to Washington in 1954, most of the war damage I had seen in Japan in 1945 had been repaired. The terrible shortages in the big cities of food, housing, and jobs had been greatly alleviated. The Japanese were struggling to get their living standard and industrial production back up to prewar levels. Nevertheless, despite the economic boost provided by the Korean War, most Americans thought Japan had little hope of developing a self-supporting economy and would probably require huge amounts of foreign assistance for years to come. They also had little doubt that the new constitution imposed by SCAP in 1946 would be quickly revised and that many of the political and economic changes instituted during the occupation would be overturned.

Fifteen years later, in 1969, after diplomatic assignments in other parts of the world, I became director of Japanese affairs in the State Department. My main task was to orchestrate the planning of the agencies in Washington for the return of Okinawa to Japanese control, an act that many Japanese and Americans considered the final step in winding up the war between our two countries. By that time we who had been so gloomy about Japan's future could see how wrong we had been. Our economic forecasts were farthest from the mark but not much worse than our predictions of political reaction. The London *Economist*, in an eye-opening report in 1962, had been among the first to tell the world about Japan's stunning rise as an economic power.[1] Soon people began to worry that Japan was too strong.

I have thought a lot in recent years about Japan's remarkable transformation and have read many explanations of how it came about. To me several aspects of the occupation have seemed particularly worth exploring. The role of the Japanese, especially of their leaders in government and business and above all of Yoshida Shigeru, who was prime minister for two-thirds of the occupation, has not received much attention in this country. In Japan, Yoshida has gradually risen from obscurity and taken on luster as a leader who stood up to General Douglas MacArthur, the supreme Allied commander, and was able to mitigate the harsher features of the occupation and pave the way for a favorable peace settlement. Yoshida is now generally considered Japan's outstanding prime minister of the postwar era,[2] although he has his detractors, as does MacArthur.

The general was, of course, the star actor in the occupation drama. But his deeds in Japan have been exaggerated by many including himself, distorted by the cult of personality he helped create, and diminished by his debacle in the Korean War. He is no longer seen as a figure of heroic proportions. Yet his role in Japan and his relationship with Yoshida, a kind of partnership between a senior and a junior, merit closer study. Yoshida was much more than a passive recipient of occupation orders. He acted as a filter through which important policies and orders passed, on occasion he offered advice about how problems should be handled, and he managed key government operations designed to carry out SCAP directives.

The two men had some important characteristics in common. When the occupation began, both were in their midsixties. Both had taken part in the rise of their countries to world influence early in the century. Both were elitist and fiercely independent. Both were considered by many of their contemporaries to be arrogant and highly conservative in their political outlook. Both were called on during the occupation to take actions they found distasteful. Both were firm supporters of Japan's imperial institution. MacArthur believed strongly in a powerful world role for the United States. Yoshida, who was once described as having "the outlook of imperial Japan," never wavered in the conviction that his country had an important part to play.[3]

Someone once compared Yoshida to Winston Churchill, and Yoshida replied, "Yes, but made in Japan."[4] Like the British wartime leader, Yoshida did not see it as his duty to preside over the wholesale liquidation of Japanese institutions and society. He did not hide his view that many actions by the occupation were "excessive." And like the postwar leader of West Germany, Konrad Adenauer, he acquired skill in blunting the blows of the occupiers.

The United States and Japan had been fierce rivals for a generation and bitter enemies during four years of war. Japan suffered enormous damage and America very little. In 1945 the United States was the most powerful nation on earth, and Japan was one of the weakest. The United States was less than two hundred years old, confident of its power and the strength of its open society and democratic institutions. Japan was more than fifteen hundred years old, a hierarchical society that had been isolated for centuries and that lacked much knowledge of the outside world even after two generations of rapid modernization. Defeat had shaken the morale of its people and undermined their sense of national purpose.

In the aftermath of the war, it became the task of Japanese and Americans to compose the profound differences in culture and outlook that separated their two countries and to build out of the carnage of war a new and enduring relationship. The occupation was one of the rare occasions in history when a modern industrial state had virtually unchallenged power to direct the destiny of another major modern state for a lengthy period, in this case eighty months. An American authority has said, "The Allied Occupation of Japan was perhaps the single most exhaustively planned operation of massive and externally directed change in world history."[5] How the two nations went about this, and how they were able to turn a Pacific rivalry into a Pacific friendship, is the basic story that needs to be told about the occupation.

A huge literature already exists on virtually all facets of that six and one-half year period of U.S. control. Yet very few books, either in English or in Japanese, have studied it from start to finish. Few have looked at all aspects of the occupation. I have tried to examine the important sources of information. I have talked to nearly one hundred persons who participated in or were close observers of the occupation. I have also familiarized myself with what writers in both countries have had to say about it. Although MacArthur's star burns less brightly than before, most Americans see the results of the occupation as almost exclusively the product of American initiatives and efforts. Japanese scholars, in their intensive research on the occupation, have been able to uncover a number of areas in which Japanese made valuable contributions to occupation reforms and even "Japanized" some of the changes made by Americans, as in drawing up the constitution. Relatively little attention is given by Americans or Japanese to the punitive aspect of the occupation, such as the war crimes trials or the "purges" of officials and business leaders; Japanese generally admit to some brutal actions during the war but see the atomic bomb as equally barbarous.

Agreement is widespread that the goals of both countries shifted during the occupation. But there is no consensus on the causes or extent of this change. That Japan's recovery became an American goal of equal prominence with reform is generally accepted. But one school of observers goes farther and sees U.S. policy as taking a "reverse course" halfway through the occupation; the term has no agreed meaning, but one formulation calls it "the shift of occupation priorities from democratization of a former enemy to reconstruction of a future cold-war ally."[6] Some adherents to this school see the reverse course as a precursor of the policies that led some years later to U.S. involvement in Vietnam.

That the cold war was a factor in the U.S. decision to help rebuild Japan is undeniable. Reconstruction was, of course, something all Japanese wanted. It is likewise undeniable that from an American point of view, world conditions were rapidly deteriorating in the late 1940s, as exemplified by Mao Zedong's victories in China and the Soviet blockade of Berlin; the Allied nations virtually terminated their occupation of western Germany in 1949, and it was only natural to expect significant shifts of U.S. policy toward Japan. In MacArthur's view the reform program was virtually completed by 1948. Japanese attitudes were also changing at the same time. The Japanese had had enough reform and tinkering with their institutions and sought refuge in a conservative government that promised more stability and economic improvement.

The Japanese press was the first to write about reverse course. This happened just before the occupation ended in 1952, when the press criticized the government for talking about modifying some of the occupation reforms. Debates like this had gone on in Japan for years. Even before World War II some writers claimed that Japan was dominated by "feudal survivals," like the imperial system, while others asserted the country had sufficiently reformed these old-fashioned institutions to be on the way to "modernization." After World War II one camp said feudal and nationalist influences were "rooted" in Japan, while others claimed Japan's militarist plunge in the 1930s was merely a kind of historical discontinuity or "stumble" that had enabled the nationalists to seize power and lead the nation to war. More recently, a few critics have argued that a clique of bureaucrats, politicians, and business leaders have been able to manipulate the political "system" to their advantage.

While noting these interpretations, I have tried to write a book that is accurate in its description of events and balanced in its judgments, so that those reading it will see how Americans and Japanese worked together and how close they came, despite the inevitable shifts and changes over a six and one-half year period, to bringing about a liberal democracy and a self-supporting economy in Japan. And the paradox will be evident that two men who had a relatively narrow concept of democracy and a considerable attachment to traditional values nevertheless played key roles in overseeing this effort. They were carried along by forces they could neither resist nor control.

In the decade that I have worked on this book, I have had help from many people and institutions. I want to thank in particular Professor Amakawa Akira, Dr. Tsuru Shigeto, Professor Sodei Rinjiro, Professor Takemae Eiji, Suzuki Gengo, and Kojima Noboru in Japan, as well as Charles Kades, W. J. Sebald, Ezra Vogel, Professor Marleen Mayo, Frank Joseph Shulman, and Justin Williams, Sr., among many others, in the United States. I made extensive use of the resources of the National Diet Library and the Yoshida Foundation in Japan, the National Archives in Washington, and the MacArthur Memorial Foundation in Norfolk, Virginia. I relied heavily on two dedicated archivists, Edward J. Boone, Jr., in Norfolk and John Taylor in Washington. I owe special thanks to my daughter Allison for her editorial advice and to Jean and Brad Coolidge and Vicki and Cromwell Riches for the extensive help they gave me from their libraries on the occupation period.

PART I

Enemies Face to Face

On August 8, 1945, two days after an American B-29 dropped an atomic bomb on Hiroshima, General Douglas MacArthur said to news correspondent Theodore White, "Wars are over, White, wars are over. There will never be another war. Men like me are obsolete. There can't be any more wars."[1] This inspiration seems to have come on MacArthur, a lifelong warrior, like a flash of light. It remained with him for a long time and had a profound effect on his thinking.

The bombing of Hiroshima was an awesome event. A 4-ton bomb containing uranium 235 was detonated over Japan's seventh largest city, an important regional and military center with a population of 400,000. The most powerful weapon in history, its explosive force equaled 12.5 kilotons of TNT, the same as a conventional bombload of two thousand B-29s. It destroyed 90 percent of the city. Within the next four months probably between 90,000 and 100,000 persons died as a result, including a dozen or so American prisoners of war and thousands of imported Korean workers. Many more Japanese died thereafter from injuries directly attributable to the bomb.[2]

Two days later the Soviet Union, in a speedup of its schedule, declared war on Japan and attacked Imperial Army forces in Manchuria and Korea. The day after, August 9, a second atomic bomb, of 4.5 tons and made of plutonium 239, was dropped on Nagasaki, with an explosive force of 22 kilotons of TNT. Within a month between 60,000 and 70,000 people died as a result. Ironically, the bomb was dropped about

two miles off target when the plane was getting low on fuel and detonated not far from the Urakami Cathedral, a large Roman Catholic
church. The military necessity of dropping a second atomic bomb has
become one of the more debated issues of World War II.

Yet Japan was not ready to surrender. It was a nation with a long
and proud history of military valor. This samurai tradition, sometimes
called the "spirit of Yamato," had not disappeared during a century of
modernization. The conflict in the Pacific had been tough and brutal,
aptly described as a "war without mercy," but the imperial forces had
fought without surrender in a series of bloody battles in the western
Pacific. Japanese leaders had had great difficulty in deciding how to
react to the Potsdam Declaration issued in Germany by the major Allied
powers on July 26, 1945, calling on Japan to proclaim the unconditional surrender of its armed forces or face "prompt and utter destruction."
Prime Minister Suzuki Kantarō, an octogenarian retired admiral and
hero of the Russo-Japanese War, decided after a tense debate with his
advisers that Japan would "ignore" the Allied statement. The word he
used, *mokusatsu*, somehow got into the press the next day. The *New
York Times* reported that Japan "formally rejected the Allied declaration."[3]

But staggered by the cataclysmic blows received during the month of
August, Japan's leaders had to choose between vague Allied peace terms
that might be a disaster for the nation and continuation of a war Japan
could not win. The Supreme Council for the Direction of the War,
a six-member body of senior officials created a year earlier to make
defense policies, met on August 9 to decide what to do.[4] Three of its
members, all military men, were determined to fight on until one final
"decisive battle" would show both sides the futility of further combat
and compel them to agree to negotiate an armistice. But the events of
August made even these ardent warriors waver. They had no defense
against this terrible new American weapon, although in the confusing
period after the bombing of Hiroshima very few people knew what had
hit them. The USSR's entry into the war wiped out the last hope of
enlisting Soviet mediation and dividing the Allies. The council, and the
cabinet that met soon afterward, were hopelessly deadlocked after tense
meetings that lasted much of the day. In desperation the prime minister
requested another meeting that night to put the issue directly to the
emperor, an action without precedent in Japanese history.[5]

Despite General MacArthur's flash of inspiration, World War II was not over. Nor could it be said—yet—that Japan was ready to give up, despite all its battle losses in the Pacific, the fearful pounding from the air it had been undergoing, the Allied peace offer, two atomic bombs, and Soviet attacks on the outposts of its empire.

CHAPTER 1

Tense Beginnings

World War II ended when the emperor decided that Japan should accept the offer of terms made by the Allied powers. Two *gozen kaigi*, "meetings with the emperor," were required before the bitter division in the Supreme War Council could be bridged. In this unique crisis, only the emperor could make the decision. And only he had the authority to ensure that it would be carried out. At the first meeting the emperor said, "I cannot bear to see my innocent people suffer any longer." He added that he did not believe his armed forces could repel an invasion. He felt regret for all those who had died in the war and said it would be "unbearable" to see "the loyal fighting men of Japan disarmed" and some "punished as instigators of the war."[1]

After this meeting on the night of August 9, the Japanese government sent a note to the United States stating that it accepted the Potsdam Declaration on the understanding that acceptance would not prejudice "the prerogatives of His Majesty as a sovereign ruler." The United States replied artfully that "the authority of the Emperor and the Japanese Government to rule the state shall be subject to the Supreme Commander for the Allied Powers, who will take such steps as he deems proper to effectuate the surrender terms." At the second meeting on August 14, the emperor said he thought the U.S. response was "evidence of the peaceful and friendly intentions of the enemy" and reiterated that he could "not endure the thought of letting my people suffer any longer."[2] At this point the United States was intensifying the bombing of Tokyo.

The Japanese then sent a reply accepting the Potsdam terms and giving assurance that they would carry out the surrender arrangements. President Harry S Truman announced the same day that he considered the reply "a full acceptance of the Potsdam Declaration, which specifies the unconditional surrender of Japan."[3]

The Japanese people heard the voice of their emperor for the first time when he broadcast to the nation on August 15. Despite the stilted court language used by the man known as Tennō to his subjects and as Hirohito to the outside world, his meaning was unmistakable. Speaking of the Allied powers' statement at Potsdam, he said, "Our Empire accepts the provisions of their joint declaration." He did not use the word *surrender*. He added, perhaps optimistically, that Japan had "been able to safeguard and maintain the structure of the imperial state."[4]

The willingness of the Japanese to respond to "the voice of the crane" by abandoning a policy of militant nationalism and calmly facing an unknown and frightening future was strikingly illustrated that day.[5] Historians debate what caused Japan to surrender, but the intervention of the emperor was crucial. Nevertheless, despite all Japan's troubles, including the shock of the atomic bomb, the emperor's intervention would probably not have been effective or even possible before August 10. After his death in 1989 the Tennō became known as Emperor Shōwa, meaning "enlightened peace," a title that his deeds in 1945 and afterward may well justify.

A new cabinet was soon organized, headed by Prince Higashikuni Naruhiko, an uncle-in-law of the emperor and a career army officer. The cabinet's greatest concern was that the armed forces might not obey the emperor's cease-fire order of August 16. Hotheaded rightists might try to seize control of the government, or army forces on the Asian mainland might decide to fight on. But the authority of the imperial order prevailed, and after a few tense days and a number of suicides by recalcitrant rightists or military men carrying out the code of loyalty to the throne, compliance was complete throughout the empire.[6]

General MacArthur was at his headquarters in Manila when the war ended. He had been told officially on August 15, 1945, that he would be named supreme commander for the Allied powers to receive the Japanese surrender and command the Allied forces of occupation. He did not return to Washington or receive any special briefing for his new assignment.

Yoshida Shigeru, who had retired from the diplomatic service in 1939, was living at his country home in Oiso, thirty-five miles southwest of Tokyo, at that time. He was not feeling well, but he was not so sick that he could not get up to Tokyo to celebrate with his friend Prince Konoe Fumimaro. Yoshida, who enjoyed parties and whiskey, got so tipsy that he fell asleep and missed his stop on the train back home.[7]

The first U.S. forces landed in Japan on August 28, two weeks after the imperial pronouncement. That interval provided a respite for both sides, giving time for emotions to simmer down and for future steps to be planned. A sixteen-member Japanese delegation went to Manila on August 19–20 to receive advance copies of the surrender documents and work out details for the ceremony. The businesslike discussions covered all the necessary ground in two meetings. The Americans were firm, but, according to one of the Japanese, they were "gentlemen."[8]

MacArthur had decided that he would go to Japan at an early time, just as he had accompanied his invading forces during his campaigns in the Southwest Pacific. "To prevent regrettable incidents," the Japanese wanted a longer delay than MacArthur would accept. Although staff members worried about his security, they finally reached a compromise with the Japanese on a three-day delay in the arrival of the advance party—to August 26, with the general to come in on August 28.[9]

Providentially, a typhoon blew up on August 22, and the Americans decided to wait two more days. On August 28 the advance group of 146 communications and engineering specialists landed at Atsugi air base, thirty miles southwest of Tokyo, to make final arrangements for the arrival of the main elements. Two days later, on August 30, U.S. troops arrived in force both at Atsugi and at the big naval base of Yokosuka, fifteen miles east of Atsugi. Every four minutes another big transport plane arrived and unloaded troops and equipment. When MacArthur came in on his command plane, *Bataan*, at 2 P.M., the sky was bright and Mount Fuji stood out clearly forty miles to the west.[10]

As the plane neared Japan, MacArthur's military aide and close confidant, Brigadier General Courtney Whitney, nervously mused to himself: "Had death, the insatiable monster of battle, passed MacArthur by on a thousand fields only to murder him at the end?" Whitney's worry was not unfounded. The Imperial Army had some 3 million men in Japan's home islands, and 300,000 of its best troops were in the Tokyo area, trained for a last stand. Only 4,200 U.S. soldiers were in the vicinity when the supreme commander slowly descended from his plane at Atsugi. Winston Churchill later termed this act "the outstanding accomplishment of any commander during the war . . . in the face of several million Japanese soldiers who had not yet been disarmed."[11]

Except for the spirited music offered by the Eleventh Airborne Division band, there was no ceremony. MacArthur had wanted no massive display or parades and had passed the word that there should be no delegation of Japanese to meet him, although Japanese reporters and photographers would be permitted to cover his arrival. For the benefit of those assembled there, the general pronounced the less-than-immortal words, "Melbourne to Tokyo was a long road, but this looks like the payoff."[12]

The Japanese press wrote up the event in detail for the intensely interested nation. It made much of the general's informal dress—khaki uniform, open collar, no jacket or ribbons, aviator glasses, and even his corncob pipe. The photo of MacArthur emerging from his plane and calmly surveying the situation attracted worldwide attention. One Japanese writer compared MacArthur's descent from his plane to the well-known actor Kikugorō descending the *hanamichi*, or passageway to the stage of the kabuki theater. The general always took care that his dramatic arrivals, like the one a year before when his forces invaded the Philippines, were well photographed.[13]

An astute Japanese editor who knew the United States well termed MacArthur's exploit "an exhibition of cool personal courage; it was even more a gesture of trust in the good faith of the Japanese. It was a masterpiece of psychology which completely disarmed Japanese apprehensions. From that moment, whatever danger there might have been of a fanatic attack on the Americans vanished in a wave of Japanese admiration and gratitude."[14]

Nevertheless, the general realized he had taken a big chance. A few weeks later he proclaimed that "probably no greater gamble has been taken in history than the initial landings where our ground forces were outnumbered a thousand to one."[15] But it had been a carefully considered gamble. The parleys at Manila and the treatment of the advance party had given powerful evidence of Japan's determination to cooperate and of its well-known ability to maintain order. Disciplined cooperation with the occupation forces replaced fear and tension and continued as the order of the day for the next six and one-half years.

The Japanese were taking a gamble, too, although the savage beating they were suffering every day at the end of the war left them little room for bargaining. Japanese moderates had calculated that the United States would not be a vengeful conqueror, and they had all but convinced themselves that the victors would not seek to destroy or mutilate the emperor system.[16] The initial actions of MacArthur and the U.S. troops reinforced these hopes.

On September 2, two days after MacArthur's arrival, the occupation of Japan formally began with the surrender ceremony on the battleship *Missouri*. In that interval the general was busy working out Allied surrender arrangements, drafting the two speeches he was to give (one at the ceremony and the other to the people back home) and, most difficult of all, trying to coordinate Allied plans for the surrender of Japanese forces in China, Southeast Asia, and the western Pacific.[17] His office was in the cavernous customs building in Yokohama, which was one of the few big structures in the area to survive the air raids in fairly good shape.

The arrangements for the surrender had given both sides some trouble. The victorious Allies had difficulty in deciding which of them should sign the surrender papers, finally agreeing that representatives of the Big Four—the United States, China, the United Kingdom, and the Soviet Union—should sign first, followed by representatives from five other Allies. The U.S. Army and Navy had to work out some service differences over which should have the bigger role, senior navy officials believing, not without reason, that the navy had done more to bring about the defeat of Japan than the army had. But since General of the Army Douglas MacArthur had been designated supreme commander for the Allied powers to accept the surrender and carry out its terms, Fleet Admiral Chester W. Nimitz, the navy's top commander in the Pacific, was given the honor of signing as the representative of the United States of America. The navy got the bonus of a decision by President Truman that the event should take place on a U.S. battleship named after his home state and christened by his daughter. The rivalry did not end there, however, because even as the main American units started to land in Japan on the morning of August 30, reports from Yokosuka circulated that navy landing boats were "full of admirals trying to get ashore ahead of MacArthur."[18]

Japan had a more acute problem: no one wanted to sign a "surrender" document. The United States had abandoned its first plan—that the emperor sign—and had accepted a British suggestion that his authorized representatives would be good enough. It then became necessary for two Japanese to sign—one for the government and the other for the military command—to conform with Japan's constitutional division between civilian and military authority. Prime Minister Higashikuni was ruled out because he was a relative of the emperor. The army chief of staff, General Umezu Yoshijirō, threatened to kill himself if he were pressed to sign. The one senior official willing to accept this onus was the minister of foreign affairs, Shigemitsu Mamoru, who appeared genuinely to believe that surrender was good for the nation and would give it a chance to start over on a wiser course.[19] Under pressure from the throne, Umezu gave in and agreed to sign for the imperial general staff. He and Shigemitsu were accompanied on the *Missouri* by a group of nine officers and diplomats.

The surrender ceremony was the most photogenic event of the occupation. It was not the dramatic scene John Trumbull portrayed of Washington receiving the British surrender at Yorktown. No band played "A World Turned Upside Down," although this would have been even more fitting for the Japanese in 1945 than it had been for the British in 1781. But the *Missouri* did have one outstanding historical touch: mounted on a huge bulkhead for all to see was the Stars and Stripes (bearing thirty-one stars) flown by Commodore Matthew C. Perry when his "black ships" entered Edo Bay in 1853 to force the opening of Japan to the outside world. And the American flag that had flown over the U.S. capitol on December 7, 1941, the day Pearl Harbor was bombed, flew over the *Missouri*.

The ceremony began at 9 A.M. on September 2. The Japanese delegation had come aboard the *Missouri* a few minutes before. Several hundred Allied officers were waiting along with reporters and photographers, including some Japanese. The U.S. officers, without ties or decorations, contrasted with the other officers, who were in dress uniform, and the Japanese diplomats, who wore formal morning attire with top hats. No one carried side arms. There was no ceremonial surrendering of swords.

General MacArthur presided over the ceremony, which took only twenty minutes. In accepting the surrender, the general expressed the hope that "out of the blood and carnage of the past," a better world would emerge. "Nor is it for us here to meet. . . in a spirit of distrust, malice or hatred. But rather it is for us, both victors and vanquished, to rise to that higher dignity which alone befits the sacred purpose we are about to serve."[20]

After MacArthur signed the two copies of the surrender documents, one in English and the other in Japanese, the two Japanese representatives signed, followed by the nine Allied representatives. The foreign minister was not sure where to sign and had to be shown. The Canadian representative signed the Japanese copy on the wrong line, forcing the three remaining signatures out of place. When a troubled Japanese official pointed out the error to MacArthur's chief of staff after the ceremony, a considerable colloquy took place. The chief of staff then inked in and initialed the necessary corrections The performance on the *Missouri* was at least better than the German surrender four months earlier, when the wrong documents were signed at Rheims on May 7 and a second surrender ceremony had to be held two days later in Berlin to do it right.[21]

The key clauses in the surrender instrument read, "We hereby proclaim the unconditional surrender to the Allied Powers of the Japanese Imperial General Headquarters and of all Japanese armed forces and of all armed forces under Japanese control wherever situated. . . . The authority of the Japanese Emperor and the Japanese Government to rule the state shall be subject to the Supreme Commander." The emperor's rescript of September 2 commanded the Japanese government and armed forces to "faithfully carry out" the provisions of the surrender document.

After the signing ceremony, General MacArthur made a radio broadcast to the American people, which was delayed in transmission so that President Truman could make a speech right after the surrender ceremony. The general was eloquent and statesmanlike: "We are committed by the Potsdam Declaration of principles to see that the Japanese people are liberated from this condition of slavery. . . . If the talents of the race are turned to constructive channels, the country can lift itself from its present deplorable state into a position of dignity."[22]

The occupation had officially started. The emperor's decision to end the fighting had been indispensable. General MacArthur had set the tone—low-key and businesslike but firm and decisive. The tensions on both sides began to dissipate. U.S. troops went around unarmed. Japanese men and women began to appear again on the streets of Yokohama and Tokyo in their usual numbers. In place of the hostilities of the past, the two countries started to look for ways to resolve in peace the clash of their conflicting purposes and different cultures.

Japan was in bad shape at the end of the war. About two million of its people had lost their lives. Of these some six hundred thousand were civilians killed or injured in air raids, in the fighting on Okinawa, and in the atomic bombings.[23] More than half a million military men were reported missing at the end of the war, most of them captured by the Russians in Manchuria and taken to Siberia as prison laborers. The British also detained a large number of prisoners of war in Southeast Asia and employed them as laborers for several years.

Sixty-six of Japan's larger cities, including Tokyo and Yokohama, were about half-destroyed. Eight and one-half million persons were homeless. More than one-quarter of Japan's residential housing was wiped out or badly damaged. The country had lost one-quarter of its national wealth, equal to $26 billion worth of its capital stock, such as buildings, machines, and equipment.[24]

During World War II Allied leaders had declared that Japan would be compelled to give up all territory it had "taken by force and greed."[25] Defeat meant that it would lose half its territory, leaving it with only 142,644 square miles, almost identical to what it possessed in 1853 when Commodore Perry first arrived. The loss of the southern Kuriles was a particularly hard blow because Japan had legally established its claim well before its colonial expansion. If Roosevelt and his advisers had known this piece of history, they might have qualified their agreement at Yalta in early 1945 that "the Kurile Islands shall be handed over to the Soviet Union." In August 1945 Washington decided only at the last minute that Soviet forces rather than U.S. forces should occupy the Kuriles.[26] A generation later the Japanese government and many of its citizens were still protesting the loss of the southern Kuriles and the adjacent islands off Hokkaido, the Habomais and Shikotan, that are geologically distinct from the Kuriles but were also seized by the Soviets in 1945.

The United States took control of the Ryukyu Islands in June 1945 after a bloody campaign. The islands were returned to Japanese control in 1972 after twenty-seven years of U.S. administration. Except for the Ryukyus and a few other small islands to the south, including the historic battleground of Iwo Jima, all of which were returned to Japan by the United States, Japan's territory has not changed since the surrender.

At the end of the war Japan's population was about 72 million. Around 7 million more Japanese, military and civilian, were located outside of Japan, mostly in China. About 2 million Koreans and Taiwanese lived in Japan as conscript laborers or farmers. Soon after the war ended, massive repatriations took place. More than one-half the Koreans and Taiwanese returned to their homelands, although many Koreans came back to Japan because of unsettled conditions in Korea. The net balance of all these shifts in population added more than 6 million to Japan's total in the years after the war, bringing it close to 80 million in 1950.[27]

There had been no panic or breakdown in morale or control during the war. The cohesiveness and discipline of Japanese society, reinforced by strict police surveillance and tight organization by neighborhoods throughout the country, seemed equal to any disaster. Japanese populations on Saipan and Okinawa had gone to their deaths by the thousands as the U.S. forces swept over the islands, thereby providing strong evidence that the people in the homeland would not waver if they, too, had to face the supreme holocaust. Harry Truman's hope that the United States "could avert an Okinawa from one end of Japan to another" was probably a factor in his decision to use the atomic bomb and seek to end the war quickly.[28]

Forceful resistance to the war had been almost totally absent, although there were many examples of dissatisfaction and noncooperation during the war. Popular opinion was carefully controlled in wartime Japan, the people knew little about the disasters that had befallen the imperial forces, and the few incidents of dissidence that did occur were ruthlessly suppressed. As a result, evidence of revolutionary antiwar resistance was minor. The decision to surrender came as a great blow to most Japanese, even if many of them realized the situation was all but hopeless.

With the war finally over, a flood of emotions swept over the country—fear, humiliation, and even relief. The government tried for a time to whip up a campaign of "national penitence" for the "mistakes of the government, the bureaucrats and the people,"[29] but little came of it. The people seemed to feel little sense of guilt about the war or about what Japan had done. But they did feel the war had been a surpassing disaster, and many thought their military leaders had misled and failed them. People seemed to feel more resentment toward their leaders than penitence about themselves, and some spoke of the Americans as "a liberation army" rather than as conquerors. Other euphemisms soon came into common use: people did not say "the surrender" but "the end of the war," and "garrison force" was used instead of "occupation force."[30]

In contrast to Japan, the United States was at its zenith of power and prestige when the war ended. In defeating the Japanese empire almost single-handedly, the United States had won its greatest victory since the founding of the republic. It was the richest and most powerful nation in the world. It was the sole possessor of the atomic bomb. America had also made a large contribution to the defeat of Nazi Germany and was a leading player in Allied negotiations to reach a postwar settlement in Europe. Pax Americana was at hand. Its executor in Japan was Douglas MacArthur.

CHAPTER 2

First Encounters

Japan's sudden surrender forced Washington and Tokyo to throw their war machines into reverse and improvise new arrangements. Americans and Japanese spent much of the month of September getting organized and learning more about each other. Except for a few diplomats, military attaches, and businessmen in both countries and some American scholars and missionaries, the rival nations did not know each other very well. Although Douglas MacArthur and Yoshida Shigeru were well-traveled men, neither had more than a passing acquaintance with the other's country. MacArthur's meetings in September 1945 with Shigemitsu, Yoshida, and the emperor were therefore of capital significance as a learning experience for both sides and as a means of determining the basic procedures and style of the occupation.

Before going to Japan in 1945 MacArthur had spent sixteen years in Asia, served four tours of duty in the Philippines, and been in Japan briefly four times. After a lengthy trip around Asia in 1905 and 1906, he spoke of its "mystic hold upon me" and grandly observed, "It was crystal clear to me that the future and, indeed, the very existence of America were irrevocably entwined with Asia and its island outposts." After meeting some of the Japanese military men who had distinguished themselves in the Russo-Japanese War of 1904–1905, he described them admiringly as "grim, taciturn, aloof men of iron character and unshakeable purpose." He added that he "was deeply impressed by and filled with admiration for the thrift, courtesy and friendliness of the ordinary citizen" of Japan.[1]

At the outbreak of World War II MacArthur was in command of U.S. and Philippine forces in the Philippines. After putting up a brave but hopeless defense against the invading Japanese, his forces were on the point of surrender in 1942 when President Franklin D. Roosevelt ordered him to Australia to command Allied forces in the Southwest Pacific. MacArthur led U.S. and Australian forces in a number of well-planned and skillfully executed operations through New Guinea and the Philippines. In June 1945 he was appointed to command the forces scheduled to invade southern Japan five months later. No doubt his confidence that "destiny had called him to the Orient" was bolstered when the Soviet Union and the United Kingdom concurred in his selection by Truman as the supreme Allied commander in Japan.

Commanding in both stature and personality, MacArthur rarely displayed doubt in his ideas or uncertainty in his action. His talent for managing situations and influencing people was almost theatrical. Lord Mountbatten, the Allied commander in Southeast Asia, remarked that "he does not look at all fierce or commanding until he puts his famous embroidered cap on. As we went out together to face the photographers and he pulled his cap on, his whole manner changed. His jaw stuck out and he looked aggressive and tough, but as soon as the photographers had finished, he relaxed completely, took off his hat, and was his old charming self."[2] The hat was for MacArthur what hair was for Samson.

MacArthur had some remarkable attributes of body and mind. He was unusually healthy. He could stand at attention for an hour at a Fourth of July review and show no weariness. He caught cold only a couple of times during his five and one-half years in Tokyo. He took no exercise. Even more remarkable was his memory. After one reading he could remember a document clearly for a long period. Or he could remember people and what they had talked about for years after he met them. He memorized the names and pertinent facts about luncheon guests and would astonish them with how much he knew about them. His command of the facts made him a formidable advocate in any discussion. Yet he was not above tailoring his views in ways he thought would appeal to his listeners. And his memory seems to have been selective, for he sometimes failed to remember important things he had said or done.

His personal life was uneventful. He made a happy marriage in 1937 after the failure of his first try. In the interim between marriages he had an interlude with a Eurasian mistress. His only child, a son who was named Arthur after his distinguished grandfather, was born in 1938 and lived with his parents throughout the war and the occupation.

MacArthur knew the Philippines well and had an affection for its people. He admired Japan's military capabilities but knew little of the country's people and politics. In his memoirs he characterized Japan as a "feudal society of the type discarded by the Western nations four centuries ago," terming it a "theocracy" where the "God-Emperor was absolute" and where there were no civil or human rights. During the war he liked to say, as he told Roosevelt's emissary, the playwright Robert Sherwood, in early 1944, that the destruction of Japan's military power would eliminate the concept of the emperor's divinity, thereby creating a spiritual vacuum and an opportunity for concepts such as democracy and Christianity to flow in. The general went on to say perceptively that enlightened leadership by the United States in the occupation of Japan "will make us the greatest influence on the future development of Asia. If we exert that influence in an imperialistic manner, or for the sole purpose of commercial advantage, then we shall lose our golden opportunity, but if our influence and our strength are expressed in terms of essential liberalism, we shall have the friendship and the cooperation of the Asiatic people far into the future."[3]

During his tenure in Tokyo the general met with more than one hundred Japanese, singly or in small groups. On a few occasions he met with big delegations, such as thirty-five new women Diet members on June 20, 1946, or a group of swimming champions on August 10, 1949. He met only about fifteen Japanese more than once. He received the emperor every six months, for a total of eleven times, always at his residence, the American Embassy. The crown prince with his American tutor, Elizabeth Vining, called on MacArthur once. He saw Yoshida some seventy-five times, far more than any other Japanese.[4] In his memoirs MacArthur made only passing reference to Yoshida and Japan's other postwar leaders. He gave the emperor more space than any of the others.

In September 1945 the supreme commander saw more Japanese than in any other month of the occupation. He seemed eager not only to convey his views but also to hear what they thought. He saw the emperor, the prime minister, the deputy prime minister, two different foreign ministers, the finance minister, the leaders of the Diet, mayors of the big cities, and some former military men. Rarely did MacArthur summon Japanese to meet with him. He called in Yoshida once or twice but almost invariably let the Japanese take the initiative if they wanted to see him.

MacArthur once told his political adviser he would "never break bread with the Japanese." He had no social contacts with any Japanese, although he did not object to others on his staff doing so. He did not impose any broad restrictions against "fraternizing" with the Japanese. The general did not travel about the country. He did take one long sightseeing ride around downtown Tokyo in the early days of the occupation, and he occasionally motored to the airport ten miles away to greet senior visitors. Otherwise his routine seven days a week was strictly limited to going back and forth from his residence to his headquarters in the Dai Ichi Insurance building one mile away.[5]

After the first few months, MacArthur confined his meetings with Japanese in most cases to only a few senior officials. His style of leadership seemed to change at that point. General Charles A. Willoughby, his longtime intelligence officer and one of the "Bataan crowd" (the group that had left the Philippines with MacArthur in 1942), used the term *grand seigneur* to describe MacArthur during the occupation; he began to keep his distance from all but the most important Japanese and an inner circle of his top staff officers.[6] His immediate staff found him relaxed and easy to get along with.

The most significant of MacArthur's early meetings took place a day after the surrender on board the *Missouri*. On September 3 Foreign Minister Shigemitsu rushed to Yokohama to persuade the general to suspend action on three proclamations he had already signed. These decrees would have placed all powers of government under the authority of the supreme commander, set up military courts to deal with violations of occupation orders, and established occupation currency as legal tender in Japan. This meeting, MacArthur's first with a Japanese cabinet minister, was critical for the losers as a test of what they might expect from the conquerors. The proclamations seemed to point to direct military government by the occupiers.[7]

Shigemitsu told the general that the Japanese government would faithfully carry out the Potsdam Declaration and the surrender terms and would issue whatever orders the supreme commander required to give these documents effect. Shigemitsu said that the occupation authorities could, of course, act directly if they were not satisfied with the government's performance. MacArthur replied, "There would be no difficulty if the content of the proclamations were carried out by the

Japanese Government and people" acting in good faith. He added, in a remarkable display of flexibility, that the U.S. government "had no thought of destroying or enslaving the Japanese nation" and was indeed "considerering ways to assist Japan somehow in its difficulties." Following the meeting the proclamations were suspended. For the duration of the occupation, orders were issued to and executed by the Japanese government. Its bureaucratic system was thus preserved intact, thereby affording an important element of continuity but at the same time, according to some critics, enabling Japanese bureaucrats, one of the pillars of the prewar administrative system, to remain in office and possibly dilute the impact of occupation directives.[8]

That MacArthur signed the three proclamations was surprising because the notes exchanged by the United States and Japan on August 10 and 11 made it clear that the emperor and the Japanese government would continue to function. In the rush of events at the time of the surrender, this new policy may not have been clearly understood. In any case, MacArthur removed any doubts by his concession to Shigemitsu. The Japanese had been particularly exercised by the proclamation that U.S. military scrip would be valid currency in Japan, a practice the Japanese had freely employed in areas occupied by their forces.

The Japanese probed for other soft spots in the U.S. position. They had resisted an Allied order in August to turn over their diplomatic records in neutral nations on the ground that this did "not correspond to any provision" of the Potsdam Declaration. Obviously, the Japanese hoped to carry on diplomatic relations with neutral nations. After Shigemitsu was so indiscreet as to leak to the press the results of his talk on September 3 with the supreme commander, MacArthur requested Washington to issue a statement that because Japan had surrendered unconditionally, he should not entertain any question as to his supreme authority. Faced with this display of U.S. firmness, the Japanese carried out a new order to turn over these records and also terminated all relations with neutral nations.[9] Throughout the occupation Japan deftly skirted the issue of "unconditional surrender," and the United States obliged by never pressing it. Although a few Japanese legalists have continually asserted that the surrender was in fact conditional by virtue of the wording of the Potsdam Declaration and the notes exchanged at the time, this has not been an important historical issue.

After seeing Shigemitsu, MacArthur met with other cabinet members. He saw the first postwar prime minister, Prince Higashikuni Naruhiko, a bluff career army officer, but did not find much common ground. The supreme commander lectured the prince at their first meeting on the role women could play in a democracy, and two weeks later, at a meeting with the prince on September 29, the general said he saw no reason for any change in the cabinet.[10]

The general also met twice with the deputy premier, Prince Konoe, scion of one of Japan's oldest families and prime minister three times in the years leading up to the war. At their first meeting, on September 13, MacArthur held forth on the evils of Japan's prewar nationalist zealots . Three weeks later Konoe delivered his favorite lecture on the subversive threat to Japan during the war from "the union of the military forces and the left" and on his fear that "if you wipe out in one blow the established feudal forces and the zaibatsu (powerful family combines) as well, Japan will immediately go communist." MacArthur did not respond to this dire advice, which was much like what Konoe said to the emperor eight months before. Instead, the general asserted that the constitution should be revised and suggested to Konoe that he was still young enough to lead liberal elements in the country.[11]

At MacArthur's behest several staff officers met with Konoe and passed on suggestions for constitutional change. The emperor and his close adviser, Marquis Kido Kōichi, the privy seal, decided to use Konoe as a special consultant to study constitutional issues from the point of view of the palace, possibly because they thought this might please MacArthur.[12] Konoe and his team energetically rushed ahead with their study.

On September 17 SCAP headquarters moved to the imposing head office building of the Dai Ichi Insurance Company in downtown Tokyo, across the moat from the imperial palace. The Japanese had hoped to be spared the indignity of occupation of their capital, but the Allied commander decided to rule Japan from an office within sight of the palace.[13] And for years to come American GIs would look on Tokyo as the Mecca of the Orient and visit there in droves.

The same day the prime minister summoned Yoshida Shigeru from Oiso to the capital. Higashikuni offered Yoshida the portfolio of foreign minister to replace Shigemitsu, who had not got along well with either the occupation or his cabinet colleagues and had been forced to submit his resignation. After some hesitation Yoshida accepted and was invested by the emperor late that evening. Yoshida did not even have time to change his creaky brown shoes for a proper pair of black ones.[14]

The new foreign minister had been born in Yokohama in 1878, two years before MacArthur. Yoshida's natural father was Takenouchi Tsuna, a businessman and minor political figure. His mother was probably a geisha. He was soon adopted by Yoshida Kenzō, a childless, well-to-do merchant in Yokohama. The young Yoshida received a good education and inherited a considerable patrimony that enabled him to live comfortably for the rest of his life. He attended Tokyo Imperial University, which even then was at the apex of the educational system. He married the daughter of Count Makino Nobuaki, who was himself the adopted son of one of modern Japan's founding fathers, Ōkubo Toshimichi, and influential in public life until well after World War II.[15]

Yoshida lived the first thirty-five years of his life in the reign of Emperor Meiji and had many of the characteristics attributed to the leaders of that era, the "men of Meiji," such as education in the Chinese classics, patriotic pride, loyalty to the throne, and, in many cases, a broad international outlook. As a diplomat in China in the 1920s, Yoshida supported Japan's tough policies and pursuit of "special interests." As consul general in Mukden from 1925 to 1928, however, he squabbled with the militarists, whose policies of force, intrigue, and assassination he considered extreme. The Foreign Office in Tokyo did not back him up, and he was recalled. He landed the job of vice minister of foreign affairs in 1929 in the cabinet of the ill-famed Tanaka Giichi, considered one of the architects of Japan's tough policies in China, and was lucky enough after that to find pleasant postings in Europe. He remained keenly interested in Chinese affairs throughout his life. He served as ambassador to Rome in 1931–1932 and turned down an offer of the ambassadorship to the United States in 1932. He never served in the United States, but he visited there twice, in 1932 and 1935. Yoshida was not an admirer of U.S. foreign policy; he described it as "irresolute and indecisive" and once asserted, "The national character of the United States is such as to make it basically not very dependable in diplomacy."[16]

In 1936 Yoshida almost became foreign minister. On February 26 of that year a number of prominent public figures were assassinated in the most notorious coup attempt of the prewar period, the "2–26" incident. Yoshida's daughter, Kazuko, saved the life of her grandfather, Count Makino, when right-wing militarists tried to assassinate him. When a new government was formed in the aftermath of the coup attempt, Yoshida was proposed for the post of foreign minister in the cabinet of his friend and diplomatic colleague Hirota Kōki. Imperial Army leaders vetoed his nomination. As it turned out, if he had got the job, he might have been foreign minister when Japan invaded China in

1937. In that event he, like Hirota, might well have been tried as a war criminal after the war.[17]

Yoshida ended his prewar career as ambassador to the Court of St. James from 1936 to 1938. In London he developed considerable admiration for the British political system, with its parliamentary politics and combination of aristocratic and democratic traditions. In his later political career he seemed to prefer the classic liberalism of British democracy, with its stress on parliamentary government and free-enterprise economics, to the more populist version found in the United States. Britain's success in economic diplomacy also appealed to him. While in England he again incurred the wrath of the militarists at home by firmly—and unsuccessfully—opposing Japan's joining with Nazi Germany in the Anti-Comintern Pact of 1936. Out of favor with the groups running the government, he retired in 1939.

He used his numerous diplomatic contacts in Tokyo in an effort to halt the slide toward war in 1941, again futilely. Yoshida was not a pacifist, but he did feel that the Axis nations could not win a war against Britain, which would certainly be joined by the United States. After the war began he struggled as a patriotic and strong-willed man to find ways to get Japan out of it on favorable terms. He helped Konoe prepare a memorandum for the emperor in February 1945 stating that the war was lost and that Japan should end it quickly before the throne itself was endangered and the threat of a communist revolution became serious. The "Konoe Memorial" bore no fruit at the time, but the Tennō may have had had it in mind in August when he made his decision for surrender.[18]

The immediate result of the Yoshida-Konoe appeal was to arouse Japan's military police, the Asian version of Hitler's Gestapo, to the threat of what they called the "Yoshida antiwar movement." They arrested Yoshida in April 1945, grilled him for forty-five days, and released him in late May, after the second ferocious firebombing of Tokyo burned down the prison in which he and two fellow prisoners were being held. This experience gave Yoshida a halo of martyrdom that made him a symbol of resistance to militarism ever after.

Barely five feet tall and chubby in build, Yoshida was a witty and acerbic man with strong likes and dislikes in both people and ideas. He had an independent mind and a stubborn personality that set him apart from most Japanese, who are often reticent in expressing personal views. He was a far cry from the typical bureaucrat. He had great confidence in his own judgment, especially in diplomatic matters, and scorned those who did not see things the way he did. He was close to his daughter, Kazuko, who learned perfect English as a girl in England and was of great help to him in dealing with the English-speaking world. His wife died in 1937, and he had an agreeable association thereafter with a well-born geisha. In a personal allusion, he is reputed to have said that "sons of geisha like geisha."

In taking on the job of foreign minister, Yoshida faced the greatest challenge of his career—representing a defeated nation before the supreme commander for the Allied powers, a senior and an imperious officer of the U. S. Army. Late in the morning of September 20, three days after Yoshida's appointment became official, he was ushered into General MacArthur's spartanly appointed office. As usual, Yoshida was dressed like a European gentleman of the old school in a dark Western suit and white shirt with wing collar. It was the first time the two men had ever met.

Yoshida had two goals. First, he wanted to get to know the top Americans because he was confident his background and official position would make him Japan's most effective representative in dealing with them. Second, he wanted to talk about the emperor. To "protect the emperor" had in fact been the paramount goal of nearly all Japanese at the time of the surrender. Now, one month later, the Tennō was still sitting undisturbed on his throne. Because the Allies had not made their plans clear, Yoshida decided to raise the delicate matter by proposing that the Tennō call on MacArthur, although Yoshida was himself a little fearful about the emperor's making a call in "enemy territory."[19]

Speaking in somewhat quaint but quite understandable English, the foreign minister opened by saying he would like to convey the cordial regards of the emperor as well as his own pleasure in welcoming the general to Tokyo. He then asked, "for his information," if the general expected the emperor to pay a visit. Without hesitation MacArthur replied that it "would give him the greatest pleasure to see the Emperor" but that he did not want to "embarrass or humiliate" him. Yoshida then asked about the time and place for a meeting "if the Emperor should call." The general suggested the American Embassy.

The two men then discussed stories in the press about Japanese war atrocities and the atomic bomb.[20] Yoshida commented that the Japanese press got some of its ideas from the American press. He and MacArthur both carefully followed the press and resented press criticism.

MacArthur thereupon launched into one of the short speeches (the

Japanese called them *sekkyō*, or sermons) he liked to give all his visitors. Japan's military leaders had been foolish to start the war, he said, and they had followed a foolish strategy. The general then ticked off some of the problems Japan would have to act on. It would have to deal with devastated cities and 7 million demobilized men. More people would have to be given the right to vote. Freedom of the press would have to be recognized. He emphasized the power of "democracy" and Japan's need for better leaders.

Yoshida responded with a little speech of his own. "Democracy" had swept through Japan after World War I. Political parties had carried democracy to such an extreme that military men hesitated to appear in public. But the situation had changed when the Depression began in 1929, giving rise to Nazism, fascism, and communism. In Japan support for the military increased. Yoshida said democracy takes time to develop and needs an affluent country in which to thrive. The conversation ended with MacArthur commenting on the poor quality of textbooks in the schools.

This first encounter was reassuring to the new foreign minister. He had won the supreme commander's ready agreement to a meeting with the emperor. He had got across one of his favorite ideas: Japan could not become democratic until economic conditions improved. And he found he could exchange ideas with the general on sensitive matters, something they would often do in the future. Yoshida said later that MacArthur was not like generals in the Imperial Army, who conceitedly strutted around clutching their swords.

After this first meeting, Yoshida told his daughter that MacArthur seemed to be somewhat theatrical. The general liked to pace up and down his office as he talked, thereby causing Yoshida to turn back and forth to hear the general's words. Yoshida began to imagine that he was locked up with a pacing lion, and he burst out laughing. The general asked what was so funny. Yoshida thought he might be in trouble but replied nonchalantly that he felt as if he were hearing a lecture inside a lion's cage. MacArthur, who was not used to cheeky people, Japanese or American, glared for a moment, and then he, too, laughed. Yoshida was famous for his puckish humor, and, although MacArthur was not, it is just possible that this episode happened the way the foxy old diplomat described it.[21]

The Tennō called on the supreme commander a week later. The visit was the emperor's idea and broke with court tradition: emperors had often received foreign dignitaries but had never called on them. With a small retinue he drove the short distance from the palace to the American Embassy in midmorning, stopping for traffic lights, unlike the general, for whom the Tokyo lights were always turned green. The emperor was ushered into the embassy residence and presented to MacArthur, who led him into a large reception room. There, no doubt to the emperor's surprise, a military photographer snapped several pictures. The general had carefully planned this photographic opportunity.

The two men began a forty-five-minute conversation,[22] with only the emperor's interpreter present. The Tennō asked about the general's health after his many years in the tropics, and the general replied that he was in good condition. Then, speaking firmly, MacArthur launched into a twenty-minute speech on the destructiveness of modern war, especially air power and atomic bombs. A future war would mean the end of humankind. It was the duty of statesmen and experienced leaders to guide the world toward peace. If Japan had continued the war, it would have been destroyed. Therefore, the emperor's decision to end the war was a wise one that avoided immeasurable suffering. Some feelings of hate and revenge might persist in public attitudes, which were difficult to control in any country, but clearheaded people did not feel that way.

The emperor said that he had wanted to avoid the war and that he had been most pained when it started. The general observed that it was hard for one person to change the direction of events when they had gained momentum. The emperor responded that he and the Japanese people knew they had lost the war, adding that he wanted to devote all his efforts to building a peaceful Japan and that the Potsdam Declaration would be carried out fully. MacArthur commented that the emperor could guide the Japanese people in carrying out the many orders they would receive; he emphasized that he would be grateful for the emperor's advice at any time.

Evidently in a genial mood, the general recalled some of his previous visits to Japan. He also thanked the emperor for sending flowers on the occasion of Mrs. MacArthur's arrival a few days before. The meeting ended with pleasantries about the general's family and the weather. The general showed the emperor to the door as a special courtesy.

The meeting became known to the whole world two days later, September 29, when the front page of the minuscule Tokyo dailies carried a photograph showing the two men standing side by side in the embassy living room. The Tennō looked small and stiff in his formal morning attire. The general, towering over his guest, was in summer

khakis without tie, jacket, or ribbons, looking older without the familiar braided cap of a field marshal in the nonexistent Philippine Army to
cover his receding hairline. This was without doubt the most sensational photo of the occupation.[23]

Many Japanese felt humiliated when they saw the picture. Not only
did it show that the emperor was very much a human being; it was also
a grim reminder of the defeat and subservience of their nation. The
general said later that he had rejected the advice of his staff to summon
the emperor as a show of power because he felt this "would outrage the
feelings of the Japanese people and make a martyr of the Emperor." But
MacArthur felt no such compunction about insisting on publication of
the photograph. One discordant report on the meeting has been attributed to former Foreign Minister Shigemitsu, who said the emperor
wanted to see the general because he was nervous about his war responsibility and was playing the role of flatterer to sound out MacArthur's
intentions.[24]

MacArthur did not make any record of his talk with the emperor or
even tell Washington that they had met. A Japanese official, however,
briefed the foreign press on October 1 about the meeting, saying the
emperor was particularly impressed "that General MacArthur did not
make any reference as to who was responsible for the war." MacArthur
was reported to have stated that "the smooth occupation was really due
to the Emperor's leadership." The official added that the Japanese expected the supreme commander to pay a return call on the emperor.[25]

In his memoirs published in 1964 MacArthur quoted the emperor as
saying, "I come to you, General MacArthur, to offer myself to the judgment of the powers you represent as the one to bear sole responsibility
for every military and political decision made and action taken by
my people in the conduct of the war." The general added, "This
courageous assumption of a responsibility implicit with death, a responsibility clearly belied by the facts of which I was fully aware,
moved me to the very marrow of my bones." In that instant, "I knew I
faced the first gentleman of Japan in his own right." The available record from official Japanese sources does not contain any reference to
war responsibility. Nevertheless, the emperor may indeed have felt responsible for the nation's wartime actions, it being the Japanese tradition for a superior to claim responsibility and often resign when those
under him become involved in some untoward happening.[26]

When MacArthur wrote that he had facts belying the emperor's
assertion of war responsibility, he was probably referring to the

Japanese constitutional practice in which the emperor did not decide national policy but acted in accordance with the recommendations of his cabinet and advisers. Despite the provision in the Meiji Constitution that "the emperor is the head of the empire, combining in himself the rights of sovereignty," the Tennō always acted as a constitutional monarch. On military matters, he acted on the advice of the military. On civilian matters, he acted on the advice of the cabinet. The emperor played the role he had been taught by his mentor, Prince Saionji Kimmochi, the last genrō, or "elder statesman." This view of the emperor's constitutional role was consistent with the doctrine of imperial will that grew up in Japan's modern era; it prescribed that actions taken in the name of the emperor reflect the overwhelming consensus of all those about the throne, even if the emperor had a different personal view. A corollary was that no decisions should be taken in the emperor's name if they were controversial or risked bringing discredit or disadvantage to the nation. The decisions that led to the war in 1941 were made unanimously by the cabinet, the emperor was fully informed about them, often they were made in his presence, he knew in advance of the plan to attack Hawaii, and he even made suggestions about how to carry it out.[27]

In this situation the views of those who had access to the emperor and to his closest advisers became critical. This very small group was almost totally isolated from the rudimentary political process that existed in Japan before the war. For example, no more than fifteen men made the decision to begin war against the United States in 1941. The emperor's power of supreme command under the Meiji Constitution was interpreted to mean that the nation's military leaders could make decisions on national defense in the name of the emperor without restraint by the cabinet or Diet. In addition, the emperor system spawned various supraconstitutional and advisory bodies, notably the Privy Council, that were not subject to cabinet or parliamentary control and that advised the emperor directly.[28]

Marquis Kido, the lord privy seal, had said in 1939 that because the emperor was a scientist, a pacifist, and a liberal, the danger existed that a gulf could grow between him and the right wing. Kido thought the emperor should show "a little more understanding of the army." In 1941 Kido probably thought that the military nationalist elements, the "renovationists," had become stronger than the more internationalist and democratic elements, the "constitutional monarchists." He therefore supported the appointment of General Tōjō Hideki to succeed

Konoe as prime minister in October 1941, hoping Tōjō might try to restrain the militarists. Tōjō did for a time work with the Foreign Office in an effort to find a diplomatic solution to the crisis in relations with the United States, but within a few weeks his cabinet voted unanimously to carry out the decision of the Konoe cabinet to go to war because diplomatic measures had not succeeded. The emperor "displayed no signs of uneasiness. He attended the cabinet meeting that took this fateful action and seemed to be in an excellent mood." Actually, the emperor seemed to like Tōjō.[29]

The distinguished British historian Sir George Sansom once recounted a tale told him by MacArthur. In discussing the events that led up to the attack on Pearl Harbor, the general asked the emperor, "Why did you not at this point just tell your ministers that this could not be done?" The emperor replied, "But I am a constitutional monarch. If I am advised by my prime minister and other ministers that this must be done, I must do it, even if I do not like it." According to Sansom, this "shattered the general."[30]

In speaking later of his eleven meetings with the Tennō, MacArthur said that these talks ranged over most of the problems of the world and that he always carefully explained the underlying reasons for occupation policy. He commented that the emperor "had a more thorough grasp of the democratic concept than almost any Japanese with whom I talked. He played a major role in the spiritual regeneration of Japan, and his loyal cooperation and influence had much to do with the success of the occupation." At another time the general said of the emperor: "He's a gentleman. He is well educated and well informed. He would ask the right questions. . . . When you consider the ancestry, all the inbreeding and so on, I think he's quite remarkable." It was clear the supreme commander felt the emperor was a valuable asset for the occupation.[31]

MacArthur's respect for the emperor, like the good relationship he had begun with Yoshida, was, as a prominent Japanese historian has recognized, of basic importance to the occupation. Yet in September 1945 the Allied nations had not yet decided whether the emperor's leadership in ending the war freed him of any responsibility for the events leading up to the war.[32]

CHAPTER 3

Planning and Organizing the Occupation

The occupation of Japan was the largest foreign policy operation in the history of the United States in its duration, the number of Americans involved, and the tremendous authority they wielded. Washington made the basic plans and preparations; the organization and implementing actions were largely the handiwork of General MacArthur and his staff. The Japanese had not made any advance plans to be occupied—the very word *senryō* (occupation) was for some time taboo—but they proved to be quick and clever improvisers.

Several features of the plans for the occupation were significant. The planning was almost entirely the work of Americans. Its purpose was to reform and punish Japan, not to help rebuild it or make it an ally. The planning ignored the problems of how the Japanese were to feed themselves and revive production of consumer goods, let alone rebuild their industrial machine. It paid no attention to what was going on in the world around Japan and seemed to assume that Japan would have only a modest and unimportant international role. It presupposed that Nationalist China would be a major power in Asia and the most important U.S. ally in the region. It also assumed that the Soviet Union would follow cooperative policies. It said nothing about Korea or Taiwan or Okinawa. Pax Americana, as Washington saw Asia in 1945, seemed to be based on short-term, localized, and sometimes ill-conceived policies.

MacArthur played almost no role in planning these policies. He read about the Potsdam Declaration in the newspapers. He did not know about the atomic bomb until a few days before it was dropped on

Hiroshima. But as a self-assured officer with long experience at senior levels of military command and as the obvious choice for the top job in Japan, he felt no qualms about his new eminence. For a time the United Kingdom questioned whether his mission was simply to receive Japan's surrender on behalf of the Allied powers or to go ahead and implement the surrender terms. This doubt soon faded. The supreme commander remained and his authority grew.[1]

The general came to consider himself an international officer responsible not only to the U.S. government but to all the major Allied nations. In fact, he received 111 directives during the occupation, of which 60 were decisions by the Allied powers and the rest actions by the United States.[2] Many of the early U.S. plans he received were the work of academic and diplomatic experts who knew Japan well and had been able to avoid the pressure for draconian solutions that planners for Germany experienced.

The most concise summary of U.S. plans was composed by MacArthur himself. "From the moment of my appointment," he later wrote in his memoirs, "I had formulated the policies I intended to follow, implementing them through the Emperor and the machinery of the imperial government." Flying in to Japan on August 30 a few hours after he had received from Washington the text of the initial policy he was to carry out, he paraphrased the actions he was to take:

> First, destroy the military power. Punish war criminals. Build the structure of representative government. Modernize the constitution. Hold free elections. Enfranchise the women. Release the political prisoners. Liberate the farmers. Establish a free labor movement. Encourage a free economy. Abolish police oppression. Develop a free and responsible press. Liberalize education. Decentralize political power. Separate the church from state.[3]

This was MacArthur's recipe for making the new Japan: a summary of the U.S. policy paper he had just received from Washington. Several of his goals, such as suffrage for women, liberation of farmers, and political decentralization, went beyond the Washington guidance. He did not mention reparations. MacArthur's formulations showed his direct approach to policy issues: long and complex analyses were not his style, and he left them to the staff to wrestle with.

The most significant policy statements he received were the Potsdam Declaration and two papers prepared by the United States—the initial policy statement and a basic postsurrender directive. These three documents gave MacArthur a lot of policy, more in fact than he wanted.

The Potsdam Declaration provided the fundamental statement.

Based on an original draft by the State Department with a few emendations by British officials, it was drafted for the most part in the Pentagon. In thirteen short paragraphs the declaration set out in sweeping language the "terms" the Allies would impose: unconditional surrender and disarmament of Japan's armed forces, punishment of war criminals, payment of reparations, limitation of Japan's territory, "strengthening of democratic tendencies," and a peacefully inclined and responsible government established by the freely expressed will of the Japanese people. The occupation would end when these goals were attained.[4]

An early version of the declaration contained a provision allowing the Japanese to retain the monarchy if it was suitably reformed, but this was dropped when American leaders could not agree on it.[5] Even so, Japanese diplomats drew some reassurance because the Allies had gone on record stating that "the authority of the Emperor and the Japanese Government...shall be subject to the Supreme Commander for the Allied Powers," thus meeting, at least for the time being, Japan's one condition for surrender—retention of the emperor. Moreover, Japanese experts were confident that if given the choice, the people would certainly choose to keep the imperial institution.[6]

The second key document was the "Initial United States Post-Surrender Policy," approved by President Truman on September 6, 1945. In mid-August John J. McCloy, the assistant secretary of war, who had been the principal redrafter of the Potsdam Declaration only a few weeks earlier, produced a draft of the initial policy by hastily revising a much longer policy draft to align it with the Potsdam statement. The initial policy set out many general goals, such as demilitarization, freedom of religion, creation of democratic political parties, and protection of civil rights. It provided more specifically for three major reforms. First, "active exponents of militarism and militant nationalism" were to be excluded from public office or responsible private positions; this was the basis for a later "purge" of top officials. Second, "organizations in labor, industry and agriculture organized on a democratic basis" were to be favored; this authorized support of a free labor movement. Third, "a program for the dissolution of the large industrial and banking combinations which have exercised control of a great part of Japan's trade and industry" was to be favored; this aimed at the notorious zaibatsu and their banks. Another key clause stated that U.S. policy would be to use the Japanese government, not support it.[7]

A significant provision that reflected the liberal trend of some postwar thinking in Washington stated that "changes in the form of govern-

ment initiated by the Japanese people or government in the direction of
modifying its feudal or authoritarian tendencies are to be permitted and
favored." If force had to be used to make these changes, "the Supreme
Commander should intervene only where necessary to ensure the
security of his forces" and the attainment of all his other objectives.
MacArthur was shocked by this wording, which seemed close to an
invitation to violence.[8]

The United States was the only Allied power to engage in detailed
planning for postwar Japan. When British policymakers were shown an
earlier draft of the initial U.S. policy, they commented that a large and
direct occupation, which might be expensive and risky, could be
avoided if the Allied powers applied external controls to Japan's trade
and foreign relations and confined themselves to occupying easily held
key points and putting on occasional demonstrations of military power.
These were the views of Sir George Sansom, probably the outstanding
authority in the West on Japanese history. He thought sweeping reforms were not needed and that only a few changes in basic institutions
would be required to convert Japan into an acceptably democratic state.
This was far from what U.S. policymakers had in mind.[9]

When the initial policy was made public on September 22, 1945,
U.S. public opinion seemed to welcome it. The British Foreign Office
commented that the economic provisions went much farther than the
terms of the Potsdam Declaration. The Japanese were reported to be
"aghast." Nevertheless, the Japanese government decided to wait
and see. Yoshida commented later that the policy's "objectives were,
in essence, our own from the moment the war had ended."[10]

The policy paper was formally approved with minor changes one
and one-half years later by the eleven-nation Far Eastern Commission
(FEC), formed in 1946 to make Allied policy for Japan. Before submitting the paper to the commission, the State Department discreetly deleted a provision that the policies of the United States would govern in
case of differences among the Allies. MacArthur praised the commission, for which he had scant respect, for producing this "great state
paper,"[11] which the FEC entitled "Basic Post-Surrender Policy for
Japan."

The third key policy document was the "Basic Directive for Post-
Surrender Military Government in Japan Proper" sent to MacArthur on
November 3, 1945. This was the longer, more detailed paper from
which the initial policy had been cloned in mid-August. When Mac-
Arthur saw a version of the new directive in early September, he pro-

tested that it was a "rigid and stringent directive...which all but removed from him the detailed method of execution of the mission which has been assigned to the Supreme Commander." He thought it was "in certain respects far beyond the principles set forth in the surrender terms and the Potsdam Declaration" and "would require a much greater force for a greater length of time than is now contemplated."[12]

The War Department hastily replied that the directive "was primarily the concern of the State Department" but could be construed merely as guidance for MacArthur, who could recommend changes and exercise "reasonable latitude" in executing it. Guidance rather than directive had become the standard way for the Joint Chiefs of Staff (JCS) to deal with MacArthur during the occupation, an approach that reflected Washington's special deference to the Far Eastern commander. The State Department considered the directive something the War Department wanted so that people in the field would know exactly what they were supposed to do.[13]

The basic directive was an interagency document that had not been submitted to the president or the FEC. In structure and some wording it was similar to the famous JCS 1067, the governing statement of policy for the occupation of Germany that reflected the drastic Morgenthau concept of severely limiting the level of the losing nation's industrial production.[14] The directive for Japan was three times as long as the more authoritative initial policy and contained some severe and punitive provisions, especially in the economic field:

—The supreme commander would "not assume any responsibility for the economic rehabilitation of Japan or for the strengthening of the Japanese economy." Helping the economy would not be a task of the victors. This became the best known of all provisions in the basic directive, especially in Japan.

—Strikes would be prohibited only when the supreme commander considered they would interfere with military operations or directly endanger the occupation forces. This was another provision intended to give democratic forces freer rein. MacArthur and his staff prohibited several strikes during the occupation, but they did not cite this provision as the basis of their action.

—The supreme commander could import supplies only to supplement local resources and only when needed to "prevent such widespread disease or civil unrest as would endanger the occupation forces or interfere with military operations." This provision, also contained in

JCS 1067 for Germany, authorized import of food and raw materials to combat starvation and, eventually, to enable industry to get started up.

Despite MacArthur's misgivings, the basic directive became an important fount of policy for SCAP. One enthusiastic liberal on the staff asserted that the directive provided the authority to put the principles of Franklin Roosevelt's New Deal into effect in Japan.[15] In fact, U.S. planning for Japan went far beyond the New Deal, especially its provisions for radical reform of political and social institutions, not to mention its stern demands for punishing war criminals and purging nationalist leaders. The Japanese did not see the basic directive until 1949, when it was released for publication in the massive study on Japan's "political reorientation" by the Government Section (GS) of SCAP.

These American policy papers drew on many sources, including the Bill of Rights, trust-busting legislation, New Deal social programs, and several state constitutions. Added to these were the traditional powers of victors to destroy the enemy war machine, exact reparations, punish war criminals, and remove political leaders. Washington guidance was strangely silent on several key points: How extensive the "purge" of public officials should be? What kind of changes should be made in the constitution? Should Japan be permanently disarmed? How should "large industrial and banking combinations" be defined? Enfranchisement of women and land reform were not mentioned. In the economic field the supreme commander was told to make extensive reforms, but he was not told how to keep the badly battered Japanese economy afloat or feed the people, problems that he was soon to face.

MacArthur was not a man to want much guidance from his nominal superiors. He once commented in the early days of the occupation that it had been impossible during the war to obtain any clarification of the basic policies he received from Washington, and as a result he had found it necessary to improvise. The general indicated he himself would therefore interpret general policies such as the Potsdam Declaration, "which is broad and capable of varied interpretation."[16]

Contrasting sharply with the massive U.S. planning effort was the Japanese preoccupation with the present and the immediate future. During the war Japanese diplomatic planners had studied American policy statements, especially the Potsdam Declaration. Additional planning was undertaken by government and academic economic experts, who examined matters such as Allied reparations policy and the Bretton Woods monetary arrangements worked out by the Western powers in early 1945. The Japanese were particularly anxious to figure out the economic implications of possible limitations on Japan's standard of living.[17]

One man who had some ideas about what to do was Yoshida Shigeru. On August 27, 1945, twelve days after the emperor's historic broadcast and the day before the first Americans were to arrive, he dashed off a couple of notes to an old friend, Kurusu Saburō, who had been in Washington as a special emissary at the time of Pearl Harbor. Yoshida started his note with a sentence in English: "If the devil has a son, surely he is Tōjō." Tōjō was no doubt the most unpopular man in Japan at that point, and Yoshida was suspicious of most military men. Yoshida sketched a hopeful blueprint. "The way we have accepted de-feat is a performance without parallel anywhere. Now we should apply all our efforts to rebuilding our empire. The cancer of militarist policies must be cut out. Political activity must be reformed. Public morals [must be] promoted. Our diplomacy will have to be totally recast." He then optimistically forecast, "The business world will be improved not only by the advancement of science but also by inviting in American capital." His final words were that he had been reading the English historian G. M. Trevelyan and was filled with admiration for the way British leaders had rebuilt their nation in the nineteenth century after the loss of the American colonies and the long wars against Napoleon.[18]

Organizing for the occupation was a major task for both Americans and Japanese in the month of September. Running big military opera-tions was one of the supreme commander's strong points. General Dwight Eisenhower, who served under MacArthur in the Philippines for four years, said later he was "deeply grateful for the administrative experience he gained under General MacArthur," without which he did not believe he "would have been ready for the great responsibilities of the war period."[19]

Along with organizing his staff, MacArthur felt it was essential to start disarming Japan's forces and forestall any threat of dissidence. On October 4, 1945, in a meeting with Karl T. Compton, president of the Massachusetts Institute of Technology, MacArthur said that he wanted to establish his control in Japan within thirty days, before armed guer-rilla bands started operating in the mountains. Although there had been a few reports of the existence of dissident groups, MacArthur wanted to hold off taking actions that might be seriously disruptive—for example, a purge of wartime leaders. He also rebuffed an invitation from President Truman to return to Washington for a victory parade in his honor, citing the "extraordinarily dangerous . . . situation" in Japan.[20]

SCAP had given the Japanese responsibility for demobilizing their armed forces. Huge amounts of military materiel were destroyed, and military production facilities were set aside for reparations to be awarded later to the Allied powers after they agreed on how war material should be divided up. On October 16, 1945, MacArthur announced that Japan's armed forces "are now completely abolished. . . . Approximately seven million armed men . . . have laid down their weapons. In the accomplishment of the extremely difficult and dangerous surrender in Japan, unique in the annals of history, not a shot was necessary, not a drop of Allied blood was shed."[21] Without doubt, the demobilization of all Japanese forces within two months of the surrender was a remarkable feat and powerful evidence of Japan's desire to carry out the surrender terms. Any threat of armed resistance had dissipated.

From the moment of surrender the occupation launched a barrage of orders to the government. During the eighty months of its life, SCAP issued some six thousand SCAPINs, or SCAP instructions, on an enormous range of matters, mostly small but on occasion monumental. Other instructions—letters, memoranda, and verbal orders—were also issued. The stream never stopped, but the early months produced the heaviest flow.

The general believed in clear and simple lines of control, leaving no one in doubt that he was the boss. He would permit no American or Allied activities in Japan that he did not control. At the outset, he set up two headquarters, one to control Japan (GHQ SCAP) and the other to command U.S. forces in the Far East (GHQ FEC). MacArthur felt that if an organization "is right at the top, it will be right at the bottom."[22]

GHQ SCAP had fifteen staff sections at its peak strength. The most influential were the Government Section, which dealt with the Diet and political matters; the Economic and Scientific Section (ESS); the Civil Information and Education Section (CIE), which handled education and religion; and G-2, which controlled intelligence and censorship.[23] At its peak strength GHQ SCAP numbered about 5,000 persons. MacArthur also commanded the Eighth Army under Lieutenant General Robert L. Eichelberger in Yokohama and the Sixth Army under General Walter Krueger in Kyoto. At the outset the two armies each had about 230,000 troops. The Sixth Army was disbanded at the end of the year, leaving the Eighth Army with about 200,000 troops. By the end of 1948 the Eighth Army numbered 117,580, including a small British

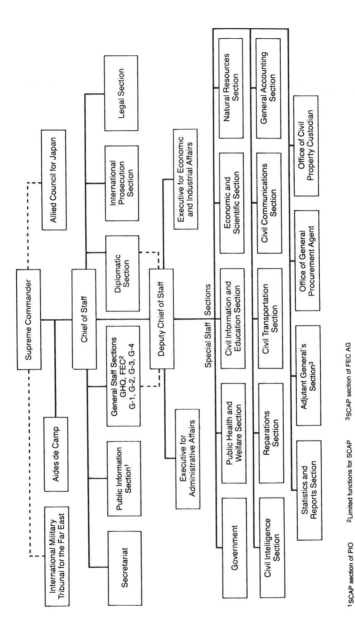

SCAP Organization Chart

International Military Tribunal for the Far East

Allied Council for Japan

Supreme Commander

Secretariat

Aides de Camp

Public Information Section[1]

General Staff Sections GHQ, FEC[2] G-1, G-2, G-3, G-4

Chief of Staff

Diplomatic Section

International Prosecution Section

Legal Section

Executive for Administrative Affairs

Deputy Chief of Staff

Executive for Economic and Industrial Affairs

Special Staff Sections

Government

Civil Intelligence Section

Statistics and Reports Section

Public Health and Welfare Section

Reparations Section

Adjutant General's Section[3]

Civil Information and Education Section

Civil Transportation Section

Office of General Procurement Agent

Economic and Scientific Section

Civil Communications Section

Office of Civil Property Custodian

Natural Resources Section

General Accounting Section

[1]SCAP section of PIO   [2]Limited functions for SCAP   [3]SCAP section of FEC AG

Commonwealth contingent. Large military forces were never needed for the occupation of Japan.

The general held few staff meetings and saw very few members on his staff outside of section chiefs and staff aides. Those who had ready access were the chiefs of the important sections—GS, ESS, G-2, and the Diplomatic Section (DS), which dealt with foreign diplomats. The general saw a few outsiders fairly often, such as the British and Canadian ambassadors and a few American newsmen. He did not have a lot of meetings, perhaps three or four a day, and often they were quite lengthy.[24] MacArthur delegated freely to his section chiefs. He made decisions after reading a one-page abstract or summary prepared by staff officers on the basis of the often complex and lengthy memoranda submitted by the staff sections, as, for example, on the reorganization of the Yokohama Specie Bank. He was not one to delay or agonize over intricate problems. Press releases were important and were often issued in his name, even if he had little to do with the subject matter.

The occupation staff was short of people who had more than a passing knowledge of the country. Only two of MacArthur's section chiefs, William Sebald of DS and Lieutenant Colonel Donald R. Nugent (USMCR), the second chief of CIE and a former high school teacher, had had extensive prewar experience in Japan. Japanese-Americans, a number of whom were professionally trained, were almost all engaged in language work. Nevertheless, the occupation could boast of many persons well qualified in specialized fields.

MacArthur occupied a small office facing an inner court on the sixth floor of the Dai Ichi Insurance building. The occupation took over many office buildings in downtown Tokyo as well as many of the Western-style houses still standing in the city. At one point it had been suggested that Tokyo University might be requisitioned to serve as the headquarters for the occupation, but this idea was not pursued. The Japanese government paid to owners as "occupation costs" the cost of rentals and maintenance of buildings taken over by U.S. personnel. Japan paid more than $4 billion in occupation costs during the eighty months of the occupation; this was about twice as much as Japan received from the United States in economic assistance.[25]

Finding a role for the U.S. State Department was a knotty problem. State wanted a separate office that would handle international political and economic issues, as was the case in the American zone in Germany, but MacArthur insisted that the office be under his control. State finally yielded, and the staff of the political adviser, called POLAD, found a niche serving as a sort of foreign office in SCAP. Later POLAD took on some political and economic responsibilities, but the role of the State Department was minor for most of the occupation.[26] Under Secretary of State Dean Acheson, a supporter of tough policies toward Japan, decided in 1945 that he did not want a "Japan hand" to head the Tokyo office and selected a China expert, George Atcheson, Jr., to be the first political adviser.

The organization of local U.S. military government teams posed another problem. Initially set up in fifty-three places around Japan to observe and assist in carrying out SCAP policies and consisting on an average of about fifty persons each, these teams were useful in keeping contact with local Japanese officials and even in helping the police ensure that rice collection quotas were filled and taxes paid, but many teams were inadequately staffed and poorly informed of what the Tokyo headquarters was doing. In 1948 they were renamed civil affairs teams, and their operations were significantly reduced.

The Japanese had the daunting task of preparing themselves to deal with an administration whose purposes and methods they could only dimly fathom. But they plunged ahead resolutely. They set up a central liaison office (CLO) on August 22, 1945, at the request of MacArthur's headquarters in Manila, to serve as a channel between the occupation and the Japanese government.[27] The CLO had representatives from other agencies and established field offices all over Japan to match the American local government teams. These field offices were useful for placing unemployed officials from the Foreign Office, some of whom, such as Okazaki Katsuo and Asakai Kōichirō, were later top diplomats. The head of the CLO's Yokohama office, Suzuki Tadakatsu, was especially valuable in his relations with General Eichelberger. Handling criminal incidents by Americans, particularly in the early days of the occupation, was a special test of the liaison system. The Japanese meticulously reported these cases, and the Americans investigated them with equal care, although they did not always prosecute suspects vigorously. Incidents continued throughout the occupation, some of them serious, but each side usually felt the other was acting in good faith. The occupation forces won much goodwill from the Japanese population for their friendly behavior. Former Imperial Army officers were impressed by the good conduct of American enlisted men. Recognizing the crucial importance of the CLO in keeping good relations with the occupation forces, Prime Minister Yoshida kept a firm grip on its operations until it was disbanded in 1948. By then SCAP sections were dealing directly with their counterparts in the Japanese government and no longer needed a liaison agency.

To put occupation orders on a legal basis, the Japanese either passed enabling legislation or issued ordinances under the blanket authority of imperial ordinance no. 542 of September 20, 1945. This decree gave supralegal effect to occupation orders and imposed severe penalties on Japanese for violations. A total of 293 imperial ordinances (called cabinet ordinances after the new constitution went into effect in 1947) were issued during the occupation.[28]

The pressure exerted by the occupation led to the resignation of the caretaker Higashikuni cabinet on October 5, six days after MacArthur told the prime minister he saw no reason for a cabinet change. Installing an imperial prince as prime minister and for good measure making another prince from the old nobility the prime minister's deputy, neither of whom was able to make much headway with MacArthur or his staff, had clearly been a stopgap device that had run its course by early October.

The resourceful lord privy seal, Marquis Kido, decided that the new prime minister should be someone with a clean record and a diplomatic background. Yoshida said he did not even want to be considered. Baron Shidehara Kijūrō, a former foreign minister known for his scholarly ability in English and his prewar advocacy of "peaceful diplomacy," was chosen. Shidehara was seventy-five and had been out of the public eye for ten years. Some even asked, "Isn't Shidehara dead?" He told the emperor he had no confidence he would be adequate as prime minister, and the emperor replied, "Who has confidence under today's conditions?" The only questions MacArthur asked Foreign Minister Yoshida about Shidehara were how old he was and if he spoke English.[29]

On October 9 the Shidehara cabinet was installed and included Yoshida as foreign minister. George Atcheson, the political adviser, called it "mediocre." Shidehara was eager, despite his frail health and long absence from public life, not to be a passive agent of the occupation but rather to carry out some of the urgent tasks facing the nation. One of his first projects, to strengthen the police, was turned down by SCAP, which was not yet ready to deal with that sensitive issue.[30]

Yoshida, one of the activists in the cabinet, thought economic reconstruction should be Japan's number one goal. He enlisted the help of a number of specialists from business and academic circles with whom he met regularly for advice. Several of the country's outstanding economists helped him, including Ōkita Saburō, an electrical engineeer by training who became a world-famous authority on economic development, and Tsuru Shigeto, a Harvard Ph.D. and later president of Hitotsubashi University, Japan's equivalent of the London School of Economics. Several of these men, foreseeing the inevitable disaster, had met in secret even before the war ended to plan for the future.[31]

On October 11 Shidehara called on the supreme commander. One observer made the witty comment that new prime ministers now had to call on the supreme commander in addition to visiting the Grand Shrine at Ise. At the outset the general took the unusual step of first reading to Shidehara, and then giving him, a short paper listing five basic reforms MacArthur wanted instituted "as rapidly as they can be assimilated." Prefaced by the statement that unquestionably "liberalization of the constitution" would be necessary, the points listed were:

1. Give women the right to vote, which would make "government directly subservient to the well-being of the home."
2. Encourage labor unions and correct child-labor practices.
3. Institute a more liberal education to make clear that government is "the servant rather than the master of the people."
4. Eliminate practices "which through secret inquisition and abuse have held people in constant fear."
5. Promote "a wide distribution of income and ownership of the means of production and trade."

The selection of points and wording was MacArthur's own, probably with some staff help, and, except for the last point, was not taken from any instruction he had received from Washington. Presurrender planning had made no direct reference to women's suffrage and may have taken for granted that it was a basic policy goal. In Washington the State Department told the British ambassador it did not have the text of what MacArthur had given Shidehara.[32]

The prime minister said his government would try to carry out these policies. It was already taking steps to include women's suffrage in a new election law and was looking into some of the other points raised by the general. Encouragement of labor unions and "antitrust" action seemed to give Shidehara some concern, but he said his government would study them. He then commented that Japan had been on the road to a liberal and democratic state some years earlier, before a "malign influence was allowed to prevail." The principle of respecting the will of the people would emerge again but "in the shape of Japanese democracy" and not like democracy in Western countries. MacArthur said he realized there had been an "interruption" in Japan and added that he wished the new government well. MacArthur's espousal of the "interruption" theory was somewhat at variance with his frequent characterization of prewar Japan as "feudal" and seemed to put him in the camp of those, such as Yoshida, who thought Japan had been on the road to democracy but had temporarily "stumbled."[33]

Nothing seems to have been said about the constitution, but there was almost surely a gap between the thinking of the supreme commander and that of the prime minister about how far constitutional revision should go. Nevertheless, two days later Shidehara appointed a special cabinet minister, Matsumoto Jōji, to study the constitutional issue. At the emperor's request, Konoe was hard at work on the same problem. In early November two New York papers wrote editorials criticizing this "acceptance of Konoe as the man to lead Japan to democracy." SCAP quickly issued a press release denying any connection with Konoe and warned Atcheson not to have any further association with him. Konoe's connection with the occupation thus ended abruptly.[34]

The Shidehara cabinet, true to its word, went ahead with election reform. On December 15 the Diet passed a law giving the right to vote to all citizens older than twenty; this action more than doubled the electorate, which had been limited to males older than twenty-five. The law also increased the size of electoral districts, long an issue in Japanese politics. General MacArthur and his Government Section decided not to intervene in the Japanese legislative process, despite the strong SCAP propensity, especially in the early days of the occupation, to press for Japanese adoption of U.S. models. Paradoxically, the Japanese decided in 1947 to go back to the former system of medium-sized districts.[35]

By the fall of 1945 the political parties were busy getting organized. They tended to repeat the late prewar pattern of two large conservative parties and a scattering of smaller parties. The first to organize after the surrender was the Socialist Party, set up on November 2, which preferred to be known in English as the Social Democratic Party because this had a sweeter ring to American ears. Katayama Tetsu, a former Diet member and a prominent lawyer, was its leader. For the first time in Japanese history, the communists formed a legal party. They began to organize after their leaders were let out of prison in early October, with Tokuda Kyūichi and Shiga Yoshio in the vanguard. Early in 1946 another prominent figure, Nosaka Sanzō, returned from exile in China to join the leadership. The communist newspaper *Akahata*, or "Red Flag," began publication on October 20, its daily circulation soon growing to six hundred thousand.[36]

The two large conservative parties had only barely discernible differences in doctrine. The head of the Liberal Party, which had 50 seats in the lower house, was the most skilled politician to emerge on the early postwar scene, Hatoyama Ichirō, with more than thirty years of experience as a political leader. The Progressive Party, with 249 members, was the biggest in the "Tōjō Diet" elected in 1942. By December 1945 thirty-five other political parties had declared their intention to participate in the forthcoming election.

The four major parties—Liberal, Progressive, Socialist, and Communist—all advocated in varying ways strict execution of the surrender terms, political and economic reform, and respect for individual rights. The liberals and progressives supported the emperor system, the socialists were silent on this score, and the communists advocated its abolition. The conservatives favored free economic enterprise, the socialists promoted a socialized and planned economy, and the communists wanted participation by the people in the management of industry and confiscation of idle agricultural land. Hatoyama spoke out strongly against communism.

The political pattern that emerged right after the war shaped the entire future of the Japanese system—strong conservative and centrist forces, with socialists to the left of center and communists to the far left. A two-party system never developed.

PART II

MacArthur's
Two Hundred Days

Of the six and one-half years of the occupation, the first two hundred days were the most dramatic and the most significant. This period resembled the first "one hundred days" of the Roosevelt New Deal in 1933 for the initiative and enthusiasm of the reformers. It was a time when the Japanese seemed almost eager for change, even though they were understandably confused and dazed by the kaleidoscopic turns in their national life.

The overwhelming thrust of the SCAP program was on reform. The models followed were almost universally from American experience, highlighted by a liberal constitution, representative government, full adult suffrage, a strong labor movement, educational opportunity for the many, widespread ownership of all means of production, and autonomous local government. Britain provided the model for a constitutional monarchy and parliamentary government.

Writers about the occupation wage verbal war about whether the Japanese were ready for democracy in 1945. Some argue that Japan's society was still pervaded by feudal elements; others claim that Japan had been steadily modernizing for nearly a century. In any case, it seems safe to say that the Japanese in 1945 were not unprepared for many of the American changes, having had a half century of experience with their own diluted form of constitutional government and parliamentary democracy. Even though Japan's prewar government had had some of the trappings of a police state, it had been far from the brutality and massive repression of Hitler's Germany.[1] Japan had held a relatively

free parliamentary election in 1942 at the height of the nation's war
fervor. Yet overall, the prewar period had been a catastrophic setback
for liberal forces in Japan, even if some democratic seeds had remained
in the soil.

In mid-October 1945 the mood of the Japanese leaders and people
was so receptive that MacArthur spoke of their "complete docility" and
of the "sense of liberation" they seemed to feel.[2] Most Japanese were
far more preoccupied with desperate shortages of food, clothing,
shelter, and jobs than with the intricacies of occupation reforms. Yet
they were hearing a lot about *demokurashii* (for a long time they used
the English word) and knew it was something the Americans thought
very important. To many Japanese the term seemed to mean "working together in a spirit of harmony" rather than the more abstract
"freedom" or "equality." The draft of a new and liberal constitution
devised by MacArthur's staff soon gave the vague concept a concrete
form.

Punishment was an important counterpart to reform in the early period
of the occupation. Persons who had led the nation to war or committed
crimes in military campaigns during the previous fourteen years were put
on trial. Those who had played a significant role in Japan's nationalist
surge before the war were removed, or "purged," from important positions in government and barred from responsible posts in the future. The
Japanese were told they would have to make reparations for the damage
they had done in East Asian countries.

The supreme commander was the guiding hand for these far-ranging
programs. Although he was directly involved in only a few projects, the
style and the tone of the occupation were his, and he commanded the
support and even the confidence of the Japanese politicians and people.
No leader emerged from the ranks of the Japanese. Hatoyama, the head
of the Liberal Party, seemed to have the best credentials, but MacArthur
purged him as a right-winger. Yoshida Shigeru distinguished himself as
foreign minister by his energy and bustle. He tried to foster rapport
between Americans and Japanese, but he incurred the implacable suspicion of some of those on MacArthur's staff as an old-guard reactionary.
The emperor made signal contributions to the new order by renouncing
his divinity and endorsing the new constitution. The supreme commander seemed to place the emperor beyond reproach when he told
Washington that tampering with the position of the Tennō would be
ill-advised. The State Department found a role in the occupation for
America's Allies, to which MacArthur gave grudging assent.

By May 1946 the occupation seemed to have been successfully launched. Japanese and Americans were pretty well adjusted to each other. Washington had reason to be happy with MacArthur's smooth administration in Tokyo.[3]

CHAPTER 4

The First Wave
of Reform

SCAP's initial campaign in 1945 dealt with the press and civil rights. In the first weeks of the occupation the press in both Japan and the United States gave SCAP a good deal of trouble. Guidance for the media—newspapers, magazines, and radio—designed to eliminate practices of the past and open the way to greater freedom of expression became urgent as news and views of all sorts began to appear in the newly unleashed press. "There shall be an absolute minimum of restrictions upon freedom of speech," was the positive note sounded by the first SCAP order of September 10, 1945, called the press code. At the same time, relying on general authority to censor communications and the press, SCAP prohibited "false or destructive criticism of the Allied powers, and rumors."[1] Censorship of Japanese newspapers, radio, magazines, and films was heavy in the early days and continued to the end of the occupation in 1952, though precensorship of most magazines was terminated in December 1947 and of newspapers in July 1948. In retrospect it is hard to escape the feeling that General Mac-Arthur permitted far more censorship than seemed necessary for the security of his forces.[2] Criticism of SCAP censorship policy has been an enduring complaint by the Japanese.

The press in the United States gave vent to some unhappiness about events in Japan. The *New York Times* carried a think piece on September 14 arguing that "the enemy has succeeded in perpetuating the same traditions, customs, processes, habits and institutions that did so much to bring on this war." The *Times* was particularly disturbed by "our acceptance of the emperor as sort of a 'junior partner' in the surrender and occupation." MacArthur countered the same day, noting the "impatience of the press based on an assumption of a so-called soft occupation policy in Japan" and asserting that "the surrender terms . . . will not be applied in kid glove fashion."[3]

Also on September 14, the Associated Press carried a story of an interview with Prime Minister Higashikuni, who asked, "People of America, won't you forget Pearl Harbor? . . . We people of Japan will forget the devastation wrought by the atomic bomb. . . . The war is ended. Let us now bury hate." This report touched off a barrage of criticism in the United States. Dean Acheson commented that "nothing could show more clearly than this statement the failure of the Japanese to understand the nature of their conduct or the mind of the American people. . . . Pearl Harbor is not a symbol of hate for Japan but a symbol of Japanese perfidy." Despite Acheson's lawyerlike distinction, the Japanese have often tended to equate Pearl Harbor with the atomic bomb and have sometimes added atrocities in Vietnam for good measure, trying to show that war horrors are not confined to one nation. It is remarkable that the reaction of the only people to have endured the atomic bomb remained as controlled and muted as it did during the occupation and afterward.[4]

MacArthur himself got into trouble. He issued a press statement on September 17 that because of "the smooth progress of the occupation," within six months not more than 200,000 men would be needed, "which will permit the complete demobilization of our citizen Pacific forces." Senior officials in Washington were worried at that time that demobilization of the armed forces was proceeding too rapidly, and they were annoyed by MacArthur's apparent assertion of authority. Acheson issued a stinging comment to the press that "the occupation forces are the instruments of policy and not the determinants of policy." MacArthur, who was not accustomed to hearing such firm talk from higher authority, in turn sent a cable to the War Department that was uncharacteristically apologetic, saying he thought he was "acting in complete conformity with the War Department's announced policy of demobilizing just as rapidly as conditions permitted."[5]

In a conversation with General Eichelberger a month later, MacArthur was bitter about the way he had been handled by Washington. He attributed this to Truman's fear that MacArthur might be a serious political rival. The general said he might have been dropped from his position if the Soviets had not "come out against me," but "thanks to the Soviets I am on top. I would like to pin a medal on their a —."[6]

On October 4 General MacArthur issued one of the most powerful directives of the entire occupation, a "bill of rights" ordering the government to remove all restrictions on political, civil, and religious liberties; free all political prisoners; abolish secret police organizations; permit unrestricted comment about the emperor and the government; and remove the minister of home affairs and all high police officials responsible for the enforcement of measures limiting freedom of thought, speech, religion, and assembly.[7] Japanese reactions were understandably cautious. Some welcomed the first of the basic reform directives as a long step toward freeing their society of nationalist shackles, while conservatives were shocked by its assault on the reactionary practices and habits of thought that had become embedded in their society.

The provision for freeing political prisoners jolted the Japanese most. As far back as 1887 Japan had instituted measures to punish persons expressing unorthodox political views. It had subsequently toughened the restrictions until the wide-ranging Peace Preservation Law of 1925, one of the most infamous laws on the books, made it a crime to advocate overthrow of *kokutai*, the mystical "national polity," by criticizing the emperor or calling for basic political change.[8] Thousands of suspected leftists had been imprisoned for attacking the government or criticizing the political system. Professors had been dismissed for supporting free speech or for describing the emperor institution as an "organ" of the state when people were being told the emperor was the incarnation of the state.

The directive brought about the release of 439 political prisoners and ended the surveillance of 2,026 others; it forced the removal of 4,800 special thought police from their positions, as well as the home minister, Yamazaki Iwao, whose order to the press on September 29 not to publish any more photos of MacArthur and the emperor had been canceled by SCAP.[9]

Old-line Japanese thought the October 4 directive was "excessive." Moderate Japanese officials, like the "social bureaucrats" who handled labor and welfare issues, thought it was "foolish" for SCAP to liberate communist leaders. Yoshida proposed to MacArthur's chief of staff, General Richard K. Sutherland, on October 5 that in the future there should be better consultation before such important actions were taken. Yoshida complained a few days later to the president of the United

Press news service that the occupation was making it hard for the police to preserve order and respect for the law. One of Yoshida's subordinates in the Foreign Office, Sone Eki, commented in his memoirs that Yoshida wanted to play down the impact of the October 4 directive by applying it only to noncommunists, so that the Peace Preservation Law would stay in effect for communists. This Yoshida gambit failed.[10]

The release of sixteen prisoners from Fuchu prison in the outskirts of Tokyo on October 5, 1945, became one of the more publicized incidents of the occupation. Two SCAP officials, E. Herbert Norman, a Canadian diplomat attached to Civil Intelligence Section, and John K. Emmerson, a U.S. diplomat serving in POLAD, both prewar experts on Japanese politics, went to see the political prisoners in Fuchu and invited three of them to come to GHQ for a talk. Two of these prisoners, Tokuda and Shiga, later became leaders of the Japanese Communist Party. Norman and Emmerson were attacked by Americans and Japanese on and off for many years after this event on suspicion of having given support to the communist movement in Japan. Their previous records were given the minutest scrutiny, especially Norman's communist activity while a university student, and their later careers were profoundly affected.[11]

Economic reform proved to be the most complicated and intractable field of endeavor for the entire occupation. The disastrous economic situation was compounded by an ill-defined U.S. policy. Labor, the most volatile and dynamic element in postwar Japan, took full advantage of SCAP's early liberalism and then wanted to go farther and faster than SCAP would permit. In the field of business regulation SCAP moved slowly; it tried to get the big Japanese conglomerates to break themselves up but met pockets of resistance. Land reform, by contrast, was well planned and smoothly worked out with the Japanese; the program was rooted in fertile soil.

The Japanese economy was close to collapse at the end of 1945. Food was extremely scarce in the cities, industrial production was less than one-fifth of the wartime high, and the consumer price level was nine times the prewar standard of 1934–1936. Foreign trade, including imports of food and raw materials, was totally cut off. For many months unemployment was hard to keep track of. It may have reached as high as 13 million at the end of 1945 amid the flow of demobilized soldiers and refugees returning from the mainland; it fell to about 3 million later in 1946.[12]

The Japanese government and military leaders bore a heavy responsibility for the catastrophic inflation that swamped the country for many months. At the end of the war military pay officers hastily disbursed all existing appropriations, paying out huge sums of money between August 15 and the arrival of the Americans at the end of the month. Military pensions were paid off for years ahead. A SCAP order in September 1945 to end these payments may have been too late to have any effect. Stockpiles of military equipment and precious metals worth several billion dollars were handed over to unscrupulous dealers, who either hoarded the goods or sold them on the black market at huge profits.[13]

The food shortage became alarming when the 1945 crop fell to two-thirds the normal level. The caloric intake for adults in the cities was for many months approximately one thousand calories, compared with a normal adult level of eighteen hundred. People living in the big cities were forced to buy on the black market and barter their personal possessions in order to survive. In October 1945 Japanese officials asked for more than 4 million tons of food from the United States. SCAP challenged Japanese statistics, and Yoshida ruefully admitted to Mac-Arthur that the data given him by his experts were bad, adding that poor statistics were one reason Japan had lost the war. SCAP released some of its local stocks, but Japan did not receive food imports from the United States until 1946. Rumors spread in the press that 10 million persons might die of starvation, but the Japanese managed to scrape through. Although malnutrition was serious, it was difficult to establish whether anyone actually starved to death.[14]

Contagious disease was a threat. SCAP's Public Health and Welfare Section rose to this challenge, although such assistance was not mentioned in Allied policy. Massive campaigns against diphtheria, typhus, typhoid, cholera, smallpox, and tuberculosis achieved dramatic reductions in the incidence of these diseases. Agricultural land was sprayed with DDT. General MacArthur stated in his memoirs that 2 million lives were saved by these measures in the first two years of the occupation. He solemnly added, "With the dreadful loss of lives in the war fresh in my mind, these statistics brought much comfort to my soul."[15]

The economic results of the war were not all bad. Japan's militarist decade had witnessed several remarkable innovations in industry, some with long-term effects in strengthening productivity. Heavy industry developed rapidly, as did chemical production. The training of engineers and skilled workers intensified. Large firms became expert in subcontracting to small ones, thereby erecting the two-tier industrial system that is now entrenched in Japan. The seniority wage and lifetime employment systems in big companies expanded greatly in the period before and during World War II. Government "guidance" to business and industry, which was not far from control, became the general practice during the war period.[16]

MacArthur's main instructions from Washington in the economic area were to free the labor movement, break up the big industrial and banking combinations, and leave it to the Japanese to revive their economy. U.S. goals were not to try out social experiments but rather to broaden the ownership of productive assets in agriculture and industry and widen the distribution of economic benefits in the form of wages and consumer goods. To reach these goals SCAP decided it would be necessary to break up the prewar system, which confined ownership of enterprises to relatively few families and individuals, encouraged large industrial concentrations, and opposed efforts by workers and farmers to organize for better treatment.

Some critics saw a contradiction in these policies. A leading British authority asserted, "Whatever the political and social merits of those measures, they certainly made no contribution to economic recovery. Most of them actually impeded it." A Japanese financial expert, Watanabe Takeshi, was more trenchant: these policies were "reforms that New Dealers wanted to realize in Japan but could not carry out in the United States." Conservative Japanese often grumbled about the "New Dealers" in SCAP.[17]

In the field of labor, legislation enacted well before World War II recognized a role for labor unions in dispute mediation; regulated the employment of women, children, and young workers; and set up a limited system of insurance and pensions for some employees. Government surveillance and interference in labor activities were frequent, as were disputes and violence. By the mid-1930s trade union membership was at its prewar peak, about 420,000, a small part of the labor force. In the late 1930s when government policy turned oppressive, left-wing unions were banned and their leaders were jailed. A "labor front" organized at that time and controlled by the government in effect destroyed the labor movement.[18]

Labor conditions right after the war were dreadful. Wages were abysmally low, with a wage base in early 1946 of only ¥213 a month; foreign exchange values were not very meaningful in the early period of the occupation, but this was probably the equivalent of a little less than $10. The labor movement started slowly, with only six unions consisting of 3,800 members formed by the fall of 1945. But the movement soon took on momentum and responded more powerfully to the stimulus of reform than did any other group in Japan.[19] Early SCAP actions dissolved the government's wartime front organizations, banned the use of prison labor in projects competitive with the regular labor force, and tried to curb the labor-boss system, by which bosses recruited gangs of workers and extracted a substantial part of the laborers' pay for their own pockets.

Not long after the surrender labor troubles began. Korean and Taiwanese coal miners fled from their enforced servitude, causing coal production to plummet. The three big Tokyo newspapers became a battleground, with militant liberals trying to eject senior editors and managers accused of having actively supported the war effort. *Asahi* and *Mainichi* eliminated the nationalists without strife, but the struggle at *Yomiuri* went on for months in 1945 and 1946 before a settlement was finally reached. The *Yomiuri* battle was an early instance of "production control," an unusual Japanese phenomenon whereby the workers took over and operated a factory or business and then, after settlement had been reached, turned over the operation and any profits to management. Similar struggles took place at Toshiba Electric and Japan Steel Tube Company. Between January and June 1946, 255 such incidents involving 157,000 workers occurred. The government considered these takeovers illegal, and the Supreme Court of Japan eventually agreed. SCAP experts asserted that legality depended on the specific circumstances. Production control bore some resemblance to a revolutionary takeover of the means of production, but one authority said in March 1946, "The distance yet to be traveled to a revolutionary transformation of the capitalist system in Japan was great."[20]

On December 21 the Diet enacted the first important piece of labor legislation, the Labor Union Law, drafted after Prime Minister Shidehara met the supreme commander on October 11. The moderate "social bureaucrats" who had long pressed for more liberal treatment of the labor movement played a key role in drafting labor legislation during the occupation and in rolling some of it back later. The new law was based on both Japanese and U.S. practice, in particular the Wagner Act of 1935, and, of course, had SCAP approval. It not only legalized trade unions and the right of workers to organize and join trade unions but also encouraged collective bargaining and set out procedures under which workers had the right to strike. Provision was also made for public workers to organize and strike, an important and controversial matter in Japan, where the government operated railways, communications, and other activities that were conducted by the private sector in the United States. Commissions of labor, management, and "public interest" representatives were established on a national and prefectural level to oversee the execution of the law, the first of many pieces of such legislation setting up similar commissions to curb the power of the bureaucracy and the central government.[21]

The Labor Union Law was revolutionary for Japan in somewhat the same way the Wagner Act had been for the United States; both laws were catalysts for the emergence of more powerful and aggressive labor movements. In Japan the new law seemed to release the pent-up energy of the working groups. The number of unions and their members began to skyrocket. By the end of 1945 union membership had surpassed the prewar peak, and by the end of 1946 there were 17,266 unions with nearly 5 million members. Even the Tokyo geisha formed a union.[22]

Japanese unions were in effect company unions. Following their pre-surrender structure, they were enterprise unions formed by all the workers in one company, not craft or industrywide unions, as in the United States. In many cases white-collar workers joined the company union, and union leaders sometimes later became management officials. Enterprise unions often joined other enterprise unions in labor associations, but the core unit was the union in each plant.[23] True to Japanese social custom, the work force of a Japanese company was closely knit, forming groups not unlike military units and even lining up every morning to sing the company song.

Speaking a year later of the postwar growth of the labor movement, General MacArthur commented, "I do not think the history of labor throughout the last two thousand years has shown such an extraordinary, magnificent development in such a short space of time. They had gone far beyond my expectations and I was delighted."[24] Neither the general nor the chiefs of ESS knew much about labor. They both gave wide discretion to the heads of the labor division, who in the early days of the occupation gave free rein to moderate Japanese experts and were even willing to tolerate some communist influence within organized labor.[25]

Agricultural land reform, one of the more ambitious and draconian operations of the occupation, deeply influenced the status and income of almost half the population. With an area of 142,811 square miles, Japan is not quite as large as California. Only 17 percent of its land is arable. Its chief crop is rice, occupying more than half of the cultivated land. At the end of the war about 30 million Japanese, or 5.7 million families, lived on farms; this was about 40 percent of the population. About 65 percent of the farmers were tenants in whole or in part, and they tilled about 50 percent of the nation's 15 million acres of farmland. Farm plots averaged about 2.4 acres, sometimes scattered among several pieces of land. Half of the tenants rented less than 1.2 acres each. Nearly 1 million landlords were absentee owners, many of them living in villages near their land.[26]

Tenants turned over about 50 percent of their crops to the owner as rent. Out of the rest they had to procure housing, food, fertilizer, and equipment. They had little security of tenure because there were rarely written contracts and tenants could be dispossessed without compensation. Nevertheless, the paternalistic nature of Japanese society, which was particularly strong in rural areas, tended to alleviate the harsh features of the tenant system.

The countryside was a source of workers for the cities and recruits for the army. This heavy flow into industry impeded the growth of a strong trade union movement and served as a drag on wages. Supported by the nationalists, rural landlords had joined with urban industrialists before the war to obtain protective legislation from the Diet that would keep workers and tenant farmers in their place.[27]

Living conditions during the war had not been disadvantageous for farmers. They had food to eat, and their income was high because rice was in great demand. The government authorized payments of rent in money rather than in produce, a distinct advantage for the farmers. Although many tenants were given greater security in their holdings, the rapid rise in the value of agricultural land and products caused many landlords to try to dispossess their tenants and take over themselves.

Early U.S. policy papers did not call for action on land reform. A few experts in Washington explored the subject, notably Russian-born agronomist Wolf Ladejinsky, who joined SCAP in January 1946 and eventually became a leading authority on land reform in Asia. The State Department office in Tokyo sent the supreme commander a report based on the Washington research. MacArthur became interested and ordered a staff study, possibly because, as he said in his memoirs, "I felt that any man who farmed the land should, by law, be entitled to his crops, that there should be an end to sharecropping, and that even more fundamental, perhaps, was the need to make land itself available to the people."[28]

The Japanese had been moving ahead on their own. In response to increasing pressure for improvement of rural landholding conditions, the Shidehara cabinet decided in 1945 to enable tenants to buy the land they tilled. This was another of Japan's "independent initiatives" toward democracy after the surrender. Late in the year the Diet passed legislation setting a limit of 12.25 acres on absentee ownership. Conservatives like Yoshida felt that this legislation went far enough because the improved status of farmers had markedly reduced any inequities. SCAP experts disagreed. On December 9 they ordered suspension of part of the law and indicated that 12.25 acres was too much for absentee owners to retain; SCAP requested a more comprehensive plan. Further action regarding land reform was then held up until a new government was formed after the general election of April 1946.[29]

Probably the best known of all occupation reforms was the breaking up of the zaibatsu, the large industrial and financial conglomerates, usually family controlled, that flourished during Japan's modern century. It was American policy to "favor a program for the dissolution of the large industrial and banking combinations" and encourage "a wide distribution of income and of ownership of the means of production and trade."[30] Great bureaucratic battles were fought over these general propositions.

For the Japanese, *zaibatsu kaitai* (trust-busting) was the epitome of New Deal activism, especially when the program applied not only to the relatively few family-dominated companies but to hundreds of other lesser business "concentrations." Yet the New Deal trust-busting program never had the toughness or wide scope of the SCAP campaign, which an authority has described as the "most ambitious anti-trust action in history."[31]

Some able and zealous economists in Washington thought the zaibatsu had been a powerful force behind Japan's will to war and thus had to be smashed. For example, an official report concluded in 1945 that "not only were the zaibatsu as responsible for Japan's militarism as the militarists themselves, but they profited immensely by it. . . . Unless the zaibatsu are broken up, the Japanese have little prospect of ever being able to govern themselves as free men."[32]

Paradoxically, when the top suspects were indicted a few months later for having plotted aggressive war, not a single zaibatsu representative was included. The American chief prosecutor decided that the evidence was inadequate to support a charge of war crimes against any of the business barons. (In Nazi Germany several were put on trial, including the financial wizard Hjalmar Schacht.) Some of the Allies were skeptical about trust-busting. In commenting on U.S. policy, an official British staff paper remarked, "The principle has encountered formidable obstacles in its application in the United States, but the Americans are apparently determined to confer on their late enemies the benefits of an economic regime which they find difficulty realizing at home." Other skeptics argued on economic grounds that large concentrations were integral to Japan's economic development.[33]

The Japanese military had mistrusted the "old" zaibatsu as pro-Western and hostile to nationalist goals. A few zaibatsu leaders had been assassinated in the 1930s, including Baron Takuma Dan, the managing director of Mitsui Gōmei, the central holding company of Mitsui. The military reportedly preferred to deal with the "new" zaibatsu, many of which had been established to promote armament production and the industrial development of Manchuria. By the time of the China Incident in 1937, when the Japanese Army invaded China, all the zaibatsu were cooperating with Japan's military leaders, often expanding their activities in military fields and acting as agents for the government. After Pearl Harbor cooperation was virtually total.

General MacArthur thought the zaibatsu were one of the pillars of Japanese feudalism that would have to be torn down by the occupation. In his memoirs he described the zaibatsu as "about ten Japanese families who practiced a kind of private socialism. They controlled 90 percent of all Japanese industry." In a scornful vein he once said the zaibatsu were like "the most effete New York clubmen."[34]

A good part of prewar Japanese industrial, commercial, and banking ownership was, in fact, in the hands of ten family groups. The four largest—Mitsui, Mitsubishi, Sumitomo, and Yasuda—controlled more assets than the other zaibatsu combined. By the end of the war the ten controlled about 68 percent of Japan's machinery and equipment production, about 53 percent of the financial and insurance business, 50 percent of mining production, and 38 percent of chemical production. The zaibatsu were what are now called conglomerates, companies with strong positions in diverse industries. None of them had monopoly control in any important economic area, and they generally avoided serious competition with each other.[35] The top holding company of each zaibatsu group operated through a wide network of subsidiaries and affiliates by means of intercorporate stockholding, interlocking directorates, management agreements, and financing by the combine bank. To "break up" the zaibatsu involved dissolving the holding company at the top of the network and cutting the links that bound the principal companies in the group.[36] In effect, not only would the zaibatsu be dissolved; the large economic concentrations they controlled would be divided up.

Official Japanese views about zaibatsu dissolution were guarded. In one of the few Japanese utterances on the matter, Yoshida, who had Mitsui connections, showed some temerity at a press conference on October 19: "Mitsui, Mitsubishi, and other old zaibatsu... themselves suffered losses during the war.... The government obliged them to build ships and planes...ignoring their losses.... Those who enjoyed great profit and worked hand in hand with the militarists were the new zaibatsu.... The old zaibatsu, having their interests in peacetime industries, rejoiced at the war's end." To correct possible misinterpretation, another ministry issued a statement three days later saying the government did not oppose zaibatsu reorganization.[37] Japanese officials other than the foreign minister were obviously following that sage advice often cited by Yoshida—*Nagai mono ni wa makarero* (Don't fight City Hall).

The first SCAP trust-busting action was to restrict transactions by the fifteen big holding companies. The head of the SCAP economic section, Colonel Raymond C. Kramer, a New York businessman and former textile manufacturer, then tried to persuade the big companies to submit their own plans for dissolution. Yasuda, the fourth biggest zaibatsu, came up with a plan on October 16, and SCAP cabled Washington recommending approval. In a few days the War Department told MacArthur to go ahead and accept the Yasuda plan on a tentative basis. Mitsubishi led a rear-guard action but finally gave in.

On November 4 the Japanese government produced a comprehensive plan for the dissolution of the four biggest holding companies. According to the plan, their securities would be transferred to a new holding company liquidation commission (HCLC), and their shareholders would be compensated by nonnegotiable government bonds. These actions took place in late 1945 and early 1946, with a fifth zaibatsu, Fuji Industrial, added to the SCAP chopping block. Other combines were to be dissolved later. SCAP issued a directive accepting the Japanese dissolution plan and on December 8 listed 18 holding companies and 326 subsidiaries as "restricted companies" that could not sell or transfer securities without approval.[38]

In December Colonel Kramer returned to the United States with at least two achievements to his credit. He had overcome the resistance of the old-guard conservatives, whose objection to the breakup campaign was stronger than that against any other American policy in the early months of the occupation. And he had made probably the most prescient forecast uttered by any American official in Japan during the occupation when he told a presidential representative visiting Tokyo in October 1945 that in fifteen years Japan would have a far more important position in world trade than ever before and would be a very serious competitor to the United States and Great Britain.[39]

MacArthur often showed suspicion of "big business" and "Wall Street." He mistrusted outsiders and high-powered businessmen, at least those he did not know. When the top jobs on his staff came open, he preferred to pick someone he knew he could count on to be entirely his man regardless of professional skill. In this case MacArthur replaced Kramer with Major General William F. Marquat, a career coast artillery officer who had served with MacArthur on Bataan. Marquat's experience in economic affairs was modest indeed, but he had the redeeming virtues of being nice, witty, hard working, and a good manager.

Although the labor movement and agricultural land changes each affected millions of people, educational reform and the abolition of official support for the state religion, Shintō, reached into the lives of virtually everyone. Sweeping changes in these fields began early under the direction of CIE, which accomplished much with little controversy; in fact, many Japanese worked with CIE to advance the new ideas.

The Japanese have consistently attached great importance to education. The first six years of elementary school were free and compulsory, and literacy was almost universal. An excellent system of technical education, *semmon gakkō*, provided an alternative to high school. Admission to state-supported schools that included the best universities was by examination. University fees were modest.

Nevertheless, the system had many defects. Girls were restricted to their own schools, including a few universities, with a limited curriculum after the period of compulsory education. Less than 1 percent of elementary school graduates went to university. A few elite schools at the top level dominated the system: attendance at Ichikō and Tokyo Teidai (the First Higher School and Tokyo Imperial University) was a guaranteed passport to success in later life.

The cancer of nationalism spread throughout the education system. Although the imperial rescript on education, issued in 1890, was fairly innocuous in its pietistic wording, it had been laid over with the ultranationalist commentary and cant of the Education Ministry. Retired military men, widely used as teachers and military instructors in the schools, enforced and fed the cult of nationalism. Generals were made ministers of education; reactionaries controlled teaching appointments and the writing of textbooks. The purpose of education was to train students to become effective servants of the state.[40]

The school system was in chaos at the end of the war. Because most of the schools had been closed, 18 million students were idle. Four thousand schools had been destroyed in the war, about 10 percent of the total, and many more had been damaged. One of SCAP's early steps was to advise the Japanese to reopen their schools (in Germany schools were kept closed in the early months of the occupation).

General MacArthur had only skimpy guidance regarding education. The basic Washington directive provided that nationalist teachers and opponents of occupation goals be replaced, military training prohibited, and democratic principles used in teaching.[41] The first chief of CIE, Colonel Kermit R. Dyke, a former NBC executive who had MacArthur's confidence and a smooth manner with the Japanese, supervised a number of dedicated men including Harold Henderson, an authority on Japanese art and literature; Robert King Hall, an education specialist; and Kenneth Bunce, a former schoolteacher in Japan. As SCAP's religions expert, Bunce showed great finesse in handling the clashing advocates of differing religious viewpoints, among them General MacArthur. Dyke was replaced in May 1946 by Lieutenant Colonel Donald R. Nugent, a Marine reserve officer who had also taught school in Japan before the war. Nugent was a cautious chief who relied heavily on advice from experts, both American and Japanese, and worked earnestly to win Japanese support for SCAP reforms. In early dealings with officials of the Ministry of Education, CIE found them "technically unqualified to plan and initiate complete reforms."[42]

After trying to persuade the education minister, Maeda Tamon, an old-fashioned liberal who had lived in the United States, to take the lead in liberalizing the system, CIE issued several directives in late 1945 to eliminate all nationalist teachers, textbooks, and ideology; revise the history and geography texts; and ban the teaching of "moral education," or *shūshin*. Even before the screening, 115,778 teachers and officials resigned from the schools. By April 1949, after a screening of some 700,000 persons, nearly 6,000 more had been removed or had voluntarily left education positions. The education purge was in many ways more sweeping than the political purge and was carried out almost entirely by Japanese.[43]

Under a revised method instituted by SCAP, textbooks were written

by individual scholars and published by commercial concerns, subject
to review by the Ministry of Education and CIE experts. The Japanese
were accustomed to considerable government interference in their education, and so the new way did not surprise them. The ministry has
continued to exercise a supervisory role in the selection and content of
textbooks. A few liberated spirits have tried in recent years to free the
system of government interference but without great success. The early
occupation period witnessed the rise of large and powerful teachers
unions. One of these, known as Nikkyōso (Japan Teachers Union),
became a militant and often radical force in Japanese education.

The U.S. program for demilitarizing Japan had one immediate effect
on academic research. In November 1945 General MacArthur directed
that two Japanese cyclotrons be destroyed in response to a Washington
order that turned out to have been issued by mistake. Press stories in the
United States made it appear that MacArthur had been responsible, an
interpretation that he took pains in his memoirs to correct. In the aftermath of this strange episode, the Allied powers decided in 1947 that
Japanese research in atomic energy, primitive as it was, should be prohibited. But the resulting damage to the principle of freedom of research
was repaired in good part when a scientist from the Massachusetts Institute of Technology, Harry Kelly, was sent to serve on MacArthur's
staff to oversee Japanese scientific activity; Kelly got to know Japanese
scientists and was valuable in helping guide the peaceful development
of Japanese science and in promoting cooperation with the United
States.[44]

Undoubtedly the most significant force in education reform was the
report of the U.S. education mission to Japan, made on March 31,
1946. The mission, requested by MacArthur two months before, arrived early in March to study "education for democracy in Japan." The
twenty-seven-member group, headed by George D. Stoddard, soon to
become president of the University of Illinois, spent three weeks in
Japan meeting with a wide cross-section of people, including Mac-
Arthur and the emperor. The education minister, Abe Yoshishige,
advised the mission in frank terms not "to use Japan as a kind of labo-
ratory in a rash attempt to experiment."[45]

The mission's report was elevated in tone and general in approach.[46]
It made several significant recommendations:

—Compulsory, free education should be coeducational and should
include six years of primary school, three years of lower secondary

school, and, eventually, three years of upper secondary school. (This was the 6-3-3 system that would precede four years of higher education.)

—"Higher education should become an opportunity for the many, not a privilege of the few." Higher schools and technical schools should be liberalized to provide a general college training. Women should have free access to higher education.

—Teaching should rely not only on textbooks but also on cooperative give-and-take between teacher and student.

—Administration should be decentralized. The Education Ministry should be retained for professional guidance but its control function should be transferred to local elected agencies.

—"Some form of *romaji*," the "roman alphabet," should be brought into common use so that "language would be a highway and not a barrier."

Action on the report was postponed until a new Diet was elected in April 1946.

Early in 1946 Nambara Shigeru, president of Tokyo Imperial University and the leading educator in Japan, became the head of the Japanese Education Reform Council, an influential body set up to advise the Education Ministry and CIE. A brilliant and dynamic man, and a Christian, he played a key role in liberalizing Japanese education between 1945 and 1952.

Religion was of great interest to General MacArthur, who clung to the hope that Japan might experience a religious reformation. U.S. policy was to encourage freedom of religious worship and prevent religion from being used by nationalists. This meant separation of religion from state control and from the nationalist trappings of state Shintō (*kokka shintō*). General MacArthur went further by actively promoting Christianity in the early years of the occupation. At one point he advised Washington that his policy was "to increase greatly Christian influence in Japan." President Truman, reading this in a briefing memorandum, penciled in the notation, "I approve."[47]

MacArthur reportedly told the American evangelist Billy Graham that the emperor had privately declared his "willingness to make Christianity the national religion," but the general had rejected the offer "because he felt it wrong to impose any religion on a people." The general evidently said similar things to other American Christians, but

Japanese sources do not throw any light on the surprising assertion attributed to the Tennō.[48]

Seeing visiting churchmen and answering correspondence on religious matters took up a good bit of the general's time. An Episcopalian but not a churchgoer himself, he viewed the values of democracy and Christianity as complementary. At the same time, he saw little conflict between Christianity and the "Oriental faiths" and thought "each might well be strengthened by a better understanding of the other." Apparently with this in mind, he "asked for missionaries, and more missionaries." At war's end there were 900 Christian missionaries in Japan, whose presence reflected a considerable degree of Japanese religious toleration during the war, and near the end of the occupation there were 1,700. MacArthur also requested and received 10 million Bibles translated into Japanese.[49]

SCAP's first significant action based on the bill of rights directive of October 4 provided that freedom of religion be guaranteed to everyone. On December 15 another directive, based on Washington guidance, provided for the separation of religion from the state and placed all religions, including Christianity, on exactly the same legal footing. The directive cut off Shintō from all state support, but its purely religious functions were permitted to continue. This directive also prohibited official support of "the doctrine that the Emperor of Japan is superior to the heads of other states because of ancestry, descent or special origin." The directive banned, somewhat to the surprise of the Japanese, use of the term *Greater East Asia War*, the standard reference to Japan's wars from 1937, against China, through World War II. Thereafter, the Japanese substituted the "Pacific War" or even the "Fifteen Years' War," beginning with the Manchurian incident of 1931.[50]

The theological status of the emperor was clarified, at least for foreigners, by a revealing event on New Year's Day of 1946. On that day the emperor issued a "declaration of humanity," or *ningen sengen*, in which he declared that he was a human being. Possibly at the emperor's initiative, he and his advisers had begun in late 1945 to consider ways of dispelling the mythology and cult of the emperor.

In late November Harold Henderson of CIE suggested to a British acquaintance, R. H. Blyth, a tutor to the crown prince, that it would be appropriate if the emperor would renounce his divinity as American policy suggested. A few days later Blyth excitedly asked for suggestions about how the emperor might do this. Somewhat reluctantly Henderson dashed off a short paragraph to the effect that the ties between the emperor and the people were not based on myths or the mistaken idea that the emperor was divine or that the Japanese people were superior to other races. Blyth took this paper back to the imperial household but returned it the next day, asking that the paper be burned. This was done on the spot. A day later Blyth returned with a longer text containing the Henderson paragraph. This draft was given to recently promoted Brigadier General Dyke, who reportedly showed it to MacArthur. Both men were said to be pleased.[51]

Prime Minister Shidehara and his aides revised the draft and translated it into English. Education Minister Maeda reworked the Japanese version, not in the stilted language of court documents but in the colloquial form requested by the emperor. The Tennō also asked that the announcement include the famous charter oath issued in 1868 by Emperor Meiji, which declared in vague and impressionistic phrasing that "all measures of government should be decided in accordance with public opinion."[52] By the end of December the rescript was finished. Yoshida sent an advance copy to MacArthur on December 30, and the rescript was issued the next day.[53] Its key sentences, almost identical to the Henderson draft, provided that "the ties between us and our people have always stood upon mutual trust and affection. They do not depend upon mere legends and myths. They are not predicated on the false conception that the emperor is divine and that the Japanese people are superior to other races and fated to rule the world."

General MacArthur issued a statement, which appeared on January 1, 1946, at the same time as the rescript, saying the emperor's action "pleases me very much. By it he undertakes a leading part in the democratization of his people." Although the general said in his memoirs that the emperor's statement was made "without any suggestion or discussion" with him, MacArthur was kept informed about the rescript and saw a copy before it was issued.[54]

It surprised Americans that the emperor's announcement did not create a big stir in the Japanese press, which gave the announcement only routine play. One observer familiar with both societies explained that the Japanese had never thought of emperors as divine, only as unusual and elevated persons meriting special veneration.[55] The Japanese used the word *kami* (god) in regard to many things, including emperors and natural phenomena (like *kamikaze*, or "divine wind"), but the term had a broader and less theological meaning for Japanese than the word *god* had for people in the West.

To humanize the emperor even further, General MacArthur urged him to travel around the country and be seen by the people. His subjects had rarely been permitted to look upon the Tennō, and they were intensely curious about him. By 1952 he had visited almost every region and prefecture. Only one untoward incident marred these trips: on November 21, 1951, students at Kyoto University surrounded his car and shouted questions and slogans critical of his wartime role and the policies of the government.[56]

A young U.S. naval officer played a part in the process of humanizing the emperor. Otis Cary, who had been born and brought up in Japan, met several times in late 1945 and early 1946 with Prince Takamatsu, the younger brother of the emperor. Having perfect command of Japanese and a deep understanding of the people, Cary pressed on the prince some ideas for bringing the emperor closer to his subjects, suggesting, for example, visits around the country and a public expression of sympathy with those suffering in the food crisis.[57] In the following weeks many of Cary's suggestions came to pass, although the veil of secrecy that surrounds the Japanese court makes it impossible to know exactly what inspired these actions. It is obvious, however, that the emperor was quite willing to act in ways that would meet with Allied approval.

The emperor showed another human touch at Christmastime in 1945. Through Yoshida the imperial family sent an ink-writing set to General MacArthur, a box of *hina matsuri* dolls (used for the Girls' Festival) to Mrs. MacArthur, and dolls and candy to their son, Arthur. The general's aide, Colonel L. E. Bunker, sent an effusive letter of thanks to Yoshida.[58]

CHAPTER 5

The Allies

Their Role and Reparations

The surrender ceremony on the *Missouri* had been a remarkable display of Allied unity. It reflected the idealistic flavor of presurrender planning in Washington and the high hopes around the world that the victor states would work together to drive "irresponsible militarism" from the earth.

In the late years of the war U.S. policy documents often referred to "United Nations policies" or to the "United Nations Commander," and the spirit of internationalism ran high. But by the time Japan surrendered in August 1945, the ecumenical impulse was on the wane, and Washington planners were referring to the "Allied powers." The Potsdam Declaration and the ceremony on the *Missouri* made clear that the Big Four would have the deciding voice in the control of Japan. By then U.S. leaders had agreed that in case of any differences with the other powers, U.S. views would be controlling.[1]

In the days right after the Japanese surrender, the other big powers were willing to recognize the primary position of the United States. They offered no objection to the U.S. proposal that General MacArthur be named supreme commander to receive Japan's surrender. Stalin did not press his proposal for a separate zone of occupation or for a Soviet officer on the "Allied high command."[2] Yet the major Allies, in particular the British and the Soviets, were reluctant to accept U.S. dominance in Japan. They wanted a bigger voice.

The selection of MacArthur proved to be the masterstroke in preserving U.S. primacy. A strong commander who believed in complete unification of authority in his own hands and who sought to reduce as much as he could guidance and advice from outside sources, he felt no need to conciliate Allies and coordinate his actions with them. He had had some experience dealing with the Allies—in Europe during and after World War I and in Australia during World War II—but the role of supreme commander was far more congenial to him than that of diplomatic negotiator.

The occupation began with only a few of the Allies having any role. The British and Soviets had liaison officers attached to General MacArthur's headquarters, and although relations were harmonious, the liaison officers had no agreed function. Other nations also wanted representation in Japan and a voice in occupation policy, but the United States was reluctant to concede any of its hard-won authority. A number of issues, however, such as dividing up reparations, would obviously depend on Allied agreement, and it was understood that the Allies would in some form play a significant part in the occupation.

On August 21, 1945, the United States proposed to ten of its Allies that an advisory commission be set up in Washington to advise on occupation policies. This proposal was accepted, and the Far Eastern Advisory Commission (FEAC) held its first meeting on October 30, with nine governments participating. Although the Soviet Union had accepted the invitation to take part, it did not attend. The FEAC held ten meetings, devoted largely to reviewing actions the United States had already taken, but the commission reached no agreement on what its functions should be.[3]

From the outset both the British and the Soviets showed their unhappiness over the limited role the advisory commission gave them. Australia, believing it had played as big a part as any nation other than the United States in the war against Japan, was even more resentful. Its assertive foreign minister, H. V. Evatt, made painfully clear in Washington and London that Australia expected to be the spokesman for the British Commonwealth on Pacific matters.[4] Australian restiveness and rivalry with the United Kingdom were to be recurring problems during the occupation.

Bowing to the pressure, Secretary of State James F. Byrnes agreed to consider a five-power Allied control council to sit in Tokyo, with General MacArthur acting as its chair and invested with authority to decide on policies for Japan.[5] A control council of any type proved to be anathema to the U.S. government and even more so to MacArthur. On October 22 he dashed off one of his potent messages objecting to the whole concept, "which negatives every basic principle of unity of command...and could empower subordinate military commanders by combined action to practically negative the views of the senior commander."[6] Thereupon Byrnes overrode the arguments of the British and the Soviets for a control council and searched for another solution.

Finally, on December 26, 1945, the Big Four foreign ministers reached agreement at a meeting in Moscow on a formula for Allied participation.[7] It created two bodies: the Far Eastern Commission and the Allied Council for Japan (ACJ). The FEC, sitting in Washington and consisting of the eleven major Allied powers, would formulate policies and standards for Japan's fulfillment of the surrender terms and would review upon request of any member any directive or action taken by SCAP involving commission policy decisions. The Big Four nations would each have a veto power.

The ACJ was to be a four-member advisory body to consult with and advise the supreme commander on the implementation of the surrender terms and on the occupation and control of Japan. The supreme commander or his deputy would be the chair. The supreme commander could decide when and how to consult with the ACJ, and he would be "the sole executive authority for the Allied Powers in Japan."

The United States and the supreme commander were thus well protected by the veto power in the FEC and by their controlling voice in the ACJ. And the recognition that the supreme commander was the sole executive authority in Japan constituted a sweeping grant of power to MacArthur, who interpreted it liberally. The United States also gained the right to issue interim directives in certain urgent situations not covered by commission policy. Byrnes had indeed won a signal diplomatic victory in Moscow.

Despite all these safeguards, MacArthur, who was sometimes remarkably heavy-handed in his approach to diplomacy, had a jaundiced view from the start about the new arrangements. In response to a Washington statement that the general had been advised and had not objected to the "new Japan control plan," an obvious reference to the two Allied bodies, MacArthur issued a press release on December 30 saying that he had sent his "final disagreement" to Washington on October 31 and that he had not been consulted during the Moscow conference. He added, however, that he would "try to make it work." This was the first of a number of occasions in which MacArthur publicly disagreed with Washington. Moreover, he later criticized the State Department several times for having "surrendered unilateral U.S.

control over Japan" at the Moscow meeting in 1945.[8] In his memoirs he wrote that "not one constructive idea to help with the reorientation or reconstruction of Japan ever came" from the FEC or ACJ.[9]

The very day the Moscow communiqué was issued, the about-to-die FEAC left Washington for a trip to Japan. On January 31, 1946, the supreme commander met the FEAC members in Tokyo. He told them the occupation should last from three to five years and suggested that the commission soon begin to consider a peace treaty for Japan. He added that "the most likely way of ensuring the development of a peaceful and democratic Japan" was to make "a friend of an enemy."[10]

The Allies also discussed the composition of the occupying forces for Japan in late 1945. The United States wanted Allied units to be part of the garrison forces, including forces from Asian nations. But MacArthur insisted that these units be under his operational control and not be assigned separate zones of occupation.[11] The British Commonwealth went ahead with plans to set up an occupation force in Japan.

The USSR did not agree to the condition, however. Stalin had asked Truman in August to permit Soviet forces to accept the Japanese surrender not only in the Kurile Islands but also in the northeastern half of Hokkaido, where Soviet forces would presumably stay on as an occupation force. Truman agreed to the Kuriles but made clear that MacArthur would accept the Japanese surrender throughout the main islands of Japan, including Hokkaido. Had Truman agreed to Stalin's proposal, Soviet forces or their communist agents would no doubt have controlled at least part of Hokkaido for many years.[12] The Soviets withdrew their forces from Manchuria in May 1946.

General MacArthur asserted in his memoirs that the Soviets in Tokyo came directly to him early in the occupation with a request for a zone of occupation in Hokkaido. This he turned down "point blank." The record does not indicate that MacArthur knew of Truman's rejection of Stalin's request in August 1945 or that MacArthur informed Washington of the Soviet request in Tokyo. It seems odd that even as independent an operator as MacArthur would not have reported an important Soviet demarche like this to Washington, especially because Allied policy encouraged participation in the occupation by other Allies.[13]

On October 24, however, Stalin commented to Ambassador Averell Harriman that "to preserve the freedom of action of MacArthur, it perhaps might not be advisable to send other troops to Japan." Stalin seemed to want either a big role for the Soviets, as might have been expected, or virtually none at all, possibly because he felt that Japan was in the U.S. zone of influence and the USSR should not poach upon it. Harriman took issue with him, indicating that the United States wanted the forces of other Allies in Japan. Nevertheless, once President Truman told Stalin that the Soviets could not have a separate zone of occupation, Stalin seemed to lose interest in sending forces there.[14]

In January 1946 Harriman found Stalin "perfectly content" with the role assigned the USSR in Japan "because the United States and the Soviet Union have found common ground." Stalin may well have decided tacitly to recognize the American position in Japan in return for U.S. recognition of the Soviet-supported situations in Rumania, Bulgaria, and Hungary. In the eyes of Prime Minister Yoshida, one of MacArthur's greatest contributions to Japan was his refusal to permit the USSR to set up a separate zone of occupation. But Stalin may have deserved more credit than MacArthur for this.[15]

Another significant issue of concern to the Allies was war reparations to be exacted from Japan. The major Allies had agreed at Potsdam in August 1945 that Japan would be permitted "to maintain such industries as will sustain her economy and permit the exaction of just reparations in kind." The initial U.S. policy had refined this vague formula by providing that reparations be made by the transfer of Japanese property outside Japan and by "the transfer of such goods or existing capital equipment and facilities as are not necessary for a peaceful Japanese economy."[16]

American leaders wanted to avoid a replay of the disastrous consequences of the Versailles Treaty of 1919; the treaty's excessive demands for reparations from defeated Germany became one of the causes for the breakdown of the peace settlement. Accordingly, the first U.S. reparations mission to Japan, led by Edwin W. Pauley in late 1945, planned that reparations be estimated on the basis of Japan's ability to pay, not on the cost of the war damage it had done.[17]

Economists on the Pauley mission, however, wanted to apply a further criterion. They wanted to correct the imbalance that Japan had established in its own favor by exploiting the raw materials of other Asian nations so as to build up its own industrial capacity. On the basis of this criterion, Pauley's experts concluded that "in the overall comparison of needs Japan should have the last priority."[18] This unrealistic approach, which would have outdone the Morgenthau pastoralization plan for Germany, was short-lived.

The Pauley report was presented to the president on December 18, 1945, and filed with the FEC in April 1946, a time when U.S. policy-makers were still planning that other nations in East Asia, led by China, would establish a new balance of power and would make good use of Japanese reparations. Pauley recommended the removal of Japan's war industries, including the aircraft industry, and drastic reductions in iron and steel, shipping, and machine tools capacity. To many Japanese and some Americans, this was a punitive policy designed to prevent Japan's revival as an industrial nation.[19]

From the start of the occupation, MacArthur had reservations about making plant and material available for reparations. He told the FEAC on January 30, 1946, that as a former engineer he knew how hard it was to move a plant and make it work in a new place.[20] But the Allied powers' determination to exact reparations continued to take a lot of the general's time, although he never mentioned the subject in his memoirs.

For the Japanese government and businesses, reparations were a crucial issue. Until the Allies decided what to do, the Japanese could not make plans for industrial development. A diplomat, Asakai Kōichirō, assigned to the CLO, had the luck to get some early information out of Pauley about U.S. plans. In November 1945, when Pauley was taking a holiday trip to Nikko, a shrine city north of Tokyo, Asakai went along and engaged Pauley in conversation on the train and was told that two key industries to be limited were ball bearings and steel. The Japanese cabinet was pleased to hear Asakai's report that Pauley would accept steel-making capacity of "over two million tons a year," which was much more than the Japanese had expected. Pauley's report actually recommended an annual capacity of 2.5 million tons.[21]

On January 20, 1946, SCAP issued a directive designating the first wartime facilities to be reserved for reparations. The directive listed aircraft factories, military and naval arsenals, and research laboratories to be placed under SCAP control. By August 1947, 504 installations had been designated for removal as reparations.[22]

On another key issue, the role of the emperor, the Allies played an inadvertent but pivotal role in crystallizing U.S. policy. In late 1945 when lists of war crimes suspects were being drawn up, Australia, with the support of New Zealand, maintained that the emperor should be put on trial. The United Kingdom disagreed, and the Soviet Union, which had not stated its position, was expected to favor indicting the Tennō. Equally strong differences had arisen in Washington. State Department experts felt that the emperor should not be implicated in any way, but some officers in the Navy and War departments disagreed, recommending at least an investigation into the emperor's role in the events leading up to the war. Dean Acheson, the second man in the State Department, agreed with this position.[23]

The three departments most involved—State, War, and Navy—then formulated a policy: the emperor should not be immune from trial, and evidence regarding his activities should be collected in Tokyo and sent to Washington for study. MacArthur was asked on November 10 to examine information that might warrant or permit "proceedings against Hirohito as a war criminal." Former ambassador to Japan Joseph C. Grew, who was sympathetic to retention of the institution, reportedly felt that the emperor ought to be tried because he had approved the rescript authorizing a declaration of war against the United States in 1941. Whereas Grew believed that many factors including political expediency should be considered before reaching a final decision, the political adviser in Tokyo, George Atcheson, wrote President Truman on January 4, 1946, that "the emperor system must disappear if Japan is ever to be wholly democratic." Thus, at that stage the United States had no definite policy about the emperor.[24]

MacArthur had not yet put his views on record. On November 26, 1945, he saw Admiral Yonai Mitsumasa, a former prime minister and a prominent military and naval figure who had been handling demobilization matters for the navy. The admiral had no compunction about asking the general what he thought about "the position of the Emperor." According to the Japanese account, MacArthur candidly replied, "I have no thought at all of making any change in the position of the Emperor."[25]

The issue came to a head on January 21, 1946, when the Australian representative to the United Nations War Crimes Commission in London urged that the emperor be charged with war crimes. On the same day Washington informed MacArthur of the Australian action. The general responded on January 25, 1946, with a long message drafted by his acting chief of staff, Major General Richard J. Marshall, that made several crucial assessments.[26] In what was probably the most dramatic telegram MacArthur sent Washington about occupation policy, he asserted that the role of the emperor in past Japanese actions was "largely ministerial and automatically responsive to the advice of his counsellors." Some even believed that if he had acted to thwart the dominant military clique, this "would have placed him in actual jeopardy. . . . He is a symbol which unites all Japanese." If the emperor were indicted or tried as a war criminal, MacArthur continued, "a vendetta for revenge will thereby be initiated whose cycle may well not be complete for centuries, if ever. It is quite possible that a million troops would be required, which would have to be maintained for an indefinite number of years. In addition, a complete civil service might have to be recruited and imported, possibly running into a size of several hundred thousand." MacArthur concluded, somewhat modestly, that it would be inappropriate for him to make a recommendation as to whether the emperor should be tried because the decision would have to be made on such a high level but that if the decision were affirmative, he would "recommend the above measures as imperative." By sending this message, overdrawn though it was, MacArthur hardly needed to make a recommendation.

On January 30, the State Department requested the U.S. embassy in London to take measures to forestall the Australian proposal to try the emperor. The U.K. Foreign Office also took the position that consideration of the Australian list by the U.N. commission should be postponed.[27] The commission took no further action.

On April 3, 1946, the FEC approved a policy regarding war criminals with the understanding that the U.S. directive to the supreme commander would be worded to except the Japanese emperor from indictment as a war criminal "without direct authorization."[28] American agencies decided on April 13, 1946, that MacArthur should take no initiative regarding the elimination of the imperial insitution, particularly because the Japanese "were showing a willingness to eliminate [its] most objectionable aspects." MacArthur's advice to the emperor to take some trips around the country and see the people had been in accord with this policy.[29] The Washington decision in effect ended the American debate about the future position of the emperor.

MacArthur told the visiting FEAC on January 31, 1946, that the natural evolution of Japan would be in the direction of a constitutional monarchy, which the occupation should promote. He added that he thought "it would be a disaster to indict the Emperor as a war criminal. . . . The present Emperor had been from the beginning to the end a 'complete Charlie McCarthy,' who had neither begun the war nor stopped it. At every point he had acted on advice and could not have done otherwise." George Sansom reported to London that he was "convinced the Supreme Commander's judgment is correct." Speaking somewhat dramatically to the British ambassador a year later, Mac-

Arthur said the emperor had once confided that if he had opposed his advisers before the attack on the United States in 1941, "I should most certainly have had my throat cut."[30]

When MacArthur called the emperor a puppet who did only what his advisers told him to do, he seemed to be espousing the view that the emperor and his advisers wanted to foster in the early days of the occupation. Since that time, however, much evidence has been adduced to show that the emperor was well informed about Japan's cabinet discussions and military planning for war. In the months before the war began he showed some concern that diplomatic solutions were not being actively pursued, but he made little effort to restrain the preparations for war. Before World War II the emperor seems to have acted for the most part as a constitutional monarch, not making political decisions but putting his stamp of approval on cabinet actions and occasionally offering opinions on some issues. His "supreme command of the army and navy" (tōsuiken) seems to have been largely titular or honorary, not operational. Though his actions did not seem to implicate him in political or military responsibility for the starting of the war, at no point did he use his moral authority or prestige to oppose war planning.[31]

MacArthur's role in the postwar debate over the emperor proved decisive. The emperor was not put on trial. His reputation as a well-meaning but powerless ruler gained wide currency. And the general's prediction on the way that the imperial institution would probably evolve was not far off the mark.

CHAPTER 6

War Crimes and Punishment by Purge

The execution of war criminals and the removal from high positions of those who had been influential in the prewar period were the most punitive actions taken in Japan. They were regarded by the Japanese as a form of "victors' justice." It is questionable how much these actions contributed to creating the kind of postwar peace the United States desired.

World War II was the first major conflict in history in which the victors carried out trials and punishment of thousands of persons in the defeated nations for "crimes against peace" and "crimes against humanity," two new and broadly defined categories of international crime. Early in the war Allied leaders had stated that war criminals would be punished, and in October 1943, well before the surrender of Germany, the U.N. War Crimes Commission was set up to collect evidence of war crimes by the Axis powers in both Europe and Asia.[1] Winston Churchill and the British favored making a list of the top Nazis and shooting them as soon as they were captured. The Americans strongly argued that due legal process must apply to the punishment of war criminals, and this view prevailed.[2]

The aftermath of World War II also witnessed the forced removal from important public and private positions of those Germans and Japanese who had taken a leading part in the aggressive actions of their governments. This, too, was the first time that victors had carried out a systematic and widespread removal from office of the leaders and important officials of defeated nations.[3]

The Potsdam Declaration of July 1945 provided for trials of Japanese war criminals and elimination of the influence of those who had "deceived and misled" the Japanese people. MacArthur said in his memoirs that to charge political leaders with war crimes was "repugnant to me." He also "very much doubted the wisdom" of purging extremists because purges would eliminate able officials, were punitive, and lacked popular support in Japan.[4] Despite these dark forebodings, he energetically presided over the execution of these two complex policies. Neither was well understood by the Japanese, but both satisfied a deep-seated feeling in the Allied world that those Germans and Japanese guilty of starting the war and committing atrocities should be punished for their malefactions. Both policies were administrative quagmires.

The Nuremberg trial of major German offenders started in November 1946 and finished eleven months later. One lesson the United States learned from it was that an operation in which the major Allies were expected to work jointly in collecting evidence, setting up a tribunal, designating prosecutors, and conducting a trial was cumbersome and contentious. Under Secretary of State Dean Acheson and Assistant Secretary of War John J. McCloy, a skillful duo in organizing many of the early projects in Japan, decided that MacArthur should be given the authority to conduct the trial of major offenders in Japan, with judges and prosecutors recommended by the other Allied nations. Each Allied nation would also be empowered to conduct trials of lesser offenders of interest to it.[5]

MacArthur ordered the arrest of thirty-nine suspects on September 11, one day before receiving instructions to proceed "without unavoidable delay." He wanted to start with the trial of members of the Tōjō cabinet that declared war in December 1941 and was unhappy to be told soon afterward that they should be tried by an international tribunal. He commented, "It is self-evident that no international action can be obtained here in the near future."[6] U.S. military police (MPs) were at the point of arresting the number one catch, General Tōjō on September 11, when he shot himself. He bungled the attempt and survived with the help of expert treatment by U.S. Army doctors. General Eichelberger ruminated later that it might have been better if Tōjō had succeeded. Yet to have conducted the trial without Tōjō would have emptied the proceedings of much of their meaning and excitement. Hermann Goering, the principal Nuremberg defendant, was cleverer than Tōjō; he went through the trial and then robbed the Allies of the desired consummation by taking poison before he was to be hanged.

On October 6, 1945, the supreme commander received a directive, which was soon approved by the other Allied powers, granting him authority to proceed with the major trials.[7] As in Germany, war crimes were divided into three categories:

Class A—*crimes against peace*: the planning or waging of a war of aggression or war in violation of international law or treaties, or conspiring to do so. These trials would be conducted jointly by the eleven major Allied powers and would include Class B and Class C charges against the same defendants.

Class B—*conventional war crimes*: violations of the laws or customs of war, such as cruel treatment of prisoners of war or civilians. Each Allied nation would try cases of concern to it.

Class C—*crimes against humanity*: criminal or inhumane acts against civilians, such as enslavement or deportation, also to be tried separately by each Allied power.

The basic directive of November 3 also dealt with war crimes. It listed in sweeping terms the categories of suspects to be arrested: top military officers, including the imperial general headquarters and the army and navy general staffs; all commissioned military police officers; all military officers who had been "important exponents of militant nationalism and aggression"; and all key members of ultranationalistic, terrorist, and secret patriotic societies. Very few of the many hundreds of persons in these categories were tried, but most of them were purged.[8]

The supreme commander was also directed to intern others, such as all persons who had played an active and dominant governmental or economic part in Japan's program of aggression; all high officials of the Imperial Rule Assistance Association (IRAA), sometimes considered the Japanese counterpart of the Nazi Party in Germany; and other civilians as necessary for the achievement of occupation goals.[9] SCAP did not actually imprison many persons in this category but did remove them from important positions.

Ever the efficient administrator, MacArthur moved vigorously to organize the trials of Class A suspects. An international prosecution section was added to his staff on December 8, headed by Joseph B.

Keenan, a former U.S. assistant attorney general who had been named chief of counsel by President Truman on November 30. The eleven powers on the FEC were invited to designate justices of the tribunal, who were then formally appointed by the supreme commander.

SCAP generally followed the legal definitions and framework adopted for the trials in Germany. But it found that the definitions of war crimes were vague and that the available evidence was often too skimpy and insubstantial to stand up in court.

George Atcheson suggested to the general on November 6 that the trials be expedited, and MacArthur replied that the directives he had received were so broad and general "that he is unable to determine those individuals that the American Government or the Allied governments wish to prosecute." Atcheson proposed to Washington on December 17 that the United States go ahead with a U.S. tribunal because the Allies had not yet agreed on trial procedures.[10] Washington ignored this unwelcome suggestion.

MacArthur asked the political adviser on November 7 to list persons he thought should be arrested and to provide evidence. Largely on the basis of information from Washington, Atcheson submitted four lists in November and December, compiled by Robert A. Fearey and John Emmerson of his staff with the help of Canadian diplomat Herbert Norman. Nearly all of those listed were arrested and tried. By the end of 1945, 103 major suspects had been arrested, including most of the Tōjō 1941 cabinet, former prime minister Hirota Kōki and former privy seal Kido Kōichi.[11]

Norman had prepared lengthy memoranda on Konoe and Kido, both listed by Atcheson as war crimes suspects. The memos described the influential role they had played in Japan's aggressive actions. Some of the information in these memos was probably used in deciding to charge the two men with war crimes. Konoe took poison on December 15, the day before he was to enter prison as a Class A suspect, plaintively asserting, "The victor is too boastful and the loser too servile."[12]

On January 19, 1946, the supreme commander promulgated the charter of the International Military Tribunal for the Far East (IMTFE), drafted by Keenan and his staff and based in part on the U.S. directive of October 6.[13] This followed the pattern of the Nuremberg charter, providing for just and prompt trial and punishment; "fair" trial procedures, including the right to counsel and aid in producing needed evidence; and review of sentences by the supreme commander. The tribunal would examine alleged offenses committed by defendants in the period from 1928 to 1945. The supreme commander formally appointed the justices of the IMTFE on February 15 and designated Sir William F. Webb, the chief judge of the Supreme Court of Queensland, Australia, as the president of the tribunal.

On April 29 the IMTFE returned indictments against twenty-eight Class A suspects, who were arraigned on May 3. The indictments, which were the handiwork of the British prosecutor, Arthur Comyns-Carr,[14] contained a total of fifty-five counts: thirty-six for crimes against peace, sixteen for murder of prisoners of war and civilians, and three for conventional war crimes and crimes against humanity. Several of the counts described a conspiracy by Japanese leaders to dominate East Asia and, along with Germany and Italy, the world. Chief Prosecutor Keenan stated later that he had selected the defendants with the help of a committee of prosecutors.[15] Thirty-one additional Class A suspects were not indicted but continued to be held in custody, and many of them were held until the trial ended in 1948; the other arrested Class A suspects were released earlier.

The tribunal did not indict the emperor. This decision, made by vote of the prosecutors "acting on instructions from their governments," was not unanimous, despite the assertion by the State Department in 1949 that all nations represented on the FEC had agreed to exempt the emperor from trial.[16] MacArthur, who had no doubt been consulted by Keenan before the prosecutors voted, wrote later in his memoirs that some of the Allies, notably the Soviets and the British, had pushed to include the emperor as a war criminal suspect.[17] But this was not so. The United Kingdom had consistently taken the position that the emperor should not be involved in war crimes, and the Soviet Union did not propose that the emperor be tried. Australia and New Zealand, which had initially advocated trying the emperor, gradually muted their position.

The twenty-eight suspects indicted on April 29 included fifteen senior army officers, three admirals, five diplomats, and five senior government figures or influential civilians. Most of the military officers had had important roles in the war against China or in planning the attack on Pearl Harbor. Three of the suspects were in the cabinet when Japan attacked the United States. Shigemitsu Mamoru and Umezu Yoshijirō, who had signed the surrender instrument on the *Missouri*, were included as suspects at the request of the Soviet prosecutor, who had arrived in Tokyo only a few days before the indictments were filed.[18] Not a single industrialist was indicted; one zaibatsu figure, Ikeda Seihin, former managing director of the top Mitsui holding company, was arrested but soon released.[19]

The IMTFE convened on June 3. The next day it heard Chief Prosecutor Keenan present a lengthy opening statement of the case against the twenty-eight defendants. The document most relied on by the prosecution throughout the trial was the diary of Kido Kōichi, who had been privy seal from 1940 to November 14, 1945, when the position was abolished by the cabinet. Kido kept careful, although brief and sometimes cryptic, records of all meetings held by the emperor, of the subjects discussed, and of his own talks with the Tennō.[20]

Given the atmosphere after the emperor's meeting with General MacArthur, Kido decided the diary would not raise new concerns. He and his nephew-in-law, Tsuru Shigeto, an economist who had studied in the United States, had a long meeting with Keenan, after which Kido agreed to turn the document over. A member of the prosecution staff called the diary "the working Bible of the prosecution and the main key to all further investigation."[21] As it turned out, Kido, and some of the other defendants, would almost surely have been better off if he had not turned over the incriminating evidence. The information in his diary contributed to the finding that Kido was guilty of crimes against peace. The emperor, however, would not have been tried in any case because the United States, with Allied support, had decided, largely on political grounds, that he should not be tried.

Even before the international trial began, the United States had unilaterally tried two senior Japanese generals in late 1945 for war crimes under U.S. military law. The trial of Yamashita Tomoyuki was the most publicized and most controversial of all the trials of Japanese leaders. By capturing Singapore on February 12, 1942, with a force one-third the size of the British and Australian defenders, Yamashita won the sobriquet "Tiger of Malaya" after the most brilliant victory of any Japanese general in the war. Yamashita would no doubt have had to face a British court for that operation had U.S. authorities not seized him in September 1945 in the Philippines, where he had conducted the Japanese defense against the invading Americans led by Douglas MacArthur. Yamashita had been banished to Manchuria for much of the war by a jealous General Tōjō but had been recalled to take charge of Imperial Army forces in the Philippines ten days before the U.S. invasion of October 18, 1944. The pillage, burning, murder, and rape that took place in the defense of Manila were among the most wanton and brutal of the many vicious acts the Japanese perpetrated.

His trial began in Manila at the end of October 1945 before a five-member U.S. military commission. Very liberal rules for the introduction of evidence were followed. The zealous defense staff of six American lawyers argued that Yamashita faced "insurmountable difficulties" in establishing command over his scattered forces in a rapidly deteriorating situation and that the evidence did not show that he had ordered, condoned, or even known of the atrocities. Yamashita claimed that he had no control over the naval forces that had virtually destroyed the historic Old City of Manila, that he was in Manila only part of the time, and that for the rest of it he was 150 miles away.

On December 7 he was adjudged guilty and sentenced to death. The tribunal found that Japanese officers had been present when the offenses charged had been committed and that the incidents were so widespread that Yamashita knew or should have known of their occurrence. The sentence was confirmed by the commanding U.S. general in the Philippines. The defense filed an appeal to the U.S. Supreme Court, the Philippines then being a U.S. possession. The Supreme Court denied the appeal on February 4, 1946, by a six-to-two vote on the ground that the Court did not have the power to review the judgments of military courts trying offenses against the laws of war by enemy combatants. Two justices (Frank Murphy and Wiley Rutledge) dissented, calling the verdict "legalized lynching."[22]

After reviewing the record, MacArthur confirmed the sentence on February 11, 1946, concluding that there were no mitigating circumstances and that Yamashita had "failed his duty" and "violated his sacred trust" as a soldier.[23] On February 23 Yamashita was hanged and stripped of his uniform and decorations, the most demeaning form of execution for a military man.

The United States also tried Lieutenant General Homma Masaharu, whose forces had seized the Philippines in early 1942. MacArthur had been commander of the defending U.S. and Filipino forces until President Roosevelt had ordered him to proceed to Australia on March 11, 1942. Homma had had the benefit of overwhelming numbers on his side in the Philippine campaign.

At his trial in Manila, which began in late December 1945, Homma was charged with responsibility for the bombing of Manila when it was an open city in 1941–1942 and for failure to exercise proper command responsibility to prevent the deaths of more than 8,000 U.S. and Philippine troops in the Bataan "Death March" after the surrender of the defending forces in late March 1942. Homma claimed that he had not known about the forced march of the prisoners of war; his claim contested evidence that his headquarters was near the route of the march and that he traveled along there while the prisoners were marching along it. The court found him guilty on February 11, 1946. His appeal to the U.S. Supreme Court also failed. Mrs. Homma made a personal appeal for clemency to MacArthur, who later called their meeting "one of the most trying hours of my life." On April 3, after MacArthur affirmed the judgment of the military court, Homma was executed by a firing squad.[24]

MacArthur told Averell Harriman, the retiring American ambassador to the Soviet Union, who visited Japan in early 1946, that the Yamashita decision had been a difficult one but that Homma had violated the rules of war by refusing to accept the surrender of General Jonathan Wainwright on Corregidor in 1942 unless he surrendered all U.S. forces in the Philippines, even though those forces were no longer under his commmand. Harriman claimed "tears were running down the face" of the general. MacArthur reportedly told the foreign editor of *Newsweek* in 1947 that Wainwright "should never have surrendered" and "his men should have died fighting."[25]

On December 5 MacArthur ordered all trials of war crimes suspects by U.S. military courts to be placed under his jurisdiction as supreme commander rather than as a U.S. commander. This action was intended to set his authority outside the jurisdiction of all U.S. courts. It illustrated what George Kennan called the "flealike agility" of U.S. international commanders in switching from a U.S. to an international role. MacArthur and the U.S. military tribunals have been widely criticized for their actions in the Yamashita and Homma cases, yet their jurisdiction to try the cases and impose the sentences adjudged was clear, and the evidence that atrocities had been committed was overwhelming.[26]

Far less dramatic was what the Japanese called *paaji*, their version of what the Americans called "the purge." Its formal title, as designated by SCAPIN 550, was "The Removal and Exclusion of Undesirable Personnel from Public Office." This instruction, which General MacArthur issued on January 4, 1946, struck a mighty blow against the military and political leaders of prewar Japan.[27]

To purify Japan's political, economic, and social systems of persons tainted by nationalism was a primary U.S. goal. The Potsdam Declaration said "the authority and influence of those who have deceived and misled the people of Japan into embarking on world conquest" had to be eliminated because "a new order of peace and justice will be impossible until irresponsible militarism is driven from the world."[28] The implementing basic directive was much wider ranging, aiming at those who "have been active exponents of militant nationalism and aggression, who have been influential members of any Japanese ultranationalistic, terroristic or secret patriotic society, its agencies or affiliates, . . . or who manifest hostility to the objectives of the military occupation."[29]

Agreement within SCAP on the purge was not easily reached. The supreme commander had not wanted to move too soon, fearing that a purge would damage the efficiency of the government and hurt the economy, as he thought had happened in Germany.[30] Serious questions were then raised about the draft that GS had laboriously prepared. Should all former military officers be purged or only those of high rank, such as generals and admirals, or those of the rank of colonel and above? When did Japanese aggression begin—in 1931, when Japan invaded Manchuria, or in 1937, when Japan attacked China? Some questioned whether SCAP should base the purge, as GS proposed, only on broadly defined categories of activity and not examine individual cases. General Willoughby, the intelligence chief, offered the portentous comment that the directives ran counter to the "corollary" of the Potsdam Declaration that Japan should be developed into "ultimately an adherent of the United States."[31]

Colonel Charles L. Kades, the deputy chief of GS, supervised the drafting of the purge orders. They were approved by the chief of staff, and no doubt by MacArthur, much as GS had drafted them. MacArthur personally decided that they should be issued on January 4, 1946. Purging would be done by broad categories. The period of time to be covered would be between 1931 and 1945. The chief of staff made one change in the drafts: all military officers would be liable to the purge, not just high-ranking or career officers. This decision vastly increased the number of Japanese to be purged and meant that 80 percent were military personnel. The reasons given for this change were that Japanese company-grade officers were the cruelest in combat and that young officers had often been the ringleaders in right-wing activities in Japan.[32] The number of persons ultimately purged in Japan was about one-half of the 418,307 purged in the U.S. zone in Germany.

SCAPIN 550 set forth the categories of persons to be purged:

—Arrested war criminal suspects

—Senior military personnel and key officials of the Army and Navy ministries, military police, or special intelligence personnel

—Influential members of extreme nationalist societies

—Influential members of the IRAA and its affiliates

—Officers of overseas financial and development organizations

—Other active exponents of militant nationalism and aggression

Persons whose rank or position put them in these categories were automatically purged, except for the last, which was subject to interpretation and was used for a number of individual purge actions by SCAP. Many purgees received their normal pensions, with SCAP approval.

The companion directive, SCAPIN 548, ordered the Japanese government to ban organizations or actions in support of militant nationalism as well as "resistance or opposition to the occupation forces." The directive listed 27 ultranationalistic societies whose activities were prohibited and whose property was to be seized. By February 24, when the Japanese government issued an imperial ordinance to carry out the SCAP order, the list of proscribed organizations had grown to 147, and many more were added later. The category of "resistance or opposition to the occupation forces" later became an important criterion when SCAP applied the purge to left-wing persons and organizations.

The two directives were heralded by a somewhat flatulent press release: "These directives blast from their entrenched position in the command posts of government all those who planned, started and directed the war, and those who enslaved and beat the Japanese people into abject submission and who hoped to do the same with all the world."[33] The purge in Japan was nothing like the lethal actions that Stalin and Hitler had taken against their political enemies. It was carried out by an administrative process: any person whose prewar position fell within a defined category was purged. A few women, such as Ichikawa Fusae, a well-known advocate of women's rights, were included in the purge. One high SCAP official blithely called the purge "early retirement." There was no legal proceeding, no trial, and no attempt at due process, as there was in Germany and as many Japanese thought would be more fair.

The procedures that the Japanese government instituted were relatively simple. A three-page questionnaire was given to those persons in public life and other important positions who might be affected, eventually totaling 2,308,863, and a series of boards at the local, prefectural, and national levels screened the completed papers. There were no hearings, and appeals were allowed on a limited scale only after the person concerned had been barred from office. SCAP monitored the whole process. In 1947 the Japanese set up a procedure for the "provisional designation" of all persons, especially in the military, whose positions fell under the purge criteria, eliminating most of the screening procedure.[34]

The purge directive provided not only that persons designated as purgees be removed from office but also that they be excluded from positions of authority and influence in the future. The number excluded greatly exceeded the number actually removed. The purge directive also authorized temporary exemptions for persons whose services were needed to carry out the directive or to complete the demobilization program; this provision was used to postpone the purge of several cabinet members and allowed Willoughby to hire some Imperial Army and Navy experts as historians and advisers for most of the occupation.

The way SCAP applied its instructions meant that the number of Japanese tried as war criminals was far fewer than Washington had planned but that the number purged was much greater. Many persons were simply removed from office but were not interned and tried as war criminal suspects, as they might have been under the basic directive from Washington. According to the official GS history, the essential purpose of the purge was not to punish those who had led Japan to war but rather to remove persons who could not be trusted to guide the nation in peaceful directions. Nevertheless, many in Washington had not expected that the SCAP purge program would involve such a large number of people, and they felt the purge went too far.[35] This kind of confusion is the common result when one set of people makes policies and an entirely different set carries them out.

One young officer purged in 1946 was Morita Akio, a reserve lieutenant in the navy, who was forced thereby to give up a teaching appointment in the Tokyo Institute of Technology, a government university.[36] He soon joined a small electronics company that was then struggling to get started but later became the Sony Corporation, of which he became co-chairman. Not only was Morita *not* an extremist; he was an electronics and marketing genius, and the purge was a good thing for him. It created severe hardship for most purgees, however, making it difficult to find jobs and often imposing a kind of social stigma.

The purge order was not just a shock for the Japanese; it was a thunderbolt. More than 80 percent of the members of the Diet and 50 percent of Shidehara's cabinet would be expelled. The cabinet at first thought of resigning en masse, and Yoshida so informed MacArthur soon after the orders were issued. The general was displeased, saying SCAP might have to take over the administration of the government. He also said that if the Shidehara cabinet resigned, he would not allow Shidehara to form a new government even with the consent of the emperor. The cabinet then decided to hang on; four of its five purged members were allowed to keep office temporarily.[37]

Shidehara proposed to Brigadier General Courtney Whitney, the new chief of GS, that a commission of inquiry be set up to examine and decide each case on the ground that "it seems doubtful whether the directive purports to exclude and remove" from office all persons "no matter how innocent they may be of the sinister actions defined."[38] The Japanese were trying to get some kind of due process introduced into the purge procedures.

At a meeting with the prime minister on January 25, Whitney firmly explained that full compliance with the directives was expected and that any inequities could be remedied later. Whitney did agree that the Japanese government could set up a commission of inquiry after the necessary removals of officials had taken place.[39] The Japanese then proceeded to carry out SCAP's orders. Whitney's meeting was the first important test of his leadership as the chief of GS, and he obviously felt it went well. As he reported to MacArthur, "Once your desires were *fully* understood the government went *all out* in its compliance, accepting not only the *letter* of the requirements but the *spirit* as well."[40]

Whitney had one scare. A SCAP spokesman told the press on February 11 that the government was going far beyond the requirements of the purge orders. This statement was particularly embarrassing because MacArthur had earlier told Yoshida that "the prime minister could disclaim all responsibility for the action required" on the ground that it was required by SCAP orders. Suddenly SCAP was pointing the finger of responsibility for a sweeping purge at the Japanese. Whitney insisted that all future statements of this kind be cleared with him.[41]

The initial purge was carried out in preparation for the forthcoming elections. Three hundred eighty-one members of the Tōjō Diet of 1942 were found ineligible. Of the 3,384 standing for election, 252 more were disqualified as a result of the Japanese government screening. Many political figures did not file for the election and withdrew from public life rather than risk being declared ineligible.

Carrying out the purge marked the rise to power of General Whitney and GS. A veteran of World War I turned lawyer in Manila, Whitney had handled guerrilla operations in the Philippines on MacArthur's staff in the latter days of World War II. Because he had not fought and escaped with MacArthur in 1941–1942, however, he was not a member of the elite "Bataan crowd," like Willoughby and Marquat. He left Japan soon after the surrender ceremony but came back in mid-December to replace a lackluster career officer as GS chief.

Whitney was an able and determined man totally devoted to MacArthur and happy to see the CINC (MacArthur was known inside SCAP as "the See-in-See" or "the old man") get all the credit. Whitney was liked and admired by his own staff but disliked by many Americans in SCAP and in the foreign press corps. Most of the Japanese who dealt with him seemed to fear him. He saw MacArthur several times every day, entered the boss's office without going through the protective staff guarding the entrance, and often finished the day with a long talk with MacArthur.[42]

Whitney also imparted a sense of esprit to GS. His staff members did not hesitate to tackle any issue they thought important. A perceptive Japanese diplomat described them as "good Americans of outstanding intelligence even if they were liberal New Dealers who went too fast sometimes."[43] Whitney's deputy, Colonel Kades, a Wall Street lawyer in later life, was in the view of both Americans and Japanese the epitome of the brainy, liberal American who wanted to reform Japan. MacArthur and Whitney were far from having a New Deal outlook, but they allowed the GS staff to spearhead the reform program.

As soon as Whitney took over, he set about to establish the primacy of GS and succeeded brilliantly. Early in 1946 he requested that GS be given responsibility for coordinating the work of military government teams; this proposal would have made much better use of the teams in the field than SCAP was ever able to do. G-3, a military staff section, proposed in response that it be given authority in the field of civil affairs. Whitney then counterproposed that a separate deputy chief of staff for civil affairs be named, a position that he no doubt aspired to. None of these proposals was approved. MacArthur may well have seen them as a challenge to his own complete authority. Nevertheless, Whitney had succeeded in defending the principle of civilian supremacy on behalf of a section made up mostly of career civilians against a military staff section.[44]

In early 1947 he had a real bureaucratic triumph. A staff memo approved by the chief of staff and no doubt by MacArthur empowered GS to make recommendations to the supreme commander on policy aspects of economic matters as well as political issues, thus giving GS a hunting license to roam through much of the business of the occupation, notably in regard to the broad jurisdiction of ESS. This action did not make GS popular but did give it power. In effect, Whitney became MacArthur's right-hand man for much of the work of the occupation.[45]

Whitney devised the SCAP policy of governing the Japanese by advice and pressure tactics rather than by directive. As a result, GS issued only one more formal directive after the purge orders. This clever technique not only created the illusion that SCAP was not telling the Japanese what to do but also cut away the legal basis for any objection to SCAP actions by the FEC and the ACJ, since there were almost never any written orders for these bodies to challenge.

An important lesson was learned from the purge, Whitney wrote the supreme commander. Japanese delays should not be attributed to "unwillingness or indifference" before patient efforts were made to ensure that SCAP instructions were fully understood.[46] Whitney's own section did not learn this lesson easily because its members were to complain often and bitterly of Japanese "resistance" to their instructions.

CHAPTER 7

The New Constitution

From February 4 to February 13, 1946, GS drafted a new constitution for Japan. With only minor changes it became the law of the land in May 1947 and has remained in effect without amendment ever since. General MacArthur termed it "probably the single most important accomplishment of the occupation."[1] It was surely the most far-reaching—and audacious—of the many actions he took in Japan.

Making the new constitution led to serious clashes between SCAP and the FEC, strained MacArthur's relations with his own government, and raised doubts about his candor in reporting what he was doing in Japan. The SCAP draft constitution aroused consternation among Japan's leaders, and thereafter it provoked intense feeling and debate. But for all these frictions, the result was a remarkable political instrument, called by one senior Japanese "a beautiful jewel that came out of a senseless war."[2]

The inspiration for drafting a new constitution came from Courtney Whitney.[3] Fresh from his triumph in pushing through the purge in January, Whitney persuaded MacArthur to have a draft constitution prepared and given to the Japanese as a "model." The supreme commander saw this as a way to shore up the position of the emperor and to bind Japan to a policy of pacifism. He was concerned that if he did not act swiftly, the new FEC might soon tie his hands. He therefore commissioned GS to sit in conspiratorial secrecy as a "constitutional convention" to draft the charter. MacArthur took an unusually keen interest in the whole operation and followed it carefully, leaving Whitney to supervise the drafting and steer the document through the Japanese legal shoals.

MacArthur had received only general guidance from Washington about constitutional change. At no time had he been told that a new constitution would be necessary to achieve Allied goals, although he had been advised of numerous reforms that should be made in Japan's political structure to make it representative and democratic. Sir George Sansom, a member of the soon-to-expire FEAC, thought the existing constitution would be compatible with Allied goals if three changes were instituted: make the cabinet responsible to the Diet, or parliament; reduce the powers of the house of peers, the nonelected upper house; and give the Diet full power to make the annual budget.[4] American views were more ambitious.

In the fall of 1945, when Sansom gave these views, the U.S. government had not yet formulated any specific ideas about constitutional reform. On November 6, 1945, the political adviser informed the State Department of MacArthur's view that "as the Japanese Government has been directed by the Supreme Commander through the prime minister to initiate a constitutional revision, none of us should be involved until the Japanese Government itself formally submits something on the matter"; he was referring to MacArthur's statement to Shidehara on October 11 of the need for "liberalization of the constitution."[5] When Atcheson drafted a message in mid-November telling the State Department of his concern that the Japanese were moving too slowly, MacArthur added a paragraph to the effect that the message did not reflect his views, which were "very much more optimistic." The political adviser seemed to be out of step with the general.[6]

Meanwhile, Washington had been working on a statement of U.S. policy on political reform. Atcheson received an advance copy on December 13, which he sent to MacArthur with the suggestion that liaison be set up with the Japanese to make sure they were aware of the views of the United States. MacArthur did not react to this advice. He received the final copy of the Washington policy on January 11, 1946, and this document was reportedly used by GS as a guide in its drafting endeavor.[7] By that time General Whitney had taken charge of GS, leaving Atcheson with a negligible role in the making of the constitution.

Drafted largely by Hugh Borton, a Columbia University expert on Japan, the Washington policy paper bore the number SWNCC 228 (SWNCC referred to the State-War-Navy Coordinating Committee, an interagency planning group) and was entitled "Reform of the Japanese

Governmental System." First it described the major defects of the existing political system, such as concentration of power in a small group of personal advisers to the emperor; the weakness of the lower house of the Diet; the emperor's overriding prerogatives, such as the right to select the prime minister and to exercise "supreme command" of the armed forces; and inadequate protection of civil rights. The paper then recommended goals for U.S. policy: an executive branch responsible to the electorate or to a fully representative legislature, guarantees of fundamental civil rights, popular sovereignty, and "the drafting and adoption of constitutional amendments or of a constitution in a manner which will express the free will of the Japanese people." The paper contended that the emperor system could not be retained as it was: the people should decide the eventual form of government, but they should be encouraged to abolish the emperor institution or reform it. If they decided to retain it, the emperor must act only on the advice of the cabinet and should be deprived of all authority in military matters.

SWNCC 228's last caveat was that "only as a last resort should the Supreme Commander order the government to effect the above listed reforms, as the knowledge that they had been imposed by the Allies would materially reduce their acceptance and support." Inserted by the Joint Chiefs of Staff, this clause reflected concern that the "proposed reforms may foment unrest in Japan to such a degree as to require increases in occupational forces." SWNCC 228 was later referred to the FEC as a U.S. proposal. In accord with the usual procedure, it was also sent to SCAP for information so that Tokyo would know what Washington was thinking and doing. The FEC approved SWNCC 228 as Allied policy, with minor changes, on July 2, 1946. All member governments including the Soviet Union and Australia thus approved giving Japan the right to decide whether to retain the emperor institution.[8]

In early 1946 the Matsumoto committee set up by Shidehara continued to work on revising the 1889 constitution, but the scope of the planned reforms, especially in regard to the role of the emperor, was limited. The prime minister stated publicly that he saw no need for broad revision of the constitution. The political parties and several private groups prepared drafts of a new constitution; some, like that of the Socialist Party, were quite liberal, and others, like those of the Progressives and the Liberals, were quite limited. There was no contact between the Japanese government and SCAP on this matter. Indeed, at that stage GS had few contacts with the Japanese on any political matters.[9]

SCAP experts told the visiting FEAC in January 1946 that many changes were being made in Japan's system of government but that "we do not amend the constitution as such." The Philippine representative on the FEAC said he did "not understand why constitutional revision was not part" of GS's work; several other representatives appeared to think that revision would eventually be necessary. MacArthur seemed to end the debate, however, when he told the FEAC on January 30 that the matter of constitutional reform "had been taken out of his hands by the Moscow agreement" setting up the FEC. Nevertheless, three days after meeting the FEAC MacArthur instructed his staff to draft a new constitution. He acted because his most trusted adviser, Courtney Whitney, had convinced him that he had the authority he needed, that he had to move quickly before Washington intervened, and that the Japanese were stalling on reform.[10]

SCAP's role in constitutional reform having been questioned, Whitney first requested a study of MacArthur's authority. Drafted by Kades, the study was sent to the supreme commander on February 1.[11] It argued forcefully that MacArthur had both general authority from the Allied powers to take such steps as he thought proper to carry out the surrender terms and specific authority, under the surrender terms and U.S. policy, to take measures to strengthen democratic tendencies, eliminate authoritarian practices, and require Japan to develop a non-militaristic and democratic government. Only two limitations could restrict his authority: action to remove the emperor would require prior consultation with the JCS; and any directive to the Japanese government about constitutional change would, if the FEC had previously issued a policy decision on that matter, be subject to review by the ACJ and the FEC.

This legal opinion did not become generally known until 1949 when GS published it as part of a detailed and sometimes self-serving report of its activities, *The Political Reorientation of Japan*. As penetrating an analysis as it was, most members of the FEC would certainly have disputed its conclusion. MacArthur was careful, however, not to press his assertions of authority too far, and he soon avoided the whole issue by claiming that the draft constitution was a Japanese product, not a response to any "order" by him.

Having satisfied the supreme commander that he had the necessary authority, Whitney probably went on to urge him to act quickly. The new FEC, which would soon hold its organizational meeting, would take up the constitutional issue and could quite possibly, under pressure from the Soviets and the Australians, impose a constitution on Japan and on him.[12] MacArthur had little confidence in the U.S. representatives on the commission and might have thought that the United States would not veto radical solutions, such as elimination of the imperial institution, that a majority of the commission might devise. Citing these dangers, Whitney might then have persuaded MacArthur that he should take steps to forestall undesirable action by the FEC.

Whitney's clinching argument was a scoop in the Japanese newspaper *Mainichi*, also on February 1, making public what it claimed was a revision plan prepared by the Matsumoto committee.[13] Whitney immediately wrote a memorandum to the supreme commander describing the draft as "extremely conservative in character" because it left substantially unchanged the status of the emperor, with all rights of sovereignty vested in him.[14] The press widely criticized the "Matsumoto draft" as reactionary, leading the government to issue a statement that the draft was merely the working paper of one committee member. In any case, MacArthur's earlier optimism that left to themselves the Japanese would produce a suitable revision seemed to have been unwarranted.

On February 3 MacArthur decided that GS should prepare a draft constitution. Whitney was optimistic that the Japanese would accept the principles of a SCAP draft and "get into the swing of this thing as they finally did in compliance with the 'purge' directive."[15] At that point Whitney's intention was to give the Japanese a "model constitution" that would serve as a statement of basic principles but not as an order.

The next month—from February 4 to March 6, when the draft of a new constitution was made public—was one of the most extraordinary periods of the occupation. The U.S. military command wrote a basic national constitution for the defeated nation in utmost secrecy and then made sure it was approved by Japan's political leaders with only a few changes. The document was then made public, and other governments were told it was the joint product of the Japanese and SCAP.

On February 4 Whitney summoned members of the public administration division of GS and told them they would "sit as a constitutional convention."[16] He said he planned to submit a draft to General MacArthur in a week and then give it to the Japanese. Twenty-seven persons— officers and civilians, professionals, and secretaries—prepared the draft. Some were lawyers; others were teachers, civil servants, or military professionals. There were no constitutional lawyers. Only a few had any background in government or prewar experience in Japan. For reference material, they had the Meiji and U.S. constitutions, those of several European and American states, and a few charters drafted by Japanese scholars and political parties.[17]

Whitney told the group the Japanese would be advised that the only way to retain "the Emperor and the remnants of their own power is by their acceptance and approval of a constitution that will force a decisive swing to the left." To do this, General MacArthur had "empowered him [Whitney] to use not merely the threat of force, but force itself."[18] MacArthur would insist on only a few points, Whitney told his GS staff. He had a sheet of yellow paper on which three numbered paragraphs were written in longhand, either MacArthur's or Whitney's. The main points were:

I

The emperor is at the head of state. . . . His duties and powers will be . . . responsible to the basic will of the people. . . .

II

War as a sovereign right of the nation is abolished. . . . Japan renounces it as an instrumentality for settling its disputes and even for preserving its security. It relies upon the higher ideals which are now stirring the world. . . . No Japanese army, navy or air force will ever be authorized and no rights of belligerency will ever be conferred upon any Japanese force.

III

The feudal system of Japan will cease. No rights of peerage except those of the imperial family. . . . Pattern budget after British system.

In his remarks to Whitney, MacArthur also said he preferred that Japan have a unicameral legislature rather than two houses.[19]

GS was divided into seven committees to produce drafts of various parts of the proposed constitution. In addition, a steering committee of three lawyers headed by Kades supervised the drafting and resolved differences. Taking his cue from MacArthur, Whitney delegated all the drafting work to the staff and intervened on only a few matters. No one outside the section was to know what was being done, and the project was to be treated as top secret.

Whitney worried particularly that the State Department political adviser might get wind of the project and tell Washington what was going on. POLAD and Washington learned nothing about the operation until they saw the draft constitution in the press on March 6. Kades wrote a memorandum of record in early March asserting the supreme commander was not required to consult the JCS about constitutional changes unless they involved the removal of the emperor and reasserting that MacArthur's powers were absolute so long as he acted within the scope of his basic directives. Kades added that SCAP actions were in "complete conformity with SWNCC 228." The secrecy of this operation demonstrated the confidence MacArthur and Whitney had in themselves and their lack of confidence in the rest of the U.S. government.[20]

The draft, which was finished by February 10, took seven days, almost surely a record time for the drafting of any constitution. Writing the U.S. Constitution of 1787 had required 127 days' work for fifty-five persons, many of them experts with long experience in government.[21] The three overriding principles of the SCAP draft were popular sovereignty, pacifism, and protection of individual human rights. The draft provided for retention of an emperor as the "symbol" of the state, a popularly elected and representative legislature, and a cabinet responsible to it.

In light of Japan's constitutional history, the group adopted the British system of parliamentary supremacy rather than the U.S. system of checks and balances among three branches of government. A prime minister would appoint and dismiss cabinet ministers. A supreme court would have the power to determine the constitutionality of laws and official acts. The draft included lengthy definitions of civil and human rights. Two provisions in the SCAP draft soon fell quietly by the wayside, however: one providing that the Diet could reverse Supreme Court decisions by a two-thirds vote in certain cases and the other prohibiting the Diet from voting appropriations in excess of anticipated income.

The preamble was notably eloquent in its borrowing from the Constitution of the United States: "We, the Japanese people, acting through our duly elected representatives in the National Diet, determined that we shall secure for ourselves and our posterity the fruits of peaceful cooperation with all nations and the blessings of liberty throughout this land, and resolved that never again shall we be visited with the horrors of war through the action of government, do proclaim the sovereignty of the people's will."

Chapter One provided, "The Emperor shall be the symbol of the state and of the unity of the people." According to Kades, a number of Americans in Washington and Tokyo had come to the view that the emperor should have only a symbolic and ceremonial role and that if he were to have the role of "head of state," as MacArthur proposed, the suspicion might arise that the emperor had retained some political power.[22] Chapter Two, on renunciation of war, was drafted by Kades much as MacArthur had directed, although the stricture that Japan should not resort to war "even for preserving its own security" was dropped, a crucial change as it turned out later.

Chapter Three, on the rights and duties of the people, was a comprehensive recital of thirty-one civil and human rights. One provision stated that laws with regard to marriage and the family would be enacted "from the standpoint of individual dignity and the essential equality of the sexes." As a result, the civil code was later amended to break up the old family system, the *ie*, in which the oldest living male member inherited the family property and exercised certain legal rights over the extended family, which consisted of a number of his close kin.[23] Under the new system the core family consisted of the husband, the wife, and their children. Although a logical consequence of the principle of individual equality, this radical change provoked stormy debate and considerable opposition.

The GS draft provided for a unicameral legislature, as MacArthur had proposed. No executive veto would limit the legislative power of the Diet. The Diet could be dissolved only by a vote of no confidence or by defeat of a resolution of confidence. The GS draft provided that the appointment of supreme court justices would be reviewed in a general election at ten-year intervals after their original appointment. Kades had at one point advocated popular election of judges but was persuaded to give up this idea.

Amendments would require a two-thirds approval of all members in each house of the Diet and a majority vote in a nationwide referendum. The amendment procedure was made particularly complex because SCAP wanted to be sure that the new constitution would not be quickly changed once the occupation ended.

When MacArthur approved the GS draft on February 12, he made only one change, deleting an article that would have prohibited future amendment of any of the provisions dealing with the rights and duties of the people. He approved a sonorous article that Whitney had personally drafted (Article 97) according to which "the fundamental human rights . . . guaranteed to the people of Japan are fruits of the age-old struggle of man to be free; they . . . are conferred upon this and future generations in trust, to be held for all time inviolate."[24]

On February 13, in one of the tensest meetings of the occupation,

Whitney, Kades, and several of their experts presented the GS draft to Japanese officials, including Yoshida; Matsumoto, who was in charge of constitutional reform; and Shirasu Jirō, Yoshida's confidant and a member of the CLO. Expecting to get comments on the authentic Matsumoto draft, which had been officially presented in summary form to Whitney on February 8, the Japanese were "aghast" to be presented with a brand-new draft of a constitution for their nation.[25]

Whitney told them that their draft did not show that Japan had learned the lessons of the war and was ready to act as a responsible member of the international community. The supreme commander had therefore prepared, in the form of a draft constitution, a detailed statement of those principles he deemed basic. Whitney advised the Japanese to give the draft the fullest consideration in the preparation of a revised constitution. According to a record made by one of the American participants in the meeting, he also said, "MacArthur was firmly resisting pressure from other Allied nations to put the Emperor on trial as a war criminal, but if Japan would agree to this constitution, the Supreme Commander thought the Emperor would be safe."[26]

Whitney told the Japanese that they were under no compulsion to take further action but that MacArthur was determined that the people should have the opportunity to consider and express their will on the issue of constitutional reform well in advance of the general election. If the cabinet did not act, MacArthur was prepared to put the issue before the people himself. MacArthur later told Whitney he would back this strong assertion. Finally, Whitney said that MacArthur "feels this is the last opportunity for the conservative groups, considered by many to be reactionary, to remain in power and that this can only be done by a sharp swing to the left."[27]

According to the Japanese report of the meeting, Whitney also said that MacArthur was concerned about how to overcome U.S. domestic opposition to the retention of the emperor. According to Yoshida's memoirs, Whitney stated that if the SCAP draft was not accepted, "GHQ could not answer for whatever might happen to the Emperor."[28] Whitney then gave copies of the draft to the Japanese and said he and his aides would step outside for a few minutes while the Japanese looked it over. When he reentered the room twenty minutes later, according to his memoirs, he said he had been enjoying Japan's "atomic sunshine." Just at that moment a B-29 flew overhead. Kades stated afterward that a B-29 did fly over but that Whitney was merely joking and not making any kind of threat. Whitney was not ordinarily known for his sense of humor, but he did seem to appreciate "psychological shafts."[29]

The Japanese did not comment at any length other than to question the provision for a unicameral legislature. Kades had previously suggested this might be a "throwaway" proposal useful for bargaining if the Japanese objected strongly. That MacArthur was the author of the idea did not seem compelling to his staff. Yoshida said little at the February 13 meeting because he thought it was up to Matsumoto to speak for the Japanese. Yoshida said later he thought the draft might have come from Washington; Shirasu thought it had been prepared months before in Australia. It was not until publication in 1949 of the GS opus on political reorientation that the Japanese learned that the draft was not an Allied policy document but rather the last-minute creation of MacArthur and his staff.

Shirasu, who had a good command of English and a mordant sense of humor, wrote Whitney on February 15 that the Japanese were more than a little shocked at the direct American way of dealing with the problem but that they, too, wanted a democratic constitution and felt they should proceed carefully. Whitney sent a firm reply the next day asserting that MacArthur wanted to place the emperor "in a position of dignity, honor and respect" while placing political power in the hands of the people. Whitney added that if Japan did not act forthrightly, a far more drastic charter might be forced on it "from the outside . . . a constitution which well might sweep away even those structures and traditions which the Supreme Commander by his instrument makes it possible to preserve."[30]

On February 18 Matsumoto gave Whitney a written "explanation" of his draft constitution, but Whitney dismissed it as frivolous and contentious. He told the Japanese they must state their position within forty-eight hours or MacArthur "will take the constitution to the people directly." Shirasu got a two-day extension from Whitney so that the English draft could be translated and explained to the cabinet.[31]

On February 19 the cabinet began for the first time to discuss the SCAP draft and soon found itself sharply split, especially regarding the status of the emperor and the no-war clause (Article 9). The prime minister and several others thought the SCAP draft should be rejected. They decided Shidehara should see MacArthur to find out how strongly the Americans felt.[32]

Whitney was accustomed to sending MacArthur memos with tidbits of information. On February 19 he labeled Matsumoto and Yoshida "as the most reactionary element of the cabinet." On February 21, just before MacArthur was to see Shidehara, Whitney asserted that the cabinet was "playing its final card" and that MacArthur should ignore any threat to resign because he was giving the people the "essence of human freedom" as required by the Potsdam Declaration.[33]

Shidehara's meeting with MacArthur was surely one of the most significant meetings the general held with any Japanese during the occupation. They had a full discussion of Article 9 and its relation to the emperor system. There was no confrontation or argument, but Shidehara clearly reflected the deep concern he and his cabinet felt about these two provisions. MacArthur said to the prime minister, "I think the emperor system should be kept for Japan's sake, but the Soviet Union and Australia are worried that Japan will carry out a war of revenge, and so they oppose Japan's having the emperor system and armaments. . . . What will foreign countries say if a provision is retained that Japan will keep armed forces? They will obviously think that Japan is planning to rebuild its armed forces. Therefore, if you think about what is the good thing to do, Japan should take moral leadership by stating clearly that it renounces war." Shidehara then broke in, "You talk about leadership, but other countries may not go along with Japan." MacArthur cut him off in a positive tone of voice: "Even if no other country goes along, Japan will lose nothing. Those who will not give their support are in the wrong."[34]

In his report to the cabinet, Shidehara said he thought changes in the SCAP draft would be possible, except for the provision regarding the emperor and the no-war clause. Some members of the cabinet felt that if the constitutional issue were taken to the people, as Whitney had threatened, the conservatives might lose strength and even be voted out of office. Thereupon, the cabinet concluded, in the most far-reaching decision of any cabinet during the occupation, that there was no alternative to accepting the SCAP draft but that Japan should try to get the best deal possible. Some cabinet members even wept during this emotional meeting.[35]

In the afternoon of February 22, Shidehara reported to the emperor that the cabinet felt it must accept the U.S. draft. Accounts vary as to what the emperor said, but they agree that he gave his approval. Yoshida did not attend Shidehara's meeting with the emperor but later said the emperor's temperament was such that he probably said something like, "It [the SCAP draft] is all right this way, isn't it?" In any case, according to Yoshida, the Tennō's endorsement was decisive in winning government support for the SCAP draft.[36] The emperor's approval of the new constitution must rank with his influence in ensuring a smooth surrender in August 1945 and with his "declaration of humanity" in January 1946 as signal contributions to the occupation and the evolution of postwar Japan.

GS was able to get some inside information from Narahashi Wataru, a minister in the cabinet, when he invited several members of GS to a Sunday picnic at his country home soon after the meeting with the emperor. Narahashi described the "furious struggle" that took place in the cabinet and how several ministers were thinking of resigning even after the emperor had expressed "unqualified approval" of the GS draft. Narahashi categorized Yoshida as part of the group favoring acceptance of the new charter, thus contradicting unshakable GS suspicions.[37]

On the day Shidehara met with the emperor, February 22, Yoshida, Matsumoto, and Shirasu saw Whitney, Kades, and other members of GS. Quoting what General MacArthur had said the day before to Shidehara, Whitney asserted that "it is the basic principles and structure that we are insistent upon," adding that the terms of the SCAP draft were basic, though modifications in form might be permitted to make the meaning clearer or to conform with Japanese procedure. Matsumoto commented that the opening words of the GS version, "We, the people of Japan," posed a problem because the Meiji Constitution required the emperor, not the people, to initiate amendments. Whitney and Kades saw no difficulty if the new draft was approved by the emperor and adopted through the procedure required by the Meiji Constitution.

Whitney offered one concession: "If the cabinet feels strongly about the desirability of a bicameral legislature, and both houses are elected by popular vote, General MacArthur will interpose no objection." In regard to the clause on renunciation of war, Whitney insisted that it be a separate article in the constitution, not a general principle in the preamble, because "this article affords Japan the opportunity to assume the moral leadership of the world in the movement towards lasting peace." Speaking as one lawyer to another, Whitney told Matsumoto, an authority on commercial law, "You have the satisfaction of knowing that your fee for this work will be the highest possible—the welfare of the Japanese people."[38]

During the next week the Japanese reworked the SCAP draft to in-
corporate language they thought more appropriate for Japan. At 10
A.M. on March 4 the top experts of the two sides began discussions and
met continuously until 4 P.M. on March 5. At this critical meeting in
the drafting of the Shōwa Constitution, the Americans insisted that
agreement on the draft be reached at once. The Japanese presented their
revised draft but found the Americans unyielding on all but minor
changes in the SCAP draft of February 13. The model had become
absolute.[39] Early in the meeting Matsumoto walked out after a quarrel
with Kades over the translation of provisions defining the powers of the
emperor. Matsumoto claimed Kades was attempting to alter not only
the constitution but the Japanese language as well. Matsumoto's assistant, Satō Tatsuō, a skilled legal craftsman, carried on as the main
Japanese representative, and the marathon meeting then proceeded
without incident. The negotiators agreed, among other things, that the
legislature would have two chambers. Shirasu, a participant throughout
the negotiations, kept a somewhat cryptic record of the sessions. At the
end he wrote, "This is the way the constitution that exposed our defeat
was born. Now see what happens."[40]

The cabinet reviewed successive drafts of articles as they emerged
from the conference, as did senior SCAP officials. The final version received the emperor's approval late in the day on March 5, when he
issued a rescript stating his "desire that the constitution of our empire
be revised drastically upon the basis of the general will of the people
and the principle of respect for fundamental human rights." General
MacArthur issued his own statement of deep satisfaction with the "decision of the Emperor and government of Japan to submit . . . a new and
enlightened constitution which has my full approval." He noted that it
had been "drafted after painstaking investigation and frequent conferences" between the government and his staff. A "gist of the revised draft
of the Imperial constitution," which was in fact an extensive summary,
was made public on March 6. The press reaction both in Japan and
abroad reflected some surprise at these announcements but was generally favorable.[41]

A week after the FEC's opening meeting on February 26, 1946,
the members in Washington read about the new Japanese constitution
in the newspapers. They were dismayed, to say the least, that a new
charter drafted without their knowledge had received the approval of
the emperor and the supreme commander. Nor were they enlightened

by the U.S. member, Major General Frank R. McCoy, the chairman of the commission and a retired officer with close ties to MacArthur. McCoy and the State Department knew no more than the FEC did.[42]

The commission's first significant action was to pass a policy decision on March 20, with the U.S. member concurring, instructing MacArthur to inform the Japanese government that the commission must be given an opportunity to pass on the final draft of the constitution and to permit the Japanese to consider drafts other than the government draft just made public. Secretary of State Byrnes had already stated on March 12 that the commission would review the constitution in some way before it went into effect.[43]

MacArthur told the Pentagon he thought the FEC's action was based on "an invalid premise" and that the United States should have vetoed it. But he carried out the FEC's instructions by telling the newly organized ACJ on April 5 that changes might be made in the draft as a result of "ultimate consideration by the National Diet and the Allied powers," certainly an oblique way to refer to a direct instruction by the body set up to make policy for the occupation. The U.S. representative on the commission staunchly defended MacArthur's method of executing its first decision.[44]

The commission's second step was a request on April 10 that MacArthur send a member of his staff to consult with the FEC on constitutional questions. Well over a month later, the State Department conveyed MacArthur's reply that close understanding was desirable but that no officer on his staff was in a position to express his views because he was personally dealing with constitutional matters. It turned out that MacArthur had replied on April 13, but "due to a misunderstanding" the reply had not been sent to the commission promptly. Washington had been negotiating with MacArthur to persuade him to make a more helpful reply, which was finally given to the commission on May 29.

On June 4 the commission received another exposition of the supreme commander's views. This message, drafted by Whitney, stated that MacArthur wanted to avoid "any implication . . . that reform resulted from Allied pressure." His own "personal approval" was designed to give "moral support and encouragement to the liberal forces struggling in Japan for reform against tradition, prejudice and reaction." The SCAP message concluded disingenuously by remarking that the new charter "will probably have been the most freely discussed and considered constitution in history" and that the commission could render no better service than to permit the Japanese "as I propose to do, to proceed unshackled, unhindered, and in complete freedom to work out their constitutional reforms."[45]

The FEC was understandably unhappy with this reply. Members disagreed with MacArthur as to what was policy and what was implementation; they felt they had a responsibility to ensure that the charter reflected the "freely expressed will of the Japanese people." They also wanted to avoid a "trial of strength" with the supreme commander,[46] but they had just had a tilting match with him. He got his way and made no concessions.

Several points in this four-month period are noteworthy. First, changes in the SCAP draft were few and minor. Kades said later the Japanese could have made more changes, but they "chose the easy way."[47] The record is clear, however, that SCAP opposed all but minor changes. Second, MacArthur's role was mostly that of an observer, except for his instructions at the outset regarding the status of the emperor and the no-war clause and his persuasion of a doubting Prime Minister Shidehara.

Third, Article 9, the no-war clause, was conceived in mystery and confusion. MacArthur later said he got the idea from Shidehara, who confirmed this statement some years later.[48] MacArthur himself had been outspoken in the years after World War II that society should outlaw war. He said this to *Time* journalist Theodore White on August 8, 1945, to the emperor on September 27, and to president-elect Eisenhower in 1952 as a proposal to make to the Soviets in an effort to settle the Korean War. MacArthur made an eloquent antiwar speech in Los Angeles on his seventy-fifth birthday in 1955, dilating on how "war has become a Frankenstein to destroy both sides." The idea of a no-war clause in the Japanese constitution was almost certainly MacArthur's, and the responsibility for having it inserted was surely his. It was ironic, as Theodore McNelly, an authority on the origin and meaning of Article 9, has pointed out, that in later life MacArthur reverted to the view he held during most of his career that the profession of arms, wars, and sacrifice for the nation were still necessary and that "in war there is no substitute for victory."[49]

For MacArthur to insist on the no-war clause without giving Washington the slightest hint of what he was doing was an arrogant act. Although the initial U.S. policy of September 1945 provided that Japan was not to have an army, a navy, or an air force, it was evident that this measure was to apply during the occupation. In fact, Secretary of State

Byrnes was at that time trying to win Soviet agreement to negotiation of a twenty-five-year treaty of disarmament and demilitarization with Germany and Japan, implying there had been no derogation of Japan's sovereign right to have armed forces. Nevertheless, Under Secretary Acheson told an Australian diplomat in 1947 that "the United States does not approve of the idea of Japan's having armed forces," thus seeming to ratify the concept underlying Article 9.[50]

In spite of this tangled background, the "peace constitution" is considered by many Japanese to be the legal basis and the symbol of their pacifism, and they associate it with the name of Douglas MacArthur. U.S. leaders have consistently pressed Japan since the late 1940s to take a larger role in collective security actions to counter threats to peace in East Asia. The Japanese have played only a modest part in these efforts, citing as one reason their constitutional barrier against offensive military forces.

Finally, the question of pressure arises. No doubt all military occupations are based on implied force and direct pressure. MacArthur and GS acted forcefully to win acceptance of their draft constitution. The emperor saw no reason to oppose it. The Japanese, according to Shirasu, understood and accepted U.S. pressure. Yoshida, a devoted patriot and conservative, had reservations about the draft when he first saw it, but he soon came around to accepting it and later vigorously supported it. Many Japanese wanted a new and democratic constitution. They were sympathetic then, and remained so later, despite the pressure applied by SCAP.

After the constitution went into effect in 1947, the imperial household sent all members of GS a memento in appreciation of their contribution to the new Japan. Initially, the gifts were to go only to the supreme commander and the chief of GS. Upon the suggestion of Whitney, however, all who took part in drafting the constitution were honored with a chalice bearing the imperial crest or with a certificate. MacArthur personally intervened to make silver available for the cups. The Tennō seemed to feel no resentment that he had become a "symbolic emperor."[51]

PART III

Japan's Search for Stability

The thirty months from April 1946 to October 1948 were a long plateau with virtually no signs that Japan would reach the high ground of political stability and economic growth. The main cornerstones of the SCAP reform program had already been set; it was up to the Japanese to rebuild their institutions on the foundation that had been laid. They would have to find leaders of a new mold, men—and women, MacArthur hoped—who could cope with the mountain of economic troubles the nation faced: the food shortages, unemployment, racing inflation, lack of raw materials, and cutoff of foreign trade.

The Japanese slowly started to come back to life. An early sign was their vigorous election for a new lower house. When MacArthur rejected the man who was sure to be elected prime minister, Yoshida Shigeru emerged from obscurity to take over the government, even though he lacked both experience and a political base. Moving energetically, he created overwhelming support for the new constitution and the legislation to implement it. Another exception to the postsurrender lethargy, called *kyodatsu* by the Japanese, was the surging labor movement. Workers, particularly in the government employee unions, made up the most dynamic political force in Japan throughout the occupation. Labor showed its strength even before Yoshida took office in May 1946, and by the end of 1946 it was planning a general strike that could have threatened the security of the occupation and the stability of the government. At the last minute MacArthur prohibited the strike. Some critics, both American and Japanese, have claimed that at that moment the occupation turned away from liberalism and reform. Eighteen months later MacArthur reinforced this impression by denying government workers the right to collective bargaining as well as the right to strike. Yoshida and the conservatives welcomed these steps.

MacArthur directed that a new election be held in 1947, and Yoshida resigned in May. Following an election that produced no clear winner, Japan experimented with two different governments. Both were coalitions, the first headed by a socialist and the second by a conservative. Despite SCAP's preference for the social democratic approach, the right and left wings of the Socialist Party found their differences irreconcilable. A huge bribery scandal in late 1948 put an end to moderate coalition government.

Political instability deepened. Three different prime ministers—a conservative, a socialist and a middle-of-the-roader—had all tried to get the nation going. But none was able to stabilize the political situation or gain much support from the people. MacArthur's grip as supreme commander did not weaken, but his attention wandered for a time as he looked toward Washington and saw visions of high public office.

CHAPTER 8

The Emergence of Yoshida Shigeru

The most important political action Japan took after its surrender was to elect a new lower house on April 10, 1946. The FEC, worried that an early election would "give a decisive advantage to the reactionary parties," asked MacArthur if he shared this concern. He countered that "the new Diet will be the most truly responsive body to the will of the people that has ever served Japan and will provide the basis for a much more representative cabinet."[1]

Because the Allies had agreed at Potsdam that Japan would consist of the four main islands, with minor islands to be determined later, it became necessary to define Japan's territory for electoral purposes. After consulting Washington, SCAP issued an order on January 29, 1946, that for electoral purposes Japan would exclude the Bonin Islands and the Ryukyu Islands to the south and the Kurile Islands, the Habomai Islands, and Shikotan Island to the north. The denial of Japanese administrative rights in these areas, even with the caveat that this action was not definitive, seemed to weaken Japan's chances of getting them back. Korea was also separated from Japan by MacArthur's order but remained under his supervision for U.S. military purposes until American forces were withdrawn in 1949.[2]

As the election neared, it was evident that the dominant political figure was Hatoyama Ichirō, the founder of the Liberal Party, who had a mixed record of cooperation with nationalist elements in the prewar period. Yoshida Shigeru was not a candidate and no doubt anticipated that his short spell as a cabinet minister was about to end. The socialists seemed to promise real change, but their leader, Katayama Tetsu, was an unknown quantity dealing with a turbulent and divided party. The Communist Party had several active and popular leaders, notably the intellectual Nosaka Sanzō, who returned to Japan in January 1946 after a long exile in China, where he had worked with communist leaders, and the dynamic Tokuda Kyūichi, who had spent seventeen years in prison. Then as now the Communist Party was more unified in its policies than the other large parties. Most Japanese, however, remained highly suspicious of communism and the Soviet shadow.

More than 3,000 candidates ran for the 466 seats in the House of Representatives. The electorate of 37 million voters, consisting of all adult men and women, was far larger than in any previous election. Voter turnout was high, with 73 percent of those eligible voting. It was a fair and orderly election. Hatoyama's Liberal Party, which won 140 seats, received a distinct plurality. The Progressive Party won 93 seats; the Socialists, 92; and the small People's Cooperative Party, 14. The Communists won 5 seats, with 3.8 percent of the votes.

The right-of-center parties had thus obtained 246 seats, more than 50 percent of the total. Most of the independents and minor party figures were also conservative, making the final result a distinctly conservative victory. Thirty-nine women were elected, the record for Japan's entire postwar period. Some said that so many women were elected because voters, who could vote for three candidates, gave them a "courtesy vote" as the second or third choice on their ballots. Three hundred seventy-five members of the new house were elected for the first time. The results seemed in an indirect way to affirm support for the new constitution because the communists, who provided the only vocal opposition to the charter, did very poorly. On April 25 MacArthur issued a lengthy press statement asserting that democracy had registered "a healthy forward advance." He said nothing about the constitution.[3]

The two most dramatic political events of the entire occupation—the purge of Hatoyama and the emergence of Yoshida—occurred in the aftermath of the elections. Widely recognized as Japan's most skilled politician, Hatoyama came out of the election as the leading candidate for prime minister. Sixty-three years old, he was an affable man who was on good terms with all political groups in postwar Japan except the communists. Although his record had been screened and cleared by the Japanese before the election, he soon became the target of intense press interest and suspicion.

On election day the Civil Intelligence Section (CIS) of SCAP asked Japanese officials to provide more details about Hatoyama's prewar activities, in particular his 1933 order as education minister dismissing a Kyoto University professor accused of "leftist leanings" and his authorship of *The Face of the World*, a report by Hatoyama on a trip to Europe in 1938 that made several favorable allusions to Hitler, Mussolini, and the way the Nazis controlled the labor movement in Germany. CIS intimated to the Japanese that if they did not take action on Hatoyama, the occupation would issue an order that would cause them to "lose face."[4] Hatoyama's confidence was not shaken. His friend Yoshida, who had had some experience dealing with SCAP purge orders, advised him that an explanation about his book might end the matter.

The Japanese began to get nervous, however, and the cabinet decided to seek SCAP approval for Hatoyama's nomination as prime minister. When informal soundings did not work, Yoshida wrote a letter to MacArthur on May 4 stating that Shidehara intended to "recommend to the Throne that Mr. Hatoyama be empowered to form a new cabinet." Whitney replied at once that a directive had already been issued covering this subject. SCAPIN 919, a two-page order, directed the Japanese government to purge Hatoyama because the supreme commander found that he was an "undesirable person" who had "denounced or contributed to the seizure of opponents of the militaristic regime." The order cited a number of specific actions.[5]

Yoshida later wrote in his memoirs that the purge of Hatoyama "came as a complete surprise to me." Actually he was aware weeks before the purge that Hatoyama was suspect. Yoshida surmised that officials in the Foreign Office were conniving with SCAP officers to bring about Hatoyama's downfall. Yoshida used this opportunity to banish a promising young diplomat, Sone Eki, to a central liaison post in remote Kyushu. Sone, one of the most talented and liberal men in the Japanese government, later resigned and became an important member of the Japan Socialist Party and the Diet. Yoshida did not stop at this one action; he used what became known as the "Yoshida purge" to transfer or demote officials he did not like, especially young diplomats.[6]

Yoshida and Hatoyama had known each other well for years. Even before he was purged, Hatoyama thought that if something untoward happened to him, Yoshida could take his place. After receiving the purge order, Hatoyama approached Yoshida about the prime ministership. Yoshida consulted with his family, in particular his father-in-law, Count Makino, and his daughter, Asō Kazuko, all of whom strongly counseled him to stay out of politics. As his daughter said, he did not have the temperament, the money, or the skill at speech making necessary for a politician. His old friend Shirasu told him he would be "a damned fool" to take the job. Yoshida turned Hatoyama down, saying there were other more suitable candidates.[7]

The political scene was in turmoil. The liberals were paralyzed by a leadership crisis. The second party, the Progressives, were discredited by Shidehara's ineptness as prime minister and all but shattered by purge losses. The third-ranking party, the Socialists, made a bid for power but lacked the strength and finesse to build a coalition. The crisis was compounded by mass disorders in Tokyo that had begun in early April before the election. Thousands of demonstrators marched through the streets demanding food and calling for the departure of the already resigned Shidehara cabinet.[8] SCAP dispatched armored cars and jeeps to help disperse the demonstrators.

Shidehara turned again to Yoshida and by a combination of persuasion and trickery got him to accept political office. Yoshida said in his memoirs that "the ending of the political deadlock and stabilization of the situation became an urgent necessity" in view of reports that "Japan had been submerged under a sea of red flags." Yoshida's friends and relatives were taken aback. His close friend and physician, Dr. Takemi Tarō, asked if he was confident he could do the job. Yoshida is reported to have replied, in words that became famous in Japan, "History shows that there can be defeat in war and victory in diplomacy." These words reflected more than anything Yoshida's determination and confidence. According to his daughter, Yoshida felt there was a job to be done and that he could do it better than anyone else.[9]

At a May 13 meeting with Hatoyama, Yoshida agreed to take over leadership of the Liberal Party on three conditions. First, he would not collect money for the party. Second, he would make all government personnel selections. Third, he could resign whenever he wanted. The two seemed to be in agreement on those conditions. Hatoyama later asserted there was a fourth condition—that Yoshida would give up the post of party president whenever Hatoyama or other leaders in the party asked him to quit. This is hardly a condition that Yoshida would have wanted, but at that time he might have been willing to accept it.[10] Hatoyama remained a power behind the scenes throughout the occupation, despite SCAP's interdiction of political activity by purgees. Neither Yoshida nor Hatoyama could have had any idea in 1946 how long the occupation would last or that Yoshida would turn into a resourceful, successful politician who wanted to keep his job.

On May 15 after the deal with Hatoyama had been cut, Yoshida, ever the punctilious diplomat, sent a note to MacArthur saying that Shidehara would propose him to the throne as prime minister and asking for the general's approval. MacArthur penciled a note on Yoshida's letter, as he often did on incoming mail, saying, "No objection from SCAP. Best of luck. MacA."[11] In accordance with the old constitutional procedures, which were still in effect, Yoshida received an imperial order on May 16 to form a cabinet. He formally joined the Liberal Party in May 1946 and became chairman of its executive committee. He was elected party president four months later.

Although new to power and politics, Yoshida was a shrewd observer and quick learner. He realized that as prime minister the key to success was to get along well with MacArthur. For Yoshida and most Japanese MacArthur was the voice of the United States and the Allied powers— an impression MacArthur wanted to convey. In time Yoshida grew confident of his ability to deal with the general and learned that SCAP was a loosely organized headquarters, that MacArthur delegated freely, and that SCAP staff sections often disagreed. The one person who really counted was the man at the top. This, too, was a viewpoint that MacArthur encouraged.[12] Yoshida came to feel little need to yield on every occasion to MacArthur's subordinates. He even took issue with Whitney and the powerful GS, but he was well aware they had MacArthur's ear and confidence. Yoshida won few bouts, but he kept trying. He also came to relish the art of maneuvering within the loose SCAP setup to get around GS.

The new prime minister's first job was to form a cabinet. He had observed this operation many times as a diplomatic official, and in 1936 he had helped his friend and fellow diplomat Hirota Kōki form a government. Yoshida decided to keep the Foreign Office portfolio himself, as he did in all four of his cabinets during the occupation, so that he could personally deal with the occupation forces.[13] Some said he kept the Foreign Office portfolio so that he could continue to live in the stately residence reserved at that time for the foreign minister, the Asoka mansion in Shiba. He had a taste for luxury—nice places to live, good food, expensive cigars, a British sedan, and French brandy—and he was well enough off to pay for these things out of his own pocket.

After some initial soundings, Yoshida concluded that a democratic government should seek to carry out the will of a majority of the electorate but would not be workable if it tried to encompass the views of many disparate elements. He therefore rejected a coalition with the Socialists. This policy has guided the Liberal Party and its successor, the Liberal Democratic Party, for more than forty years. No doubt Yoshida was motivated even more by his strong suspicion of the left wing of the Socialist Party.

Most of Yoshida's choices for the cabinet were conservatives, including Ishibashi Tanzan, editor of the *Oriental Economist*, as finance minister and Tanaka Kōtarō, a professor of law at Tokyo University and a Catholic, as minister of education. Neither was a career politician. Cabinet ministers in Japan, except in the unusual situation right after the war, have almost invariably been career politicians who deal with only a few matters of high policy, notably the budget, and leave most of the decisionmaking to subordinates in the bureaucracy.

Finding a minister of agriculture was Yoshida's hardest task. Nobody wanted the job because the food shortage was the most critical problem Japan faced in the months after the surrender. Rice on the black market was fifteen times the official price. The situation was so desperate that the emperor offered to sell some of his imperial treasures to obtain money for purchase of food abroad. Hearing of this, MacArthur asserted that it was his responsibility to obtain food and that the emperor should keep his jewels.[14]

The food crisis led to great disorder in the streets of Tokyo and to demonstrations against the government. "Give us rice!" became a rallying cry. Riots broke out around the Diet building, and across the street demonstrators attacked the prime minister's official residence. The crisis peaked during a demonstration on May 19 known as "Food May Day" in which 250,000 demonstrators marched around the imperial plaza. Led by Tokuda, they forced their way into the palace demanding to see the emperor. They broke into the kitchen, ostensibly to see if any luxury items were stored there, and presented a petition detailing their grievances to an official of the imperial household. The police finally took charge of the situation.[15]

Left-wingers were quick to seize the initiative in the chaotic conditions of postwar Japan. They were often the most experienced and dynamic people in mass movements and labor activities. They thought they had the support of the occupation and of the Allied powers. Indeed, many of them looked upon the occupation forces as a "liberation army" that would join with them in casting out the forces of reaction and liberating the masses. Yoshida wrote in his memoirs that if the farmers had made common cause with the city crowds in May 1946, the situation would have been serious for the government. He added, however, that the thorough land reform program then getting under way was an important remedy for unrest in the countryside.[16]

Yoshida had trouble filling the cabinet agriculture portfolio. To add to his burdens, the emperor telephoned Yoshida every evening to ask when he would have a cabinet. Yoshida could only reply, "I am trying." The third man Yoshida approached, Wada Hiroo, a well-known agricultural economist and career official in the Ministry of Agriculture and Forestry, accepted the offer after five days of discussions with Yoshida. Although Wada had a record of left-wing activities that aroused considerable suspicion, Yoshida stuck with him, even rejecting Hatoyama's critical advice.[17]

On May 23 Yoshida was at last able to form a cabinet. An editorial in *Asahi* on that day asserted that the Yoshida cabinet was like the Shidehara cabinet and that little could be expected of it in advancing Japan's democratic revolution. Mark Gayn of the *Chicago Sun* lampooned Shidehara and Yoshida as "Tweedledum-san" and "Tweedledee-san."[18]

SCAP did not stand aside during the food crisis. Early in 1946 General MacArthur recommended to Washington that 2.6 million tons of food in rice equivalents be sent to Japan to fill deficiencies and establish a reserve for emergencies. Opposition arose in the FEC to any action that would seem to give Japan better treatment than that received by other needy Asian nations, many of which had suffered at Japan's hands in the war. The commission decided on April 25 that Japan should not receive preferential treatment except for "imports essential immediately for the safety of the occupation forces." On this basis food could be sent to Japan.[19]

In March and April 1946 the United States provided Japan with 155,000 tons of cereal. In May 1946 former president Herbert Hoover led a food mission to Japan as part of a worldwide survey requested by President Truman. General MacArthur reported to Hoover on May 6 that the food situation in Japan was the worst in thirty years. The general dramatized the situation with a favorite simile: "Japan can only be considered a vast concentration camp under the control of the Allies and foreclosed from all avenues of commerce and trade." Hoover recommended that 870,000 tons of food be sent to Japan. Between May and September 1946, about 600,000 tons of rice equivalents were exported from the United States; this proved to be adequate to stave off the food crisis. By the summer of 1946 one-quarter of the food being consumed by the Japanese came from Allied sources, including U.S. Army reserve supplies in Japan. SCAP historians estimated that American food aid to Japan in 1946 saved 11 million Japanese from starvation.[20]

Japan's food problem remained serious for several years. But domestic rice production did begin to improve markedly. Fishing fleets increased in size, and SCAP enlarged their zone of operations in waters off Japan. With the approval of the U.S. government and in spite of much unhappiness in Allied circles, MacArthur authorized a pelagic whaling expedition to Antarctica in 1946, marking the beginning of Japan's intensive whaling activities in the postwar era. By 1948 the food crisis was over. During the postwar years the United States brought in 3.8 million tons of foodstuffs at a cost of $500 million.[21] U.S. aid, especially food in the early years, had much to do with the receptive Japanese attitude toward the occupation; the carrot was more potent than the stick.

In later years Japanese writers claimed that Yoshida delayed forming his cabinet in May 1946 to put pressure on MacArthur to bring in food. Yoshida reportedly told his associates that when the Americans saw a sea of red flags all over Japan, they would send Japan food. The general is supposed to have called Yoshida to his office in the Dai Ichi building on May 21 and said that "so long as I am Supreme Commander, I will not allow one Japanese to die of starvation."[22] This naturally elated Yoshida, who told Wada that Yoshida's one condition for forming a cabinet had been met. This account may well contain several kernels of truth, although nothing in U.S. records substantiates it.

MacArthur was not intimidated by the food demonstrators. On May 20, the day after the huge demonstration in the imperial plaza, he issued a tough statement that "the growing tendency toward mass violence and physical processes of intimidation, under organized leadership, presents a grave menace." If this continued, "I shall be forced to take the necessary steps to control and remedy such a deplorable situation."[23] His statement was the first sign during the occupation of a strong line against left-wing agitation and violence. It came as a shock to the radicals, who had looked for sympathy from the "liberation army."

Yoshida's next test as prime minister was to navigate the new constitution through the Diet without significant change, as MacArthur and Whitney expected him to do. Although only a "gist" of the new constitution had been made public, the supreme commander said that "the April election was what I had wanted—a true plebiscite." According to a Japanese study, however, the constitution was only a minor issue in the election, with voters and candidates far more concerned about issues such as food, clothing, and shelter.

The full text of the draft constitution was made public on April 17, 1946, and submitted to the soon-to-expire Privy Council as the first step in obtaining government approval. The Japanese had proposed, and the Americans had agreed, that the new constitution should be written in ordinary Japanese, not in the formal style normally used in legal documents. This has become the standard practice in Japan. To help get the constitution through the Diet, Yoshida appointed a special minister, Kanamori Tokujirō. They spent much of the summer of 1946 answering parliamentary questions by the Privy Council and the two houses of the Diet, which set up special committees to examine the issues. The constitution was finally approved on October 29, 1946, after 109 days of wide-ranging debate.[24]

The new status of the emperor was the biggest issue in the Diet. Questions elicited a variety of responses. Yoshida agreed with a questioner on June 25 that "the emperor and his subjects are one," that they are "one family." The new prime minister went on, "The national structure of Japan has not been changed by the new constitution." This seemed to mean that the emperor and the people possessed sovereignty together, an interpretation smacking of the old *kokutai*, where the Japanese people were thought to be one great family with the emperor at its head. Yoshida's view was widely challenged by, among others, President Nambara of Tokyo University, who had just been appointed to the upper house (the House of Peers) to strengthen liberal elements there. Nambara and others argued that the constitution clearly meant that sovereignty resided in the people.[25] Concepts such as "sovereignty in the people" were evidently confusing to many Japanese, and the idea of one big happy Japanese family was not about to disappear quickly.

The no-war clause came in for much scrutiny. On June 29, in one of the few dramatic interpellations of the entire constitutional debate, Communist leader Nosaka asked Yoshida if Japan should not limit its renunciation only to wars of aggression because war for defense was justifiable. Nosaka added that the causes of war—plutocracy, reactionary politics, feudal land control, bureaucratism—should be uprooted. Nosaka and other questioners shared the view that Japan should join a world federation before it agreed to outlaw war. Many in the Diet seemed to believe in the desirability of abolishing war, but they were concerned about renunciation by Japan alone. Yoshida replied to Nosaka that nations often used the cloak of "defense" to justify war of any sort; by outlawing war in any situation, including war for defense, the new constitution would prohibit this kind of subterfuge.[26]

The issue, however, remained one in which the Diet showed considerable independence. Ashida Hitoshi, a former diplomat, lawyer, and politician, was chairman of the lower house subcommittee that studied the draft constitution intensively during the summer. His subcommittee proposed a subtle amendment to Article 9 designed to stress Japan's new devotion to international peace.[27]

> Aspiring sincerely to an international peace based on justice and order, the Japanese people forever renounce war as a sovereign right of the nation and the threat or use of force as a means of settling disputes with other nations.
>
> For the above purpose, land, sea, and air forces, as well as other war potential, will never be maintained. The right of belligerency of the state will not be recognized.

Minister of State Kanamori, who handled constitutional amendments on behalf of the prime minister, evidently thought up this amendment and drafted its wording. The key changes were the introductory phrases inserted at the start of each paragraph, which seemed to limit Japan's renunciation only to war as a means of settling international disputes; war for other sovereign purposes, such as self-defense, would not be prohibited. This change proved to be a Pandora's box. When Ashida proposed it to Kades, he approved it although he realized it meant Japan could use its forces for defense and for purposes other than settling international disputes. Others in GS and many Japanese shared this view, which is now the standard interpretation of amended Article 9. The interpretation is strengthened by general agreement among legal experts that the "right of belligerency" inserted in the constitution at MacArthur's behest is virtually meaningless in international law.[28] But nothing in Ashida's records, including his detailed diary, throws light on what he had in mind or exactly what his role was.

The Ashida/Kanamori amendment was easily the most far-reaching of any in the constitutional debate of 1946. As interpreted by successive Japanese governments, it spawned a new international concept of a conventional military force that could be used only for defense of the nation's territory but could not have "offensive" weapons and could not engage in collective defense measures, except perhaps inside its own territory. The United States never formally agreed with these limited interpretations of Article 9, and while recognizing that determining defense policy is Japan's prerogative, the United States has constantly and often vigorously urged Japan to expand greatly its defense power and liberalize its interpretations of Article 9.

A significant amendment with idealistic overtones proposed by the Socialist Party was approved as part of Article 25 of the constitution: "All people shall have the right to maintain the minimum standards of wholesome and cultured living." This clause has been cited to justify various pieces of progressive legislation.[29]

Japanese legal experts also used the Diet consideration of the draft constitution to amend several provisions along lines more in keeping with conservative Japanese practice. The most notable was the elimination of earlier SCAP language providing that "aliens shall be entitled to equal protection of the law" and prohibiting any discrimination in social relations on account of "national origin." As amended, the constitution provided in Articles 10 and 14 that the conditions for nationality and guarantee of equal protection applied only to *kokumin*, or persons of Japanese nationality. Significant protections for aliens, in particular Korean and Chinese minorities, were thus eliminated. One could say, however, that this process of "Japanizing" the constitution, as one Japanese authority called it, facilitated its acceptance by the Japanese people and countered fears that SCAP applied undue pressure.[30]

GS followed the Diet proceedings closely and sometimes challenged the Japanese on legal interpretations or translation points. The issue of sovereignty gave GS particular concern. Whitney sent MacArthur a memorandum in July complaining about Kanamori's explanation that the constitution would bring no change in *kokutai*. Whitney's staff was upset that Japanese interpretations of this sort would undermine the new charter. While acknowledging MacArthur's "view that much weasel-worded explanation is offered to persuade the two-thirds majority required" for adoption of the constitution, Whitney was concerned that "the will of the people will be constantly subjugated to the mystic concept of the 'national polity.'" The file copy of this memorandum bears the notation "Read by CINC. No comment." Nevertheless, GS raised the issue of sovereignty with Yoshida, and they quickly agreed on a precise statement in the preamble that "sovereignty rests with the people."[31]

The occupation authorities satisfied themselves that the new constitution could legally be considered as an amendment to the old one, thus ensuring legitimacy and preserving continuity from one to the other. In an extensive memorandum on this point, Alfred Oppler, GS's German-born expert on constitutional law, concluded that the emperor possessed unlimited power to initiate constitutional amendments and sanction revisions. Oppler believed that acceptance of the Potsdam Declaration committed Japan to alter its national structure along lines consistent with the declaration.[32]

The FEC watched the proceedings in Tokyo intently. It had already tilted with MacArthur over its prerogative to pass on the final draft. On May 13, 1946, it decided that the method of adopting the constitution should show that it "affirmatively expresses the free will of the Japanese people." It took heavy pressure from State and Defense to win MacArthur's consent to carry out this directive, which he did on June 21, 1946, in the form of a press release incorporating the words of the FEC policy without, however, making any attribution.[33] The general showed he was sullen in his attitude toward the FEC but not mutinous.

The FEC made a significant substantive decision on July 2, 1946, when it approved a statement of basic principles that closely followed the U.S. policy paper, SWNCC-228, "Reform of the Japanese Governmental System." Its key provisions for inclusion in the constitution were that sovereign power reside in the people and that a majority of the cabinet members, including the prime minister, be members of the Diet. These changes were inserted in the draft. The FEC policy asserted that "retention of the emperor institution in its present form is not considered consistent with the foregoing general objectives" and enumerated the safeguards that the Japanese would have to apply if they decided to retain the emperor institution. The FEC went along with MacArthur's opposition to releasing this decision to the press on the ground that "the voluntary character of the work now in progress would instantly become clothed with the taint of Allied force."[34]

The next FEC action, decided on September 25, 1946, reaffirmed that all members of the cabinet should be civilians. It took this action at the urging of the Chinese representative that this position be reaffirmed in light of the adoption of the Ashida amendment to Article 9. MacArthur and the Japanese were unhappy about this decision, which they thought unnecessary because Japan planned to abolish its military forces. But on the theory that Article 9 might be amended later to permit the establishment of armed forces, the FEC amendment was duly implemented. A new Japanese word for "civilians," *bunmin*, was invented to capture the right nuance.[35] No reference to the crime of treason was included in the draft charter because Japan would have no armed forces and presumably no national secrets to protect.

The final decision by the commission on constitutional issues, on October 17, 1946, specified that between one and two years after the constitution went into effect "the situation with respect to the new constitution should be reviewed by the Diet" and the FEC. MacArthur again opposed publicity, which "would result not only in the collapse of the constitution but would give rise to serious deterioration in the whole Japanese situation."[36] He informed Yoshida of this decision in January 1947.

Neither the Japanese nor the FEC ever formally reviewed the constitution. Yoshida said later that SCAP had suggested in the summer of 1948 that the Japanese government should review the constitution, but his government had no desire to do so.[37] The FEC decision formally advising the Japanese that they could review the constitution and even amend it may have mitigated some of the feeling of pressure in Japan. The Diet debate plus FEC interventions resulted in amendment of the preamble and twenty-five articles, the addition of four articles, and the deletion of one, a total of thirty-one changes, beyond a number of minor alterations in wording.[38]

The enactment of the constitution was Yoshida's greatest achievement during his first term in office. Whatever his initial doubts, he loyally supported the American-made charter. He recognized that "international circumstances" dictated change for his nation. But beyond that he came to believe that new ideas and new institutions could be good for Japan. His advocacy, aided Kanamori and Ashida, erased many of the doubts and frictions that MacArthur and GS had created by their strong-arm methods earlier in the year. The successful launching of the constitution owed much to Yoshida's adroitness.

On October 7 the lower house passed the constitutional revision bill by 342 to 5. The five opponents were all Communists. In the upper house a voice vote was overwhelmingly in favor, with only a few votes of no. The bill thus easily won the required two-thirds vote in favor. The Privy Council mandated its own extinction by approving the bill on October 29 at a session attended by the emperor.[39]

Only a few days later, on November 3, the constitution was promulgated by the emperor at a large ceremony held in the House of Peers. Both the emperor and the prime minister made statements. According to the emperor, the constitution would enable the nation to establish the "basis of national reconstruction in the universal principles of mankind." Yoshida said, "This constitution is indeed one which has been decided by the will of the Japanese people, seeking the reconstruction of their nation on the basis of democratic principles. Moreover, we feel unbounded pride and responsibility in leading the world by our renunciation of war."[40]

The choice, suggested by Yoshida to MacArthur, of November 3 as the day for promulgation of the constitution was curious because this was the birthday of Emperor Meiji and had been a national holiday for some time. Some in SCAP thought that a day so revered in the old Japan was a poor choice for adoption of a democratic constitution. MacArthur, however, went along with Yoshida's suggestion.

On May 2, 1947, the general wrote the prime minister, "To mark this historic ascendancy of democratic freedom. . . . I believe it particularly appropriate that from henceforth the Japanese national flag be restored to the people of Japan for unrestricted display." Although the flag was not in Japanese eyes the hallowed symbol it was for Americans, this was a welcome gesture.[41]

On only one occasion since the end of the occupation has the new constitution received searching scrutiny, and that turned out to be not very serious. In 1956 the Diet enacted a bill to set up a commission of distinguished people to recommend possible changes in the 1947 charter. Socialists and leftist parties refused to take part, making clear they thought the operation was a conservative device to undermine the constitution. The commission, consisting of thirty-eight persons including one woman, filed its report in 1964.[42]

Neither MacArthur nor Yoshida appeared in person, but both filed statements regarding the origins of the constitution. In a letter of December 5, 1958, the general asserted:

> A new charter was immediately imperative if the structure of Japanese self-government was to be sustained. The choice was alien military government or autonomous civil government. The pressure for the former by many of the Allied nations was intense, accompanied by many drastic concepts designed to fracture the Japanese nation. . . . The preservation of the emperor system was my fixed purpose. It was inherent and integral to Japanese political and cultural survival. The vicious efforts to destroy the person of the emperor and thereby abolish the system became one of the most dangerous menaces that threatened the successful rehabilitation of the nation. . . . The suggestion to put an article in the constitution outlawing war was made by Prime Minister Shidehara. . . . Nothing in Article 9 prevents any and all necessary steps necessary for preservation of the safety of the nation. I stated this at the time of the adoption of the constitution.[43]

This letter illustrated the general's propensity for sweeping statements, historical reinterpretation, and prediction of dire consequences if his views were not accepted.

In a letter dated December 17, 1957, Yoshida said he had believed quick approval of the constitution would help expedite action by the Allies on a peace treaty.[44] He thought that the no-war clause was MacArthur's idea but that Shidehara probably agreed with it. Yoshida observed that MacArthur had almost religious views about the evils of war. Yoshida stressed that the Diet had been free to discuss the draft charter and make amendments. He noted that occupation authorities had also suggested that the Japanese try the new constitution, see how it worked, and change it if experience showed it was not suitable. Yoshida concluded that from the vantage point of 1957 he saw no reason to change the constitution, even in the respects that had been most discussed, such as Article 9 or the family system.

As part of the final report, twenty-nine members of the commission signed a memorandum concluding in a guarded way that the constitution might not have been adopted on the basis of the free will of the people. As they put it, "In essence, it is clear that the constitution of Japan is the product of a lost war and that it was enacted under the very special circumstances of a military occupation as well as in the very center of the chaotic environment of the people's lives. . . . It is not too much to say that Japan's future was decided in reality by the acceptance of the Potsdam Declaration."[45] Commission member Nakasone Yasuhiro, then a conservative Diet member from the Liberal Democratic Party, who was a Diet freshman from the Democratic Party in 1947, commented in the report that the liberals and the progressives had agreed to the constitution in 1947 "with deep regret." (Nakasone was prime minister of Japan from 1982 to 1987.)

A majority of the members of the commission favored revision of the constitution in a number of respects, especially Article 9. But the commission made no specific recommendations for change, and the government took no action on the report. In 1985 the Nakasone cabinet did consider some minor modifications in the constitution, but there was little public interest or support. Japanese do not look upon laws and the constitution as having the same fixed and binding quality that Westerners see, and accordingly they do not seem to feel any urgency to amend the constitution, even to correct an apparent contradiction,[46] as in the case of Article 9 and the existence of military force labeled a "self-defense force."

The 1947 constitution, for all the haste and pressure surrounding its birth, now enjoys almost general acceptance in Japan. It is one of the monuments of the MacArthur-Yoshida era. When the new emperor made his first speech to the nation on January 9, 1989, he pledged to uphold the constitution. His reign had already been designated Heisei, meaning "the achieving of peace."[47]

CHAPTER 9

The Second Reform Wave

On September 27, 1946, as the Diet was nearing the end of its debate on the draft constitution, Prime Minister Yoshida wrote a letter to General MacArthur about a report that greatly disturbed him. At a meeting the day before with GS, Japanese liaison officers had been told that "you had informed me that because of many instances of non-compliance by Japanese Government officials with the desires and directives of the general headquarters, you were being forced to consider dealing with problems by issuance of directives instead of by negotiations and discussions and to consider altering occupation policy from 'a soft one to a hard one.'" Yoshida asked the general for clarification.

MacArthur wrote back immediately saying, "There has been no change whatsoever in my position as outlined to you in our recent conversation. . . . Upon inquiry from the Government Section [I] find that their comments have been completely misinterpreted and misunderstood. This I attribute to language difficulties and welcome your action in seeking immediate clarification with me."[1] In his memoirs Yoshida included a brief recollection of this episode by his chief liaison officer, Shirasu, to the effect that GS "was merely playing games." The Japanese obviously drew wry satisfaction from seeing the general put down his zealous staff officers. Yoshida recounted how MacArthur would call in senior officers on matters Yoshida had raised and give orders to them, "to which all they could answer was 'Yes, sir.'"[2]

Several SCAP sections had for some time been concerned—and annoyed—about the Japanese failure to comply with orders and requests as well as about some Japanese actions: Japanese police had arrested and treated harshly some strikers at the *Yomiuri* newspaper, the government had failed to enact important antimonopoly legislation, and it was late in submitting required reports. General MacArthur's soft touch with the Japanese, which he displayed several times during the occupation, smoothed over the friction.[3]

Yoshida and MacArthur gradually evolved a modus operandi by which they exchanged letters on important subjects and often met personally, before or after, to discuss the issue. The two men exchanged some 130 letters during the occupation. Letters from MacArthur no doubt helped Yoshida show hardheaded politicians that he was doing his best. Some Japanese even thought that letters to Yoshida beginning "My Dear Mr. Prime Minister" reflected MacArthur's special esteem for Yoshida.[4]

The supreme commander and the prime minister both relied heavily on their staffs, although neither was averse to overruling his experts. Neither got himself too involved in details. Whitney was the closest man to MacArthur, and he in turn relied heavily on Kades. Kades had no background in Japan before he arrived in late August 1945, but he was a quick and eager learner who drank in the knowledge and insights of the Japan experts. When Yoshida first met Kades, the prime minister said, "So you're the man who is going to make us democratic. Ha, ha."[5]

Yoshida's alter ego in dealing with the Americans was Shirasu Jirō, a handsome and shrewd man who had been educated in the 1930s at Cambridge University, where he got to know Yoshida. Shirasu served as Yoshida's personal chief of staff for much of the occupation. His English was nearly flawless, and he exhibited great assurance in dealing with Westerners.

Shirasu was the architect of Yoshida's strategy of avoiding GS and taking issues to General C. A. Willoughby, G-2, or Colonel Laurence Eliot Bunker, the military secretary to General MacArthur. A burly man with a right-wing outlook and a volatile temper, Willoughby had considerable diplomatic and linguistic skill. He showed marked deference to the Japanese, reflecting a view he held from the outset of the occupation that Japan could become a valuable friend of the United States in the struggle he foresaw with Communist China and the Soviet Union. His staff was also a conduit for cigars procured in Hong Kong to be passed to Yoshida by Shirasu. Willoughby thought SCAP was loaded with leftist employees and wrote several memos to MacArthur in 1946 and 1947 listing civilians in SCAP, mostly in GS and ESS, whom he considered undesirable leftists.[6] Willoughby's evidence was in all but a couple of cases pretty flimsy, but his accusations caused continuing harassment for those on his lists. MacArthur paid little attention to them.

Colonel Bunker was a good-looking, socially graceful bachelor who sat in MacArthur's outer office and knew more than most people about what was going on in GHQ SCAP. Bunker had an easy relationship with the general, to whom he passed tidbits of information along with official papers. Officials such as Shirasu and Watanabe Takeshi, a senior Finance Ministry official with an international background, as well as officials from the imperial household, often dropped by to see Bunker, whose own political and economic viewpoints were more conservative than most occupation policies. He was friendly with a number of Japanese women, including Yoshida's daughter. When they wanted to ask a favor or complain, they called him up.[7] Mrs. Asō herself played an important role in the male-dominated occupation as her father's confidante and hostess.

After the constitution had been safely passed by the Diet in September 1946, a new wave of SCAP reforms engaged these and many more actors. The most contentious plan was labeled "extension of the purge." Many Japanese looked upon the first purge in 1946 as one of the most hateful of SCAP actions, and they were understandably shaken when they got a second dose of the same medicine a year later. The second purge was to include local government officials, senior economic positions, and influential figures in the media. ESS had trouble winning support within SCAP in early 1946 to go ahead with the economic purge, so GS moved in and won MacArthur's agreement on August 19, 1946, that an economic purge should be carried out.[8]

Not all Japanese were against the purges. SCAP received thousands of letters from ordinary Japanese urging that the purge be widened and even naming people the writers considered ultranationalists. Education experts in SCAP had been impressed in the same way by the strength of the liberals during the early battles between liberal and conservative elements in the nation's biggest newspapers.[9] Public opinion polling began later in the occupation, but even in the early days there were ways to find out that many Japanese wanted change.

SCAP wanted the Japanese to take responsibility for carrying out the new purges. Responding to this pressure, Yoshida sent a letter to MacArthur on October 22, 1946, stating that the government would submit proposals for extending the purge to local officials and to economic positions. But to show his true feelings, Yoshida cited the comments of an American congressman on the bad effects of the purge in Germany and somewhat flippantly added that Japan might face the same results of "anarchy, chaos and communism" cited by the congressman.[10] The government entrusted the media purge to committees of Japanese writers charged with examining the writings of those suspected of nationalist views and determining who should be purged.

Fearing that the Japanese were going to come up with an unsatisfactory plan, Whitney sent his boss a remarkable piece of advice on November 8, 1946: the Japanese "government manifests a continuing tendency to negotiate with you... rather than to proceed to implementation within the letter and spirit of your policy and decisions already determined and communicated to it.... I strongly recommend that you decline to discuss this matter further with the prime minister, making clear to him that the same is now my responsibility for implementation, controlling policy having already been determined and enunciated by you."[11] Whitney was evidently trying to protect MacArthur from himself.

Yoshida was particularly unhappy about the local purge. He sent an impassioned letter to MacArthur on October 31 asserting that the "regimentation of the military regime had been engineered by a clique of professional soldiers, of government officials, right-wing reactionaries and some members of the zaibatsu, and the people were merely the target of this scheme of regimentation." MacArthur replied that the chief purpose of extending the purge was "to afford the people new opportunity for new local leadership."[12]

Yoshida got some satisfaction out of the economic purge by a translation ruse: the word *standing director* in the U.S. draft of the purge order was translated into the Japanese for "managing director," which was one notch higher in the Japanese corporate hierarchy. In this way the number of company officers purged was considerably reduced.[13]

When SCAP insisted that the economic purge apply for ten years to relatives "within the third degree by blood, marriage or adoption," Yoshida wrote MacArthur on December 21 that when a man committed an offense in ancient China, all his relatives were sentenced accordingly but that modern concepts of justice did not attach blame even to the family of a murderer. MacArthur countered that "the vital and irrepressible issue of collusion" must be met.[14] The SCAP position seemed to fly in the face of the stress on individual rights SCAP was trying to nurture in Japan.

A valuable insight on MacArthur's thinking about both Yoshida and the purge was provided by a conversation on November 14 with the British ambassador. Sir Alvary Gascoigne mentioned rumors that the Yoshida cabinet "was on its last legs." MacArthur riposted that "solid results which he and his ministers had obtained during the first seven months of office had won them considerable merit." He was no doubt referring to the government's success in winning Diet approval of the new constitution, for which MacArthur showed marked appreciation.[15]

MacArthur then said that he had tried to persuade Yoshida to carry out the extension of the purge on his own initiative but that "Mr. Yoshida had at first shown signs of considerable perturbation and had begged General MacArthur publicly to assume the responsibility for ordering the purge." On the "strong recommendation of General MacArthur," however, Yoshida had decided that the purge should appear to be executed spontaneously by the Japanese government so as to avoid the charge that it was "nothing but an American puppet." This was a good example of MacArthur's well-known power to persuade.[16]

On January 4, 1947, exactly one year after the initial purge orders, Yoshida finally acted. Six imperial ordinances were issued. Included were:

Local officials, such as mayors and prefectural assemblymen; 3,960 persons (less than 1 percent of those screened) were purged.

Economic positions, applying to managing directors and above in 154 important companies; 8,309 persons were screened, and 1,973 were purged.

Important persons in the media, including government officials, scholars, journalists, and writers; 605 institutions were involved, 1,328 persons were screened, and 1,066 were purged.[17]

Soon after, Ambassador Gascoigne asked MacArthur about the purge ordinances. The general replied that "this purge had been carried out at the express orders of Washington and that he would have been in trouble if he had failed to carry it out." He went on to say that he agreed with his government that the purge should be carried out, noting that those being purged were not being imprisoned as in Germany. The ambassador commented to the Foreign Office that MacArthur was worried that the purge had gone too far.[18]

One of the most prominent Japanese purged in 1947 was Finance Minister Ishibashi Tanzan, who had clearly resisted SCAP's anti-inflation policy. Soon after the occupation began, SCAP insisted that the Japanese enact two taxes to recoup both the wartime profits of individuals and institutions and the indemnity payments that the government had authorized corporations or individuals to receive during and after the war. Ishibashi stoutly opposed the proposals, arguing that these taxes would seriously damage corporations and banks. A wide difference in outlook separated Ishibashi from SCAP experts: Ishibashi claimed that government spending was necessary to prime the pump of industrial production, while SCAP economists argued that inflation was already excessive and that the volume of currency in circulation should be reduced. The feeling was also strong in SCAP that the Japanese who had financed the war should pay for their mistakes. After long and acerbic negotiations, the legislation required by SCAP was enacted on October 18, 1946.[19]

On May 16, 1947, soon after the general elections held in April, Ishibashi was purged, even though General Marquat had told him only a short while before he did not have anything to worry about. GS had won MacArthur's approval, however, arguing that Ishibashi, as chief editor and president of the prestigious *Oriental Economist*, was accountable for its prewar editorial policy, "which supported military and economic imperialism, advocated Japan's adherence to the Axis, . . . [and] justified suppression of trade unionism." His "hostility to the objectives of the occupation" was also cited. Ishibashi wrote a long rebuttal to the purge decision and even held a press conference on October 27, 1947, attributing his purge to General Whitney and General MacArthur. SCAP's refusal to take punitive action in response to this display of "resistance" was a tribute to Ishibashi's guts and to SCAP's tolerance. The Ishibashi case was one of the most obvious examples in which SCAP decided hostility to the objectives of the occupation was as important as "militant nationalism."[20] Ishibashi was relieved from the purge in 1951 and became prime minister of Japan in 1956.

Purge policy was largely the work of SCAP. But missions from the United States determined both the policy of breaking up the zaibatsu and education policy. In 1945 SCAP had wrested out of the reluctant Japanese a kind of consent decree for breakup of the Big Four zaibatsu holding companies. From January 6 to the end of March, an American mission explored the complex zaibatsu issue. Led by Corwin Edwards of Northwestern University, it submitted a report defining excessive concentration as any private enterprise or combination of enterprises that by reason of its relative size or cumulative power "restricts competition or impairs the opportunity for others to engage in business independently, in any important segment of business." The report recommended that these excessive concentrations be dissolved into nonrelated units.[21]

After extensive review within the U.S. government and some debate with SCAP experts, SWNCC approved a proposal on the zaibatsu and submitted it to the FEC in October 1946. Labeled FEC-230, it became the best-known and most controversial of all FEC papers, although it was never approved by the commission and never formally transmitted to the supreme commander for execution in Japan.[22]

No case better illustrates the confusing lines of policy during the occupation than the zaibatsu issue. At the very time the United States was asking the FEC to formulate a specific policy on the basis of the recommendations set out in the Edwards report, MacArthur and his staff were going ahead on the basis of the vague and general authority contained in the initial U.S. policy statement, to which some months later they added an advance copy of FEC-230, which SCAP received for information and not for action. While the FEC was debating FEC-230, the SCAP staff was pressuring the Japanese to adopt major parts of the policy contained in the document.

In late 1946 and early 1947 the Holding Company Liquidation Commission (HCLC) raised from eighteen to eighty-three the number of designated holding companies whose stock was to be sold along with the stock of fifty-six zaibatsu "persons." All this stock was transferred to the HCLC, which was eventually able to sell it to the general public. The former zaibatsu owners received as compensation ten-year nonnegotiable government bonds, which turned out to be virtually worthless. These operations redistributed some ¥67 billion of securities (worth about $670 million in early 1947). Of the eighty-three designated holding companies, sixteen were dissolved, including the fifteen zaibatsu family companies; twenty-six were dissolved and then reorganized; eleven were reorganized; and no action was taken regarding the remaining thirty. Two hundred fifty holding company subsidiaries were made independent.

The zaibatsu breakup was only the first part of the SCAP antitrust program. It was later diversified by actions to prevent monopolies and excessive concentrations of economic power and by the economic purge. In addition, the Law for Prohibition of Private Monopoly and Methods of Preserving Fair Trade that was passed on March 12, 1947, outlawed "unreasonable restraints of trade" and unfair competition and set up a fair trade commission as an enforcement agency. This commission was alive and well a generation after the end of the occupation.

A paradoxical feature of the SCAP campaign was the virtual exemption of financial institutions. Although U.S. policy called for the dissolution of large banking combinations, they were not placed under the same limitations as nonfinancial institutions, nor were they seriously damaged by the capital levy or the cancellation of wartime indemnities. One reason for this special treatment was bureaucratic: banks were under the control of a branch of ESS operated by American banking experts who were able for a year or so to ward off the inroads of the trustbusters in other sections of the occupation on the ground that breakup of the banks would produce chaos. Another reason was that the ESS finance divison vigorously pressed the financial industry to create more banks and promote competition, arguably a healthier approach than dissolutions and forced sales. It is noteworthy that after the occupation, banks bought large amounts of zaibatsu stock and thus established a powerful position in Japan's later industrial growth.[23]

Action on another major reform, agricultural land redistribution, also began in 1945, and the government submitted a new plan in March 1946. In a rare gesture of Allied amity, MacArthur referred it to the new ACJ for advice. At four different meetings beginning on April 30, the council discussed the plan. To strengthen it, the Australian member, W. Macmahon Ball, offered a series of proposals drafted by his economic adviser, Eric Ward, such as reduction in the holdings landlords could retain, ceilings on rent payments, and written contracts for tenants. The council's recommendations based upon the Australian proposals were for the most part accepted by SCAP. The Soviet member, General Kuzma Derevyanko, proposed that payments to landlords with larger holdings be virtually eliminated, but he got no support.[24]

On July 26, 1946, the cabinet approved a new bill that Agricultural Minister Wada had taken the lead in working out with SCAP. MacArthur congratulated the cabinet for its "courage and determination to strike at the roots of an archaic landlord system." Yoshida commented that SCAP action on this issue, "affecting as it did the fundamental structure of our society, could only bear fruit if it was planned by the Japanese people themselves and of a nature genuinely acceptable to the Japanese people. . . . I think that the methods employed in this matter of land reform, at least, enabled GHQ and the Japanese Government to work well together, which was not always the case."[25]

On October 11 the Diet finally approved the land reform program in the form of two bills. The first provided that tenant cultivators would be given the first option to buy the land they worked, either outright or by installment payments over thirty years at low interest. The price of the land would be based on an official evaluation, a low figure soon rendered almost nominal by raging inflation. Owners would be paid in long-term government bonds, which proved to be equally valueless. Yoshida said in his memoirs that the tough Soviet line in the ACJ "probably helped in reconciling the landowners."[26] The landlords did not in fact get much more than Derevyanko had originally proposed.

The government was given the task of serving as agent for the transfers to ensure they were done efficiently and honestly. When the program did not move as quickly as SCAP wanted, it had to be expedited by an occupation order in February 1948. Rural land commissions were established with both landlord and tenant representatives to oversee administration of the program, which the law provided should be put into effect in two years. Setting up commissions on a nationwide basis was still novel in Japan and reflected another vigorous policy of the occupation—the promotion of local management of local issues. The commissions did a remarkable job throughout the country in dealing with a host of complicated issues whose resolution required a lot of time and patience.[27]

The second bill on land reform passed by the Diet in October stipulated that all future lease agreements would have to be in writing, that payments in kind would be prohibited, and that the amount of rental payments would be limited. These were all remedies for past abuses. The SCAP program reduced tenant-tilled land from 46 percent in 1941 to about 10 percent in 1949. More than 3 million tenants became owners of 5.5 million acres.

On October 11, 1946, MacArthur issued a public statement lauding the land reform program as "one of the most important milestones yet reached by Japan in the creation of an economically stable and politically democratic society." He was sitting in his office when he learned of the Diet approval of the two bills and was reported to have turned to a photograph of his father and said, "Dad would have liked this." General Arthur MacArthur had unsuccessfully advocated land reforms to benefit tenant farmers in the Philippines forty years before. The program in Japan, involving millions of farmers and vast amounts of land, with only a hundred or so incidents of violence and no bloodshed, was indeed an astonishing achievement.[28]

For many years land reform in Japan was considered one of MacArthur's most spectacular successes. The reform gave farmers independence, incentives to produce in volume, and strong purchasing power to help fuel the nation's economic growth. It also filled a need almost universally recognized by the Japanese themselves, and most of the success of the program was due to Japanese efforts. The powerful *nōkyō,* or "agricultural cooperatives," now more than 30,000 in number and including nearly all farm families, facilitated the rise of a healthy agrarian society. In recent years, however, land plots have been considered too numerous and too small for efficient operation; the high cost of rice production is one result and is exacerbated by the protective legislation farmers obtain from the politicians.

SCAP education reforms, more than any other SCAP policy, were largely determined by an expert mission from the United States. The proposals of the Stoddard mission made in March 1946 were well received by Japanese officials and educators. Inoki Masamichi, a prominent educator and writer, recalled how impressed he was by the words of George Stoddard, head of the commission: "The essence of democratic education is respect for the diversity, spontaneity and creativity of people." Sir George Sansom, however, took the somewhat jaundiced view that American education was "not of such a quality as to encourage one in feeling that it provides a good model for any other country." Prime Minister Yoshida commented later that the report "was, on the whole, sensibly inspired and sound," but in 1946 he counseled a go-slow response because he felt Japan lacked the money to carry out the changes rapidly.[29]

The report became a virtual bible for SCAP education experts. Its recommendations served as the basis for the momentous changes SCAP urged on the Japanese in the next few years. CIE's technique for handling the Japanese was different from that of GS. CIE preferred to avoid public debates and to quietly win over educators and bureaucrats receptive to American ideas for change. The vehicle for this conciliatory approach was the Japanese Educational Reform Council (JERC), a large and influential committee of forty-nine prominent educators and other leaders joined by eight Diet members. The JERC was formed in August 1946 and attached to the prime minister's office. Its moving spirit was Nambara, Japan's senior educator. He and his associates worked well with the Stoddard mission, and there is reason to believe that some of the mission's proposals, notably the 6-3-3 system, may have been the product of joint American and Japanese cooperation.[30]

The Education Ministry wanted to delay the start of the 6-3 school track of compulsory education, but CIE insisted that it begin in 1947. Japanese educators and many in the general public felt strongly that early action should be taken. SCAP received many letters from ordinary people who said that Japan's only hope for the future was education of the young and that efforts should be made to provide every opportunity. The CIE view prevailed: 6-3 would begin in April 1947. The minister of education, Tanaka Kōtarō, was made the sacrificial victim; he was removed from office in January 1947 not so much for any opposition to 6-3 but because his usefulness suffered by his being caught between go-fast SCAP and the go-slow Yoshida cabinet.[31]

One of the other contentious proposals of the Stoddard mission was to relax the strong central control of the Ministry of Education. The ministry lost a good deal of its power during the occupation, especially because CIE officials scorned the ministry bureaucrats but it has survived as a potent force in education below the university level. Another Stoddard recommendation was to increase greatly the number of universities and opportunities for higher education. The number of universities rose from 20 in 1945 to 304, including 200 junior colleges, by the end of the occupation. It is ironic that despite the vast increase in educational opportunities, competition to get into the better schools remains intense, and the elitist tradition anointing the former imperial universities, notably the University of Tokyo, is about as strong as ever.

The most controversial proposal in the mission's report was to substitute roman letters for *kanji* and *kana* in the written language. This suggestion was largely the work of Robert K. Hall, then a CIE officer and later a professor of education at Columbia University. The proposal was not pressed. MacArthur preferred to leave the matter to the Japanese, especially because they were showing some interest in language reform. The Japanese carried on a few experimental projects in the teaching of *romaji*, or "roman letters," partly at the behest of the Americans, but nothing much came of them. Not only does the Japanese written language have aesthetic and pedagogical value; it has clearly not been a bar to democratic reform or to technological advance in Japan, even though it is a high hurdle for foreigners trying to learn more about the country. MacArthur's decision seems to have been eminently sensible.[32]

The JERC's biggest achievements were the drafting, in partnership with CIE, of two basic laws intended to take effect with the new constitution in early 1947. The more significant law—the Fundamental Law of Education enacted on March 22, 1947, and called the "education constitution"—provided for academic freedom, respect for truth, equal educational opportunity for all, free and compulsory education for nine years, and coeducation. The law forthrightly maintained that "the political knowledge necessary for intelligent citizenship shall be valued in education." The second law—the School Education Law enacted in March 1947—provided for compulsory education in elementary and middle schools and required coeducation to the upper secondary level.[33]

Prime Minister Yoshida took a keen interest in education and devoted a chapter in his memoirs to the subject. He worried about the cost of building new schools, partly because, in the view of his critics, he wanted to stall the entire program. He thought that teachers were too interested in politics and not enough in teaching, especially in lower education. And he thought more emphasis should be placed on teaching discipline and character. These have been persistent concerns of conservative political leaders since the end of the war. Yoshida foresaw those problems but, like his successors, found no solutions.[34]

Amid all the turmoil of Yoshida's first months in office, he and MacArthur worked together without any serious hitches. They never became friends—MacArthur did not have close friends—but their mutual respect and rapport seemed to grow. On August 15, 1946, after Yoshida had been in office a few months, he sent the general a short note enclosing a newspaper article by Admiral Suzuki, the prime minister at the time of the surrender in August 1945. Suzuki wrote that he was happy with the progress of the occupation because he and the emperor had been confident that General MacArthur would be fair and just, as proved to be the case. The general wrote a short note of thanks to Yoshida, who had himself been advised by the admiral to be "a good loser" in dealing with SCAP. The prime minister claimed this was the policy he followed.[35]

On October 16, 1947, the supreme commander and the Tennō held their third meeting. In 1975 the Japanese press carried a report of this session, made by the Japanese interpreter. It revealed that, unlike their first meeting in September 1945, when MacArthur did most of the talking, the emperor was now a lively interlocutor. When he raised the subject of Japan's food shortage, MacArthur commented in some detail about his success in getting food from the United States, saying he told President Truman he would resign if the United States did not help Japan. Then the emperor mentioned that public opinion in the United States did not seem favorable to Japan, and MacArthur agreed. When MacArthur commented that his American visitors did not believe him when he told them the emperor's democratic attitude was very helpful, they both laughed. To the general's statement that the new constitution was an extremely good one, the emperor retorted that the ideal of renouncing war still seemed remote from the existing world situation.

The general asserted that Japan's action had been courageous and wise and that in one hundred years Japan would be a moral leader in the world. The emperor said he was concerned about the threat of labor strikes, commenting that the people showed "a low level of education and a lack of religious spirit" in thinking that strikes reflected democracy. MacArthur said he thought the labor movement would be dangerous if it was used for political purposes. They also discussed the repatriation of prisoners of war, and MacArthur said he would keep trying to speed up return of Japanese prisoners from the Soviet Union. He added that the emperor should let him know any time the general could be of service.[36]

Some Japanese students of the occupation have speculated that MacArthur and the emperor had become dependent on each other: MacArthur needed to show the occupation was going well in order to buttress his position in dealing with Truman and the Pentagon, while the emperor needed support to ward off charges in Japan and abroad that he bore some responsibility for the war. Because both of them were in a "fluid" or unsettled position in the early months of the occupation, they worked out an informal "power-sharing arrangement" for joint cooperation and mutual support, relying on MacArthur's power (*kenryoku*) and the emperor's authority (*keni*).[37]

MacArthur's respect for the emperor and his invitation to the Tennō to give him advice about the occupation, together with the emperor's full endorsement of major occupation programs, give some plausibility to this interpretation if only the opening months of the occupation are considered. But the record is clear that MacArthur was in full command throughout most of the occupation, and the emperor's role after the first year was minor. It was not MacArthur's way to be dependent on anyone else.

MacArthur avoided explanations or justifications of his actions, and so it was unusual for him to tell the British ambassador on September 9 that his efforts were not directed "towards the chastisement of a defeated enemy but to teach the Japanese the way of life as followed by the Anglo-Saxon democracies."[38] This comment surely characterized the general's own attitude, even if his staff found it necessary fairly often to be tough and at times punitive.

CHAPTER 10

The 1947 Labor Crisis and the Defeat of Yoshida

By the end of January 1947 Yoshida had spent eight hard months in office weathering MacArthur's second tidal wave of reforms. Now the two faced a truly serious crisis. More than 3 million workers were poised to begin a general strike in Tokyo on February 1. They planned strikes against railways, communications facilities, schools, government offices, and many factories. Whether there would be food, electricity, or transportation was uncertain. The largest city in Japan was sure to be paralyzed. No one knew for how long.[1]

On the afternoon of January 31 MacArthur issued a press statement, which he had taken the unusual step of writing himself. Even though the statement was not an order or even a letter to the prime minister, its meaning was perfectly clear: "I have informed the labor leaders . . . that I will not permit the use of so deadly a social weapon in the present impoverished and emaciated condition of Japan, and have accordingly directed them to desist from the furtherance of such action. . . . I have done so only to forestall the fatal impact upon an already gravely threatened public welfare. . . . I do not otherwise intend to restrict the freedom of action heretofore given labor in the achievement of legitimate objectives."[2]

Growth in the labor movement during 1946 had been explosive, raising union membership to nearly 4 million. Hundreds of unions had been formed, most of them members of one of the two large federations. The first, called the Japan Federation of Labor (JFL), or Nihon

Rōdō Kumiai Sōdōmei, claimed nearly 1 million members. It drew its strength largely from the right wing of the socialist movement, which included textile workers and seamen. The second federation, the Congress of Industrial Unions (CIU), or Sambetsu Kaigi, was more leftist and claimed 1.6 million members. It was strong in the government workers' unions, notably among railway and communications workers.

Although Communists held less than 10 percent of the membership of Sambetsu, they had great influence in the organization. Several of its most dynamic leaders were extreme leftists, such as its president, Kikunami Katsumi, and Dobashi Kazuyoshi, head of the communications workers' union. Both subsequently announced their affiliation with the Communist Party. The left provided the most aggressive and experienced labor leaders in the period after the war, and among them Communists turned out to be the most skillful.

The militance of the public unions resulted largely from the government's failure to increase wages in accord with the rapid rise in the cost of living, which had increased eightfold since the surrender. In May 1946 SCAP estimated that the salaries of government workers had increased from only 20 to 40 percent in that period, while wages in private industry had gone up two to four times.

By the summer of 1946, a few months after Yoshida took office, the labor movement was ready to put heavy pressure on the government. It forced the cabinet to abandon a plan to fire 75,000 railway workers and opposed the Labor Relations Adjustment Law enacted on September 20, 1946, which was designed to encourage settlement of labor disputes through mediation or arbitration with the help of the labor relations commissions set up nearly a year before. The unions particularly objected to the new law's prohibition against "acts of dispute" (meaning strikes) by public workers such as police, firemen, and employees of local governments; employees of public enterprises, such as railway workers, were not debarred from acts of dispute.[3]

On November 26 five of the big government workers' unions formed a joint struggle committee claiming to represent 2.4 million workers, with Ii Yashirō of the national railway workers union as chairman. The unions included not only office workers and schoolteachers but also workers in the post offices, telephone and telegraph offices, national railways, and the government monopolies of tobacco, salt, and camphor. The workers' demands were both economic—higher wages, more benefits, and enforcement of minimum wage laws—and political—the overthrow of the Yoshida cabinet. While granting labor a small "winter allowance," the government proposed to deal firmly with the strike threat but did not win the approval of SCAP to take tough measures.

The crisis took on a new dimension when the FEC approved a labor policy on December 6 providing that "trade unions should be allowed to take part in political activities and to support political parties." This provision, promoted by Commonwealth representatives, in several of whose countries labor party cabinets were in power, was approved by all of the nations on the commission. General Whitney asked SCAP labor expert Ted Cohen whether it was SCAP policy to permit labor unions to engage in political activity, and Cohen assured him that it was. Later in the occupation this clause was often cited by leftist unions to justify their support of political activism. SCAP never wholeheartedly agreed, especially when political activity meant strikes.[4] On December 17 a massive demonstration was held on the imperial plaza to support a Socialist Party resolution in the Diet calling for the resignation of the Yoshida cabinet. The resolution was voted down, but several important newspapers called for a new election.

Prime Minister Yoshida recognized that the position of his minority government was shaky. He entered into discussions with the Socialist Party to see if some of its right-wing members might be persuaded to enter his cabinet. Both sides perceived that Japan was entering a crisis, but neither was willing to give up much.

Yoshida poured oil on the flames in his 1947 New Year's broadcast by castigating the *futei no yakara* (lawless gangs) that caused labor disputes. He accused them of hampering production and trying to seize political power. This was one of Yoshida's most famous and intemperate, albeit deliberate, statements, which endeared him to neither workers, liberals, nor even commonsense citizens. By mid-January Communist Party leaders were giving open support to the labor campaign. Tokuda Kyūichi, invariably described as a fiery orator in a society that produced few orators or dynamic political leaders, addressed a rally of government workers to whip up their spirits. He and his comrades on the far left were now in charge. On January 18 the joint struggle committee of government workers, the spearhead of the strike movement, with support from thirty-three unions and representatives of the CIU and the JFL, set the date of February 1 for a general strike if their terms were not met. They also gave assurances that services to the occupation forces would be provided during any strike, making clear they did not want to confront the supreme commander. The support of the JFL was weak, however, and some of its unions decided to stay out. Nevertheless, as the end of January neared, the specter of a general strike became real.[5]

American officials had intently watched the gathering clouds, hoping that labor leaders and the government could get together and work out a solution. In late October MacArthur told the British ambassador he was not worried because the unions did not want to risk incurring his displeasure. The ambassador reported, "In the event of any serious threat of a general strike, the general would step in openly to stop it." Contacts between the government and the joint struggle leaders were unproductive, although SCAP officials tried to push them together. Within SCAP different tactics for handling the strike were debated. Those who had been in charge of labor policy were sympathetic toward the budding labor movement and stern toward Japanese employers and government officials. Their approach seemed consistent with the U.S. policy of the period. SCAP also wanted to restrain the left wing and so joined with the Japanese government at the end of 1946 in encouraging unions to form "democratization leagues," or *mindō*, to promote conservative attitudes and positions.[6]

Some critics of SCAP labor policy, Americans in the occupation as well as Japanese and others on the outside, have asserted that its top labor experts at that period, Anthony Constantino and Ted Cohen, were extreme leftists. Both were on Willoughby's lists of SCAP leftists. But it would probably be more accurate to describe them as believers in the kind of liberal policies that restored the United States in the 1930s, especially a healthy labor movement. In short, they thought a New Deal would be beneficial in a less developed country such as Japan.

Cohen, the head of the SCAP labor division, wrote a memo to his boss, General Marquat, on January 15, 1947, recommending strongly that MacArthur issue an immediate statement that he would prohibit strikes. Cohen wanted labor leaders to have no doubt that a strike would interfere with occupation operations, especially transportation, communications, and repatriation movements, and would not be tolerated. Marquat presented this view the next day to MacArthur, who decided that he would not act right away but would give the Japanese more time to work out a solution.[7]

The general's attitude was strangely reminiscent of his handling of the Hatoyama purge ten months before: he would wait and give the Japanese a chance to handle the matter. At no time during the 1947 strike threat did MacArthur meet with his labor experts. All the information and ideas he got were filtered through Marquat. This was not a good approach. Because on labor issues, and on broader economic matters, MacArthur and Marquat were often in the position of the blind leading the blind,[8] MacArthur might have profited from more expert advice in what proved to be the biggest challenge to law and order during the occupation.

Under instructions from the CINC, Marquat verbally informed government officials and workers that a strike would not be permitted. Another week of negotiations proved fruitless. On January 30 Marquat used an "informal memorandum" to tell leaders of the joint struggle committee once again that the supreme commander would prohibit any strike and that any violations of law would result in arrests. The struggle committee nevertheless refused to back off. Another lengthy meeting of the unions with the Japanese mediators accomplished little, even though the difference between the two sides in salary terms was narrowed to ¥70 in monthly wages, then worth about $1.[9]

Occupation officials began to make plans for dealing with a strike. They worried especially about the transportation of essential items such as food and coal. Marquat sent a memo to MacArthur summarizing the actions to be taken if the strike came off. Eichelberger, whose operational duties as head of the Eighth Army were far more onerous than those of the staff officers in Tokyo, was particularly worried. Like many senior military officers, he thought many occupation policies were ultraliberal and served only to weaken Japan and damage the prospects of future cooperation. He also thought left-wingers in SCAP should be removed. MacArthur paid no attention to the critics in his own camp.[10]

On the afternoon of January 31 MacArthur banned the strike. His press people simply issued copies of his statement, while his staff told the Japanese government and the joint struggle committee of his decision. The strike was called off, and February 1 was a normal working day.

To reinforce the strike ban, Marquat immediately called in the head of the joint struggle committee, Ii Yashirō, and told him to make sure the strike did not take place. Ii claimed that he reluctantly agreed only after he was subjected to great pressure. In one of the more memorable episodes of the occupation, he wept as he told a press conference that evening that workers and farmers must stand together even more resolutely as "they took one step back and two steps forward." To the end Ii "could not understand why MacArthur has suddenly blocked the strike at the last minute. Until then SCAP had been sympathetic to labor."[11]

MacArthur banned the strike to protect the fragile Japanese economy. Yet the directives to him clearly provided that he was to "prevent or prohibit strikes...only when you consider that these would interfere with military operations or directly endanger the security of the occupying forces." Moreover, his guidance from Washington provided that "changes in the form of government initiated by the Japanese people or government in the direction of modifying its feudal and authoritarian tendencies are to be permitted and favored." The strike threat of 1947 seemed to be the kind of situation in which the 1945 policy prescription would apply. Yet MacArthur ignored it. One of the most liberal persons in the occupation, T. A. Bisson, who had long been a student of East Asian economics and politics, wrote in his diary, "The one really significant challenge to the old guard Japanese establishment has been turned back." Some historians have argued that Japan was ripe for revolution in early 1947 or even a year earlier. Conservative Japanese were especially fearful of violence and chaos, but few Americans serving in the occupation felt that there was a serious threat to U.S. control. The social bureaucrats in the Japanese government, who supported moderate policies, "breathed a collective sigh of relief" when MacArthur banned the strike.[12]

MacArthur's position was clear throughout the occupation. He would not permit violence. He wanted the Japanese authorities to deal with strike threats and large demonstrations, but if they did not, then he would order American units to preserve order, as he did several times. The Japanese people seemed satisfied with his firm line, although they expressed strong sympathy for the economic plight of Japan's workers.[13] The censored press supported the decision to ban the strike. At the same time the press and public criticized the tactics and statements of the Yoshida cabinet.

Although Yoshida was, like MacArthur, a believer in "legitimacy," or solution of political problems by legal or traditional methods, he did not have the power to deter or put down violence, and so he had to rely on SCAP. Nevertheless, after MacArthur banned the strike, the prime minister set about to repair the damage done to his government and the labor movement. In a speech to the Diet on February 14, he expressed concern about working conditions and called the labor movement helpful to economic recovery and to democracy in Japan. On February 20

the government announced a new wage plan for government workers
and shortly made several collective bargaining agreements that doubled
the wage bill.[14]

A few days after MacArthur banned the strike, he told General
Charles Gairdner, the personal representative of the prime minister of
the United Kingdom, that he had been "let down by the leaders of both
sides," including the prime minister. They had assured him there would
be no strike. When the government later told him it could do nothing to
prevent the strike, he had banned it at the last minute, even though he
might have ruined "any chance he might have of becoming a 'big political figure' in the United States." He also told Gairdner he would not
"hide behind" the excuse that a strike would endanger the goals of the
occupation.

Aside from MacArthur's revelation of political ambition, his explanation that "both sides" had told him there would be no strike was
surprising. Labor's confidence that SCAP would support it reinforced
its determination to have a test of strength with the Yoshida cabinet.
For their part, Yoshida and his advisers thought MacArthur would
have to step in and stop the strike, although they had little confidence in
Marquat and even less in Cohen. The Japanese were leaving it up to the
supreme commander. Yoshida met with him only once in the period
immediately before the strike.[15]

A well-informed liberal historian has written that "spontaneous anti-
capitalist radicalism" had been stronger in the spring of 1946 than in
January 1947, but because SCAP's power and will to prevent a strike
were greater in 1947, the "struggle for national liberation" ended "with
disastrous consequences for the union movement and the working
class."[16]

Some people in Japan felt that the 1947 strike ban marked the start
of a conservative reaction in occupation policy. In late 1951 the
Japanese press coined the term *reverse course* (gyaku kōsu) to describe
efforts by the Japanese government to cut back the liberal reforms instituted by the occupation. As time went by, Japanese and American
observers applied the term to many of the actions undertaken by SCAP
and the Japanese government in the waning years of the occupation.[17]

MacArthur and the U.S. government did not see the events of January 1947 this way. In their view they were ensuring there would be no
violence or lawlessness. They did not feel that the left wing of the labor
movement could be allowed to push its claims so far that it would damage the social order or interfere with government efforts to maintain

order and rebuild the nation. MacArthur and his staff were convinced that they were aiding the development of a moderate labor movement.[18] Many Japanese agreed with them.

MacArthur also made it clear that the occupation would afford no support for a revolution, bourgeois or proletarian. Sheldon Garon, who wrote a perceptive study, *The State and Labor in Modern Japan*, analyzed Japanese policies and attitudes during the occupation, concluding that "from the perspective of the Japanese bureaucrats and ruling bourgeois parties, no reversal occurred. Although in the wake of defeat the civilian elites generally favored the legal recognition of labor unions, they never ceased to oppose the development of a highly politicized or Communist-dominated labor movement." This was the U.S. attitude as well.[19]

On February 6, 1947, General MacArthur wrote Yoshida that "momentous changes" had taken place in the previous year and that therefore "it was necessary, in the near future, to obtain another democratic expression of the people's will on the fundamental issues with which Japanese society is now confronted."[20] MacArthur had been planning well before the labor crisis to call for an election at the time the new constitution came into effect. He mentioned this plan twice to the British ambassador, in October and November of 1946, cautioning that this advance notice was for the ambassador's information only, "as he [MacArthur] had not yet informed his own government of his intentions."[21] The general also forecast a large rise in the number of Socialist seats and a small increase for the Communists, with corresponding losses by the Progressive and Liberal parties. In addition to wanting to clear the electoral slate with the advent of the new constitution, MacArthur probably thought that the moderate left had a big electoral opportunity because the Yoshida cabinet was weak and unpopular.

On February 10 Yoshida sent a short reply to MacArthur thanking him for his February 6 letter. He also expressed "the greatest possible satisfaction" with the decision to hold new elections because he thought the conservative parties would win a big victory.[22] In fact, Yoshida's political position was then low. He had just reshuffled his cabinet because of losses from the new purge. Party leaders were criticizing him for not standing up to MacArthur by opposing the purge. They felt Yoshida was not strong enough and that his negotiations with the Socialists for a coalition had been clumsy.

A preliminary item of legislative business was another revision of the election law. Yoshida and the Liberal Party had concluded that the large electoral districts adopted in 1945 gave the Communist Party and other smaller parties too big a chance to pick up seats, especially because many voters had no compunction about splitting their votes between conservative and leftist candidates. The conservative leaders therefore decided to revert to the prewar system of 117 districts in which each voter had one vote and three to five representatives were elected from each district. Whitney opposed the change, but Yoshida went to MacArthur and persuaded him to go along. The opposition parties were also against the change, but after a fistfight in the Diet the revision was approved.[23]

Yoshida was not a Diet member and had never been a politician. Nevertheless, he wanted to run, particularly because the new constitution mandated that the prime minister and a majority of the cabinet be members of the Diet. Yoshida's natural father had come from Kōchi Prefecture on the small and remote island of Shikoku and had been elected to the Diet from there in Japan's first parliamentary election. Yoshida had lived in Kanagawa Prefecture near Tokyo for many years and had only distant connections with Kōchi. Some friends in Kanagawa urged him to run from there. But a veteran politician told Yoshida that because "he was not a very amiable person," he would not please the people in Kanagawa for very long, whereas the voters in Kōchi were far enough away that he would not be criticized if he did not show his face very often. So he chose Kōchi and made a three-day visit there, bowing frequently and confining his speech-making—he was always a miserable public speaker—to brief and banal salutations.[24]

Yoshida had to jump one more hurdle. As a candidate for the Diet, he had to go through the purge screening process, along with more than 190,000 other candidates in the April elections. He was cleared after what seemed almost a perfunctory examination. If Yoshida's record as vice foreign minister in the expansionist era of the late 1920s had been given the microscopic examination that Hatoyama's had received in April 1946, Yoshida might have been in trouble. And if GS had known about Yoshida's earlier activities, it would have been sorely tempted to throw the book at him. But Yoshida was lucky. His record was not well known, and his arrest by the militarists in 1945 cast a protective aura of heroism around him.[25]

Because the lower house election would take place shortly before the new constitution was to come into force on May 3, the key legislation implementing it had to be enacted before the election. This herculean task was carried out only through SCAP pressure, bureaucratic docility, and an almost total absence of parliamentary scrutiny of the bills that were being passed. The job may have been easier for the Japanese because they do not attach a definitive and fixed meaning to laws or even to a constitution the way Western nations do but are rather more flexible in their interpretation of legal documents.[26]

Among the many significant pieces of legislation requiring revision were the Civil Code, the Codes of Civil and Criminal Procedure, and a judicial code. Normally revision of each of these would have occupied many months of careful study and debate, but instead a highly irregular solution was devised: a series of provisional bills for "temporary adjustment pursuant to the enforcement of the constitution" was submitted to the Diet. These bills were in effect outlines couched in broad language that by their terms would be valid only until the end of 1947. With SCAP and Japanese officials working together, eleven laws were pushed through before May 3, 1947. In the fourteen months after that, seventeen laws in regular form were enacted to bring the legal and judicial systems into line with the new constitution.[27]

MacArthur and Yoshida took part in this vast legislative operation on several occasions. Yoshida wanted special legislation to punish violence against the emperor. MacArthur replied, "The respect and affection which the people of Japan have for the Emperor form a sufficient bulwark, which need not be bolstered by special provisions. . . . The experience of the United States . . . demonstrates the adequacy of general legislation to punish crimes even against the head of the state." Yoshida wanted to use the court organization law to appoint the president and fourteen judges of the new Supreme Court before the constitution came into effect. MacArthur rejected this sally, which would, he said, "disturb public confidence in the court and create an undesirable impression throughout the Allied world." Other legislation defined the authority of the Diet and strengthened the powers of local government throughout the country.[28]

On March 22, three weeks before the election, MacArthur sent Yoshida a strong letter instructing the government to "maintain a firm control over wages and prices and to initiate and maintain a strict rationing program for essential commodities in short supply so as to insure that such commodities are equitably distributed," as SCAP had ordered at the start of the occupation. The general also told the government to make use of the Economic Stabilization Board (ESB), which had been created at SCAP instigation.[29]

The MacArthur letter had an unusual history. It was drafted by Tsuru Shigeto, a Japanese economist who had joined ESS a short time before at Yoshida's request. Tsuru's direct statement of the situation, written more clearly than most SCAPese, sailed right through head-quarters and received the supreme commander's imprimatur. Yoshida replied on March 28 that he had read the general's letter "with a deep sense of appreciation" and was taking a number of corrective steps, including better food collection, the setting of a production goal of 30 million tons of coal in the next year, and the strengthening of ESB.[30]

The Japanese economy was not far from collapse in early 1947. Un-employment remained in the millions and fed on returning repatriates. Industrial production in 1946 was about 31 percent of the 1934–1936 level. The total money supply was twenty-six times higher than in late 1945, and real wages were rising far more slowly than the inflation rate. Foreign trade was inconsequential in the years right after the war, reaching in 1947 a volume of $174 million for exports and $526 mil-lion for imports. Most of this trade was with the United States.[31]

The most important economic action taken by Japan in the early years of the occupation was Prime Minister Yoshida's adoption of "priority production" to revive industrial production. When he became prime minister he established the practice of meeting regularly with a group of economic experts, many of them academics, to discuss means of getting the economy going. One of these experts, Arisawa Hiromi, asserted that expanding coal production along with imports of coal and oil could lead to increased steel production; the two could be mutually reinforcing and could in turn lead to increased production in other key industries, such as electric power and shipbuilding. Arisawa estimated that 30 million tons of coal would have to be mined each year to get the process in full swing.[32]

Yoshida handed MacArthur a memorandum on December 3, 1946, requesting SCAP's assistance in obtaining the import of anthracite coal, coking coal, and crude oil to help increase steel production. The letter was drafted by Ōkita Saburō, one of Japan's best-known economists, who became foreign minister many years afterward. Four days later Marquat advised the prime minister that most of his requests for oil and coal could be met. Yoshida was so elated he told the emperor the good news. On December 11 Yoshida sent a note to MacArthur saying that "His Majesty has commanded me to convey to you his gratitude for the industrial assistance promised in the memorandum" of General Mar-quat. Coal production in 1947 was more than 29 million tons, just short of the target. Iron and steel production also began to mount significantly by 1948.[33] Japanese writers look back on the priority production program as the key step in starting Japan on the road to economic recovery. The program was particularly welcome as a sign of Japanese initiative and worked because both the Japanese and SCAP fully supported it. Planning priorities for industrial production became standard.

Some observers, including SCAP economists, felt that in the early years of the occupation many Japanese officials and businessmen showed little energy or initiative in combating their economic problems and even passively resisted occupation changes. It is true that the Japanese often seemed overcome by lethargy and confusion. Many of them obviously thought that all they could do was take care of themselves and let the Americans decide what to do about the government and the economy. People such as Yoshida and Tsuru did not fall into this feckless category. In addition, in the early postwar period two important management and industrial organizations were formed: Keidanren (Federation of Business Organizations), which coordinated the views of business and industry, and Nikkeiren (Japan Management Association), which dealt with labor policy from the point of view of business. They remain powerful today.[34]

As a final achievement, the first Yoshida cabinet won passage of the Labor Standards Law on April 17, 1947, prescribing basic rights and procedures of employment. It established an eight-hour day and a forty-eight-hour work week, with a 25 percent premium for overtime work. Wages were to be paid in cash directly to the workers. A labor-management committee in each industry was to set minimum wages. The law prohibited child labor and required additional protective measures for women and young workers.[35]

In April 1947 democracy came to Japan in full force. Virtually every elective office in the land was at stake. Five separate elections were held to choose 205,092 officials at the national, prefectural, and local levels. These elections were the first to be conducted by the local election commissions set up under the Election Law of 1946 to replace supervision by the Home Ministry and the police. They were also the first for the new elective upper house (the House of Councillors), for governors of the prefectures, for mayors, and for all local assemblies. The political parties were better organized than the year before, but they needed all their skill to meet what was probably the busiest month in the modern electoral history of any state.[36]

The Liberals' year in office had given them no advantage. Public opinion as reflected in the press was anti-Yoshida and anticonservative. Yoshida hoped to join with the Progressives in a united conservative party, but the factional rivalries endemic to Japanese politics, which revolved around personalities, fund-raising, and leader-follower relationships, made this impossible.

Instead, Ashida, a prominent and ambitious Liberal leader, moved into the Progressive camp along with a small group of Liberals. Together they formed the Democratic Party, which wanted to create a more progressive image. In line with the Japanese political tradition, the party's platform was vague: uphold the spirit of the new constitution, establish a democratic political structure, and make plans for industrial reconstruction.

The Socialists rejected the laissez-faire views of the conservatives on economic issues, advocating instead state control over the coal, iron, steel, and fertilizer industries. They strongly opposed any cooperation with the Communists. The known preference of GS for the Socialists may also have boosted the influence of the moderate left. The Communists had a radical platform: extend the purge, democratize the bureaucracy and the police, nationalize major industries, and "eliminate feudalism."

The most crucial election was on April 25 for the new House of Representatives, which was to be the most powerful organ in the Japanese body politic. More than 27 million people voted that day, or 68 percent of the electorate. As MacArthur had foreseen, the Socialists did well, coming in first with 143 seats, or 45 more than they had held in the old lower house. The Liberals came in second with 132 seats, a loss of 8. The Democrats, formerly the Progressives, were a close third with 126, a loss of 19. Surprisingly, the Communists won only 4 seats, 2 less than they had held in the old house. Fifteen women and 12 independents were elected. Of those elected, 221, or nearly one-half of the 466 total, were "new faces" in the Diet.

The share of the vote obtained by the Liberals and the Communists, the parties of the extremes, had not changed much since the 1946 election. The Socialists did much better. The Democrats did not do as well as their predecessors, the Progressives, had done in 1946. All eleven members of the Yoshida cabinet who ran in 1947 were elected. The advice Yoshida had received on where and how to run proved good. He came in first in his district and was reelected three times thereafter.

The results of the other four elections held in April were mixed. Here again the Socialists did well, even though independents, most of whom were conservative, did better, both nationally and locally. Overall, the Socialists came in first in both houses of the new Diet. As a political party, they were clearly number one. The elections showed that the people were looking for a new approach somewhat to the left of center. They had definitely repudiated the far left, where the Communists did badly because they were associated with the reckless strike threat earlier in the year.

In a high-flown statement on April 27, two days after the election for the House of Representatives, MacArthur noted that the elections were the last step before the constitution came into effect and declared that its effectuation marked "a new era in the Far East which may well prove vital to the future of civilization." He showed foresight in adding that "the Japanese people have...overwhelmingly chosen a moderate course, sufficiently centered from either extreme to insure the preservation of freedom and the enhancement of individual dignity."[37]

The politicians generally agreed that the Socialists should have the first chance to form a cabinet. Under their president, Katayama Tetsu, they drew up a statement of policies for the party to follow. It would seek to control wages and prices, stimulate key industries, reduce inflation, increase food production, foster cooperation between capital and labor, and set higher standards of education. On the basis of this program the four big parties—Socialists, Liberals, Democrats, and People's Cooperative—agreed on a coalition cabinet. On May 19 Katayama and his political strategist, Nishio Suehiro, called on Yoshida to discuss cabinet posts and suggested the Liberal Party might take the Foreign Office portfolio, thinking this offer would make Yoshida happy. But Yoshida insisted that the left Socialists should not be included in the cabinet because they advocated cooperation with the Communists. He went even farther by stating that the Socialist Party had to "rid itself of left-wing elements," an obvious impossibility for Katayama because the left wing provided a good part of his political strength. As a result, Yoshida decided that the Liberals should stay out of the cabinet. A party caucus endorsed his decision.[38]

On May 24 the House of Representatives designated Katayama as prime minister by an almost unanimous vote, including the support of the Liberals. On the next day he was invested by the emperor. Katayama's cabinet, consisting of eight Socialists (none of them leftists), seven Democrats, and two from the People's Cooperative Party, was sworn in on June 1. Although the Liberals did not enter the cabinet, they continued to subscribe to the four-party agreement, which was supposed to be the basis of the new government's policy.[39]

Yoshida's decision to stay out of the cabinet was a fateful one. At the time it seemed selfish and almost unpatriotic. But from the point of view of party politics, this seemingly self-sacrificial exclusion made sense because it enabled the Liberal Party to retain its pristine conservatism and stay clear of the troubles the coalition later got itself into.

On May 24 as he left office, Yoshida sent warm thank-you notes to General MacArthur and General Whitney. Yoshida told the supreme commander, "I consider it my rare privilege to have so largely profited from our association. . . . I leave office with an earnest expectation that this country will witness, under your superb guidance, a steady progress toward a genuine democracy."[40] There is no record of any reply by MacArthur.

The prime minister also thanked Whitney, in an artful choice of words, for his kindness and particularly "for your advice and assistance in drafting the present constitution, which owes so much to you." Whitney was equally deft in his reply of May 28: "Few understand better than I the difficult and complex problems which you have faced during your tenure as Prime Minister." He added prophetically that "I . . . know you will respond to any further call upon your energies in the public service."[41]

In his memoirs Yoshida listed a dozen important accomplishments of his year at the head of government, including the constitution, land reform, revision of labor and education laws, local autonomy legislation, and even the antimonopoly law.[42] But a knowledgeable U.S. expert on Japan, Hugh Borton of the State Department, who met with the prime minister on March 29, 1947, was not impressed. Borton noted in particular Yoshida's strong objection to SCAP's emphasis on the importance of decentralizing the government. Borton could not understand how Yoshida was able to regain power in October 1948 and remain prime minister for the next four and one-half years.[43] For most Americans, Yoshida was not a very amiable person, and the 1947 elections seemed to show that many Japanese felt the same way.

CHAPTER 11

MacArthur, the Allies, and Washington

The period from the spring of 1947, after Yoshida left office, to the fall of 1948 lacked the quick tempo and intensity of the first eighteen months of the occupation. The Allies were more querulous, MacArthur made a guarded bid for the Republican presidential nomination, American critics attacked his performance, and the pace of reform slowed down as the Japanese tried to find new leaders and new policies.

The ACJ (a miniature FEC) began its sessions in Tokyo in early 1946. MacArthur attended the opening meeting on April 5, one of his few appearances at a public meeting, and cordially welcomed the Soviet, Australian, and Chinese representatives. He reproved "those throughout the Allied world who lift their voices in sharp and ill-conceived criticism of our occupational policies," asserting that "history has given us no precedent of success in a similar military occupation."[1]

MacArthur had not had much experience in diplomacy. But he had worked with Allies in Europe in World War I and with the Australian government and army for four years during and after World War II. He knew little about the Soviets and not much more about the Chinese. But as supreme commander in Japan, where he was at least "quasi-sovereign," some twenty foreign liaison missions were eventually accredited to him, and he met periodically with their chiefs and saw several of them often.[2]

The Soviet member of the ACJ, Lieutenant General Kuzma Derev-

yanko, a heavy-set, handsome man and a career intelligence officer in
the Red Army, was new to diplomacy. His political adviser, Jakob
Malik, was a diplomat who had been in Japan for several years and
whose astuteness MacArthur respected. Malik was recalled to Moscow
in 1949, however, for being too conciliatory, according to MacArthur.[3]
At the second meeting of the ACJ, the Soviets asked to be "informed, as
fully as possible" why undesirable persons subject to the purge order of
January 4, 1946, had not been removed from office. MacArthur angrily
charged General Whitney to make an answer in the ACJ, "even if it
took all summer." Whitney spent nearly three hours at a council meeting reading long lists of organizations banned by SCAP and apologizing
that he did not have the names of the organizations' members.[4] The
ACJ became known as a forum for East-West controversy with little
relevance to the key issues in Allied policy for Japan. MacArthur's decision that meetings should be open to the public did not help matters.

MacArthur soon named his political adviser George Atcheson as
head of the newly established DS and as his deputy on the ACJ and its
chairman. DS was to be in effect a protocol office for SCAP in dealing
with the foreign diplomatic missions in Tokyo. MacArthur told Atcheson that some governments on the ACJ might have "sabotage and ob-
struction" as their goals and that he should counter them "with equally
embarrassing and nasty questions and statements." For example, the
Soviets might be asked why they did not send troops to share the
burden of the occupation. The general added, curiously, that he himself would protect the position and responsibility of the supreme commander but that Atcheson should "protect the foreign policy of the
United States in council meetings."[5] This was another instance in
which MacArthur claimed his jurisdiction was separate from that of
the United States.

The ACJ met every two weeks throughout the occupation, for a total
of 125 meetings. About one-half of these, especially in later years, were
without an agenda and lasted only a few minutes or less. Many of the
meetings, however, were informative, and some were even constructive,
as when the Soviet representative put the subject of police reform on the
agenda on June 4, 1946, and a discussion without polemics ensued.[6]

On June 26, 1946, the United States put on the agenda the subject of
repatriation of Japanese prisoners of war from Siberia. The refusal of
the Soviet Union to return any of the 760,000 men captured in North
China, Manchuria, and Korea in the first days after the war (the Soviet
government later claimed it held only 523,000 Japanese prisoners of

war in late 1946) touched the lives of millions of people. The Japanese public soon learned that the Soviet Union was forcing these prisoners to work under harsh conditions and holding kangaroo trials at which many of them were being sentenced to prison for alleged violations of Soviet laws. Lengthy U.S. presentations to the council on the Soviet failure to repatriate Japanese became a powerful propaganda weapon. The Soviet member claimed this subject was beyond the council's jurisdiction, but Atcheson overruled him. After all, the Potsdam Declaration provided that Japanese military forces should be permitted to return home. SCAP continued to prod the Soviets on this issue and reached an agreement with the Soviet government on December 18, 1946, for the return of 50,000 Japanese every month. This agreement was observed for only a few months, and the issue remained unresolved.[7]

MacArthur did not consult with the council in advance of issuing orders, one reason being that after April 1946 he did not issue formal orders. A peculiar exception was his request in February 1947 for the comments of council members on a letter he planned to send Prime Minister Yoshida stating that the time had come for a general election. No one on the council objected to what MacArthur termed an "administrative action."[8]

After Atcheson was killed on August 17, 1947, in an airplane accident off Hawaii, William J. Sebald from the POLAD office took his place on the council. An Annapolis graduate and prewar lawyer in Japan, Sebald was a calm, judicious man who knew Japan well and was able to get along with MacArthur. He tried to be a good diplomat and proved effective as a debater in ACJ forensics. Sebald started his chairmanship with agenda items such as trade, industrial production, and education, but by the end of the year, he had become discouraged by criticisms in the council. He recommended to Washington, with MacArthur's approval, that the ACJ be abolished, leaving diplomatic contacts in Tokyo to normalize relations between SCAP and the foreign diplomatic missions. The State Department informed him, as he and MacArthur must have expected, that his proposal was not practical.[9]

MacArthur and his staff were keenly disappointed by the conduct of the Australian and Chinese members of the ACJ. The Chinese said little, other than occasionally expressing concern that militarism might be reviving in Japan. Their silence annoyed SCAP, as did some of the reporting from China by U.S. diplomats about Chinese attitudes critical of American policy in Japan. The most irritating gadfly was the Australian representative, Macmahon Ball, an academic well grounded in political science and tenacious in his pursuit of liberal ideas. Ball was a protégé of the dynamic and strong-willed foreign minister of the Labour government, H. Vere Evatt, an advocate of a tough policy toward Japan. Evatt reflected the Australian position that it had made an important contribution to the Allied victory in the Far East and therefore should speak for the British Empire on Asian issues. A campaign was eventually mounted to get rid of Ball, ending in his recall in August 1948 and resignation.[10]

In contrast with the ACJ, the FEC in Washington was a model of accomplishment and decorum. It approved thirty-seven policy decisions in the first eighteen months of its operation. Many of these put the Allied stamp of approval on existing U.S. policies, but others—on popular sovereignty, Diet supremacy, education, labor organization, war crimes trials, and interim reparations—were improved by a new and hard look from Allied experts. When MacArthur wrote disparagingly in his memoirs of the Allied role in the occupation, he did not do credit to his reputation for fairness.[11]

The Japanese government and public knew little of the workings of the FEC beyond fragmentary press reports. Japan had no independent sources of information. The government's contacts with foreign diplomats in Tokyo were proscribed, although this rule was not rigorously enforced. Japanese officialdom watched the ACJ closely. Japanese reporters and one of their diplomats, Asakai Kōichirō, were permitted to attend meetings but had to enter through a back door. Asakai's reports, which were later published, provided his superiors, including Prime Minister Yoshida, with some remarkable insights into the actions of the council and the increasingly divergent attitudes of its members.[12]

Although the occupation was from the outset overwhelmingly an American show, it was U.S. policy to encourage other Allies to send forces to share the burden of what was widely expected to be a long and arduous operation. The United States wanted the United Kingdom and the Soviet Union to be major Allies, and Asian nations such as China and the Philippines to send forces. Under British auspices, a force called the British Commonwealth Occupation Force (BCOF), consisting of units from the United Kingdom, Australia, New Zealand, and India was organized. An agreement with the United States reached on January 30, 1946, placed BCOF under the operational control of General MacArthur and under the administrative direction of an Australian, Lieutenant General J. F. Northcott. BCOF's area of control was the Chugoku region in central Honshu to the west of Kobe and the island of

Shikoku. It had no military government duties. The first elements of BCOF arrived on February 8, 1946; by August the force totaled 36,154 officers and men. But it soon became clear that BCOF had very little to do. Occupied Japan was very peaceful, and the participating governments, except Australia, decided to withdraw their troops, starting in the fall of 1946.[13]

Although the United States had rejected the 1945 Soviet bid for a separate zone, it still anticipated that the Soviets would send an occupying force on the same basis as the Commonwealth nations. MacArthur planned to put the Soviet forces in central Japan in a relatively harmless location. As in the case of the Commonwealth forces, he would have had operational control over them. The U.S. offer to the Soviets to take part in the occupation was still alive as late as early 1947, but they never took it up.[14]

The Republic of China (ROC) accepted the U.S. offer in late 1945 and made plans to send a Chinese division in early 1946. But Chiang Kai-shek decided in 1947 that because of the worsening situation in his war against the Chinese Communists, he could not spare a division for duty in Japan. None of the other Allied powers offered to send forces.[15]

The issue of dividing up reparations engaged all the Allies. The FEC began grappling with it early on. The Soviets exacerbated matters by claiming that the Japanese property they had seized in Manchuria and Korea should be treated as "war booty," not as part of the USSR's reparations share. MacArthur valued this property at $50 billion, but Washington estimates were much lower.[16]

In 1946 the FEC approved eight policy decisions for "interim reparations" removals in industries such as light metals, synthetic rubber, shipbuilding, and machine tools. On August 24, 1946, SCAP sent the Japanese government lists of "reparations selections" in the eight industries approved by the FEC but did not order any removals. Prime Minister Yoshida wrote to MacArthur on October 23, 1946, pointing out that these removals would damage Japan's industrial recovery and asking that some of the plants be exempt. He also urged that final selections be made quickly. MacArthur replied that the issue was important to the FEC nations but that Japanese views would receive careful consideration.[17]

With the FEC hopelessly deadlocked over how to allocate reparations, the United States decided on April 2, 1947—over stiff Allied objections—to issue an "interim directive" authorizing limited "advance transfers" of up to 30 percent of the anticipated total. China would get 15 percent; the Philippines, 5 percent; the Netherlands, 5 percent for the East Indies; and the United Kingdom, 5 percent for Burma and Malaya. Deliveries consisting mostly of machine tools were made over a period of two years. MacArthur estimated that the total value of the deliveries was $40 million.[18]

On March 19, 1947, MacArthur held the only on-the-record press conference of his five and one-half years in Tokyo. The surprise of the foreign correspondents association when he accepted their long-standing invitation to attend a luncheon turned into excitement when he began by saying he was speaking on the record. Some reporters had to scramble for pencils and paper. Only sketchy reconstructions of the questions and answers were available afterward, but SCAP headquarters did put together a partially verbatim transcript.[19]

It was evident that the general wanted to say something dramatic. The first question was about his suggestion to a group of visiting American journalists a few days before that "the Japanese be placed under the United Nations." MacArthur's reply was a minispeech, which he had prepared well and in fact had already given to the British ambassador.[20] "The time is now approaching when we must talk peace with Japan. . . . The military purpose . . . to ensure Japan will follow the ways of peace . . . has been, I think, accomplished. . . . The political phase is approaching such completion as is possible under the occupation. . . . I believe sincerely and absolutely that [democracy] is here to stay. . . . The third phase is economic. Japan is still economically blockaded by the Allied powers. . . . But this is not a phase the occupation can settle. We can only enforce economic strangulation."

In response to another question, the general said he thought a peace treaty should be concluded "as soon as possible." Handling peace treaty matters was of course not part of MacArthur's job as occupation commander. He told the British ambassador later that he had spoken as an "international officer."[21] Acting Secretary of State Dean Acheson commented to a press conference in Washington on March 18 that further progress would have to be made on the peace treaties with European nations before a Japanese treaty could be addressed. Political adviser Atcheson played down the import of the general's press statement.[22]

MacArthur lunched on March 13 with Hugh Borton and Ruth Bacon from the State Department. The general knew they were experts working on a draft peace treaty. Borton asserted later that MacArthur "was fully aware of its contents both when he spoke to the press club and when I saw him in his office" a few days later. At a second meeting MacArthur told Borton that the occupation had outlived its usefulness and suggested that a peace conference be held in Tokyo in the summer of 1947, with formal signature of the treaty six months later. Mac-Arthur thought other Allied nations could be persuaded to sign a treaty with Japan, with or without the Soviet Union, and as a last resort the United States might even make a separate treaty. The general suggested the Japanese could attend the peace conference and might even have a vote. Borton said that would almost certainly not be possible.[23]

MacArthur's views were often at variance with those of the Pentagon, but that did not restrain him from speaking out, more often in private than in public. Some of his notions were overoptimistic or simplistic, but his vision of an early, short, and nonpunitive treaty was a helpful guide in later negotiations. He was the first American leader to advocate a liberal settlement of this kind. His ability to express without much challenge opinions independent of those held by his superiors showed how great his self-confidence and authority were.[24]

MacArthur floated his treaty trial balloon at a time when cold war clouds were gathering in East and West. Only four days earlier President Truman had announced his "doctrine" that the United States would assist friendly nations threatened by communist expansion, specifically Greece and Turkey. In Moscow the Big Four foreign ministers began one of their most fruitless meetings in March 1947, which in the words of a senior diplomat "really rang down the Iron Curtain." In China Mao Zedong's armies were sweeping over North China and Manchuria. And in Tokyo MacArthur had six weeks earlier prohibited a general strike that had seriously threatened the stability of the Japanese government. Peace was not in the air.[25]

MacArthur had said many times that all military occupations ran down and should not last more than three years. Now, only months after the surrender, he began a new refrain—Japan should have an early peace treaty. This desire to finish the job partly explains his hurry in pushing the reform program and putting the constitution in place. Yoshida ascribed this to the "impulsiveness common to military people of all countries."[26]

MacArthur may have had other reasons, particularly a fascination with U.S. presidential politics. Even in 1944 when he was fighting the Japanese in the Southwest Pacific, he had let his name be put in nomination as a presidential candidate. An overwhelming defeat in the Wisconsin primary on April 4, 1944, destroyed any chance he may have thought he had.[27]

He frequently discussed politics with Eichelberger, Whitney, and Joe Keenan, an Ohio Democrat, as Eichelberger recorded in his diaries. The general once told Eichelberger that Harry Truman thought "FDR was always afraid of MacArthur and seemed to think he might have tremendous political power." MacArthur probably hoped FDR was right. But at times MacArthur seemed to sense that General Eisenhower was the dark horse who might eventually run ahead. MacArthur denigrated Ike's candidacy by saying that "there was no Eisenhower for president movement except as a means to get rid of me" and that Eisenhower should withdraw and give his support to MacArthur. The record also contains unpleasant remarks by Eisenhower about MacArthur. The most famous was undoubtedly the comment by the hero of the European theater that during his tour of duty on MacArthur's staff in the Philippines, "he [Eisenhower] had studied dramatics for seven years." But Ike added that if MacArthur were to walk into the room and say, "'Ike, follow me,' I'd get up and follow him." President Truman may have been right in saying that these two outstanding generals of World War II seemed to suffer from "Potomac fever."[28]

When MacArthur heard from Borton in April 1947 that plans for a Japanese peace conference were being made in Washington, he was probably pleased. Not only did he think that he had accomplished much of his task in Tokyo, but he may well have felt he could look forward to the climax of his proconsulship at a dramatic international peace conference. A treaty could be signed in late 1947, and he could leave Japan for home the next day. His luster would be at its brightest. And the 1948 presidential campaign would just be getting under way.

In fact, the negotiations for a peace conference broke down in the summer of 1947 over procedural differences among the major powers. Meanwhile, MacArthur's presidential ambitions took on more steam, propelled by friends back home. In September retired Brigadier General Hanford MacNider, an Iowa cement manufacturer who had served in the Pacific under MacArthur, wrote to offer support. MacArthur replied on October 14, 1947, "I do not covet or actively seek... any other office," but if a movement for his candidacy won widespread support, "there would be no other course open to me but to accept it as a mandate and risk the hazards and responsibilities involved. . . . This is the first letter I have written on this subject."[29]

In November 1947 a group of MacArthur's supporters met in Chicago, led by General Robert E. Wood, chairman of Sears Roebuck; Philip LaFollette, a former governor of Wisconsin; and General MacNider. They thought it essential that MacArthur return home and campaign actively. MacArthur wrote back on November 16, 1947, to General Wood that he was too engaged to return but would give the matter further consideration. By not campaigning actively, MacArthur protected himself from charges that he was violating the law prohibiting federal employees from participating in politics.

In June 1948 Eisenhower made a bombshell statement in a letter to a New Hampshire newspaper: "Nothing in the international or domestic situation especially qualifies for the most important office in the world a man whose adult years have been spent in the country's military forces." Ike added that he would not be a candidate. Later he denied that he intended to discourage MacArthur from his candidacy, asserting he hoped MacArthur "feels as great a friendship for me as I do for him." Nevertheless, MacArthur resented Eisenhower's "slur upon the U.S. Army" and as a result "felt obliged to offer his own candidacy," according to the British ambassador, who sometimes liked to probe the general's inner thoughts.[30]

By early 1948 the general's backers in Wisconsin were getting agitated about his chances, even though polls were showing him to be the favorite over Governor Thomas E. Dewey of New York and former governor Harold Stassen of Minnesota. In a public statement on March 9 MacArthur responded with an almost Ciceronian touch, ending with the words, "I can say, and with due humility, that I would be recreant to all my concepts of good citizenship were I to shrink because of the hazards and responsibilities involved from accepting any public duty to which I might be called by the American people." The general still had not crossed the Rubicon, but he would do so if the right call came.[31]

The Japanese watched these maneuvers with keen interest and no doubt some puzzlement. Newspapers ran extras and editorials expressed regret that MacArthur might go. Signs appeared in downtown Tokyo, one reading, "Pray for General MacArthur's Success in the Presidential Election." Prime Minister Ashida, who had just taken office, wrote an effusive letter to MacArthur in March 1948 that "it has been my ardent hope that you would continue to remain in this country to carry on the magnificent work you are accomplishing here." He added that if the general should answer the call, "Japan's loss will be the world's gain."[32]

On March 29, 1948, *The New York Times* predicted victory for MacArthur in the Wisconsin primary, but wrongly, it turned out. MacArthur finished a poor second on April 6, gaining only eight of the twenty-seven delegates to be chosen and 36 percent of the vote. Harold Stassen from neighboring Minnesota got nineteen delegates and 40 percent of the vote. Governor Thomas E. Dewey, who eventually won the nomination, got 24 percent of the vote but no delegates. The day after the election, MacArthur's chief of staff in Tokyo said, "The general is low as a rug and very disappointed."[33] A week later MacArthur ran fifth in the Nebraska primary. He then asked that his name be withdrawn from other primaries. MacArthur's name was put in nomination to an almost empty hall at the Republican convention on June 25, 1948, at 4:30 A.M. On the first ballot he got 11 of the 1,094 votes cast. Dewey was chosen on the third ballot, with 1 dissenting vote—by a MacArthur supporter.

MacArthur wrote bitterly in his memoirs, "My name was precipitated into the struggle for the Republican nomination. . . . I was not a candidate and declined to campaign for the office. I had not the slightest desire to become the head of state, having had more than enough of such an office in the administration of Japan. . . . The attempt was abortive, and its only tangible result was to bring down on my head an avalanche of abuse from the party in power. . . . From that moment on it became only a question of time until retaliation would be visited upon me."[34]

Whether MacArthur's White House aspirations colored his attitudes and actions in Japan before 1948 is hard to assess. His name was always associated with conservative causes in American politics. In Japan he carried out with reasonable fidelity the policies he had been given, liberal though many of them undoubtedly were.[35] Nevertheless, MacArthur knew from firsthand observation of the New Deal in Washington what a spectacular success Franklin Roosevelt had been as a politician. The general may have figured that the liberal flavor of many of the policies he executed in Japan—the breakup of the big business combines and the emancipation of farmers and workers—invested him with a useful touch of New Deal populism.

Even before he became engaged in presidential politics, MacArthur was the target of press criticism back home. *Newsweek* in particular took a number of pot shots at him. On December 1, 1947, it published a lengthy article entitled "Lawyer's Report Attacks Plan to Run Occupation . . . Far to Left of Anything Now Tolerated in America."

The lawyer was James Lee Kauffman, an American attorney with pre-war experience in Japan. Quoting extensively from the copy of FEC-230 he had obtained surreptitiously in Japan, he claimed the policy set forth in this document would cause the "virtual destruction of Japanese business and the sale of its assets at nominal prices to selected purchasers, including labor unions, about one-half of which are communist-dominated." The *Newsweek* article shortly led to debate in the U.S. Senate, with Senator William F. Knowland, a Republican from California, taking the lead in criticizing the proposal embodied in FEC-230.[36]

Not one to hang back when under attack, MacArthur charged forth. In a long letter of February 1, 1948, to a private citizen that SCAP made public, the general thundered that the Japanese system "permitted ten family groups . . . to control, directly or indirectly, every phase of commerce and industry; all media of transportation, both internal and external; all domestic raw materials; and all coal and other power resources. . . . The record is thus one of economic oppression and exploitation at home, aggression and spoliation abroad."[37] The general also wrote to Senator Brien McMahon of Connecticut on February 1 that "if this concentration of economic power is not torn down and redistributed peacefully, and in due order under the occupation, there is no slightest doubt that its cleansing will eventually occur through a blood bath of revolutionary violence." The supreme commander was firing his big guns.[38]

Newsweek had attacked him early in 1947 regarding the purge program. MacArthur issued a long rebuttal claiming that Washington had imposed the purge on him and asserting that not only did the Japanese press support it but that thousands of Japanese had written to SCAP calling for its extension. A few months later, Harry Kern, the sword-sharp foreign editor of the magazine, reported from Tokyo that "the Japanese economy is about to go into a tailspin. . . . Unless really drastic measures are taken . . . the chances of making Japan into 'the workshop of the Far East' as part of the American policy of rebuilding the world and containing communism will have gone glimmering."[39]

Kauffman and Kern founded the American Council on Japan in June 1948 to "reverse the reformist orientation of the early occupation." They approached a group of prominent conservatives in Washington and New York, circulated critical and sometimes vicious literature about SCAP policies and officials, and won some hearing for their views from reputable former diplomats such as Grew and William Castle, and from James Forrestal, William Draper, and Lieutenant

General Robert Eichelberger in the Pentagon. But these attacks had little influence.[40]

MacArthur was temperamental in dealing with the press, and his press advisers were often clumsy. He was not popular with many of the foreign press corps. Seventeen foreign correspondents were expelled from Japan—reportedly with the general's approval in each case—during the first five years of the occupation. He had a few confidants, such as Miles W. Vaughn of the United Press, to whom he fed views from time to time. Otherwise, he saw few journalists other than distinguished publishers or senior editors who came on visits from abroad. He sometimes granted farewell interviews to foreign reporters who were leaving Japan. He and his staff followed the press avidly, and their sensitivity to criticism was notorious. They censored the Japanese-language press and, on occasion, the English-language press. Excessive censorship was a black mark on the occupation record.[41]

The most famous censorship incident occurred in October 1946 when the English-language *Nippon Times* carried an English translation of an article from the vernacular press cautioning the Japanese people not to look upon MacArthur with "idolatry." Willoughby, evidently unbeknown to his boss, had deliveries of the paper stopped and the offensive article deleted because it was "not in good taste." By that time millions of Japanese had already read the offending article in their own language.[42]

SCAP received criticism from liberal elements in the United States as well but handled it deftly. Well-known civil liberties advocate Roger Baldwin visited Japan in early 1947 to present a list of complaints compiled by civil liberties advocates in the United States. He received plush treatment, including two meetings with MacArthur, and left Japan with a profound admiration for MacArthur, asserting the general was as liberal as he was. But Baldwin did not get much support from SCAP for the civil liberties complaints he had advanced, and his later letters to SCAP also failed to bring about any change in attitude. MacArthur had defended the image of the supreme commander without altering his policies.[43]

CHAPTER 12

The Failure of
Coalition Politics

General MacArthur was always more intrigued by American political maneuverings than by Japanese politics. By 1947 his control in Tokyo was so sure that it did not seem to make much difference who was prime minister. Neither the departure of Yoshida nor the advent of a Socialist gave him any qualms. In fact, he and his GS were heartened that a humanitarian liberal was taking over the helm of state as the new democratic constitution came into effect.[1]

Katayama Tetsu was a sixty-year-old successful attorney who had been elected to the Diet three times before the war. A Presbyterian who believed "democratic government must be permeated by a spirit of Christian love and humanism," he was quite lacking in the cunning of many politicians. His grip on power was tenuous from the start because his cabinet was an ill-assorted coalition of Socialists, Democrats, and members of the People's Cooperative Party and his party held only a slim plurality in the lower house. To avoid attack from the powerful right and probably out of concern for American sensibilities about pure socialism, Katayama excluded the left Socialists from his cabinet and was compelled to split it almost evenly between right Socialists and Democrats, who were barely distinguishable from Liberals in political outlook. He wrote later that MacArthur suggested at an early meeting that he talk to Communist leader Tokuda about a united front of the Socialists and Communists. Katayama understandably did nothing about this far-out idea.[2]

The new National Diet was far more representative of the people than the old Imperial Diet. SCAP believed it would no longer encounter the niggling opposition to change and the laissez-faire economics espoused by Yoshida and the conservatives. It hoped the road to political reform and economic democracy would now be smoother. Indeed, Katayama was willing to cooperate with SCAP and even eager to do its bidding.

Katayama lasted eight months as prime minister, from June 1947 to February 1948. Despite his high hopes and tireless efforts, he made little headway in raising production, lowering inflation, or wiping out the black market economy. His one big push—to nationalize the coal industry—marked the high point of socialist endeavor in Japan's modern history. MacArthur told Katayama on September 18, 1947, that the Diet was free to act as it saw fit on this matter, adding that Japan should try to boost coal production to its wartime peak of close to 50 million tons a year. Well watered down by the Diet, Katayama's coal bill, passed in December 1947, in effect established government supervision, not control, over the industry. Coal production mounted steadily in the following years, but not because of the insignificant coal law of 1947.[3]

SCAP also pressed Katayama to adopt two controversial reforms: to break up large "economic concentrations" and to decentralize the police. Late in the summer of 1947 ESS received a copy of FEC-230, the U.S. antitrust proposal. At the same time the FEC was studying it, ESS called in two senior Japanese from the ESB and told them immediate action was necessary to implement an "order" from Washington entitled "Elimination of Concentrations of Economic Power." The moderately socialist Katayama cabinet was so disturbed that the prime minister wrote a letter to MacArthur on September 4, 1947, asserting that although the government supported the principle of deconcentration, the new proposal was "even more stringent than the law enacted in Germany." SCAP was unyielding, however, and pushed for quick approval.[4]

Before the bill was enacted, Secretary of the Army Kenneth C. Royall "directed" MacArthur to ensure that it was amended to contain certain modifications Washington wanted. MacArthur reluctantly instructed the Japanese to make the amendments as well as a significant change the Japanese wanted: insertion in the title of the word *excessive*. The bill was passed late on December 9, 1947, with two SCAP officials on the floor of the Diet and the parliamentary clock stopped to enable negotiations to finish before the Diet session ran out of time.[5] The Law for the Elimination of Excessive Concentrations of Economic Power, or the Deconcentration Law, was probably the most contentious piece of legislation passed during the occupation; SCAP and Washington disagreed about the plan, as did SCAP and the Japanese. Yet it proved to have a far-reaching effect on at least a few industries in Japan. For example, the law led to the split of Japan Steel Company into two companies, Fuji and Yawata, which brought about intense competition in the steel industry. This ended when the two were reunited in 1970 to form Nippon Steel Company, one of the largest in the world.

Police reform remained a sensitive issue throughout the occupation. The Home Ministry had tightly controlled the prewar police, whose many duties involved law enforcement, tax collection, election observation, customs enforcement, census taking, intelligence gathering, and thought control. The police commanded the respect and even the obsequiousness of the general public. In late 1945 Japanese requests to SCAP to approve increases of the size and arms of the police, then numbering 93,935 persons, were rejected.[6]

MacArthur moved cautiously on police decontrol, waiting for the Japanese to come up with their own plan. By the summer of 1947 police reform had become one of the more notorious footballs of the occupation, as Whitney's GS and Willoughby's G-2 fought to determine not only which section would make occupation policy but also what kind of police forces Japan should have. G-2 experts wanted larger and more centralized police. GS advocated only a small increase in the numbers of the police and bitterly opposed any centralization. As on several other occasions, GS instructed the Japanese to deal only with it on police matters. Willoughby wrote an interoffice memorandum on August 24 referring bitterly to "this new inexperienced government, completely under the thumb of the Government Section."[7]

Prime Minister Katayama discussed the subject with General MacArthur on August 26 and submitted a reform proposal on September 3, which GS found objectionable. GS and G-2 met nineteen times in the next two weeks and finally agreed on a compromise plan. MacArthur's letter to Katayama, dated September 16, 1947, provided for total police forces of 125,000 divided into two parts. One would be the national rural police of 30,000 operating in rural areas and small towns; it would have centralized units at the national level only for limited purposes such as the setting of standards and some forms of training. The other would be the autonomous local forces totaling 95,000 in cities and towns of more than 5,000 in population; the result would be about 1,600 independent municipal police forces. Public safety commissions would be set up at both the national and local levels. The prime minister could take control of the police forces if he proclaimed a state of national emergency, which would have to be ratified by the Diet within twenty days. The Police Law embodying the principles enunciated by the supreme commander was enacted by the Diet and went into effect on March 8, 1948.[8]

The official GS report paid tribute to the Police Law as typical of "the relationship that existed generally between the government and the headquarters in reaching solutions to Japanese problems."[9] In fact, the resolution of the police issue was a tribute to the power of GS to win over MacArthur, thus overwhelming the experts in G-2 and compelling a reluctant Japanese government to go along.

In 1954, two years after the occupation ended, the Yoshida cabinet amended the Police Law to organize all police into forty-six prefectural police forces, despite strong left-wing opposition. It called for a national public safety commission and prefectural commissions to supervise these forces and established a police agency at the national level to formulate operational standards for the entire country.

The Diet passed a maritime safety agency law on April 15, 1948. Japan actually maintained maritime control units throughout the occupation, an embryo navy that was never disbanded. The law established a new agency, modeled after the U.S. Coast Guard, to handle patrol and safety functions in coastal waters, with water police functions divorced from normal civil police activities. The personnel strength of the new force was 10,000. The ACJ debated the bill at the instigation of the Australian member, thereby stirring MacArthur's ire at this implied criticism of his policy.[10]

On December 31, 1947, the Diet formally abolished the Home Ministry. Long the most powerful civilian agency of the government, the ministry embodied the centralized and oppressive bureaucracy of prewar Japan, although its officials were generally considered to be among the most efficient in the government. GS had come to believe early in the occupation that the Home Ministry would have to be radically restructured but finally decided to abolish it and parcel out its functions to other agencies. Some observers have noted that a number of officials of the presurrender Home Ministry were never purged or reentered the government to serve in important positions. They were, of course, relatively young in the earlier period, and the bureaucratic institutions they now work in are very different from the old Naimu-shō. Many of these carryovers proved to be effective and moderate bureaucrats.[11]

Katayama set up the Labor Ministry on September 1, 1947. It included a women's and minors' bureau, which has played a key role in advancing the rights of women and children in postwar Japan. From the start of the occupation Japanese and American women had worked together to advance the cause of women's rights. Their efforts were crowned by inclusion of several provisions in the constitution of 1947. Later legislation provided further protections. There had been considerable support for a separate ministry for women and family matters, and setting up a bureau within the Labor Ministry was the compromise.[12] Equality of the sexes as promised in the 1947 constitution is still a long way off, but opportunities for women in politics, government, business, and education are steadily expanding.

During the short term of the Katayama cabinet, the Diet passed six of the permanent laws to implement the new constitution. The most significant items were the revised civil and criminal codes. The revised civil code, which became effective on July 1, 1948, enshrined into law the concepts of the dignity of the individual and the equality of the sexes. According to the official GS report, it was the Japanese who made the decision to radically alter the old family system, even beyond what the new constitution required. The eagerness of many Japanese legal experts in the early days of the occupation to adopt different ideas, often of Western origin, was one of the surprising aspects of that era. One is tempted to say that the Americans were not the only New Dealers in postwar Japan. The revised criminal code abolished adultery as a crime because the Diet did not want to make it equally punishable for both sexes. Provisions regarding libel and defamation were rewritten. The code protected the rights of defendants and witnesses much as in U.S. practice and circumscribed the authority of judges to conduct trials, which had been all but absolute.[13]

Japan has no trial by jury. Jury trials had been tried experimentally in the prewar period, but the test was considered a failure. The Japanese are not comfortable sitting in judgment on their fellow men and women. Western concepts of right and wrong, legal and illegal, are much tempered in their view by human feelings such as sympathy, regret, or a sense of obligation. The occupation did not try to tamper with these deep-rooted traits.

MacArthur's greeting to Katayama on May 24 spoke of "spiritual implications.... For the first time in its history, Japan is led by a Christian leader.... It reflects the complete religious tolerance which now dominates the Japanese mind and the complete religious freedom which exists throughout this land." Noting that two other Asian Christians were at the head of their governments, Chiang Kai-shek in China and Manuel Roxas in the Philippines, the supreme commander suggested that this "offers hope for the ultimate erection of an invincible spiritual barrier against the infiltration of ideologies which seek by suppression the way to power and advancement. This is human progress."[14]

Washington policy guidance spoke of religious freedom but said nothing about promoting Christianity. The general was nevertheless attentive to opinion back home on religious matters, as several incidents testify. On one occasion in late 1947 he received a letter from a Christian missionary complaining that "our own American government... informed the Japanese Government that Christianity is to be placed on the same plane with their own religion (in other words that it is no better than idolatry) and that it *must not be favored*." MacArthur's office drafted a reply that he believed "that Japan will become Christianized. Every possible effort to that end is being made."[15]

Lieutenant Colonel Donald R. Nugent, whose job as chief of CIE included religion, advised MacArthur that his section was not in fact making "every possible effort" to Christianize Japan, its policy being a maximum of freedom of religious belief. MacArthur said that so long as no religion or belief was oppressed and the legal treatment of all religions was equal, the occupation had every right to propagate Christianity and to give it every assistance. The general added that visiting church dignitaries asserted that the CIE had a "stiff-necked attitude of impartiality and did not show sufficient enthusiasm in the propagation of Christianity." Nugent said he would orient his staff about the point of view of the commander in chief.

MacArthur received a flock of letters a few months later from Christians in the United States criticizing a Japanese textbook containing the assertion that "today we cannot believe in all that is written in the Gospel (the Birth of Christ, the miracles he achieved, and his resurrection)." CIE reprimanded the author and publisher, suspended new printings of the book, and set up checks to prevent recurrence. MacArthur sent a virtually identical reply to all the critical letters describing what had happened and stating in regard to Christianity in Japan that "a whole population is beginning to understand, practice and cherish its under-lying principles and ideals."[16]

Many letters from the United States inquired about the progress of Christianity in Japan. The original CIE draft of a reply to one of these letters stated there were about 200,000 Christians in Japan. Fearing the "old man" would consider this figure too low, a staff officer added a zero before submitting the letter to the general for signature. Although he signed the letter, MacArthur reportedly thought that the figure of 2 million was too low and said later that 4 million might be more accu-rate. MacArthur's intense interest and hope for a Christian revolution began to taper off, however, and after 1949 it was rarely mentioned. The number of Christians in Japan increased by about 10 percent dur-ing the occupation, to a total of about 390,000, or 0.5 percent of the population.[17]

By the beginning of 1948 the divisions in the Socialist Party were steadily widening. Katayama's leadership was under challenge from both the left and right. In January the left wing decided to support a budget-breaking supplemental allowance for public workers. The de-fection of the leftists was largely due to differences over economic policy and dissatisfaction with the "middle-of-the-road" policies of the Katayama cabinet. Soon after, the purge of Hirano Rikizō, the minister of agriculture and one of the party's right-wing leaders, dealt another hard blow to party unity. It was widely known that Kades of GS had been pressing the Japanese to purge Hirano. According to one gossipy account by a Japanese historian, Hirano had committed two sins in the eyes of GS: he had given support to Yoshida in earlier interparty nego-tiations and had maintained good contacts with G-2. Several years later Whitney authorized his judicial expert, Alfred Oppler, to intervene directly with the president of Japan's Supreme Court to deny Hirano's appeal from his purge decision.[18] The breakaway of the Democratic Party group in Katayama's coalition delivered yet another blow. This was formalized on March 15 when former prime minister Shidehara Kijūrō and thirty of his supporters joined Yoshida and the Liberals. The Liberals soon renamed their party the Democratic Liberal Party, although cynics claimed they merited neither adjective.

By early February Katayama had decided to resign. He paid his farewell call on MacArthur on February 9. The general reportedly sug-gested he might go before the Diet and seek reelection, but the prime minister did not take up this suggestion. MacArthur then issued a statement praising Katayama for his "conscientious and patriotic leadership" and commenting that the outgoing cabinet had "been confronted with the serious political, economic, and social dislocations which are a natural consequence of the war and defeat." He added in regard to the selection of the next government that "the occupation will continue to regard the determination of such internal political issues as a responsibility of the representatives of the Japanese people."[19]

MacArthur told Ambassador Gascoigne on February 10 that "imbued as Katayama was with the highest ideals, he had been the victim of his own inherent modesty and patriotism." Katayama "had repudiated the policy of his own party to serve the interests of the nation" and "had endeavored to make the four-party coalition a reality but had failed owing to Yoshida's obstructive and selfish tactics."[20]

On February 10, 1948, Katayama called on the emperor and submitted his resignation. Two questions then arose: whether the emperor, whose sole constitutional function in such situations was to attest the documents involved, should have received the prime minister's resignation and whether Katayama had acted in accordance with the constitution, which provided clearly that the house could be dissolved only at the end of its four-year term or when a no-confidence resolution had been passed.[21] These issues became a subject for heated debate in the press and in political circles.

Yoshida had been working hard since he left office to build up his party and strengthen his own leadership. In the ten months he had been out of office, he had traveled around the country learning to be a politician and building political support. The enticement of the Shidehara faction away from the Democrats had been a major coup, encouraging Yoshida in his belief that two major parties might emerge in Japan— one conservative and the other left of center. In this way, he thought, Japan could develop a government strong enough to implement policy and avoid having constantly to placate warring political factions.[22]

The Socialist Party had failed to lead the nation, much as the conservatives had failed nine months before. It had done the nation a service by trying to provide left-of-center leadership, giving labor and left-wing forces an opportunity for a practical test of their policies. But after this one experience, the Japanese people were reluctant to give the party another chance.

In his memoirs published in 1969, Katayama recounted an event that has never been satisfactorily explained. In a private meeting before the prime minister resigned, MacArthur made a "statement on the rearmament of Japan." Katayama said that because he was personally opposed to rearmament and strongly in support of the no-war clause in the constitution, he did not feel he could respond in any favorable way to the general's suggestion. Nishio Suehiro, Katayama's top strategist, and Sone Eki, his diplomatic adviser and often his interpreter, stated they had no information about any such meeting with MacArthur or about advice from U.S. headquarters that Japan should "consider" rearmament.[23] Certainly MacArthur opposed Japan's rearmament at that time. It was not until 1950, when the Korean War broke out, that the general entertained any argument from his own government that Japan should increase its defense strength. Nevertheless, by early 1948 Washington was rethinking Japan's role, and Tokyo was soon to feel the pressure.

The resignation of Katayama violently shook the uneasy political equilibrium within the Socialist-Democratic coalition. Yoshida Shigeru, abiding by classic parliamentary principles, argued that there should be a new general election of if not, that the leading opposition party—his Liberals—should form a cabinet. GS did not welcome the prospect of another Yoshida cabinet, however. The British ambassador quoted Colonel Bunker, MacArthur's aide, as saying that GS would do everything "to make it as difficult as possible for Yoshida to return to power."[24]

In this fluid situation Ashida Hitoshi was able to build on the same three-party coalition—Democrats, Socialists, and People's Cooperatives—that had elected Katayama. On March 10, 1948, one month after Katayama left office, Ashida became prime minister. It took him two weeks to form his cabinet, which included two left Socialists. He had fought off Yoshida's challenge, but the old diplomat had made a good scrap of it. Some of Yoshida's supporters wanted him to join the coalition, but he fended them off. He was confident that another election was coming up and that his party would win.

General MacArthur did not endorse Ashida, as he had Yoshida and Katayama. A GS spokesman did state on February 24 that the election of Ashida had been "thoroughly democratic" and then rather incautiously suggested that perhaps the Diet should clarify the "true position of the Emperor" as a ceremonial symbol of the state without political power. This comment brought the emperor's interpreter, Terasaki Hidenari, running to Bunker to ask what SCAP had in mind. It was not clear whether the emperor was concerned, or only his protective servitors. MacArthur told Bunker not to get into the matter and that "no criticism of the Emperor" had been intended.[25] Some concern remained, however, that Katayama, by presenting his resignation to the emperor, may have conferred on the Tennō a degree of political power not sanctioned by the constitution.

With SCAP blessing, Ashida was safely ensconced in high office. The new prime minister had some assets for the job. A handsome and well-educated man, his diplomatic and legal background added breadth and sophistication to his political talents. He was more urbane and polished than Yoshida, and his command of English was stronger. From 1933 to 1940 Ashida had served as president of the *Japan Times & Mail*, an official organ of the Japanese Foreign Office and the voice of Japan for the English-speaking community. After the war it was renamed the *Nippon Times* and then the *Japan Times*. A GS memorandum of 1947 asserted that the editorial policy of the paper had "consistently and enthusiastically supported the government's program of naked aggression and ruthless exploitation in Asia." Nevertheless, Ashida had been able to escape being purged, mainly because the Japanese media subcommittee set up to examine purge cases felt that the *Japan Times & Mail* had only insignificant influence on popular attitudes because it was published in English.[26]

Ashida, however, was something of a trimmer more eager to win influence than to advance good causes. Nor did he succeed in establishing good relations with MacArthur, who considered him "slippery" despite his skill in organizing his cabinet.[27] The supreme commander's harsh judgment was somewhat surprising because Ashida tried mightily to curry favor with senior SCAP officials. The new prime minister got Whitney to write him a letter on April 3, 1948, asserting there was no basis for a new election at that time and supporting steps to increase attendance at Diet sessions.[28]

Ashida's first months in office seemed promising. He was active and successful on several fronts. He met with Under Secretary of the Army William H. Draper, who had obtained a large congressional appropriation in early 1948 for assistance to Japan as well as a loan of $600 million to enable Japan to buy U.S. cotton. Cotton textiles had been Japan's prime prewar import-earning industry and served as the flagship of its postwar industrial revival. Ashida pushed the ESB draft of a five-year economic development plan. His grip seemed strong.

Ashida's running start at the helm of government was greeted in the summer of 1948 by a potent letter from MacArthur calling for restrictions on the bargaining rights of government employees. The government had 2.5 million employees, about 1 million of whom were in government enterprises like the railway. Government workers were the most highly organized in Japan, making up about 40 percent of all union members and the most active group in politics.[29]

The bureaucracy had received no special attention during the first two years of the occupation, unlike the other pillars of the old order in Japan—the military, politicians, and big business. An effort was soon made to remedy this oversight. A U.S. civil service mission headed by Blaine Hoover, the president of the Civil Service Assembly of the United States and Canada, arrived in Japan in late 1946 to survey the situation. His solutions were 100 percent American. His June 16, 1947, report to MacArthur made two key proposals: establish a powerful central personnel agency and pass laws that (1) would give civil servants the right to organize but not to bargain collectively or to strike and (2) would empower government enterprise workers to organize and bargain collectively but not to strike. Government employees other than those in enterprise operations were already prohibited from striking by the Labor Relations Adjustment Law of 1946, although this provision was not strictly enforced.

When Prime Minister Katayama and his senior advisers learned of the Hoover recommendations on June 1, 1947, they felt consternation. These proposals would all but destroy the bargaining powers of the government workers, who were a powerful force in the Socialist movement. Yet there was little they could do about Hoover's recommendations. The drafting of a new bill went ahead, and much of the Hoover plan was embodied in a revision of the National Public Service Law (NPSL) passed by the Diet on October 21 while Hoover was in the United States. But the revision omitted the plan's key provision prohibiting strikes and collective bargaining by government workers, both civil servants and those in government enterprises, a compromise that SCAP sections were willing to accept, perhaps because they did not agree with Hoover's tough position. Hoover was incensed when he got back in November and set about to repair the damage.

By the early summer of 1948 new labor troubles were boiling. The settlement of the strike threat of early 1947 had left government workers dissatisfied with the wage increase they had received. The average pay of government workers was ¥2,900 a month (about $12), whereas pay in the private sector was about ¥5,087 (about $20). Work stoppages, slowdowns, refusals to work overtime, and similar tactics became frequent. As early as March 29 General Marquat had issued a memorandum banning a threatened strike by communications workers and citing MacArthur's general strike ban of January 31, 1947, as his authority.

With Whitney's support, Hoover argued that all government workers had a responsibility to the public to refrain from strikes and coercive collective bargaining, with any disputes to be settled by the national personnel authority. James Killen, the labor expert in ESS, argued that workers in government enterprises should have the right to bargain collectively but not to strike. It is noteworthy that the Japanese constitution of 1947 provided in Article 28 that "the right of workers to organize and to bargain and act collectively is guaranteed."

The two sides put the issue up to the supreme commander. In a unique resort to staff action, MacArthur held an all-day meeting with a half dozen senior staff officials on July 21, 1948. He listened carefully as Hoover and Killen presented their cases and asked many questions. Kades had dug up a quotation from Franklin D. Roosevelt that made an impression on MacArthur: "A strike of public employees . . . looking toward the paralysis of government by those who have sworn to support it, is unthinkable."[30]

At the end of the meeting MacArthur said he reserved his decision. The next day he sent Prime Minister Ashida a letter clearly embodying the view of Hoover and GS: "The paramountcy of the public interest is . . . of foremost consideration and corollary thereto is the need that safeguards be erected to ensure that the lawful authority of the government as the political instrument to enforce the people's will as expressed in the body of public law be only challengeable at the polls as provided under well-established democratic practice."[31]

The letter then proposed some major bureaucratic surgery: remove the bulk of the government enterprise workers, who were employees of the railways and of the salt, camphor, and tobacco monopolies, from the civil service and place them in public corporations under mediation and arbitration procedures and split the Ministry of Posts and Communications into two ministries to handle postal services and other communications functions. MacArthur's decision was thus a compromise. Public workers would not have the right to strike or bargain collectively, but public enterprise workers would have the right to collective bargaining without the right to strike.

Prime Minister Ashida moved immediately to carry out MacArthur's instructions. A cabinet ordinance issued on July 31 put them into operation pending legislation by the Diet. This was the famous cabinet order 201, which Japanese liberals interpreted as another move to the right by the United States and the supreme commander.[32]

The MacArthur letter of July 22 set off small bombs in many bastions—within SCAP, in the Japanese government, in Washington, and on the international diplomatic front. On July 30 Killen resigned as head of the ESS labor division after issuing a press statement that the proposed revisions of the NPSL were "ill-advised and will retard a healthy labor movement." Killen told the political adviser on August 9 that the Communists would make big gains as a result of MacArthur's action, but he put more of the blame for what had happened on Whitney and Hoover. The political adviser reported that on July 30 "the general appeared a bit worried about his letter to Ashida." MacArthur said he had "a great deal of factual material prepared" if the Soviets questioned his action. They soon did.[33]

The SCAP letter became an international issue when the Soviet Union challenged it in both the ACJ and the FEC. A key Soviet argument was that the FEC had authorized political activities by labor unions, whether government employees or not. This objection was heard with some sympathy by representatives of the Commonwealth nations, but the United States was firmly opposed. The Soviet objections won no converts.

The Australian and British governments believed that government workers should be entitled to some form of collective bargaining or arbitration. A majority in the FEC seemed to support an Australian proposal that in effect could have given the strike right to government enterprise workers, but Australia did not press for a vote in the face of adamant U.S. opposition. The Commonwealth attitude enraged MacArthur. When he met with the British ambassador in Tokyo, "for the better part of an hour the general was in such an uncontrollable temper that it was almost impossible to reason with him." When told of the concern of Foreign Secretary Ernest Bevin, a powerful leader of the British Labour Party, that the legislation proposed by the Japanese should provide for collective bargaining including arbitration, MacArthur complained bitterly that "in the most enlightened democracy in the world, the United Kingdom, it was not realized you could not give the same rights as were enjoyed in Britain to a backward, feudalistic nation such as Japan."[34]

MacArthur encountered his most serious opposition in the Army and State departments in Washington, which recommended greater flexibility in the treatment of public enterprise workers.[35] This was the nub of the issue: should government workers be entitled to some kind of collective bargaining in labor disputes? MacArthur and Whitney said no. Both Ashida and Yoshida were on their side.

In concert with SCAP, the Japanese government worked out and later in 1948 enacted the Public Corporations and National Enterprises Labor Relations Law. It set up five government enterprises, including the alcohol monopoly, and two government corporations, or kōsha, including the national railways and the tobacco and salt corporations. In 1950, when the Post and Communications Ministry was divided into two ministries—postal services and telecommunications—the Nippon Telephone and Telegraph Corporation was created as a third major public corporation. The employees of the five government enterprises and three public corporations did not have the right to strike under the new law but did have the rights to organize and bargain collectively. MacArthur hailed the amended NPSL as "a major victory for those who seek integrity of government over those who would leave the government prey to minority subjugation."[36] Yoshida and his Democratic Liberal Party passed all of the legislation flowing from the MacArthur letter soon after they returned to power in October 1948.

SCAP was not yet through with government workers. Having ensured that government employees were deprived of the right to strike and bargain collectively, Blaine Hoover embarked on one of the more bizarre operations of the occupation. He planned a series of examinations to determine whether those holding or applying for senior positions in the civil service had the necessary qualifications. The uneasy Japanese tried to get the exams postponed, but General Whitney said no: "In Allied countries there has been criticism of the Japanese higher bureaucracy for the role they played in the planning and the preparing and in the leadership of the war."[37]

The tests, held in mid-January 1950, put 2,649 positions on the line. Virtually every incumbent applied, along with about 5,000 outside aspirants. The exams were to probe knowledge, technical information, and adaptability for work in the civil service. The imaginative Japanese cooked up the term *paradise examinations* to describe the relaxed conditions under which the tests were to be given: the examinees could smoke, drink tea, and eat their lunch, and no time limit was imposed. A total of 7,432 persons took the exams. A SCAP report stated that 25 percent of the tested officials lost their jobs; another source put the failure rate at 30 percent; other sources put it much lower. Many who took the tests thought them reasonable and fair. The tests were never given again.[38]

Although SCAP is often criticized for doing little to reform Japan's bureaucracy, it did in fact carve up government personnel and agencies rather considerably. Of government employees, 1,809 were formally purged. Many thousands more were either fired or forced to resign, most of them in the opening months of the occupation: 4,800, nearly all police officials, were fired from the Home Ministry in October 1945 as a result of the bill of rights directive; 115,778 teachers resigned under pressure from the Education Ministry, and 5,211 more were in effect purged; Yoshida fired 7,500 nationalists in the Foreign Office. Of the twelve cabinet-level ministries in existence at the end of the war, the Japanese abolished three—the Army and Navy ministries and the Ministry of Greater East Asia. The cabinet quickly converted another, the Munitions Ministry, into the Ministry of Commerce and Industry, which became the Ministry of International Trade and Industry in 1949. With SCAP approval the Home Ministry was abolished in 1947, and its functions were parceled out to other agencies; and the Justice Ministry was reorganized. Several new ministries were set up during the occupation, such as the Labor Ministry, the Ministry of Welfare, the Ministry of Postal Services and Communications, and the Ministry of Transportation. All criticisms to the contrary, the bureaucracy was extensively pruned, and the structure of many ministries was significantly revised.[39]

In the summer of 1948, when the national public service issue was being debated and the new legislation enacted, one of the biggest political scandals in modern Japanese history was welling up and engulfing many prominent victims. The Shōwa Denkō (Shōwa Electric) Company, Japan's largest manufacturer of fertilizer, had obtained huge loans from the Reconstruction Finance Bank (RFB), a government financial institution set up in 1946 with occupation blessing to help finance development projects. The RFB had got the reputation of lending money without adequately checking the reliability and creditworthiness of recipients. Public prosecutors began an investigation of RFB's connections with Shōwa Denkō in May 1948, seized company documents, and in June arrested its president on charges of having bribed government officials. Among those arrested were a former finance minister in the Katayama cabinet and a senior Finance Ministry official, Fukuda Takeo, who was later acquitted and in 1976 became prime minister of Japan.

Next the deputy prime minister, Nishio Suehiro, was arrested on a charge of having received a bribe of ¥1 million (about $3,300). The day after, October 7, the cabinet decided to resign. On December 7 Ashida himself was arrested. All told, sixty-four persons were arrested and charged with having received some ¥6 million (about $20,000) in bribes.[40]

It was rumored that an even larger amount had been used to influence foreigners, meaning members of the occupation. That officers in GS were a favorite target of the rumormongers was ironic because only a few months earlier Kades had induced the government to make a thorough, but eventually fruitless, investigation of the "hoarded goods scandal," which involved possibly as much as $2 billion worth of military supplies and equipment illegally diposed of at the end of the war.[41]

In 1958 Ashida and Nishio were finally acquitted after ten years of trials, an example of the excessively protracted judicial proceedings that are so frequent in Japan. In the end, of the sixty-four persons arrested, only two were convicted and sentenced to prison terms. Almost none of the money allegedly used for bribes was ever traced or even accounted for.

Documentary evidence does not indicate that the Shōden (as Shōwa Denkō was known) case was of much concern to SCAP or that its officials were involved.[42] What is clear is that Shōden was the coup de grace for coalition government. Thereafter, the power of the Democratic Liberal Party and its leaders grew steadily, buoyed by a huge wave of popularity for Yoshida Shigeru.

CHAPTER 13

The End of the War Crimes Trials

The Emperor Decides Not to Abdicate

A few weeks after the fall of the Ashida cabinet, the trial of Japan's major war crimes suspects, which had gone on for two and one-half years, came to an end—more on a note of relief that it was over than with any feeling that justice had been done. Probably no one welcomed the end more than General MacArthur, who always sought quick and neat solutions to his management problems and abhorred the bureaucratic morass the trial had bogged down in.

On November 12, 1948, seven of the twenty-five defendants in the Tokyo trial, as it was commonly known, were sentenced to death: General Tōjō Hideki (a former prime minister), five other generals, and former prime minister Hirota Kōki, a civilian. Sixteen defendants, five of them civilians, were given life imprisonment. Of the remaining two, former foreign minister Shigemitsu Mamoru was given seven years in prison and General Umezu Yoshijirō received a sentence of twenty years. None of the defendants in the Tokyo trial was acquitted.[1]

The International Military Tribunal for the Far East had held 818 sessions, 419 witnesses had testified in court, 779 witnesses had given written evidence, and 4,336 exhibits had been admitted in evidence. The transcript of the proceedings covered 48,412 pages. It took eleven judges nearly seven months of deliberation to arrive at their judgments. There were three dissenting opinions, one—by Radhabinod Pal of India—a sweeping disagreement with the majority judgment.[2] (The Nuremberg trial of twenty-two Nazi leaders and generals had taken less than eleven months. Twelve defendants were sentenced to death, and three were acquitted, including financier Hjalmar Schacht.)[3]

MacArthur was empowered to review the Tokyo sentences. He decided to consult with the representatives in Tokyo of the FEC nations, most of whom recommended no change in the sentences. On November 24 he ordered the sentences to be executed as pronounced by the tribunal. In his reviewing statement, which he wrote himself, the general declared he could "conceive of no judicial process where greater safeguard was made to evolve justice." He called the trial "a symbol to summon all persons of good will to a realization of the utter futility of war . . . and eventually to its renunciation by all nations."[4]

MacArthur wrote in his *Reminiscences* that after Washington rejected his recommendation in 1945 that only those political leaders responsible for the attack on Pearl Harbor without a declaration of war be tried, he "was then relieved of all responsibility having to do with the actual trial procedures" in the Class A cases. Yet the general did play a significant, usually behind-the-scenes, role. This case was, after all, the longest and most complicated war crimes trial in history, engaging the full-time effort of several hundred persons (judges, prosecutors, defense attorneys, interpreters and translators, guards, and supporting staffs), not to mention the defendants and the additional Class A suspects who were kept in custody but never brought to trial.[5]

The handling of General Tōjō illustrated how carefully MacArthur monitored the trial. Tōjō was not only the best known of the defendants, often ranking in world opinion with archvillains Hitler and Mussolini; Tōjō was by common agreement the crucial witness in the prosecution's effort to prove that Japan had committed aggression in 1941. He was a sharp and articulate witness, deserving his nickname, "Razor." Taking the stand in late December 1947, Tōjō offered a lengthy and almost defiant defense of all he had done before and during the war: "I believe firmly and will contend to the last that it was a war of self-defense and in no manner a violation of presently acknowledged international law."[6]

Extensive cross-examination by Keenan did not shake Tōjō. He also defended the emperor, as Kido had done, against charges of responsibility for Japan's aggressive actions. Keenan was helpful in this endeavor. A few days after Tōjō said that no Japanese subject "would go against the will of His Majesty," Keenan took considerable pains to have Tōjō clearly state that the cabinet and the military high command decided on the war and that "the Emperor consented, though reluctantly."[7]

Japan's failure to declare war before the attack on Pearl Harbor, Tōjō asserted, was the fault of the Foreign Office and his fellow defendant Tōgō Shigenori, the foreign minister at the time. The Japanese note breaking off diplomatic relations was to be delivered to the United States about twenty minutes before the attack began, but the text was so long that the understaffed Japanese Embassy in Washington was not able to decode, translate, and type it by the deadline. It was delivered to the State Department at 2 P.M., December 7, 1941, one hour after the attack on Pearl Harbor had begun.[8]

The British ambassador asked General MacArthur on January 24, 1948, if he thought Tōjō's statements had made a lasting impression. MacArthur responded that he was "extremely concerned" at the way the prosecution had handled Tōjō and that he had arranged with Keenan that there would be no cross-examination of Tōjō, who was to be told to "stand down" after his lengthy affidavit had been read to the tribunal. But Keenan had persisted in questioning Tōjō, with unfortunate results. MacArthur worried that Tōjō's defense might have a "profound effect" on the Japanese.[9]

Keenan was not a skilled prosecutor. He did a poor job on direct examination of Henry Pu Yi, the "last emperor of China," a witness for the prosecution. As the Tōjō interrogation showed, Keenan also lacked the hallmark of a good trial lawyer—skill at cross-examination. He did not get on well with the president of the tribunal, Sir William Webb, an autocratic and acerbic man. Keenan had a drinking problem: Arthur Comyns-Carr, the chief British prosecutor, a highly able barrister who was later knighted, commented that Keenan was "incapable of distinguishing black and white even when they were in the same bottle."[10]

The trial was plagued by a number of administrative hitches in which MacArthur became involved. The first U.S. judge to be appointed to the tribunal, Chief Justice John P. Higgins of the Superior Court of Massachusetts, resigned when he realized the trial would go on far longer than he had expected, and the judge advocate general of the United States, Major General Myron C. Cramer, had to be drafted as a replacement one month after the trial had begun. In late 1947 when Sir William Webb was called back to Australia to sit on the high court there for a month, MacArthur tried to order the British judge, Lord Justice William D. Patrick, KC, judge of the High Court of Edinburgh, to fill in, but Lord Patrick declined for health reasons. MacArthur then ordered Cramer to fill in while Webb was absent. In the summer of 1948

MacArthur received advance information of the dissenting views held by three of the judges.[11]

The judgment, which took 1,218 pages, relied heavily on the opinion of the Nuremberg tribunal in reaching a number of significant conclusions:

1. The IMTFE Charter, like the Nuremberg Charter, was declaratory of existing international law and was not ex post facto legislation.

2. The Kellogg-Briand Pact of 1928 made aggressive war illegal, and by implication aggressive war is a form of murder and therefore criminal. Waging and conspiring to wage aggressive war are crimes for which individuals can be punished.

3. A defendant nation can not plead self-defense without reasonable grounds. Prewar Japan had been the object of economic sanctions but not of hostile military action or threats.

4. An order by a superior does not free an individual from responsibility where "moral choice was in fact possible."

5. Japan's plans for aggression were not the work of one man but "the work of many leaders acting in pursuance of a common plan for the achievement of a common object," which was a criminal conspiracy to wage a war of aggression.[12]

In an exhaustive review of Japan's diplomatic and military actions from 1928 to 1941, the tribunal wrote a virtual history of the period as seen by the Allied powers. It devoted more than one hundred pages to a description of conventional war crimes and atrocities committed during the Pacific War. No mention was made of the atomic bombs dropped on Hiroshima and Nagasaki; the tribunal had rejected a defense attempt to raise this issue.

Eight judges found all of the defendants guilty of some of the fifty-five offenses charged. Two of them wrote separate concurring opinions. Three judges dissented in whole or in part. President Webb brought up the matter of the emperor, saying, "If he did not want war he should have withheld his authority. . . . Even a constitutional monarch would not be excused for committing a crime at international law on the advice of his ministers." MacArthur commented later that Webb was playing "cheap politics" addressed to the people in Australia.[13] Judge B. V. A. Röling of the Netherlands dissented on the ground that defendants found guilty only of crimes against peace should not have received the death sentence, following the precedent at Nuremberg. Judge Pal's dissent was book length: aggressive war was not a crime in international law; rules of evidence were unfairly applied against the defense; it had not been proved that any of the defendants were guilty of conventional war crimes; therefore, all of the defendants were innocent on all counts. Curiously, none of the separate opinions was printed at the time the judgment was made public, but they were published later and widely read in Japan.[14]

Seven defendants filed motions with the U.S. Supreme Court, which heard arguments and decided on December 20 that because MacArthur had acted as the agent of the Allied powers, the Court had no power or authority to review the judgments. MacArthur cited the Court's decision as "striking confirmation" of his international authority as supreme commander for the Allied powers.[15]

Early in the morning of December 23, the seven death sentences were carried out at Sugamo Prison in Tokyo.[16] The condemned men wore cast-off U.S. Army clothing without insignia. A Buddhist priest ministered to them. Before mounting the scaffold, they shouted three times as a group, *Tennō heika banzai* (Long live the emperor), in the traditional Japanese manner. The four members of the ACJ attended as witnesses. No photographs were taken, MacArthur having rejected a plea by Secretary of the Army Royall that Allied photographers be admitted to take pictures, as had been done at Nuremberg.[17] Several prisoners gave the priest poems they had composed. That of Tōjō Hideki read in translation:

> Farewell to all,
> For today I cross the earthly mountains
> And gladly go
> To the folds of Buddha.

The bodies of the men were cremated and the ashes scattered over Tokyo Bay from an airplane. Occupation authorities wanted to prevent their interment in a grave that might become a memorial to the former leaders. A Japanese source claims that some of the ashes were preserved at the crematorium and buried in a mountain area near the city of Nagoya in 1960. Yoshida Shigeru, well known for his calligraphy, reportedly wrote an inscription on the tombstone: *Shichishi no haka* (the grave of seven brave men). In 1978 fourteen of the twenty-five convicted Class A war criminals were enshrined at Yasukuni Shrine, Japan's memorial in Tokyo for military men who died in war.[18]

Japan committed itself in the peace treaty signed in 1951 to carry out all the war crimes sentences imposed by the Allied powers on defendants in Japan. One of the convicted war criminals, Shigemitsu Mamoru, was released in November 1950 and became foreign minister in 1954. In 1958 the ten surviving defendants, who had already been paroled, were released unconditionally. All of these releases were approved by the Allied powers.

On December 24, 1948, nineteen Class A war crimes suspects—six others had died or been released earlier—were released from prison or house arrest after nearly three years of detention. SCAP lawyers concluded on the basis of the IMTFE judgment that it was unlikely any of them could be convicted in a second trial of Class A suspects. Two were later charged with conventional war crimes. Among those released were Kishi Nobusuke, a skillful bureaucrat who was minister of commerce and industry in the Tōjō cabinet at the time of Pearl Harbor and became prime minister in 1957, and two accomplished behind-the-scenes operators who had been active rightist agitators and later made a lot of money in dubious activities: Kodama Yoshio and Sasakawa Ryōichi.[19]

More than 5,000 Japanese were tried by national tribunals set up by the various Allied powers for Class B and Class C war crimes (violations of the laws and customs of war, such as maltreatment of prisoners of war, and crimes against humanity, such as brutal treatment of civilian populations). These figures do not include trials by the Soviet Union or the People's Republic of China (PRC), which did not release complete data on their trials.

As a result of these trials, 920 Japanese were executed, 475 were given life imprisonment, 2,944 received terms of less than life, and 1,018 were acquitted. The United States tried 1,344 Japanese, resulting in 140 executions, 145 life sentences, 877 sentences of terms less than life, and 182 acquittals.[20] The Bataan death march, the beheading of American pilots, and the Kyushu University vivisection murder of eight American fliers were among the more notorious atrocities perpetrated against American fighting men by the Japanese who were tried by U.S. military courts.

The ROC executed 148 Japanese war criminals and sentenced 310 to terms in prison. In February 1949 Prime Minister Yoshida asked General MacArthur to seek ROC approval to bring to Japan 260 convicted war criminals serving in Chinese prisons to keep them from the hands of the communist armies then sweeping southward on the mainland. MacArthur and the ROC agreed, and the prisoners were repatriated.[21]

The Soviet Union and the People's Republic of China conducted war crimes trials of Japanese independently of the authority of SCAP. Japanese sources assert that in 1956 the PRC sentenced 45 Japanese to prison terms of up to twenty years for war crimes. Information about Soviet treatment of Japanese prisoners of war came mostly from interrogation of Japanese repatriates from Siberia. Some 3,000 prisoners were punished not for war crimes but for violations of Soviet law and for "procapitalist conduct."[22]

Some time after the war ended, the Soviets came upon gruesome reports made by Japanese about germ warfare operations by the former Kwantung Army near the city of Harbin in Manchuria. The commanders of the Kwantung Army, who often operated independently of the high command in Tokyo, had reportedly set up a unit after the Manchurian incident in 1931 to experiment with ways of spreading bubonic plague over the farmlands of Manchuria or infecting Chinese and other victims with a wide variety of contagious diseases. These activities continued up to the end of World War II, resulting in a considerable number of deaths—estimates vary from several hundred to several thousand—but without any marked success in inducing bubonic plague. Army leaders in Tokyo almost certainly knew what was going on in Manchuria, but no official Japanese records were found.

U.S. military intelligence had got wind of these operations from its own prisoner interrogations well before the war ended. General MacArthur's initials appear on one such intelligence report made in early 1945. The general in charge of Japanese germ warfare operations in Manchuria at the end of the war, Lieutenant General Ishii Shirō, who had three to four thousand troops under him in Unit 731, was interrogated by American intelligence experts in Tokyo early in 1946.

Late in June SCAP sent a report to Washington summarizing in detail its information on Japanese germ warfare activities and giving the opinion of Chief Prosecutor Keenan's staff that the Japanese had in fact violated the rules of land warfare. The message cautioned that this opinion was not a recommendation that the Japanese be tried for war crimes because the prosecution had closed its case against the major war crimes suspects. It had not presented any evidence on bacteriological warfare. "It could not assure the tribunal under its rulings that the accused or some of them would be shown to have been associated with acts of the biological warfare group." Strangely, an American assistant prosecutor read a brief report into the IMTFE record about Japanese use of "poisonous serums" on civilian captives in occupied China but

under questioning advised the tribunal that further evidence would not
be presented.[23]

In 1947 the Soviets asked the U.S. government for permission to conduct interrogations in Japan about bacteriological warfare. Washington
agreed after checking with headquarters in Tokyo. Soviet officers came
to Japan in 1947 and interrogated Ishii and other suspects. U.S. intelligence experts had become friendly with Ishii and his family by that
time, and they sought to focus Soviet interest on "theoretical data"
rather than on what the Japanese had actually been doing. Official
SCAP reports reflected a keen interest in the intelligence value of Ishii's
research and expressed the view that "documentary immunity from
'war crimes' given to higher echelon personnel" of the Ishii group
would be useful to U.S. intelligence efforts, but the JCS and SWNCC
did not approve this proposal by MacArthur's headquarters.[24]

The Soviets moved slowly in exploiting the germ warfare opportunity. It was not until December 1949 that they opened a trial in Moscow
of twelve Japanese prisoners of war charged with "manufacturing and
employing bacteriological weapons," a crime under Soviet domestic
law. The indictment further charged the Japanese with "acting upon
secret instructions from Emperor Hirohito" and Imperial Army leaders.
After an elaborate and highly publicized trial lasting five days, the
Japanese all pleaded guilty and were given sentences ranging from two
to twenty-five years.[25]

The Soviet Union then sent a diplomatic note to the United States
and other Allied nations on February 1, 1950, proposing that a special
tribunal be established, as was permissible under FEC policy, to try the
emperor and four generals including Ishii for serious crimes against
humanity. The United States first planned to reply that it was too late to
begin a new war crimes trial, but on learning that Australia had only
one month earlier requested the arrest of fifty-seven war crimes suspects, it decided to treat the Soviet demarche as a propaganda ploy.
MacArthur agreed, on the ground that a Soviet trial "would obviously
be based on political and propaganda motives rather than considera-
tions of justice." On February 3, 1950, the State Department issued a
press release stating that because the USSR did not make a proposal
directly to the FEC, as would have been the normal procedure, its action in making "these belated charges in a sensational manner raises
obvious questions about the real motive behind the Soviet note."[26]

Although Washington refused to approve any deal with Ishii or his
subordinates, it was evident that SCAP officials and the International

Prosecution Section were willing to help the Japanese avoid war crimes charges in return for what the technical experts thought was useful information on bacteriological warfare. No evidence was produced that the emperor knew about germ warfare activities by his forces. Some Japanese were punished as a result of the Soviet trial, but the ringleaders in Japan got off scot-free. Both the United States and the USSR considered cold war politics more important than impartial justice.

In recent years a committee of the U.S. Congress heard testimony that U.S. prisoners of war in Manchuria were maltreated by the Japanese and subjected to bacteriological tests, resulting in a number of deaths. A Japanese official reportedly admitted in 1982 that more than 3,000 Allied prisoners of war and Chinese civilians were used in biological and medical experiments. The finger of responsibility for the failure of the United States to punish the Japanese engaged in these activities points to senior intelligence officers and even to General MacArthur.[27]

Japanese wartime germ warfare operations in Manchuria attracted heavy publicity in Japan long after the war: a best-selling book and many articles and TV shows were devoted to this subject. American media also gave the story some attention and in some cases were highly critical of the protection of Ishii and of the U.S. government's apparent willingness to condone biological warfare.[28]

In 1989 a book published in the United Kingdom charged that there appears to have been "a prolonged international conspiracy by a number of nations to conceal the crimes of Unit 731." General MacArthur is reported to have been well informed by U.S. medical experts about the Japanese activities in Manchuria and to have told an American officer to "promise as coming from General MacArthur that no one involved in [biological warfare] will be punished as a war criminal." The evidence for MacArthur's involvement all comes from this one officer, now deceased, and no other evidence has been adduced that MacArthur ever saw this officer or had any connection with his activities.[29]

It was long after the occupation before Japanese were able to write and speak freely about the war crimes trials. But once they overcame their reluctance to look dispassionately at the war years, a steady stream of critical comment poured forth. The dissenting opinions of judges Pal and Röling received widespread favorable attention.[30]

Many Japanese believe that the Tokyo trial was unfair. They feel that civilians were punished for crimes committed by military leaders, that tribunal rulings unduly restricted the defense, and that Tribunal President Webb was prejudiced against the defendants. Legal experts claim that the charge of conspiracy was a peculiar concept in Anglo-American law that had no general legal recognition and that it was in any case impossible to find a conspiracy in prewar Japan, where there had been fifteen different cabinets in fifteen years.[31] In Japan and elsewhere a number of critics claimed that the trial was based on legal principles created after the fact. Others claimed that the Class B and C trials were hasty and ill-prepared, were directed against minor subordinates rather than responsible officers, and resulted in an excessive number of death penalties.

General MacArthur wrote in his *Reminiscences* that he "was pleasantly surprised at the attitude of the Japanese people," who "seemed to be impressed both by the fairness of the procedures and by the lack of vindictiveness on the part of the prosecutors." Kawai Kazuo, a man who knew both the United States and Japan well, described the Japanese reaction as a manifestation of a prominent cultural trait—"situational ethics"—which held in this case that war crimes may have been wrong but seemed unavoidable in the circumstances of a desperate war. The punishment may have been tragic, but it was also unavoidable and therefore appropriate under the circumstances. Because atrocities and punishment were both preordained, it was futile for the victors to claim that punishment represented abstract justice and for the losers to try to justify their past acts.[32]

The execution of Hirota Kōki has ranked in Japanese eyes with that of General Yamashita as the most extreme and dubious of the war crimes punishments of major figures. Hirota was a close friend and contemporary of Yoshida. Their careers in the Foreign Office were parallel, although Hirota worked harder and rose more rapidly, becoming prime minister in 1936. Two events particularly damaged his career. Japan entered the Anti-Comintern Pact with Germany soon after he became prime minister in 1936. In 1937 when he was foreign minister under Konoe, Japan invaded China and savagely attacked the city of Nanjing. A best-seller written about Hirota painted him as a patient and flexible moderate who was overwhelmed by sinister forces, in contrast to his easygoing and opportunistic friend Yoshida. The book recounted how Yoshida, unable to see MacArthur to appeal for clemency on behalf of Hirota in late 1948, instead saw Whitney, only to be "reproved for conduct unbecoming a prime minister."[33]

While the Tokyo tribunal was mulling over its judgment, rumors began to circulate that the emperor might abdicate. The British ambassador tried to find out whether there was any truth to them. A senior official of the imperial household, Matsudaira Yasumasa, reported that the emperor was depressed, "was showing sympathetic interest in Christianity, and would no doubt be relieved to surrender his position as Emperor." Matsudaira said that many former military officers had come to feel that the emperor had let them down badly and "had become virtually a puppet of the United States."[34]

The Canadian representative then took up the matter. On June 16 he called on MacArthur, who asserted, with characteristic emphasis, that there was not a "scintilla of truth in these reports." The general added that "he would not allow the Emperor to abdicate but would require him to stay on as a matter of duty." MacArthur professed to see a plot by American business circles, which wanted "a return to pre-war Japan with the zaibatsu and an autocratic court running a docile country."[35]

On October 8, 1948, Ashida—who had resigned as prime minister two days before—told political adviser Sebald that he had come to feel, after a recent talk with the emperor, that "pressure for abdication may become great" when the verdicts in the war crimes trial were announced. Sebald confided to his diary that day that the emperor might "either abdicate or commit suicide." On October 28 Sebald mentioned his musings to MacArthur, who agreed that the emperor's abdication or suicide would be "politically disastrous."[36]

MacArthur then took the initiative. He saw Yoshida several times in early November and may well have told him to assure the emperor there was no need for him to abdicate, whatever the Tokyo tribunal decided or said. On November 12, the day the sentences were pronounced, the chief official of the imperial household, Tajima Michiji, sent a letter to the supreme commander on behalf of the emperor:

> I am most grateful for the kind and considerate message Your Excellency was good enough to send me by Prime Minister Yoshida the other day. It is my lifelong desire to serve the cause of world peace as well as to promote the welfare and happiness of my people. I am determined now more than ever to do my best in concert with the people to surmount all difficulties and speed the national reconstruction of Japan.

This message was not made public until 1978. At an informal press conference in 1979 the emperor was quoted as saying that MacArthur had persuaded him not to abdicate and that the general had asked for the emperor's message of November 12 in writing. MacArthur gave a different version to the Canadian diplomatic representative in January

1949: "Emperor Hirohito had asked him [MacArthur] what course he should adopt, and had intimated that he would be willing to abdicate if the Allies wished him so to do. If they were not, however, anxious to see him go, he would 'stick it out.'" Thereupon MacArthur had assured His Majesty that the whole issue was an artificial one and that there was no necessity for him to abdicate.[37] It would have been surprising for MacArthur to request a written assurance from the emperor; throughout the occupation the emperor was only too willing to cooperate with the supreme commander, and the general at no time felt the need to press him to put something in writing.

The general told Norman that to have compelled the abolition of the emperor system altogether would have been a great blow to Japanese pride and that he had been trying to "inculcate into the Japanese the love of the flag in place of the love of the Emperor" but had been unsuccessful. "The Emperor was, and would remain, the Japanese 'symbol.'"[38] Not only did MacArthur want the emperor to stay on his throne; he also wanted to shield the emperor from undesirable influences. He scrutinized appointments for foreigners to see the emperor. At times he also suggested to his visitors they should call on the emperor, and he was the instigator of the emperor's visits around Japan to enhance his image as a democratic ruler. In one curious situation in 1950 MacArthur vetoed a British project to bring in an English tutor for the crown prince who would also advise the court on diplomatic procedures. A piqued Sir Alvary Gascoigne concluded that MacArthur "does consider that the Emperor and the Court are entirely his own preserves—preserves which he will, apparently, not have infringed upon by any outsider whatsoever."[39]

PART IV

New Policies and New Directions

The American occupation of Japan had one clear turning point—late 1948, almost exactly halfway between the surrender in 1945 and the signing of the peace treaty in 1951. By 1948 strong pressures were mounting in both the United States and Japan for a policy shift away from reform and punishment and toward Japan's reconstruction and eventual reentry into the world community. The most powerful pressures in the United States stemmed from Japan's weak economic performance. Industrial production was not rising fast enough, the rate of inflation was still high, and the Japanese were showing little initiative in tackling their problems. Worst of all, the burden on the American taxpayer was growing, and complaints were swelling about the large sums of money being spent on a defeated enemy with little sign of useful results. The new under secretary of the army, William H. Draper, Jr., was particularly concerned about the economy-minded Republican Congress. He felt Washington had to push SCAP and the Japanese to do better.

Equally important was a shifting mood in Japan. After three years of chaos and dizzying reforms the people wanted order, calm, and more than a minimum standard of living. They wanted leaders who could stand up to the Americans and set Japan on a new course. Yoshida Shigeru, the old-fashioned conservative, soon made a dramatic comeback with a campaign designed to win more freedom of action for the government and build up the self-respect of the people.

Another strong pressure arose from growing East-West tension. In February 1948 the Soviet Union engineered a communist takeover in Czechoslovakia. In June Soviet military forces in eastern Germany blockaded access by the Western allies to their zones of occupation in Berlin, forcing them to undertake an airlift. On the other side of the world the Chinese Red Army under Mao Zedong swept over northern China in 1948, starting the rout of the Nationalist forces, which retreated to Taiwan in 1949. By the end of 1949 half of Asia, measured in area or in population, was communist. In Central Europe and East Asia rivalry between East and West was intensifying.

The American vision of universal peace and Wilsonian internationalism had vanished, to be replaced by what the eminent journalist Walter Lippmann called the "cold war." Pax Americana would no longer operate smoothly in a world of peace and cooperation; instead it would struggle in a world of growing rivalry and frequent crisis. A new policy was formulated to cope with this situation: its catchword was "containment."

Firmly ensconced "under the eagle's wings" since the surrender, Japan had been almost totally insulated from the winds of change. The occupation forces and the Japanese alike carried on as if what happened in the outside world was of little importance to them. But Japan could no longer remain isolated. It had to reenter the world.

The main designers of a new strategy for Japan were Draper and George F. Kennan, the State Department's policy planner and the formulator of the containment concept. Draper's goal was the economic revival of Japan; Kennan's was its political stability. Both wanted Japan to be able to stand on its own feet after a peace settlement, for which U.S. planning was already under way. Neither intended that Japan be an active participant in the cold war or a military ally of the United States. Initially they sought to redefine U.S. policy for Japan and develop a program for economic stabilization and growth. Draper's economic plan meshed with that of the SCAP experts in Japan, and Joseph Dodge, a Detroit banker, went to Japan to push it through.

Along with this revised policy came renewed authority in Washington. Reelected in November 1948, Harry Truman named Dean Acheson secretary of state. They were in agreement that the policies of containment already initiated by the Truman Doctrine for assistance to Greece and Turkey and by the Marshall Plan for the recovery of Europe should be expanded. Among other steps, they wanted to build "situations of strength" in key areas of the world as barriers against communist encroachment. The economic revival of Japan had taken on new urgency in the wake of the collapse of Nationalist China.

Under the confident hand of Douglas MacArthur, Japan had posed few problems for Washington, but by 1948 it had become the object of attention and concern. Washington wanted a healthier and stronger Japan than MacArthur had been able to produce. Deference continued to be paid to the general's authority and prestige, but the voice of Washington now counted for much more than before. MacArthur knew he could not ignore it.

CHAPTER 14

Washington Intervenes

Draper and Kennan

U.S. economic planning for postwar Japan was a multifarious collection of generally worded reforms, punitive measures, and a firm disclaimer of any obligation to help the Japanese feed themselves and rebuild their country. These policies were carried out by a commander and senior staff with little experience in economic matters. It was characteristic of MacArthur, as his entire career showed, that he did not shrink from responsibility and did not feel entirely tied down by Washington orders. Soon after the occupation began, he was asking for food and raw materials to enable Japan to escape starvation and stagnation. Washington went along. In the first year after the surrender the United States provided Japan with a little more than $100 million in food, fertilizer, petroleum products, and medical supplies, financed by military appropriations.[1]

By 1947 Washington wanted more action by SCAP and better performance by Japan. In a speech on May 8, 1947, Dean Acheson proposed that Germany and Japan be converted into the "workshops" of Europe and Asia, foreshadowing Secretary of State Marshall's momentous speech at Harvard only a few weeks later launching the European recovery program.[2] On August 30, 1947, the newly reorganized Defense Department in Washington filled the new position of under secretary of the Army by appointing General Draper, a dynamic man with broad business and military experience. Washington wanted to build up SCAP's economic staff as well but could not figure out how to overcome MacArthur's well-known resistance to having top posts on his staff filled by people he did not know and trust.[3] He was particularly averse to Wall Street bankers. As it happened, Draper and the new secretary of defense, James V. Forrestal, were both senior members of the New York investment firm of Dillon, Read.

One of Draper's main tasks was to supervise Defense Department management of areas occupied by U.S. forces after World War II, in particular Germany and Japan. He had served for two years on the staff of General Lucius D. Clay, the military governor of the U.S. zone in Germany, but he knew little about Japan. So Draper decided to go there in September 1947. He met with General MacArthur, his staff, and a number of Japanese including Prime Minister Katayama. Draper was impressed that "the Japanese are cooperating to an unbelievable extent with the occupation," but he got a negative picture of the economic situation. He was disturbed, as he had been in Germany, by the huge costs of the occupation and by the campaigns to break up large business concentrations.[4]

His visit to Japan came at a time when the SCAP anticartel program was going strong. The man in charge, Edward C. Welsh, was a trained economist hired to expedite the program. Welsh arrived in Tokyo in March 1947 and became one of SCAP's most zealous operators, immediately seeing that he would lose influence to GS if he did not move fast on the cartel issue. One of his first actions was to push for dissolution of the two huge trading companies, Mitsubishi Shōji and Mitsui Bussan, which had handled much of Japan's prewar export and import business. Bussan was split into 170 companies and Shōji into 120. No persuasive reason was ever advanced for the breakup of these companies, except, of course, that they were the trading agents for the far-flung enterprises of these two conglomerates. It seemed irrational to destroy them at a time when SCAP had allowed foreign traders to enter Japan and was trying to revive Japan's trade despite the resistance of many of the Allied nations. (The two companies were recombined soon after the end of the occupation. By 1985 they were the second and third largest non-U.S. companies in the world.)[5]

Draper readily perceived that staff officers directed economic operations in Tokyo and that MacArthur and his economic chief, Marquat, provided little input. Draper was not an archconservative or a Wall Streeter looking for capitalist opportunities, but he was an investment banker who carefully studied balance sheets and speedily detected financial trouble. He clearly saw that Japan's productive potential was hobbled by SCAP restrictions and red tape as well as by high inflation.

By the time he returned to Washington, Draper had formulated a broad plan of action. He wanted a policy statement stressing the importance of economic recovery as a U.S. objective. Getting such a statement was easy, despite objections in the State Department that existing policy was adequate. On January 22, 1948, the new State-Army-Navy-Air Coordinating Committee (SANACC, renamed to include the new U.S. Air Force) approved a weasel-worded statement that the supreme commander "should take all possible and necessary steps consistent with the basic policies of the occupation to bring about the early revival of the Japanese economy on a peaceful, self-supporting basis." Secretary of the Army Royall heralded the new American approach in a speech on January 6, 1948: "There has arisen an inevitable area of conflict between the original concept of broad demilitarization and the new purpose of building a self-supporting nation." He clearly implied that the latter purpose had become number one for the United States.[6] Royall's speech was one of the first signs of a new direction in U.S. policy.

The next step was a specific plan. In 1947 Washington and Tokyo were working on plans that turned out to be similar. Draper carried to Tokyo a State Department plan called Crank Up that aimed at a self-supporting Japan by 1950. SCAP's "green book" planned that the United States would provide $1.2 billion in assistance, Japan would become self-supporting in four years, and by 1953 it would be able to export $1.5 billion worth of goods and services. By 1947 U.S. aid was running at about $400 million a year and was even higher for the next two years. All these plans became outmoded when the Korean War broke out in 1950.[7]

To implement his economic strategy Draper targeted two occupation programs for reduction or elimination—reparations and deconcentration of big business—even though the State Department remained opposed to any changes. Reparations, however, were a crucial issue in the FEC, where "more time was given . . . to Japanese reparations and related topics than to any other subject which came before the commission."[8] Draper was more impressed, however, by the potent argument that the American taxpayer would eventually pay for any reparations deliveries because whatever Japan shipped out as reparations would delay its recovery and lengthen its period of dependence on the United States for assistance.

One of Draper's clever devices was to commission a group of influential businessmen to study a problem, make sure they knew his view-

point and were generally sympathetic, and then use their report to justify a shift in policy. This was the way he worked out the reparations
matter. First came the Overseas Consultants, Inc., under engineer Clifford Strike, which made two surveys in 1947 and recommended huge
reductions in the industrial facilities listed by the Pauley report of 1946.
Asked for his views on the Strike report, MacArthur asserted on March
21, 1948, that the "decision should be made now to abandon entirely
the thought of further reparations. . . . In war booty Japan has already
paid over fifty billion dollars by virtue of her lost properties in Manchuria, Korea, North China and the outer islands. . . . Except for actual
war facilities, there is a critical need in Japan for every tool, every factory, and practically every industrial installation which she now has."[9]

As his second step in the attack on reparations, Draper organized
and participated in another study two months later by a group led by
Percy Johnston, the chairman of the Chemical Bank and Trust Company of New York. After a three-week stay in Japan, the Johnston
committee recommended far larger reductions than those of the Strike
committee. Strike had recommended a 33 percent cut in the Pauley
proposals, and Johnston recommended a cut of more than 50 percent
in the Strike plan. Altogether, reparations would be 25 percent of the
1945 plan.[10] The new approach was the kind that Draper and Mac-
Arthur wanted. The State Department questioned the extent of damage that would be done to Japan's economy by the earlier reparations
proposals and argued that the SCAP-Army position would be unacceptable to the FEC nations.

On July 25, 1948, MacArthur cabled Washington that Japan would
need to retain much of its industrial capacity: "Indications are now that
Japanese export trade of the future will have a substantially different
pattern than prewar. With the rapid expansion of the cotton textile
industry in other countries in the Far East . . . it is indicated that future
Japanese exports will consist much more of machinery, other capital
goods and chemicals, and much less proportionately of textile products
than prewar. This . . . will require a larger steel and machinery capacity
to support export industries with no change involved in the internal
domestic standard of living."[11]

The coup de grace to the Allied reparations program came in 1949.
On May 6 the United States decided, in NSC-13/3, that the advance
transfer program should be terminated and that the FEC should be
advised that all industrial facilities, including "primary war facilities"
stripped of their military characteristics, should be used as necessary for
the recovery program. Many factories used for war production in

World War II were later sold to private companies for peaceful production; industrial equipment designed solely for military purposes was later destroyed by SCAP pursuant to a FEC policy decision of October 30, 1947. On May 12, 1949, the United States rescinded the advance reparations transfer directive to MacArthur and so informed the FEC.[12]

The U.S. action fueled resentment in several Asian countries, notably the Philippines and the ROC, that American policy favored Japan at their expense. This claim had much to justify it, though the American rejoinder that transplanted factories and equipment were rarely usable in backward countries was about equally true. Several points are significant: if the Allies had reached quick agreement on reparations and early deliveries had been carried out by Japanese technicians under Allied supervision, the program might have been beneficial to Asian nations. In fact, however, the Allies probably took too little from Japan after World War II and took too much from Germany after World War I.

Some critics of American policy claim that reparations were another example of a U.S. policy reversal. It did indeed reverse its position because the U.S. government decided, not without reason, that if Allied agreement could not be achieved in three and one-half years, the policy should be given up. This made all the more sense because reparations were not a reform but a punitive policy that held out little promise of assistance to the Allies.

Draper's campaign to wind up the deconcentration program proceeded more easily and quickly than the struggle over reparations. The main battle, breaking up the zaibatsu holding companies, had long since been completed, but the program to dissolve a large number of big business groupings was just getting started. MacArthur, however, began to have some doubts. Reportedly, he thought it "sounded crazy" to designate 325 companies as excessive concentrations two and one-half years after the antizaibatsu campaign began. Accordingly, he suggested to Washington in January 1948 that an impartial board of American businessmen come to Tokyo to review the deconcentration program. Draper soon put together a group of five men in whom he had confidence. The Deconcentration Review Board arrived in Japan in May 1948. By then some 150 companies had been removed from the original list of 325. The board steadily pared the list during the year of its operation, though it was careful to save SCAP face when it announced in September "there has been no change whatsoever" in SCAP deconcentration policy.[13]

While the board was swinging into action, Draper busied himself with redirecting deconcentration policy. The first step was to end consideration of FEC-230. After another protracted battle between State and Army, the U.S. representative to the FEC was authorized to state on December 9, 1948: "There is no need to lay down policies for the guidance of the Supreme Commander with respect to any remaining significant aspect of the program. . . . Hence, the United States has withdrawn its support of FEC-230. . . . The major points of procedure set out in that document already had been implemented in Japan." General McCoy noted in his statement to the FEC that "the assets of fifty-six persons who comprised the ten major zaibatsu families and the assets of the eighty-three holding companies controlled by these persons have been acquired by the government and are in process of being sold to the Japanese public."[14]

Of the original 325 companies, 297 had been exempted when the Deconcentration Review Board dissolved on August 3, 1949, orders for reorganization of 11 others had been issued, and the remaining 17 cases were in the final stage of processing. The SCAP deconcentration program actually split up only 18 companies, including Mitsubishi Heavy Industries, Mitsubishi Mining, Mitsui Mining, Toshiba, Hitachi, Oji Paper, and Japan Steel, which was split into Yawata Steel and Fuji Steel.[15]

Japan's biggest banks did not fall under the 1947 Law for Elimination of Excessive Concentrations of Economic Power. These banks, including Dai Ichi, Chiyoda (a cover name for Mitsubishi), Fuji (cover for Mitsui), Osaka, and Sanwa, played a key role along with a number of new banks in Japan's economic revival after the occupation. Thirty-six years after the occupation ended, the ten biggest banks in the world were Japanese.[16]

MacArthur told Patrick Shaw of Australia in April 1949 that the Draper mission was "the most high-powered effort of big business interests to break down his policy of preserving Japan from carpetbaggers." The Canadian representative, Herbert Norman, had commented earlier, "On more than one occasion I have noticed General MacArthur's addiction to the vocabulary of the trust-busting era; thus his determination to break up the zaibatsu in Japan is a genuine part of his political philosophy." A Japanese business leader said later that "zaibatsu dissolution was a major factor in Japan's postwar growth." It also helped bring about a managerial revolution in which stockholding was widely dispersed, managers ran companies, and in most industries competition was keen.[17]

Draper's campaign to make economic recovery the top priority of the occupation was the first serious intrusion by Washington into Mac-Arthur's autonomy in Tokyo. Soon after came a statement of national policy that provided a broad framework for the new approach. Approved by President Truman on October 9, 1948, this document was one of the early products of the National Security Council (NSC) and became well known as NSC 13/2.[18]

NSC 13/2 was primarily the brainchild of George F. Kennan, who at age forty-three was regarded as America's foremost authority on policy toward the Soviet Union. His article in the July 1947 issue of *Foreign Affairs* on the sources of Soviet conduct had won wide acceptance as a perceptive and realistic prescription for the United States and its friends to follow in dealing with the communist nations. His analysis became an essential element in U.S. foreign policy and was universally known as containment, a description he did not entirely appreciate and the meaning of which was hotly debated.

Secretary of State Marshall appointed Kennan the head of a new policy planning staff in 1947. After completing a study on European recovery that was valuable in the formulation of the Marshall Plan, Kennan and his staff decided to look at Japan. The immediate issue they faced in the late summer of 1947 was whether to go along with plans for a peace conference, for which Far Eastern experts in the State Department had made extensive preparations. The basic point, in Kennan's view, was to determine whether Japan was stable and strong enough to stand on its own feet; he was convinced that the restoration of a postwar balance of power required that Western Europe and Japan stay out of communist hands.[19]

Kennan had had no experience in the Far East. Concerned that U.S. policy in Japan might have the effect of "rendering Japanese society vulnerable to Communist political pressures and paving the way for a Communist takeover," he suggested that someone go to Japan to talk to MacArthur and examine the situation there firsthand. Kennan sensed that relations between Marshall and MacArthur were "not cordial" and that the secretary of state was "reluctant to involve himself personally in any attempt to exchange views with General MacArthur." No one in the State Department seemed to want this job, and the task soon fell to Kennan.[20]

He was the most important State Department official to visit Japan during the occupation. In the same period high officials went regularly to Europe; Secretary of State Dean Acheson, for example, made eleven trips between 1949 and 1952. Although State Department officials complained that their views did not get much hearing in Japan, they shrank from any direct tilt with MacArthur. MacArthur's military associates in the Pentagon had many of the same problems with the general, and Kennan thought they probably relished "watching a civilian David prepare to call on this military Goliath."[21]

Kennan arrived in Tokyo at the end of February 1948. His detailed reports of his three meetings with MacArthur are among the rare records of MacArthur's views that can be called complete and candid. After an uncertain start, Kennan and the general got along surprisingly well. At their first meeting, a luncheon on March 1, the general held forth in a virtual monologue, a "MacArthur sermon," about the prospects for democracy and Christianity in Japan. "Overcome by weariness," Kennan says, he had little to offer at this meeting.[22]

In advance of the second meeting, Kennan sent the general a note, which reflected his own thoughts, suggesting that the emphasis of occupation policy should be threefold: the "maximum stability of Japanese society" based on a "firm U.S. security policy," an "intensive program of economic recovery," and a "relaxation in occupational control designed to stimulate a greater sense of direct responsibility" in the Japanese.[23]

At the meeting of March 5 MacArthur responded at length. Regarding security, he asserted that the strategic boundary of the United States ran along the island areas off the eastern shore of the Asiatic continent and that Okinawa was "the most advanced and vital point in this structure," which the United States had to control completely. MacArthur further noted that it would not be feasible for the United States to retain bases in Japan after a peace treaty because other Allied nations would then have a right to do likewise. Regarding economic recovery, the general agreed that it should be made a primary policy goal. He was already doing all he could to achieve this, he said, but the difficulty was in the development of foreign trade, and in this matter the FEC nations were "shamelessly selfish and negative" toward Japan.[24]

Regarding a relaxation of control, MacArthur asserted that occupation controls were not so stringent as many in the United States thought. The general went on to describe some of the reform measures. Provisions in the new constitution renouncing war had resulted from a Japanese initiative. The zaibatsu were not men of superior competence; the real brains of prewar Japan were in its armed forces. Most reform measures had been completed, civil service reform being the only important one remaining. MacArthur said he was planning to cut down the SCAP section most concerned with subjects of interest to "academic theorizers of a left-wing variety," commenting that he had a few of these in his shop but did not think they did much harm.[25]

Changing the subject, Kennan suggested that the FEC, which MacArthur had indicated would be an obstacle to any attempt to change occupation policy, had largely fulfilled its main function and could be "permitted to languish." The general thought this was the right line to take and said he could easily certify to the FEC within a short time that the surrender terms had been carried out. Kennan summarized by saying the position should be that "the occupation is continued, not for the enforcement . . . of the terms of surrender, but to bridge the hiatus in the status of Japan caused by the failure of the Allies to agree on a treaty of peace."[26]

At the third meeting, on March 21, Draper took part and mentioned that some planners in the Department of the Army thought Japan should have a "small defensive force." MacArthur prefaced his reply by urging that the United States press for an early peace conference, suggesting that if a treaty could be negotiated, the Soviets would eventually go along with it. He then asserted that he was "unalterably opposed" to a Japanese military force because it would violate fundamental SCAP policies and alienate Far Eastern nations. A rearmed Japan would have trouble surviving economically and could never be more than a fifth-rate military power, "a tempting morsel, to be gobbled up by Soviet Russia at her pleasure." In addition, the Japanese had sincerely renounced war and would be unwilling to establish an armed force.[27]

While in Japan, Kennan formed strong and skeptical views on some occupation policies. Speaking of the purge program, he commented later, "The indiscriminate purging of whole categories of officials, aside from the sickening resemblance to the concepts of certain totalitarian governments, was a denial of the civil rights provisions of the new Japanese constitution and created an unfortunate setting for the promulgation of Japan's new legal codes." The anticartel program was in his eyes the work of people who saw problems "exclusively from the standpoint of economic theory and whose enthusiasm and singleness of purpose have sufficed to get them documented as U.S. government policy." He thought war crimes trials "were profoundly misconceived." The "hocus-pocus of a judicial procedure" belied the fact "they were political trials." Echoing Winston Churchill, Kennan asserted it would have been better "if we had shot these people out of hand at the time of the surrender." As for reparations, he said, echoing MacArthur, it was "sheer nonsense . . . and basically inconsistent with the requirements of Japanese recovery" to transfer industrial equipment from Japan to other Far Eastern countries. He was also somewhat appalled by the lifestyle of American occupationaires, commenting that "it is instructive rather than gratifying to get a glimpse of this vast oriental world, so far from any hope of adjustment to the requirements of an orderly and humane civilization, and to note the peculiarly cynical and grasping side of its own nature which Western civilization seems to present to these billions of oriental eyes, so curious, so observant, and so pathetically expectant."[28]

After three weeks in the Far East, including a short inspection trip to the Philippines, Kennan returned to Washington. Within a few days, his report to the NSC was ready. It began with a caveat that the United States should not press for a peace treaty. He explained later that "in no respect was Japan at that time in a position to shoulder and to bear successfully the responsibilities of independence that could be expected to flow at once from a treaty of peace." This was not, of course, the view of General MacArthur.[29]

The report offered twenty important policy prescriptions. Next to its security interests, the United States should make economic recovery its primary goal, stressing to the Japanese the need to increase production and exports. Kennan's proposals regarding political reform were more controversial: SCAP should undertake no new reforms and should relax pressures on those already in effect, intervening only if the Japanese sought to revoke or compromise fundamental reforms. The control system under SCAP should be maintained, but more responsibility should be given to the Japanese government. The report gave a lot of attention to Okinawa and went along with MacArthur: the United States should "make up its mind at this point that it intends to retain permanently the facilities at Okinawa."[30]

Kennan was most concerned about the weak power of the police, which had been broken up into many small units that lacked central direction, a central pool of information, and any means of coordination between the national rural police and the local police. Police officers were armed mostly with pistols, with only one for every four men. In Kennan's words, "It was difficult to imagine a setup more favorable and inviting from the standpoint of the prospects for a communist take-over." He cited as an example of his concern that police in Tokyo had no records of lawless elements in Osaka, such as dissident Koreans.

In his report Kennan recommended that the police be strengthened by better equipment, creation of a coast guard, and establishment of a central organization along the lines of the Federal Bureau of Investigation. He did not recommend any increase in the size of the police forces, and he made no recommendations regarding a military force, but he did talk with Draper about the possibility of "a strong, centrally-directed, National Rural Police." Kennan also thought the SCAP purge categories had been too rigid and should be reviewed to permit some exceptions.[31]

On another knotty issue, a greater civilian role in the occupation, Kennan partly disagreed with MacArthur, recommending that the State Department send a permanent political representative to Japan. Even this modest compromise fell by the wayside as his report made its way upward through the U.S. government, as did an ambitious scheme by some in the State Department to assume control of all nonmilitary activities in Japan. MacArthur was adamant in his opposition. He liked being supreme. There was little talk after 1948 of any change in the structure of the occupation.

Kennan proposed other ways to bring about a more normal relation with Japan. Cultural interchange between Japan and the United States should be strongly encouraged. Precensorship of the press should cease. The impact of the large American military community in Japan should be mitigated, and the costs of the occupation paid by the Japanese government should be reduced. FEC and ACJ controls over Japan could continue but should not be strengthened.

Kennan's report found wide acceptance in Washington, sailing through the bureaucracy with only minor changes. The consensus reflected a general belief that the occupation had achieved its basic purposes of disarming Japan and laying a foundation for democratic government. In this sense, the occupation was over. In Europe the United States and its Allies had by 1946 veered sharply away from reform and punishment and toward economic recovery. By 1948 they were preparing to turn over most of their control in the western zones to a new German government. They might have liked to do the same in Japan, but the thought of dumping both MacArthur and the FEC made this option uninviting.

The general had a few comments on the Kennan report. Many were minor: U.S. occupation forces in Japan could not safely be reduced; occupation costs were not a heavy burden on the Japanese economy because they were devoted largely to construction of buildings, which would be useful for the Japanese in the future; reducing the influence of the FEC and the ACJ was desirable; and war crimes trials could not be expedited. On a few points, however, he felt strongly. Any "expansion" of the police force would bring "explosive international reactions" in the FEC. He refused to alter purge policy, pointing out that it bore the approval of the FEC and that even though his execution of the policy had been "as mild as action of this sort conceivably could be," he had been bitterly attacked by five of the Allied nations for his "excessive mildness."[32]

Some of MacArthur's views resulted in modifications of the Kennan proposals. But the provisions regarding the police and the purge were retained much as originally drafted. These led to acerbic exchanges between Washington and Tokyo after the president approved the report on October 9, 1948. The State Department wanted to press MacArthur hard to carry out the provisions of NSC 13/2, and the Department of the Army went along reluctantly after watering down the wording of the messages to Tokyo.[33]

One stratagem was to send these instructions to MacArthur as U.S. commander in chief in the Far East (CINCFE) rather than as supreme commander for the Allied powers. MacArthur quickly rejoined that he had been designated an Allied commander by the Moscow agreement of 1945. Were the United States to breach this agreement by unilaterally sending him orders, other Allied powers might try to do the same. The Soviets might claim this right, "and with the present emasculated condition of our occupation force it is doubtful that we could successfully resist any thrust [they] might decide upon against Hokkaido or any other part of Japan." MacArthur added the telling comment that "NSC 13/2 has not been conveyed as an order to SCAP by appropriate directive as prescribed by international agreement and therefore SCAP is not responsible in any way for its implementation."[34] These hard-hitting messages, which were drafted by Whitney, smacked of insubordination. They did not deter State and Army. These departments knew, as did MacArthur, that the occupation was a U.S. show, and they were determined that American policy would prevail. On February 15, 1949, Washington informed Tokyo that several sections of the basic directive of November 3, 1945, regarding the purge had been rescinded, as had the important provision that the supreme commander should take no responsibility for the economic rehabilitation of Japan. These policy adjustments had little impact on MacArthur, who had decided three years earlier to ignore the injunction against economic help for Japan.

On May 2, 1949, the State Department made an internal report on the implementation of NSC 13/2, six months after the president approved it. The internal report gave MacArthur low marks for his performance: no action had been taken to reduce the psychological impact of the occupation, no specific steps had been taken to prepare long-term plans for Okinawa or to improve the facilities there, and Japanese police had been issued more pistols, but nothing had been done to set up a national investigation bureau or to increase coordination of police operations around the country.[35] Nor had there been any reduction of SCAP's supervisory role over the Japanese government. In fact, SCAP had stated that greater stress on economic recovery had "completely reversed this policy." The purge had not been modified. Occupation costs had not been reduced. Only two actions were being taken to carry out the policy: intensive efforts were being devoted to economic recovery, and precensorship of the press had been terminated.

As he often did, MacArthur decided to implement the policy his own way without acknowledging Washington's role. On May 6, 1949, he ordered all headquarters sections to review outstanding directives and procedures for the purpose of relaxing controls and stimulating a sense of self-reliance and responsibility among the Japanese. Without mentioning the NSC policy paper, MacArthur based his order on his own press statement of May 2, 1949, on the second anniversary of the Japanese constitution, in which he proclaimed, "In these two years the character of the occupation has gradually changed from the stern rigidity of a military operation to the friendly guidance of a protective force. While insisting upon the firm adherence to the course delineated by existing Allied policy and directive, it is my purpose to continue to advance this transition."[36]

One of MacArthur's senior staff officers later described this program as "little more than window-dressing." But he did point out that SCAP took a number of actions under this order to reduce its operations and interventions in Japanese activities. In particular, it reduced the civilian employee element of the occupation from 3,660 to 1,950. It removed civil affairs teams—formerly known as military government teams—from prefectural capitals and cut their personnel drastically from 2,758 to 526.[37] Moreover, SCAP continued to give the police more pistols and training. The Japanese government was permitted to establish an appeals board to review purge cases, although its jurisdiction was restricted.

A number of American and Japanese historians have labeled Kennan

the master planner of a new policy of reverse course designed to implicate Japan in cold war politics. Kennan would have denied that his
proposals were designed to turn back the clock on reform, although he
did say later he could understand how younger scholars might feel he
had taken a stern attitude regarding U.S. policy toward Japan. He
believed that the reforms should be retained, some in modified form,
and that the time had come for the Japanese to implement the reforms
their way so long as they did not try to undo them. Nor would he have
understood the argument that his policies were intended to embroil
Japan in the U.S. rivalry with the Soviet Union.

Kennan's goal was to help Japan build adequate political stability
and economic strength to make its way after negotiation of a peace
treaty, which was already an active item on the Allied agenda. He felt
Japan had to have better protection against internal threats to its security, especially a more effective police force, and he was willing to sanction firm but legal measures to control communists and left-wingers.
Kennan did think a number of occupation reforms went too far, but he
made no effort to change them. Nor did he take part in any group
lobbying for change.

Consistent with his view that containment was a political, not a
military, policy he made no recommendation that Japan should develop
military forces or even that the United States should station forces in
Japan after the peace treaty. He said in his *Memoirs* that "it was my
hope—shared at the moment, I believe, by General MacArthur—that
we would eventually be able to arrive at some understanding with the
Russians, relating to the security of the northwestern Pacific area, which
would make this unnecessary."[38] These were hardly cold war polemics.

Kennan left himself a loophole on the crucial issue of rearmament.
Two days after meeting MacArthur, he inserted an explanatory note in
his report that said in part that because of the Soviet threat and Japan's
internal weakness (he considered Japan much more vulnerable to communist pressure than MacArthur did), Japan could not be left defenseless after a peace treaty; either there should be no treaty, or "we
must permit Japan to rearm to the extent that it would no longer constitute an open invitation to military aggression." He added that if the
USSR's military-political potential became less threatening in the future, then a treaty of demilitarization with Japan would be feasible.[39]

Kennan wrote later that his efforts in 1948 made "a major contribution to the change in occupational policy that was carried out in late
1948 and 1949; and I consider my part in bringing about this change to

have been, after the Marshall Plan, the most significant constructive contribution I was ever able to make in government. On no other occasion, with that one exception, did I ever make recommendations of such scope and import; and on no other occasion did my recommendations meet with such wide, indeed almost complete, acceptance."[40]

Kennan was not optimistic about the situation. In a talk he gave at the Central Intelligence Agency (CIA) in October 1949, he said that Japan would have to make a "drastic adjustment" after the occupation and would face a "dangerous situation" in Asia because the country had been demilitarized. He felt there was a likelihood of reversion to an "extreme form of nationalism" and to a "totalitarian government," which did not bode well for the United States.[41]

The State and Defense departments did accept and apply the proposals in NSC 13/2, but MacArthur all but shunned them. They did not circulate in SCAP headquarters as new policy for the conduct of the occupation. MacArthur did not mention Kennan or NSC 13/2 in his *Reminiscences*. Yet he understood that Washington had decided on a shift in course. In a remark to Sebald on August 15, 1949, MacArthur said he was implementing the NSC policy as rapidly as possible, thus preparing Japan for eventual return of sovereignty.[42] And the new Japanese government, without knowing the bureaucratic tangle inside the U.S. government, welcomed the revised U.S. approach, which soon became evident despite MacArthur's shunning.

1. Autographed photograph of General Douglas MacArthur and Emperor Hirohito at their first meeting, September 27, 1945. Courtesy of MacArthur Memorial Archives, Norfolk, Virginia.

2. Aerial photograph of Hiroshima (taken December 22, 1945). Note the church in the foreground. Courtesy of the National Archives, Washington, D.C.

3. MacArthur relaxing. Courtesy of the Thames Collection.

4. MacArthur greeting John Foster Dulles on his first trip to Japan, June 21, 1950. Ambassador W. J. Sebald is at right. Courtesy of the National Archives, Washington, D.C.

5. Dulles, Sebald, and Prime Minister Yoshida Shigeru in conversation at a reception in Tokyo, January 21, 1951. Courtesy of the National Archives, Washington, D.C.

6. Prime Minister Yoshida signing the peace treaty, as his co-signers—
Ichimada Hisato of the Bank of Japan, Tokugawa Muneyoshi of the House of
Councillors, Hoshijima Nirō and Tomabechi Gizō of the House of Representa-
tives, and Finance Minister Ikeda Hayato—look on. Secretary of State Dean
Acheson sits in the middle behind them. Courtesy of MacArthur Memorial Ar-
chives, Norfolk, Virginia.

7. Prime Minister Yoshida signing the security treaty on September 8, 1951, at the San Francisco Presidio. Looking on are Dulles, Secretary of State Dean Acheson, and Senator H. Styles Bridges, ranking minority member of the Senate Armed Services Committee. Courtesy of the National Archives, Washington, D.C.

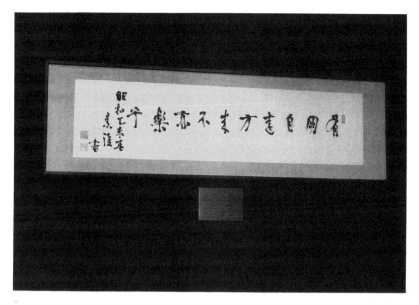

8. Yoshida's calligraphy. Yoshida Shigeru was well known for his calligraphy. He penned this quotation from the opening chapter of the *Analects* of Confucius in 1955 as a gift to the new International House in Tokyo, where it is now displayed. It means "Is it not delightful to have friends coming from distant quarters?" (Legge's translation). Courtesy of International House, Tokyo.

9. Two old friends. MacArthur and Yoshida meet at the Waldorf-Astoria on November 5, 1954. Courtesy of Wide World Photos.

10. Yoshida in retirement at Oiso. Courtesy of *Asahi shimbun*. Photograph by Yoshioka Senzo.

CHAPTER 15

New Life in Tokyo

Yoshida and Dodge

October 9, 1948, the day President Truman approved Kennan's new policy, was far more significant in the modern history of Japan for another reason. On that day, Yoshida Shigeru met with MacArthur and told the general he planned to be a candidate for the prime ministership. Within a week Yoshida succeeded in capturing the prize and thereby inaugurated a long-lasting rule of Japan by moderate conservatives.

Yoshida found the road back to the top of the political heap a rocky one. But he was spunky and determined when the crisis began in early October, despite an attack of gallstones.[1] In an effort to head off Yoshida, SCAP tried to enlist two other prospects for the job, one supported by MacArthur and Whitney and the other by their powerful subordinates in GS, Charles Kades and Justin Williams. Williams approached Yamazaki Takeshi, the secretary general of Yoshida's own party and a man with wide political experience and a liberal outlook. GS's firm support for Yamazaki and opposition to Yoshida opened up divisions in party ranks. Some of the old guard began to talk about getting rid of the party leader, who had failed once and was not strong enough to keep all his lieutenants in line.[2]

Yoshida remained spirited and steadfast. On October 7 he lectured his colleagues that party decisions should be made on the basis of democratic procedures that would set a good example for the nation, not on the basis of personal likes and dislikes. Yamazaki's attempt to oust Yoshida had sparked his ire, and he declared, "If General MacArthur forces this on me, I will obey. . . . I will go to him and find out for myself."[3]

Yoshida and MacArthur met alone on October 9. Neither made a record of the meeting. Yoshida later used various terms to describe the general's attitude toward his candidacy, varying from "understanding and encouragement" to "approval" to "I want you to do it." All of these implied MacArthur's support and reinforced the prime minister's decision to run. To be the sole Japanese source of information on MacArthur's views was a powerful weapon in Yoshida's hands, which he used often and effectively.[4]

Right after seeing Yoshida, MacArthur had a lengthy meeting with Miki Takeo, the head of the People's Cooperative Party, who had served in the Diet without a break since 1937. Miki was then forty-one, which was young for a Japanese politician; his political position was middle of the road; and he had studied for two years at the University of California at Berkeley. According to Miki's account, General Whitney had earlier conveyed "General MacArthur's request that I succeed Dr. Ashida as prime minister." On October 9 MacArthur "personally reiterated the request that I become the next premier." Miki later commented that "under the circumstances where General MacArthur was the virtual ruler of Japan, if I had acceded to the General's wish, I could have gained the post of prime minister."[5]

Miki went on, "Nonetheless I refused the offer. The line of reasoning I presented to the general for refusing his most cordial consideration was as follows: (a) I am the leader of a minority party in the Diet, the People's Cooperative Party. (b) For General MacArthur to establish the ground rules for Japan to be ruled by a parliamentary democracy, he must take into consideration the fact that the Liberal Party, headed by Yoshida, held the largest number of seats in the Diet among the opposition parties and that his governance of Japan would proceed more smoothly with Yoshida installed as premier, since that would accord with the democratic requirements of the nation at the time." Miki thus bowed out, and MacArthur did not press him. Miki did become prime minister twenty-six years later, when he succeeded the scandal-covered Tanaka Kakuei in 1974.

This was a curious episode. As Miki said, MacArthur was "the virtual ruler of Japan" at the time. He could have forced the selection of Miki or the rejection of Yoshida. Yet the general generally tried to avoid getting involved in the selection of Japan's political leaders. His tentative overture to Miki, which the evidence clearly shows he made, was the farthest he ever went in intervening in what he considered a Japanese process. Surprisingly, no word leaked out at the time about what Miki and MacArthur had discussed, despite intense curiosity in political circles. It was, of course, even more surprising that MacArthur and Whitney were going one way while two of their senior staff officers were going another.

Yoshida's political strategy worked well. He had argued skillfully against "plot politics" at a time when many Japanese politicians were disturbed by GS's interference in their affairs. And MacArthur's apparent endorsement was no doubt decisive. Yamazaki was talked out of making a challenge, and he soon resigned his seat in the lower house. Williams wrote a memo offering a psycho-historical explanation: "Yamazaki's action is strictly in keeping with the tenets of *bushidō*, which require that a samurai commit *harakiri* if he causes his lord and master any embarrassment. That Secretary General Yamazaki has caused his feudal lord, President Yoshida, considerable embarrassment during the last several days, there is no doubt. In fact, the immediate threat of overthrowing and replacing his feudal lord is so imminent that the Democratic Liberal Party has coerced him into accepting the most drastic fate of all, political suicide."[6] Actually, Yamazaki was reelected in January 1949 and had a long and successful career thereafter in the Democratic Liberal Party.

The British ambassador saw MacArthur on October 16 and reported to London that the general "showed little pleasure" at Yoshida's nomination but "stressed that this was, of course, entirely a matter for the Japanese and that he had not interfered in any way in the recent political crisis."[7] Sir Alvary's version rings truer than Yoshida's account. Clearly, the general had talked to both Miki and Yoshida. MacArthur probably listened to Yoshida explain his intention to stand for the premiership and said something like "good luck," as he had said to Yoshida in May 1946. This would have been all Yoshida needed to pass the word to his cohorts—and to the opposition—that MacArthur had "encouraged" him to seek the top job. MacArthur stretched the truth when he said he had not interfered in any way in the recent crisis, but Yoshida stretched it more when he let on that he had been supported by MacArthur.[8]

On October 14 the House of Representatives elected Yoshida prime minister by a vote of 185 to 1 with 213 blank votes cast. At a press conference soon after the vote, Yoshida expressed regret for the recent "troubles" but stressed his goal of national reconstruction and appealed for public support. A few days later he let Colonel Bunker, MacArthur's aide, know he wanted to thank MacArthur for his "sympathetic interest and assistance during this period."[9]

Yoshida sensed that public opinion was on his side. The other political parties were not doing well. A huge scandal had engulfed the Ashida cabinet. Difficult economic conditions prevailed throughout the country. And the occupation's meddling in domestic politics was stirring resentment among Japanese politicians. In Williams's words, "It was at this very time that GHQ intervention in Japanese affairs reached unprecedented heights, characterized by SCAP seeming to run afoul of Washington's instructions, the minority party government doing battle with the majority opposition parties, . . . Government Section clashing with ESS, and General Whitney tilting with Prime Minister Yoshida."[10] Modesty may have deterred Williams from including the "Yamazaki affair" in his critique.

Yoshida wanted to call an election while his popularity was high and his opponents were in headlong retreat. Although the Democratic Liberal Party was the largest in the House of Representatives, with 153 seats, this figure represented only one-third of the 466 seats. The Socialists and the Democrats with their small party helpers still held a solid majority of 235 seats and could block a vote to dissolve the Diet. It took Yoshida two months of abrasive bargaining with both his political opposition and SCAP before the Diet could be dissolved and an election called.

Yoshida's subservient position became painfully clear when SCAP insisted that amendments to the NPSL be passed before the Diet was dissolved. GS went even further and insisted that the dissolution could take place only after the lower house of the Diet passed a resolution of no confidence in the new cabinet. Yoshida and the Democratic Liberals strongly supported the amendments to the NPSL, having consistently advocated that government workers should not have the right to strike or bargain collectively with the government. Yoshida was not keen on the provision for an independent national personnel authority, another of Blaine Hoover's borrowings from U.S. practice, but this was a detail the prime minister could accept. Hoover complicated the issue by insisting on a pay raise for government workers,[11] which MacArthur supported on the theory that it would mitigate the workers' bitterness over the new restrictions. SCAP's financial experts shuddered at the prospect of additional spending, but they were overruled.

Diet dissolution raised a serious question of constitutional interpretation, one of the few presented in the early years of the constitution's operation. Article 69 provided that the House of Representatives
could be dissolved if it passed a resolution of no confidence in the
cabinet or rejected a confidence resolution. Article 7 provided that the
emperor could dissolve the House of Representatives with the advice
and approval of the cabinet. The question was whether the House of
Representatives could be dissolved only by a vote pursuant to Article 69
or whether it could also be dissolved under Article 7 by decision of the
cabinet or the prime minister alone, with the emperor giving his approval as a mere formality. No one argued that the emperor had the power
unilaterally to dissolve the lower house.[12]

To head off the impasse, Williams suggested a solution: the amendments to the NPSL would be enacted, the bills for a pay raise and the
supplemental budget would be approved, and then a resolution of no
confidence would be presented and passed, with opposition support.
This proposal led to the famous "collusive dissolution," which acquired
considerable notoriety in Japanese politics. According to the terms of
this stratagem, the major parties would all commit themselves in advance to vote for the bills on the legislative agenda, and then the opposition would introduce and vote for a motion of no confidence in the
government, which would dissolve the lower house pursuant to Article
69 of the constitution. Yoshida went along reluctantly with this deal,
which he felt was not sanctioned by the constitution and violated parliamentary principles.[13]

On November 27 Whitney and Kades called on the prime minister
to force the issue. Whitney reported MacArthur's fear that the political situation would seriously worsen if the wage increase were not
approved before the Diet was dissolved. Whitney asserted that to go
through the emperor for authority to dissolve the Diet would raise
grave concern among the Allied powers that an attempt was being made
to restore governmental powers to the throne. Yoshida replied that the
emperor could dissolve the lower house with the advice and approval of
the cabinet. Whitney countered that the emperor's role was a ministerial function to be performed only after the lower house passed, or
failed to pass, a motion of no confidence. When the prime minister
asked Whitney what should be done next, the general coyly replied that
he was not there to suggest but to act as "messenger for General
MacArthur."[14]

Yoshida decided to try pinning MacArthur down. And so the next day, November 28, he wrote the general a letter that began with pointed irony, "General Whitney was kind enough to call on me this morning to give advice on the current political situation. I feel I have to express my sincere appreciation for his valuable assistance at this juncture. May I take the liberty of asking you to convey to General Whitney my feeling of deep gratitude?" The prime minister then summarized his understanding of the agreement and concluded that "General Whitney will see to it that the opposition parties act in good faith in accordance with the line set as above."[15]

Yoshida may have been the head of a government under military occupation, but he was acting more like a negotiator than a subordinate. And he seemed to be putting MacArthur into the role of an arbitrator. The general still wanted to stand aside, for on November 29 Whitney replied that MacArthur had "noted with satisfaction the compromise agreement which had been determined upon by all major political parties." Whitney then informed the prime minister that General MacArthur and General Marquat had decided to leave it to the Japanese government to set the wage level for public servants.[16]

Nevertheless, SCAP officials insisted on higher figures than Yoshida wanted, and he was forced to give in after meeting with MacArthur, Whitney, and Marquat. Yoshida stated in his memoirs that the result was a "defeat" because ESS changed its position. After much scrambling by both occupation and Japanese finance experts to figure out where to get the money for the pay raise, the wage bill and the supplemental budget were approved on December 21 and 22, 1948.[17]

One victim of the budget battle was the minister of finance, Izumiyama Sanroku. At a late meeting of the Diet on December 13, his inhibitions loosened by sake, he made advances toward a woman member of the Democratic Party, reportedly asserting, "I like you better than the supplemental budget." Later he fell asleep on a couch in the Diet lobby. A photograph of the recumbent minister got wide play in the press the next day. He immediately resigned.[18]

In keeping with the plan for a collusive dissolution, a motion of no confidence in the Yoshida cabinet was passed on December 23, and the lower house was dissolved. Yoshida called a new election for January 23, 1949. The sixty-eight days of the second Yoshida cabinet had been stormy, but he was confident of his leadership ability and his good relations with MacArthur. Yoshida sensed, too, that the strong-arm methods of the occupation and the evident animus of GS toward him were stirring some resentment among the Japanese.[19]

Yoshida had been preparing for an election since leaving office nineteen months before. After putting down the Yamazaki insurrection and finally meeting SCAP conditions for a general election, he was ready. In his campaign he focused on Japan's two main requirements—economic stabilization and an early peace treaty. He also promised tax reductions and called for self-reliance by the Japanese people, with an overtone of greater independence and freedom from interference. These ideas turned out to be appealing.

True to his hopes, the election gave Yoshida and the Democratic Liberals an absolute majority of 264 seats, one of the few times in Japanese history that a party won so sweeping a victory. In comparison with the election of 1947, Yoshida's party doubled the number of Diet seats and the percentage of votes it obtained. The Socialists suffered a catastrophic defeat, falling from 143 seats to 49.[20] The Democrats dropped from 90 to 68. The Communist Party, however, skyrocketed from 9 to 35 seats. Thus, the two extremes—the Communists and the Democratic Liberals—profited from the failure of the former coalition parties in the middle. A number of Socialist leaders, including Katayama and Nishio, were defeated. The husband and wife team of Katō Kanjū and Katō Shizue, left Socialists of moderation and intelligence, went down.

The day after the election MacArthur issued a remarkably brief and simple statement: "The people of the free world everywhere can take satisfaction in this enthusiastic and orderly Japanese election, which at a critical moment in Asiatic history has given so clear and decisive a mandate for the conservative philosophy of government."[21]

A few days later the indefatigable British ambassador saw MacArthur and Yoshida to get their slant on the election. MacArthur said he was "delighted" that a strong conservative party would be in power for four years. He did not consider the Communists' sharp success, 35 seats and 9.6 percent of the votes cast, as "anything very serious" because he thought they had now "reached their peak in Japan." Nevertheless, he said, "he would watch them 'like a hawk'; if they broke the law they would pay for it."[22]

MacArthur commented, "Yoshida was an astute diplomat and he had learned a lot lately regarding the internal politics of his country and the conditions in occupied Japan." Gascoigne told London that the general had changed his opinion of Yoshida, "for in the past he had severely criticized him to me, inter alia, for his efforts to circumvent occupation regulations." Some historians have questioned Yoshida's ability as a diplomat, but he was winning plaudits from the supreme commander.[23]

Sir Alvary found Prime Minister Yoshida "jubilant" over his victory. He assured the ambassador he would not be too stern with the labor movement. Saying he was a "good liberal," with a horror of the extreme right and the extreme left, Yoshida asserted that he wanted to bring to Japan a moderate, two-party system in which the party of the left would resemble the British Labour Party. The prime minister showed some prescience in observing that communism in Japan had reached its high-water mark; he added that it would never be successful because the people "hated" Russia and "feared" communist ideology.[24]

The big victory of the conservative Democratic Liberals was undoubtedly the most important result of the election, and the jump in Communist representation in the new lower house was the most surprising. These results were readily explained by the dismal failure of the middle-of-the-road parties to give Japan any sense of purpose during their one and one-half years in office.[25] The Democratic Liberal Party became the dominant force in Japanese politics, buttressed by later coalition with the main wing of the Democratic Party and rechristened the Liberal Democratic Party in 1955. The Communists were never able again to reach the high level of votes and seats they had attained in 1949. The Socialists managed to regroup themselves and do better in later elections, but they never became a fully unified party and finally split in 1960.

The principal engineer of these results was Yoshida Shigeru. He had rebuilt his party and taken charge of the conservative movement. He markedly influenced the course of Japanese politics by injecting new blood into the conservative forces. SCAP had expected that its reform programs would develop new and enlightened leaders, particularly among the Social Democrats, but the Socialists proved too weak in doctrine and too divided by factionalism to nurture strong principles and leaders.

Yoshida, however, began in 1949 to bring in from the ranks of the bureaucracy a group of younger men who were to provide some of Japan's best leaders in the years to come. Among them were Ikeda Hayato from the Finance Ministry, Satō Eisaku from the Transportation Ministry, both of whom became highly successful prime ministers, and Okazaki Katsuo from the Foreign Ministry, who became foreign minister in 1952. Fifty-five former bureaucrats were elected to the Diet in 1949, nearly all of them Yoshida supporters. Although most of them had held positions in government during and before the war, their technical expertise and lack of roots in old-guard politics made them desirable as legislators.[26] Yoshida's program for finding leaders no doubt succeeded because of the openings created by the occupation purges and reform policies, but it was his inspiration that created the "Yoshida school," as the Japanese call it. The program also fortified Yoshida against old-guard politicians and purgees when they made their bid for power several years later.

Yoshida felt so strong after the election that following lengthy discussions with the political adviser, he was willing to sign a one-sided agreement with the United States waiving Japan's claim for the sinking of the merchant ship *Awa Maru* by a U.S. submarine in April 1945. The sinking occurred after the United States had granted safe conduct to the vessel, which had delivered relief goods to Allied prisoners of war in Southeast Asia and was returning to Japan with two thousand Japanese passengers, all but one of whom were lost.[27]

MacArthur's confidence in the prime minister had risen markedly. Instead of criticizing Yoshida as lazy, as he had done in the past, the general told Herbert Norman, the Canadian representative, on February 11, 1949, that "Yoshida's political philosophy was comparable to that of the Conservatives in England or the Republicans in the United States. Yoshida was free from political ambition, anxious to do the right thing and realized the dangers of abusing the majority respect he now enjoyed in the Diet." MacArthur thought it was wrong to describe Yoshida as reactionary or ultraconservative; "these forces were represented by the zaibatsu and the military and were now eliminated." Yoshida was so annoyed by these labels, which the foreign press, joined sometimes by the Japanese press and persons in the occupation, often attached to him and the Democratic Liberal Party, that he made a speech defending himself at the foreign correspondents club on May 11, 1949.[28]

American observers noted a sense of protest in the Japanese election. A leading State Department expert, Max W. Bishop, reported in February after a trip to Japan that the election was a protest vote against the occupation and that "Yoshida has become a symbol of Japan's ability to stand up to the occupation." Edwin O. Reischauer of Harvard University, who became ambassador to Japan in 1961, observed at the same time that "whereas several years ago the Japanese looked upon the occupation as a unified, all-powerful force, centering around an infallible leader, they have come to see it today as a conglomeration of persons having conflicting views and widely varying abilities. . . . Even General MacArthur has lost his aura of sanctity. . . . This irritation with the occupation was significantly demonstrated by the returns of the recent election, which resulted in a resounding defeat of those parties which were tainted with 'collaboration' with general headquarters." Both Bishop and Reischauer thought that the communists were expanding their influence in this disturbed situation.[29]

Another sign of the changing times was the departure in December 1948 of Charles L. Kades, the powerful driving force in SCAP for political reform. He had remained in Japan much longer than he had originally expected because he was fascinated by the challenge and importance of his job. In 1947, in a rare meeting with lesser staff officers, MacArthur had asked Kades to stay on until the reform job was done. By the end of 1948 Kades was out of sympathy with some of the ideas coming out of Washington, and he was discouraged by the return of the conservatives to power in Japan. The general asked Kades to explain the situation in Japan to the top officials in Washington and persuade them not to change direction. Kades conducted a one-man campaign and made several important speeches, with the approval of the supreme commander.[30] But the pressures for change in both Washington and Tokyo were too strong to resist.

The signal conservative victory may have caused Yoshida and MacArthur to feel optimistic about the direction of events in Japan. Yet it was evident by 1949 that occupation policies and leadership roles were evolving. Washington was taking a much more active role than before, especially in pressing for economic recovery. MacArthur was still supreme, but no longer unchallengeable. And Yoshida was prepared to play the part designed by U.S. policymakers for a more active Japan and a less interventionist SCAP. MacArthur correctly believed that Yoshida had developed remarkably as a politician and leader. His views on national issues and occupation policies had not changed, but fed no doubt by his election victory, his self-assurance in handling people and problems had grown. The Japanese press thought he was so strong-willed it began to call him "one man," by which the press meant one-man rule.

One of the first fruits of the Draper-Kennan approach to Japan was a directive sent to MacArthur in December 1948 "to achieve fiscal, monetary and price and wage stability in Japan as rapidly as possible, as well as to maximize production for export." The general relayed the directive to Yoshida by letter on December 19, making the rare acknowledgment that he had received it as an "interim directive."[31] This important instruction had been prepared by the National Advisory Council (NAC), a top-level economic advisory body, and approved by the president. Its impact was somewhat blunted a few days later by the no-confidence vote against the second Yoshida cabinet and the hanging of five major war criminals.

The directive set out nine goals, including a balanced budget, increased production, better tax collection, stronger price controls, improved foreign trade procedures, and more efficient food collection. A target date of three months was set for instituting a single exchange rate in place of the existing maze of multiple prices. Most of the points in the directive, other than the exchange rate, had been incorporated in instructions to the Japanese during the previous several years. General Marquat had given the Ashida cabinet a ten-point program very similar to the NAC directive on July 15, 1948. But this time Washington, not merely the economic specialists of SCAP or even MacArthur, was speaking.

Yoshida immediately replied to MacArthur's letter, thanking the general for his "earnest advice and detailed analysis" and noting, somewhat undiplomatically, that the U.S. objectives were ones "which you have repeatedly indicated to my government and I am happy to say that their importance is fully appreciated."[32] The NAC directive had aroused a heated debate in Washington. The Department of the Army and MacArthur opposed stringent stabilization measures and a single exchange rate. Against them were State and Treasury. They compromised by sending the stabilization directive and a special mission to look over the situation.[33]

Yoshida knew little of the battling within the U.S. government over economic policy and probably did not fully appreciate the significance of the new directive. During his subsequent election campaign he said nothing to indicate that a new and tough U.S. program was about to be applied to Japan. He even talked about eliminating the sales tax and providing more government support for struggling industries, almost in contradiction to the new policies. Nor did Yoshida know that Mac-Arthur was worried about the impact the new program would have.

MacArthur had wired Washington on December 12, 1948, expressing strong reservations about the new directive:

[It] calls for the imposition of economic controls probably without historical precedent. Its implementation will require the reversal of existing trends toward free enterprise . . . and negation of many of the fundamental rights and

liberties heretofore extended to...Japanese society.... Imposed at this
time when the Japanese are registering such marked and decisive strides toward their own economic rehabilitation and when the austerity of Japanese
life is already reflected in an average monthly wage equivalent to less than
twenty dollars United States currency and for whom a 1,500 daily calorie
basic ration is still an objective rather than a realization, its effect on the local
situation is impossible accurately to gauge.... If the Japanese people follow
us...if capital and management move with vigor and determination...and
if Japanese politicians and political parties faithfully subordinate themselves
and their policies and political efforts to the stated objective...we will succeed. If any of these human forces fail...explosive consequences well may
result, but I shall do my best.

A few months later MacArthur took a less anguished attitude. In a talk
with the Australian representative on March 15, 1949, the general said
that Draper had insisted on the directive "in order to have something to
show to Congress." MacArthur went on to say that "the nine-point ESP
[economic stabilization program] was designed to hustle the Japanese."
The general was not sure of the wisdom of hustling.[34]

On February 1, 1949, the American whose impact on the Japanese
during the occupation was second only to that of MacArthur arrived in
Tokyo. Joseph M. Dodge came as financial adviser to the supreme commander to begin what the Japanese called the "Dodge whirlwind." A
self-made man who had risen to be president of the Detroit Bank and
served as adviser to General Clay in Germany in the early years of the
occupation there, Dodge was a determined and tough-minded banker
who was nevertheless unassuming in his personal relations, although he
was not very popular with some of the SCAP staff, who made him out
to be a kind of penny-pinching accountant. He had been recruited for
the Japan job by Draper, with MacArthur's consent. President Truman
personally asked Dodge to take the job and assured him of full
support.[35] Dodge won the confidence of MacArthur, with whom he
worked closely, and he gained the respect and friendship of the
Japanese leaders, who came to value his judgment and willingness to
talk fairly and candidly with them about the issues they faced together.

The goal of both the SCAP and the Japanese economic experts was to
reduce the costs of the occupation and prepare Japan for a competitive
role in the world economy. Dodge felt the necessary preconditions were
price stability and a balanced budget. By the time Dodge arrived, conditions were slowly improving, but indicators were still well below prewar levels. Industrial production had reached about 70 percent of the
benchmark 1934–1936 period. The Tokyo price level at the start of

1949 was more than twice that of the year before. Industry and banks were desperately short of capital, so the government facilitated capital accumulation by providing generous loans and subsidies to producers. Foreign trade was entirely controlled by SCAP, although foreign traders had been allowed to do business in Japan since 1947. The trade deficit went up from $352 million in 1947 to $426 million in 1948.[36]

Yoshida told his new cabinet at its first meeting on February 18 that he wanted the nine goals of the stabilization program fully realized. This meant reversing some of the easy-money policies he had advocated during the election campaign. After consulting business leaders, he chose as his new finance minister Ikeda Hayato, a veteran Finance Ministry official and tax expert. Yoshida had come to think that in dealing with Americans new faces and younger men were often preferable to the politicians and businessmen of the old school. This appointment launched Ikeda on one of the most brilliant postwar political careers in Japan, which culminated in his becoming prime minister eleven years later.[37]

Dodge first met with senior Japanese officials on February 9, even before the new cabinet was formed. In a crisp and direct manner, he told them, "The budget will have to be balanced. Unpopular steps will have to be taken. Austerity will have to be the basis for a series of economic measures." One Finance Ministry expert, Miyazawa Kiichi, who later entered the Diet and became a senior political leader, said of Dodge, "We thought he was a terrible old man, but in several years things turned out the way he said." Miyazawa related how the Japanese often found it a useful tactic to play off one group in SCAP against another; this time they decided they would side with Dodge against the "New Dealers."[38]

Dodge and Ikeda met on March 1 for their first serious discussion of the budget, which the government was preparing for the fiscal year beginning April 1. In vivid language, Dodge stressed three points. First, Japan's economy was walking on stilts made of price subsidies and U.S. commodity assistance. These would have to be cut, or "Japan would fall on its face." The budget should show clearly how large these items were. Second, spending by the Reconstruction Finance Bank, then at the ¥40 billion ($111 million) level, was undesirable. It would be a crime for Japan's inflation-bloated economy to spend money labeled for "investment." It was high time to turn off this spigot. Third, excess liquidity in the system had to be sopped up.[39]

Dodge felt Yoshida's political promises to cut the income tax and eliminate the sales tax were wrong. The sales tax was said to be a bad tax, but no tax was a "good tax." At a press conference on March 1, Dodge restated these thoughts in his pungent way. His stilts metaphor became famous in Japan.[40]

Dodge and the Japanese, led by Ikeda, spent more than one month in almost constant negotiation over the fiscal year (FY) 1949 budget. Both kept in close touch with their principals, General MacArthur and Prime Minister Yoshida, neither of whom knew much about budget complexities but both of whom carefully followed and approved all significant actions. The most contentious items were the income tax and the sales tax, which the Democratic Liberal Party had promised during the election campaign to reduce. Dodge would not permit this. His insistence on an increase of 50 to 60 percent in railway fares and postal fees also gave the Japanese serious problems.

Ikeda became so discouraged early in the negotiations that he wanted to resign, but Yoshida bucked him up and persuaded him to stay. The political pressure on both men from their conservative colleagues was intense, but Yoshida, buttressed by his overwhelming majority, refused to yield an inch. Ikeda said later in his career that he owed all his success to Yoshida *sensei*, meaning "my mentor Yoshida." Without Yoshida's backing at that point, Ikeda might not have had a later career. The success he and Dodge ultimately achieved in turning around the economy proved to be a tremendous asset for him.[41]

By March 20, 1949, agreement was reached on the budget for fiscal year 1949, which authorized revenues and expenditures of ¥741 billion. The budget also placed anticipated American aid (¥86.9 billion, or $248 million) in a counterpart fund. Dodge insisted that Bank of Japan note issue be kept to the 1948 level. By careful monitoring and control in FY 1949, the Japanese were able to reduce the 1949 note issue by ¥1.2 billion (about $3.5 million) and to achieve a dramatic reduction in spending. The net result was FY revenue of ¥758.6 billion and expenditure of ¥596.5 billion, a huge surplus of ¥162 billion (about $460 million) at the end of the year. The Japanese called this a "superbalanced budget" because it had such a large surplus, for the first time since 1931.[42]

On April 23, just before he left for home, Dodge decided after lengthy calculations that Japan should institute a single exchange rate of U.S. $1.00 to ¥360, and SCAP so instructed the Japanese government. The single rate put powerful pressure on Japanese exporters to cut costs and improve their products to meet foreign competition without the cushion of variable prices that could be adjusted to promote sales. Amazingly, the 360-to-1 rate lasted until the Smithsonian conference of 1971; the yen became increasingly undervalued, thus buttressing exports in the 1960s. Dodge made the decision to set the rate, and he proved farsighted.[43]

To complement Dodge's attack on inflation through budget reforms and to rationalize the tax structure, an American tax mission under Carl Shoup of Columbia University came to Japan in May 1949 on the first of two visits. Shoup's report advised the government to emphasize direct taxation of corporate income and personal income as principal sources of revenue; over time the revenue from the two taxes tended to equalize. The report also struck a blow for local autonomy by recommending that the revenue base of local governments be strengthened. Most of Shoup's recommendations were adopted in 1950, including repeal of the sales tax on a number of basic commodities. The value-added tax he suggested was enacted, then repealed in 1953. The tax structure he recommended lasted for thirty-five years. It had the effect of steadily increasing revenue from corporation taxes, as improving economic conditions enabled corporations to grow in size and profitability.[44]

The Japanese government took a series of important steps to stimulate economic activity. The Ministry of International Trade and Industry was created in early 1949. Yoshida Shigeru, always a firm believer in economic diplomacy, and Shirasu Jirō, his trusted adviser, played key roles in the ministry's establishment. MITI, as it is universally known, served as an economic general staff for government planning and government-business coordination. Its contribution to Japan's later economic growth testified to Yoshida's acumen in economic policy-making. Chalmers Johnson called MITI "the single most powerful instrument for carrying out [Japan's] industrial policy."[45]

Foreign exchange operations and controls were strengthened. In late 1949 SCAP turned control over to the Japanese government, which passed a foreign exchange and foreign trade control law in December. Foreign capital transactions by Japanese, investment by foreigners in Japan, and repatriation of profits by foreign companies were all carefully limited and required MITI approval. This system, set up under the watchful eyes of SCAP experts, has been described as "the most restrictive foreign trade and foreign exchange control system ever devised by a major free nation." The antimonopoly law passed in 1947 was also significantly relaxed in June 1949. These arrangements went a long way toward establishing the governmental policy and structure for facilitating rapid growth in the next two decades.[46]

Increasing foreign trade, a high priority, was rendered more urgent by the communist takeover of China in 1949. U.S. planners gave attention to Southeast Asia as a possible alternative to the markets and raw material sources China had provided before the war. Various plans were drafted, especially in Washington and Tokyo, to strengthen the security and economies of Southeast Asia and to increase Japan's trade with them. Defense Department planners in particular came up with some imaginative ideas for using U.S. assistance to build up Japan and increase its ties with Southeast Asian nations. In February 1950 MacArthur referred to the ideas circulating in the Pentagon as a "fantastic scheme for Asiatic trade." A generation later, in the aftermath of the Vietnam War, some American writers detected in the voluminous staff papers on this subject a U.S. intention to build a "great crescent" of anticommunist nations stretching from Japan to Pakistan and to bring about "Japanese economic integration with Southeast Asia." They concluded that these plans ultimately "helped lead the United States to its long and costly intervention in Southeast Asia."[47]

U.S. policy in that period was actually far less ambitious. NSC working-level papers and speeches by senior officials reflected a cautious approach, stressing moderate economic and military assistance to a few key Southeast Asian nations to help them strengthen internal security and resist communism. One of the basic policy papers, NSC 48/2 of December 30, 1949, provided that $75 million of already appropriated funds were to be used in Thailand, Indonesia, and the Indochina states for internal security. President Truman approved the paper with the comment, "A program will be all right, but whether we implement it depends on circumstances." In his famous speech of January 12, 1950, defining U.S. interests in Asia, Secretary of State Acheson made it clear that beyond a defense perimeter running through Japan and the Philippines, "initial reliance must be placed on the people attacked to resist" an armed attack; the United States could "do no more than help." He noted that Japan was having a hard time buying raw materials and selling goods. Eventually about $50 million was appropriated for security and technical assistance to Indochina and three other Southeast Asian nations; by 1951 only $10 million of this had been delivered. The record shows that no U.S. policy was adopted or funds appropriated for "building an anticommunist barrier" in Southeast Asia or for "integrating the economies of Japan and Southeast Asia." The Japanese were also cautious about Southeast Asia, preferring to avoid any security involvement and to slowly expand their modest trade relations with the region.[48]

The Korean War brought about a huge increase in Japan's exports and foreign exchange earnings, thereby causing Japanese interest in foreign markets to shift from Southeast Asia to the United States, the beginning of a dynamic and tempestuous trade relationship.

The Dodge Line, as the Japanese began to call it, had a number of beneficial results. Soon inflation fell markedly and consumer prices went down. The budget deficit of ¥62.5 billion in FY 1948 (about $175 million) was transformed into a surplus of ¥125 billion in 1950 (about $350 million). Dodge established a policy of balanced budgets that the Japanese followed religiously for two decades. He also gave a strong impetus to the enterpreneurial spirit of Japanese businessmen by telling them that the United States wanted them to take the lead in bringing about recovery under stable conditions and free of occupation restraints.[49]

There were some ill effects of the Dodge Line: tight money, a big jump in unemployment, lower industrial production, and a rise in the number of bankruptcies. Farmers were deprived of black market sales and higher food prices. Laborers were thrown out of work or deprived of wage increases. Businessmen had trouble getting credit and were put under pressure to export rather than sell on the easier domestic market. Nearly everyone complained bitterly about depressed conditions. The deflationary Dodge Line was by no means an engine of economic revival.

Dodge realized that his program would have serious internal effects. He met a number of times with politicians and businessmen to explain what he was trying to do and to alleviate their concerns. He was entirely willing to accept responsibility for the actions the Japanese government was being forced to take and offered to help Ikeda in any way possible. Dodge sometimes complained that occupation policy was misguided in trying to confer on the Japanese a standard of living like that of the United States,[50] but he was not as wise a long-range economic forecaster as he was a stern-minded banker.

MacArthur was rarely much impressed by visitors from the United States, but he had a good opinion of Dodge, whom he described as "primarily a banker, extremely honest, cautious and thoroughly reliable." Yoshida's daughter recalled that her father had many sessions with Dodge in which the prime minister argued vehemently, but unsuccessfully, that some of Dodge's budget actions were too harsh and would do damage to Japan.[51]

Dodge is much admired in Japan for the unflinching line he took on balancing, or "overbalancing," the budget; for many years Japanese budget managers tried to adhere to this policy. He also gets credit for wiping out inflation, although SCAP economists and some Japanese feel that the supply-demand gap, the main cause of inflation, was narrowing by the end of 1948. The *Economist* pointed out, however, in its startling feature of September 1962, that by then Japan's real national product was increasing at an average rate of more than 9 percent a year while "continuing and following almost precisely the policies which Mr. Dodge had castigated and opposed." For example, Dodge had opposed Japanese banks' practice of overloaning heavily, yet the banks continued this practice for many years, relying on the Bank of Japan to provide a safety net. Many economists also feel that without the Korean War, the Dodge Line would have plunged Japan into a serious depression.[52]

One point does seem to be clear. The Dodge Line posed a hard test for Shigeru Yoshida. He had been overwhelmed by a labor crisis during his first term in 1947. In the summer of 1949 he faced an equally serious challenge to hold his party together and stave off the attacks he faced from labor, business, and the public, all of which were being subjected to the harsh rigors of the Dodge whirlwind and the new U.S. policy. Nevertheless, Yoshida firmly supported Dodge, while Dodge was of the view that "Yoshida is our best asset in Japan." Dodge ended up with surprisingly good relations with Japanese politicians, bureaucrats, and businessmen. It may not be too gross an exaggeration to say, as one American observer has, that Dodge "engineered the historic tacit alliance between America and the Japanese conservative and business elements that endured for the decades that followed."[53]

CHAPTER 16

Unrest and Violence on the Left

The tough budgetary and personnel programs of the Dodge Line in 1949 and 1950 led to tension and violence in the Tokyo area, the epicenter of political shocks in Japan. The government and the private sector discharged thousands of working personnel and, with SCAP approval, took a number of repressive measures against liberal and left-wing elements in politics, the media, and the labor movement. The summer of 1949 was a time of more trouble than any other in the postwar period, but the occupation's control and the government's stability were never endangered.

Reduction of government spending was a key element in the Dodge Line. Prime Minister Yoshida was only too happy to comply. In early 1949 the government employed about 1.63 million workers. Government offices were often heavily overstaffed as a means of holding down unemployment, with repatriates and demobilized military men receiving preferential treatment. General MacArthur expressed the view in March 1949 that both public and private employment rolls "had been padded quite unnecessarily to include twenty to forty percent more workers than required."[1]

On April 19, 1949, the prime minister wrote a letter to the supreme commander stating his reduction plan would save the government about ¥7 billion (nearly $20 million) in annual wages.[2] Because the national railways had incurred a ¥50 billion deficit (about $140 million) in FY 1949, particularly sharp reductions were to be made in the railway staff of 610,486 employees. A new ceiling was set by law at

506,734, thereby necessitating a cut of more than 100, 000 workers. The national railway workers union was the largest in Japan in early 1949 and the most active politically. The leading force in the labor strife of 1949 and 1950, its central committee was almost evenly divided between moderates and leftists, some of whom later became communists.

Along with the government's "administrative retrenchment," private industry carried out a massive reduction program. Persons discharged in 1949 under the various administrative retrenchment programs totaled about 160,000 government workers and 330,000 private-sector workers. About 100,000 more were fired by the private sector in 1950.[3] Although efficiency and rationalization of operations were usually the announced reasons for the cuts, many workers were discharged because they were considered left-wingers.

As soon as the government decided on its personnel retrenchment, a series of incidents occurred—work stoppages, worker takeovers of railway operations, demonstrations, and a strike threat (which SCAP's labor chief personally, and without specific authority, ordered canceled). In fact, SCAP officials interpreted MacArthur's statement of January 31, 1947, banning the threatened general strike as a legal prohibition against all strikes. Unrest increased as it became common knowledge that leftists and labor activists would be among the first to be fired in both government and the private sector. The largest number of railway sabotage incidents of the entire occupation took place in 1949, the worst month being July, with 1,574 reported cases.[4]

The Communist Party, with Tokuda in the front line, decided to take the lead in opposing the government's plans. At a meeting of the party's central committee on June 18 and 19, Tokuda announced a "September revolution thesis" in which he called for the overthrow of the Yoshida cabinet by September. The communists had no specific battle plan. They knew that a strike would be banned, as had happened when they called a general strike in February 1947. But Tokuda wanted to rally all the forces on the left against reactionary capitalism. Although his appeal seemed to be empty theatrics at the time, it proved to be the first salvo in a series of terrorist actions that soon followed. The return to Japan on June 27, 1949, of 2,000 prisoners of war from the Soviet Union, waving red flags and singing communist songs, added to hopes and fears that the communist revolution might not be far off.

Three notorious incidents took place within six weeks during the summer of 1949.[5] The first was the death on July 5 or 6 of the president of the national railways, Shimoyama Sadanori, whose name had frequently appeared in the press when the plans for a huge personnel reduction began to receive attention. He had received threatening letters. On July 4 the first set of dismissal orders was sent out to 37,000 railway employees. Shimoyama was at work on the morning of July 5, but his whereabouts became a mystery after he went shopping at the Mitsukoshi department store in downtown Tokyo later in the morning. Shortly after midnight his body was found on the railway tracks near Kitasenju in the northern part of the Tokyo metropolitan district. Although the body had been run over by a train and was dismembered, it was quickly identified, but no one ever determined how the body got there or even whether Shimoyama had been dead before the train ran over him. Prime Minister Yoshida was so concerned at the time that he called in the head of the national police and asked why he did not "go to the scene of these incidents and assume direction of the operations, only to be told that the national police could not intervene unless the local police requested their aid."[6]

The Shimoyama incident became the most famous unsolved crime in postwar Japan. No credible evidence was ever unearthed regarding his activities immediately before the train ran over his body. No arrests were ever made. Suicide was never conclusively ruled out. Twenty years later a group of educators and intellectuals made a study of the incident, which had reached the proportions in Japan of the Sacco-Vanzetti case in the United States in the 1920s, but their investigation produced no new explanations. Rumors even sprang up, and were reinforced by a popular book, that American or Soviet agents had perpetrated the deed to cause political agitation and advance their own purposes.[7]

The second major incident took place at Mitaka railway station in western Tokyo on the evening of July 15, two days after the second round of dismissal notices, affecting 63,000 employees of the national railways, had been posted. An empty electric train that had been parked for the night was somehow released from the car barn. It rolled down a hill for a half mile, hurtled over a guard rail, and smashed into the station area; six persons were killed, and twenty others injured. The police concluded that the incident was an act of sabotage because the train "could not have been moved without deliberate human action." Police arrested ten persons, nine of them Communist Party members. After a lengthy trial, one of them, the noncommunist, confessed and was convicted. His sentence of life imprisonment was confirmed on appeal, and he died in prison eighteen years after the incident. The nine communist defendants were acquitted, and this verdict was sustained on appeal.

The last of the three big cases—the Matsukawa incident—took place early in the morning of August 17. A passenger train loaded with 630 persons was derailed at Matsukawa, in Fukushima Prefecture, 168 miles north of Tokyo. The engineer and his two assistants were trapped in the wreckage and killed, while many passengers were injured, three seriously. Someone had tampered with the tracks, removing the bolts and joining plates and throwing them into a nearby field along with the tools that had been used.

Twenty persons were arrested, most of them acknowledged communists, after one of them had confessed. At their trial, seven more defendants confessed. All of the defendants were found guilty by the Fukushima district court, but after ten years of litigation and appeals, including a retrial and a second hearing by the Supreme Court, all were acquitted on the ground that the retrial had turned up important new evidence. This was Japan's most publicized postwar court case, one that well illustrated the complexities of the judicial process in Japan.

Following the Shimoyama and Mitaka incidents, a struggle for control of the central committee of the national railway workers union took place. The communist members had a bare majority, but the national railways fired all seventeen of them, leaving in control the Democratic League (Mindō) faction, which some Japanese thought was a tool of the occupation. The impression was inescapable that the occupation and the Japanese government were taking quick and firm action, in contrast to their hesitant reaction in January 1947 to the strike threat. The leftists also seemed to be alienating public opinion, thereby making it easier for the Yoshida cabinet to isolate them from moderate elements in the labor movement.[8]

Many companies had serious labor problems in those years. The Toyota Motor Company, for example, had managed to rebuild itself after the war. It developed a small car, having decided that the only hope for the Japanese auto industry lay in producing superior small vehicles, but found by 1949 that it could not sell all the cars it produced. As a consequence it could not meet its payroll. In April 1949, after Toyota started to make salary cuts and plans for dismissals, the company union founded at the end of the war went on strike. Red flags waved from the top of buildings, and workers demonstrated for an end to employee reduction proposals and delays in wage payments. The company was on the edge of bankruptcy when agreement was reached in June 1950. The union agreed to reduce the work force from 8,000 to 6,000, and the top management of the company including founder Toyoda Kiichirō resigned. This was the only strike in Toyota's history.[9]

Americans and Japanese, including MacArthur and Ikeda, agreed that the wages of government workers should be increased.[10] As in the case of the National Public Service Law in 1948, MacArthur saw that a wage increase would assuage the workers' bitterness. But it was not until the beginning of 1951 that a supplemental budget raised the monthly base pay of government workers by 22 percent to the princely total of ¥9,000 ($22 a month plus about $3 a month in allowances). Workers in the private sector continued to receive substantially higher pay than those working for the government. One promising result of the 1949–1950 negotiations was the successful resort to the national personnel authority and to arbitration procedures to settle pay issues. These mechanisms contributed markedly to labor peace and stability in future years. The Labor Union Law was amended in late 1948 to strengthen the hand of managers in several ways, notably by prohibiting full-time union officials from taking salaries from the company.

On July 4, 1949, at the height of the labor violence, MacArthur made a statement referring to the Communist Party and asking "whether any organization that persistently and publicly advocated a program at variance with the aims of democracy and opposed established order should be permitted to function as a legal party." Paradoxically, on September 3, 1949, the fourth anniversary of Japan's surrender, he said that "the threat of communism . . . is past." Then, on May 3, 1950, the third anniversary of the coming into force of the Japanese constitution, he issued a tough statement asserting that the Communist Party "has cast off the mantle of pretended legitimacy and assumed instead the role of an avowed satellite of an international predatory force and a Japanese pawn of an alien power policy, imperialistic purpose and subversive propaganda. That it has done so . . . raises doubt whether it should be regarded as a constitutionally recognized political movement." For the first time MacArthur had attacked the Communist Party by name in one of his most ringing pronouncements. Communist strength in Japan in 1948, according to SCAP sources, was about 16,200 party members and 80,000 supporters.[11]

By early 1950 Japanese leaders were talking about making the Communist Party illegal or setting up an un-Japanese activities committee on the model of a similar committee in the U.S. Congress. At the urging of SCAP the government enacted the Organization Control Law in April 1949, which prohibited "antidemocratic associations" and required all political organizations to register and submit their activities to public scrutiny. Riding the anticommunist wave, Yoshida appealed to MacArthur in June to release "small fry" from the purge orders to give them hope and enable them to join the struggle against communism. On July 15, 1949, Yoshida also sent a public statement he had made on the "tense and explosive" situation caused by the violence of the labor movement. Both MacArthur and Yoshida seemed to be groping for ways to deal with what they considered a serious subversive threat.[12]

Two events in the first half of 1950 intensified these fears. On January 6 the official journal of the Cominform, a propaganda arm of the Soviet Communist Party, carried an editorial in Moscow branding the "lovable Communist Party" line of Secretary General Nosaka Sanzō as "anti-democratic, anti-socialist, anti-patriotic and anti-Japanese." According to the editorial, the party in Japan should take a more militant and active line and abandon its policy of accommodation with the Allied occupation. Nosaka quickly admitted that mistakes had been made and that "the important mission assigned to the Communist Party of Japan as a link in the international revolutionary movement" must be fulfilled. Yet this assault by the citadel of communism did not seem to weaken Nosaka's position.[13]

The second event was a demonstration on May 30 held on the imperial plaza in downtown Tokyo. In one of the very few incidents during the occupation when Americans were physically assaulted, five American soldiers taking pictures were roughed up by leftist demonstrators. Eight of the demonstrators were arrested, tried by a U.S. military court, and given sentences ranging from five to eight years at hard labor. Yoshida issued a strong statement castigating communists for this "shameful affair" and asserting his government might consider outlawing the Communist Party.[14]

The campaign to rid the labor movement of leftists did not end with the retrenchment programs of 1949. In June 6 and 7, 1950, a few weeks before the Korean War started, the twenty-four members of the party's central committee and those responsible for the editorial policy of the party newspaper, *Akahata*, were barred from public service by virtue of letters from the supreme commander to the prime minister. On June 26 publication of *Akahata* was suspended indefinitely.[15]

The Japanese government hastened to carry out the occupation's orders. Communist Party leaders were expelled from office. Nine of the twenty-four central committee members went underground, including Tokuda, who died in Beijing in 1953. Itō Ritsu, who also fled to China, returned to Japan in 1980. Nosaka remained in Japan and returned to public life after the occupation ended. *Akahata* continued under suspension for the duration of the occupation, but it, too, resumed activity

in 1952. In 1950, however, no one challenged the legality of Mac-
Arthur's orders. The 1946 purge orders had been put above the law
of Japan, and the Supreme Court of Japan had been advised to reject
any challenge in the Japanese courts to the purge.

General Willoughby had earlier recommended that the Communist
Party be outlawed, but GS under General Whitney opposed this
approach. MacArthur was also against outlawing the party, but he
agreed that action had to be taken against the party because it was
becoming openly defiant of the occupation. Using the purge device
obviated the need for a massive campaign to suppress all communist
activity and served to split the communist leaders from the rank and
file of the party.[16]

MacArthur based his purge of communist leaders on his orders of
January 4, 1946, which had been directed against nationalist and militarist policies and leaders in the prewar era. It was not easy to stretch
the reference in these orders to "ultra-nationalistic, terroristic or secret
patriotic societies" far enough to apply to the Communist Party and its
leaders. The general's letter of June 6, 1950, purging party leaders, dealt
with this issue directly: "Their coercive methods bear striking parallel
to those by which the militaristic leaders of the past deceived and misled
the Japanese people, and their aims, if achieved, would surely lead
Japan to an even worse disaster. To permit this incitation to lawlessness
to continue unchecked, however embryonic it may appear, would be to
risk ultimate suppression of Japan's democratic institutions in direct
negation of the purpose and intent of Allied policy pronouncements,
forfeiture of her chance for political independence, and destruction of
the Japanese race."[17] This was muscular MacArthurian prose, but its
legal argumentation was anemic.

MacArthur's letters kicked off what has become known as the Red
Purge—the discharge of left-wingers in government, industry, and the
media and the purge of a number of leading Communist Party figures.
The purge was carried out by the government and by private companies
without any legal procedure or statement to justify it. Ultimately about
1,200 persons were discharged from government jobs, mostly teaching,
railways, and communications, and about 11,000 persons from private-
sector jobs. According to Japanese sources, GS gave verbal orders for
the purge of leftists in government and industry and advised the
Supreme Court of Japan "not to touch" the discharges in court.[18]

MacArthur's purge of communist leaders was probably welcomed
by Yoshida and by many Japanese citizens, who had become increasing-

ly disturbed by the violence of communist actions and rhetoric. The success of the Communist Party at the polls in January 1949 had caused widespread dismay, and Mao Zedong's takeover of control in China and the Soviet test of an atomic weapon later that year seemed to foreshadow a huge jump in communist international power.

Yet for many Japanese the Red Purge was ironic. Few actions by the occupation upset conservative Japanese more than the release of communists from prison in October 1945. People like Yoshida always considered that action a grave error, even if their deep-rooted fear of communism eventually subsided. To see MacArthur make an about-face on the communist issue in 1950 seemed to them to justify their earlier apprehensions and to reflect an inconsistent U.S. policy. SCAP appeared to be taking a reverse course, but so had U.S. policy toward the Soviet Union. Liberal Japanese may well have felt the Red Purge was reminiscent of some of the attitudes that prevailed in their country before the war.

Yoshida wrote about this issue in his memoirs. As to whether fundamental human rights guaranteed by the constitution had been violated, he commented that "the men concerned were not deprived of their employment because they were communists, or because of their belief in certain ideas which the government and public opinion did not share, but because the behavior of the communists up to that time and during the purge period indicated that these men were potential menaces to the offices and industries employing them; so that in order to protect these from more trouble in the future, the government was justified in removing the men concerned." Yoshida, like MacArthur, did not worry about legal niceties.[19]

MacArthur's appraisal of the communist movement in Japan had hardened noticeably since the general election of January 1949. He had put himself on record before the voting that the communist threat was not much more than "a nuisance factor" and that the communists had tried to capture the large labor unions in communications and transportation but failed because his preemptive action had stabilized the status of public service employees. In March 1949 he told the Australian representative that "there was no evidence of any connection between the Japanese Communist Party and Moscow. For three years his G-2 had been looking for it and it had not been found yet. In his view, the Japanese were essentially conservative and essentially individualist. . . . SCAP said that he was not worried by communism in Japan. There were more socialists than genuine communists in the JCP."[20]

Other than the Katayama cabinet of 1947 and 1948, Japanese leaders did not play a helpful role in labor relations during the occupation. Yoshida clearly felt the labor movement was communist dominated and beyond redemption. He was outraged by its frequent resort to violence. Two chapters in his memoirs were given to labor; he made the far-fetched point that its leaders were much like the militarists in prewar days, both being small minorities of extremists who forced the rank and file to go in directions it did not want to take. The labor experts in the government were more moderate than Yoshida: they were hostile to "left-wing political unionism" but supported Sōdōmei, the middle-course federation.[21]

SCAP experts joined by Japanese conservatives decided in 1949 that the breakup of the principal international labor organization into two conflicting wings, the leftist World Federation of Trade Unions and the International Confederation of Free Trade Unions (ICFTU), could be the key to labor peace in Japan. In the words of Valery Burati, an Austrian-born American who played a valuable role in making labor policy during the latter period of the occupation, a new council should be formed of the most important labor leaders in Japan in the hope that "around the issue of affiliation with the ICFTU they will be able to unify the Japanese labor movement." In approving the sending of a delegation to the ICFTU meeting in London in 1949, MacArthur expressed the hope to the new joint council that the delegation would return to Japan as the core of a unified labor movement and "a bastion impervious to the scourge of totalitarian ideology."[22]

The selection of a delegation had the paradoxical effect of splitting the right wing of the labor movement as well as the left. Even so, the new council, called Sōhyō, was formally inaugurated on July 11, 1950, after approval by MacArthur. It consisted of unions with a total membership of 3,770,000, or about one-half of all organized labor. Sōhyō was intended by its leaders to be "non-communist and middle of the road." Some called it "the bastard child of GHQ." But Takemae Eiji, an authority on the labor movement during the occupation, considered it a genuine initiative of Japanese labor.[23]

Sōhyō became the dominant force in the Japanese labor movement. But it was far from a tool of SCAP or U.S. policy. It soon became a liberal-left organization, taking many positions independent of U.S. and Japanese government views but not subservient to communist dogma. Sōhyō attacked the economic stabilization program, called for the overthrow of the Yoshida cabinet, opposed rearmament, and advocated a peace settlement that included the Soviet Union. From its inception, Sōhyō's viewpoints were close to those of the socialist left in Japan. Many Americans and Japanese were not happy about Sōhyō, yet it offered an alternative to the dominant groups on the right-center of the Japanese political spectrum. After the occupation a moderately conservative labor federation, Dōmei, was set up as a counterbalance to Sōhyō.

The tough and often arbitrary actions of SCAP and the Japanese government during the occupation decimated the influence of the far left in the Japanese labor movement and in politics. A number of Japanese in the labor movement and intellectual circles remain suspicious of U.S. motives even now, more than a generation later. Yet the labor movement remains alive and active. Workers have shared in the nation's affluence. Unions exert considerable influence on the policies of the two Socialist parties and have in recent years posed no threat to law and order. Management and labor are usually able to solve their problems effectively and amicably, with the government playing a helpful role. In late 1989 Sōhyō and Dōmei joined with most of the centrist labor unions to form Shin Rengō, a new trade union federation with 8 million members, two-thirds of Japan's organized labor. The leftist unions, including the railway workers, have also reorganized. The new structure of the labor movement is expected to have an important impact on Japanese politics.[24]

The labor movement was not the only source of unrest and tension in 1949. SCAP and the Japanese government became worried in the summer about the leftist threat in the education system. SCAP sent Walter C. Eells, an American professor of education at Stanford University who was a member of the headquarters education section, to visit universities around Japan and preach the evils of communist influence in higher education. Eells was greeted everywhere by crowds of jeering students and seemed to win few converts on the campuses, although he claimed that hundreds of communist teachers resigned as a result of the Red Purge campaign.[25]

In 1950 Yoshida and his education minister, Amano Teiyū, made plans to issue a "national code of conduct" for educational use. The public reaction, as Yoshida ruefully noted, was "one of uniform disapproval," and the idea was abandoned. The Japanese people were more liberal than their prime minister. Yoshida steadily pressed for more action to get rid of leftist teachers, but it was two years after the occupation ended before the Diet passed legislation more to his liking.

Yoshida and Amano also endeavored to win more respect and popularity for the national anthem and the flag. They did not make much progress in this regard, but their successors kept trying. Early in 1989 the Education Ministry decided that state-supported elementary and high schools should fly the *Hi no maru* and play the *Kimi ga yo* at entrance and graduation ceremonies. An opinion poll supported this decision, but considerable opposition remains both in the teachers union and in Okinawan schools.[26]

The Korean community in Japan was watched carefully by SCAP and suspiciously by the Japanese throughout the occupation. The 600,000 Koreans who remained in Japan after the end of the war were initially treated as "liberated people," meaning that they would not be treated as Japanese; would have certain privileges, such as separate schools; and would be repatriated if they wished.

A year after the occupation began, SCAP announced in a press statement that Koreans voluntarily residing in Japan would be treated as Japanese nationals but that they would not be obliged to obtain Japanese citizenship and could remain in Japan until a duly established Korean government recognized them as Korean nationals. SCAP continued to facilitate their return to Korea, but not many wanted to go.

In time the Japanese sought to eliminate privileged treatment for the Koreans. In the eyes of the Japanese, who had historically looked down on many other Asians as inferior peoples, the Koreans were a disruptive and unassimilable element. After a few years in Japan, many Americans tended to sympathize with Japanese attitudes. On at least one occasion U.S. troops had to come out in force to support the Japanese police in their efforts to compel Koreans in Kobe who were not entitled to attend Korean schools to attend Japanese schools.[27]

The political polarization of the Korean peninsula came to be reflected among the Koreans in Japan. At least one-half of them were under leftist influence by 1948, when the Republic of Korea (ROK) was set up and established a liaison office with SCAP in Tokyo. Both SCAP and the Japanese government hoped that a Korean liaison office would be able to mitigate the obstreperous and left-wing tendencies of the Korean residents. The unrest and turbulence Japan experienced in 1949 and 1950 made this a vain hope.

A SCAP staff study in 1948 concluded that the Korean liaison office in Japan should be allowed to register Koreans as Korean nationals if they executed a document with the Japanese government relinquishing Japanese nationality; these persons would then be treated as foreign nationals, and their repatriation to Korea would continue to be encouraged but not compelled. Those who did not register as Korean nationals would remain Japanese nationals but without full rights of citizenship. MacArthur decided not to go along with even this small step "since a partial solution will cause more trouble to arise than if we leave this matter alone."[28]

Yoshida stirred up the issue in 1949 by giving MacArthur an unsigned and undated letter—a technique he used to indicate an unofficial and informal approach—proposing that all Koreans in Japan be repatriated at Japan's expense but that those who desired to stay be permitted to do so if they could "contribute to reconstruction." Yoshida said later that MacArthur had opposed forced repatriation of the Koreans, partly because they were mostly North Koreans and "would have had their heads cut off" by the ROK. The Japanese government would have liked nothing better than a forced exodus of most of the Koreans in Japan, with the occupation taking the onus for the action, but Yoshida's heavy-handed ploy did not succeed.[29]

In 1950 Japan passed a nationality act providing that only persons born of a Japanese father could be registered as Japanese nationals; this in effect barred Koreans. In 1952 the government issued an alien registration order disenfranchising the Koreans and Taiwanese in Japan as of April 28, the effective date of the San Francisco peace treaty.[30]

Most of the Koreans in Japan now live in a kind of legal limbo. Many are permanent resident aliens under Japanese law, but a large number of second- or third-generation residents have not been accorded this status. A small number of Koreans have been naturalized as Japanese nationals after meeting a strict test of "assimilation." Intermarriage with Japanese is widespread. The Japanese have continued to discriminate against Koreans, making it very difficult for them to get government jobs or receive benefits such as social security and subjecting them to close police scrutiny. The ROK has sought to intervene diplomatically on behalf of Koreans in Japan but so far without much success.

Along with the *burakumin* or *eta*, long relegated to the bottom of the social ladder, Koreans in Japan continue to fight for better conditions, but they are still a long way from receiving equal social and economic treatment. Feelings of ethnic pride and superiority run strong among the Japanese. Japan may be compelled to make more concessions in the future if it wishes to maintain good relations with the ROK.

PART V

Peace Settlement

June 1950 marked the beginning of the end of the occupation. In that month John Foster Dulles arrived in Tokyo to explore the prospects for a peace treaty with Japan and war broke out in Korea. No less an authority than George Kennan believed that the U.S. decision to try making a treaty with Japan that did not include the USSR "probably had an important bearing on the Soviet decision to unleash the attack in Korea."[1] This thesis has been much debated, and it poses several problems. For example, there is the matter of timing: the United States had not decided by June 1950 that it would go ahead and try for a treaty. But one point is clear. The Korean War strengthened the resolve of the United States and of Japan, as well as the willingness of close U.S. Allies, to go ahead with a peace treaty.

The three key players were Dulles, Yoshida, and MacArthur. Dulles was the strategist who identified the problems, worked out the solutions, devised much of the wording of the treaties, and ultimately won the approval of the Washington establishment, notably the military, and of nearly all the Allies. Yoshida was in full command of the Japanese side, an unusual feat for a prime minister in modern Japan; he decided what Japan could and could not accept, and he ensured the support of the Japanese government and people. MacArthur was the first American leader to publicly advocate a nonpunitive peace settlement. He stuck to this liberal point of view in 1947 and 1948 as the State Department churned out complex, punitive drafts; he gave Dulles and the State Department full support after the outbreak of war in Korea; and he was instrumental both in solving the problem of how the United States could retain bases in Japan and in encouraging Yoshida to go along with the treaty arrangements.

The treaty negotiations and the outbreak of war in Korea marked a turning point in relations between Japan and the United States. Washington had been groping since the end of the Pacific War for a firm and reliable Asian policy. Its early hope had been that a strong and friendly Republic of China under Chiang Kai-shek would be the dominant power in East Asia. The rise of Mao Zedong destroyed that vision. Chiang was forced to flee to Taiwan, and the People's Republic of China was formally inaugurated on October 1, 1949. On February 14 of the next year, Mao and Stalin signed a treaty of cooperation, alliance, and mutual assistance in Moscow committing each to come to the assistance of the other in case of an attack by Japan or a state allied with Japan, meaning the United States. Washington concluded that it could expect little cooperation from the new China. U.S. concerns were heightened by the rise of dynamic communist movements in Indochina, Indonesia, and the Philippines.

U.S. policymakers began to look to Japan as an anchor for U.S. interests in East Asia. Their initial impulse was to encourage Japan's economic revival. U.S. policy in 1948, as set forth by Kennan and endorsed by MacArthur, was that with an effective government and a revived economy Japan could be a stabilizing force in East Asia. Both men felt Japan should not be pressured to rearm, although their thinking on this score got fuzzier after the war started in Korea. Then MacArthur launched Japan on the path to limited rearmament by ordering the establishment of a paramilitary police force.

Dulles had stronger and clearer perceptions than Kennan, MacArthur, or Acheson of the role Japan should play. Dulles wanted Japan to become a U.S. ally like the Federal Republic of Germany. He wanted Japan to rearm so that it could make a large contribution to the common defense and thus be entitled to the protection of the United States. With the support of President Truman, Secretary Acheson, and the Pentagon, Dulles's thinking became U.S. policy. But Yoshida refused to budge: limited rearmament was enough for him, and many Japanese seemed to be doubtful of even going that far. Japan would not be an ally but only a limited partner.

In the last two years of the occupation SCAP dismantled the purge program, created a paramilitary force, and harassed the political left. These actions constituted reversals of earlier reform measures. In the tense atmosphere of 1950–1952, they did not meet much opposition in Japan or elsewhere.

CHAPTER 17

The Search for Peace

As early as November 1945 the United States had proposed to the Big Four Allied powers that draft treaties of demilitarization and disarmament be negotiated with Germany and Japan, but the Soviet Union had backed away after treaties were drafted. In June 1947 the United States proposed to the other ten nations on the FEC that a peace conference be held in August of that year, but the Soviets insisted that the Big Four powers draft any treaty.[1]

The United States prepared two more treaty drafts. The three drafts differed in some respects, but all contained restrictive provisions. Heavy reparations would be exacted. Japan would not be permitted (1) to have a military force, other than internal police and a coast guard; (2) to establish military industries; (3) to carry on military research; and (4) to maintain any civil aviation. These restrictions would remain in force for twenty-five years and would be enforced by a council of ambassadors representing the FEC nations. No provision was made for the posttreaty security of Japan.[2]

General MacArthur did not think much of the draft treaties. He called the 1947 draft "imperialistic," adding that the Japanese were ready for peace negotiations and that a treaty should "avoid punitive or arbitrary and complex provisions." He thought that a control council of Allied ambassadors would continue the occupation by another name and that a posttreaty right to reenter Japan with military force would imply that the Soviets could do the same. He felt strongly that the United States should control Okinawa and the Ryukyu Islands, which the draft would have permitted Japan to retain.[3]

The Japanese had been busy from the start of the occupation looking at peace treaty issues. Under the direction of Foreign Minister Ashida the government worked up a list of optimistic "hopes" in 1947 for an early and generous treaty, which Ashida showed to General Whitney and several other Allied representatives. Whitney returned the list with the comment, "It would not be advantageous to Japan in the present delicate situation for such documents to be put out officially." A version of this document was leaked to the American magazine *World Report* in late 1947. The Foreign Office prepared a number of studies on treaty issues such as territory and reparations, which it passed to the State Department office in Tokyo. Some of these studies were sent to Washington, but there is little evidence that policymakers there used them.[4]

In Europe Germans had drafted, with the approval of the Western Allies, a basic law or constitution for the three western zones, which went into effect in 1949. The Western Allies soon turned over to the Federal Republic of Germany all authority over domestic matters of government pursuant to an "occupation statute," and a government was set up with Konrad Adenauer as chancellor.[5] As a practical matter the occupation of the three western zones had ended by 1949.

Dean Acheson, who became secretary of state in 1949 after Harry Truman was unexpectedly reelected president, did not agree with Kennan's recommendation to the NSC in late 1948 (NSC 13/2) that action on a treaty be postponed until Japan had more economic strength and greater internal security. Acheson said in his memoirs, "To me, one conclusion seemed plain beyond doubt. Western Europe and the United States could not contain the Soviet Union and suppress Germany and Japan at the same time. Our best hope was to make these former enemies willing and strong supporters of a free-world structure."[6] In his view an early peace treaty with Japan would serve this end.

The British government under Prime Minister Clement Attlee and its Commonwealth allies also wanted a peace treaty, though not for the same reasons. They wanted the United States to give up its monopoly of control over Japan. They also feared that MacArthur and the United States were taking actions detrimental to their interests, such as reviving Japan's textile industry, ending reparations, and favoring Japan with a higher standard of living and more generous food supplies than some of the Commonwealth nations enjoyed. Containing Soviet communism was a lesser concern for them.

Foreign Secretary Ernest Bevin came to Washington in September 1949 to urge that a new peace effort be made. He requested an updated version of the U.S. position to show his Commonwealth colleagues. The State Department quickly produced a new draft based on the concept of restoring sovereignty to Japan with only a few restrictions. According to this draft, Japan would be required to preserve a democratic government, observing such basic rights as free speech and freedom of religion; occupation reforms in agriculture, labor, and economic deconcentration were not specifically mentioned and were to be left to the discretion of the Japanese. Japan would remain obligated to make reparations. An accompanying commentary stated that the primary motivation of the new draft was to align Japan with the United States in world affairs, the first time this had been explicitly stated in a U.S. policy document. This new approach moved away from punitive and restrictive clauses and toward a more liberal and equal relation between Japan and the World War II victors. According to Frederick Dunn, an authority on the making of the peace settlement, this draft deserves credit as a precursor of the kind of settlement that was finally negotiated.[7]

Unfortunately, the new draft contained no provisions on defense or the security of Japan because the Department of Defense failed to produce any. Military leaders believed that a peace treaty with Japan was premature, and they went on record that any treaty must permit the United States to retain forces and bases in Japan *and* include the Soviet Union and "the *de facto* government of China" as signatories. The State Department was therefore not able to provide the full draft Bevin had requested, and the 1949 draft proved abortive. The issue of Japan's security had risen to the fore, where it remained to the day the treaties were signed and indeed thereafter.[8]

Before 1951 the United States did not consult with Japan about peace treaty issues. Senior U.S. officials visiting Japan avoided any discussions with Japanese about treaty issues. The U.S. view at that time held that the peace would be made without any input from the Japanese.

Secretary of the Army Royall, who liked to make dramatic statements, gave the Japanese and Washington a scare when he told a background press conference in Tokyo on February 6, 1949, "I have doubts as to the strategic importance of Japan. Its position must be seriously reconsidered." This portentous comment rapidly entered the public domain and caused a great stir. MacArthur himself added to the confusion in March 1949 when he told a British correspondent on the record that Japan should be neutral and that it was premature to talk of a Japanese army. MacArthur told other reporters at different times that Japan should be the Switzerland of the Pacific, perhaps forgetting that the Swiss have maintained a small, well-trained army.[9]

Yoshida Shigeru was wise in the ways of diplomacy. Ringing pronouncements by important Americans did not upset him, and he understood that defeated nations got short shrift at the peace table. Yoshida realized that several of the Allied powers remained distinctly hostile to Japan. Nevertheless, when Yoshida returned to power in 1948 he was determined to find a road to peace. He knew that the dominant power the United States would have to take the lead and that a treaty would have to be acceptable to the United States. Given the growing rift between the United States and the Soviet Union, the two superpowers might not be able to agree on a settlement; Japan might therefore have to side with the United States by accepting a treaty that not all the Allied nations would sign. The prospective treaty became a bone of contention as anticonservative forces in Japan led by socialists and intellectuals declared their opposition to one excluding the Soviet Union. In May 1949 Yoshida told a group of prefectural governors that a "treaty with many" (including the United States and the Western European nations) but not with all of the Allied powers would give Japan its independence and freedom of action much sooner than would a "treaty with all" the Allied powers, which might even be impossible. A "treaty with many" should therefore be acceptable to Japan.[10]

The security issue was even more far-reaching and divisive in Japan. Pacifist sentiment remained strong, abetted by MacArthur's conviction that Japan should not have armed forces. Yoshida and some of his conservative associates swung to the view, formulated first by Ashida Hitoshi in 1947, that Japan could not be neutral or defenseless in a dangerous world and that it would have to rely on the United States for protection. Other than the United States, none of the Allied nations wanted Japan to have military forces.

Yoshida had to play an adroit game for many months to thread his way through these obstacles. On April 7, 1950, he told a State Department officer that "Japan must rely on the United States for protection as it will possess no armaments of its own." Yoshida embellished his views by asserting that when Japanese said they feared Japan would become a U.S. colony, he replied that "just as the United States was once a colony of Great Britain but now is the stronger of the two, if Japan becomes a colony of the United States, it will also eventually become the stronger."[11] This was a typical Yoshida sally, which usually brought forth from Americans a wan smile or puzzled expression. But the wily diplomat may have spoken more truth than even he realized.

Observing the confused ranks of the Allied powers and the standstill in American efforts to move ahead, Yoshida decided in early 1950 to take some action of his own. In April he sent his trusted lieutenant, Minister of Finance Ikeda, to Washington to convey his views on how Japan might be defended after a peace treaty. Ikeda had emerged as a minor hero from the ordeal of the Dodge whirlwind and was entrusted with another delicate task by the prime minister.[12] Ikeda was the first Japanese official of cabinet rank to go to the United States after the surrender. He took with him Shirasu Jirō, Yoshida's confidant and expert on the Anglo-Saxons, and a bright young finance expert, Miyazawa Kiichi, who wrote afterward of the trouble Yoshida and the Japanese had in managing to send a senior official to the United States without arousing the suspicions of SCAP: "The biggest problem was the mentality of MacArthur. Since he was in charge of things in Japan, he felt a certain pride in avoiding meddling by his own government. He liked to pose as the new emperor. . . . After a person listened to his opinions for an hour or so, he would get the impression this was a great man but one who was arrogant and would not accept criticism. . . . If someone got out from under his control and had important contacts abroad, he would immediately impose his veto and afterwards his attitude might be unfavorable to the Japanese Government."[13]

To avoid trouble, Yoshida told MacArthur that Ikeda was going to Washington to study economic conditions but said nothing about a peace treaty. Nevertheless, Yoshida instructed Ikeda to convey to Washington that Japan would be willing "to request the stationing of U.S. forces" there after a treaty.[14] Ikeda had no trouble getting permission to go to the United States, despite Japanese worries, because SCAP was by that time trying to increase overseas travel by Japanese.

Ikeda's most significant meeting in the United States was with Joseph Dodge on May 2. After a discussion of economic conditions, Ikeda said that he had a personal message from the prime minister: Japan desired "the earliest possible peace treaty. As such a treaty would probably require the maintenance of U.S. forces to secure the treaty terms and for other purposes, if the U.S. government hesitates to make these conditions, the Japanese government will try to find a way to offer them." Ikeda added that if the treaty required retention of U.S. bases, Japan "would make such a treaty easier to conclude." Miyazawa later characterized this conversation as the foundation for the security treaty signed by the United States and Japan sixteen months later in San Francisco.[15]

Dodge distributed several copies of the memorandum reporting his talk with Ikeda. One went to Walton Butterworth, assistant secretary of state for Far Eastern affairs, who forwarded it to Acting Secretary of State James E. Webb with a notation that "this conversation is regarded as significant because it is the first expression we have had at an official level of the attitude of the Japanese government on the peace treaty and related questions."[16] Despite this appreciative comment, the record does not show that the conversation had much impact on thinking in Washington.

It was ironic that in 1947 Foreign Minister Ashida had sent a similar message to Washington through General Eichelberger. The "Ashida memorandum" had been prepared following a press report that General MacArthur had assured the emperor the United States would guarantee Japan's security. In the memorandum the Japanese government recognized for the first time that it and the United States might make an agreement permitting U.S. military forces to remain in Japan after a peace treaty. Such an agreement would, of course, make it easier for U.S. forces to protect Japan. Yoshida and other leaders had seen the memo and agreed with its position. Eichelberger received it on September 13, 1947. He took it to Washington, where it evidently circulated among some of the interested offices. There is no record, however, that any senior officials saw it or that any use was made of it then or later. U.S. officials were not much interested in Japanese views on defense in either 1947 or early 1950.[17]

Dodge also sent a copy of the report of his conversation with Ikeda to MacArthur. As a result, the finance minister got a chilly reception from SCAP officials when he returned to Tokyo. The generals on MacArthur's staff refused for a while to see him, and Yoshida had some difficulty getting an appointment with MacArthur. General Marquat made it plain that SCAP felt it was improper for the Japanese to go over SCAP's head and raise treaty issues in Washington. The tempest blew over in a few days, and relations returned to normal. MacArthur was rarely petty with the Japanese, and in this case his protective staff members may simply have been venting their spleen.[18]

Ikeda's end run produced no immediate result. In fact, by early 1950 the prospects for a peace treaty with Japan were distinctly dim. Describing this stage of the treaty negotiations in his memoirs, Dean Acheson wrote, "In planning content and method, four groups had to be reckoned with: the Communists, the Pentagon, our allies and the former enemy. Of these the Communists gave the least trouble. Their opposition to any tenable ideas was predictable and irreconcilable. It could only be ignored. The most stubborn and protracted opposition to a peace treaty came from the Pentagon."[19]

The top officials of State and Defense met on April 24, a few days before Ikeda arrived in Washington. The secretary of state, known for his cutting wit, commented that "in view of the mutually exclusive character of the two requirements insisted upon by the joint chiefs for a peace treaty, viz., that U.S. forces remain in Japan and that the USSR and the *de facto* government of China be parties to the peace treaty, he regarded the joint chiefs' statement that a peace treaty was 'premature' as a masterpiece of understatement, since these requirements would make the conclusion of a peace treaty impossible." The secretary of defense, Louis A. Johnson, riposted that "the only propaganda for a peace treaty was that which came out of the Department of State." State argued that early treaty action was essential. Defense countered that a treaty would undermine U.S. rights in Japan and might provoke the USSR to try to retain its rights to military occupation there. The meeting ended amicably enough, with each side agreeing to write a memorandum setting forth its views. Obviously, they were far apart.[20]

To put new life in his campaign for a treaty, Acheson decided on May 18, 1950, with the approval of the president, to put John Foster Dulles in charge of the negotiations. Acheson commented to the president that Dulles had had no "prior contaminating contact with the subject... was competent, ambitious—particularly to succeed me"—and had good political connections. Truman later kidded Acheson that in giving the Japanese peace treaty job to Dulles, he had opened the way for Dulles to become secretary of state.[21]

Dulles thus got the chance to achieve his first and greatest diplomatic success, even before he became secretary, by negotiating the peace settlement for Japan in 1950 and 1951. Few persons had as good credentials as Dulles to deal with international issues of great import and complexity. The grandson of one secretary of state and the nephew of another, he had attended the Versailles peace conference in 1919 as a reparations expert on the U.S. delegation. A highly successful corporation lawyer, he had built a large international practice in addition to engaging in Republican politics and the works of the Presbyterian church. Dulles had all but asked for the treaty job by telling Acheson, "You will never get anything done unless you select someone in whom you have confidence, give him a job to do, and then hold him to results. Look at the Japanese peace treaty. The department has been discussing it for four years without result. Why don't you give someone one year in which to get action?"[22]

Dulles had come into the State Department in April 1950 as a special consultant to the secretary. A staunch Republican who had served briefly as an appointed U.S. senator from New York, he had joined Truman's Democratic administration not only because he relished public life but also because several leading figures in both parties agreed that Democrats and Republicans should try to mitigate partisan differences over foreign policy issues, especially in the Far East after the takeover of China by Mao Zedong.

Intellectual and physical energy controlled by a disciplined mind and a moralistic outlook was the hallmark of John Foster Dulles's approach to the world. His only contact with Asia had been some service on the U.S. delegation to the United Nations dealing with Korean independence in 1948, but he picked three assistants well versed in Japan: John Allison, a Nebraska-born career diplomat with extensive service in Asia; Robert Fearey, who had been private secretary in Japan to Ambassador Joseph Grew before the war; and Colonel C. Stanton Babcock, a West Pointer who had served in Japan before the war and on MacArthur's staff after the war. In their initial interview, Dulles asked the colonel about thinking in the Pentagon on the treaty. Babcock replied that there were many different views and that the only thing the military agreed on was its opposition to the ideas of General MacArthur.[23]

Dulles soon produced a paper analyzing the problem, which he wrote himself, as he usually did with his speeches and many of his policy proposals. The final version, dated June 6, 1950, reflected the concise, logical, and occasionally casuistic cast of his mind. As Allison once said, "When Dulles felt he had to do something," he showed "all the marks of a Jesuit."[24] Dulles defined his goal as a peaceful, friendly Japan that would respect human rights and become a member of the "Free World. . . . It may be that the principal attraction to hold Japan in the Free World will be a capitalizing on their desire to be an equal member of the family of free nations." He thought a peace treaty should provide for a minimum of restrictions, enable Japan to pursue peaceful economic development without a duty to pay reparations, and free it of any treaty obligation to abide by its constitutional renunciation of war. He also believed that Japan would need a strong police force to deal with the threat of internal subversion and that Allied occupation forces should remain in Japan for a period of years until arrangements under the U.N. Charter could provide for its security. He thought both Nationalist China and Communist China should be invited to attend the peace conference. Dulles won the support of Acheson and other senior officials of the State Department for this approach.[25]

The document was unusual for the attention it paid to Japanese customs and attitudes. In the eyes of this conservative and moralistic New York lawyer, Japan's social institutions discouraged "individualism in favor of family, group and national interests." He thought the Japanese assumed that people in the West felt a sense of superiority toward them, while they themselves felt a sense of superiority toward the Chinese. He also wrote that "extreme Japanese conformity has a close affinity with the conformity idea which is fundamental in Soviet Communism" and has led the Japanese people to "have a tendency to totalitarian forms and to authoritarian rule."[26] While perceptive, these assertions had more than a touch of Anglo-Saxon ethnocentrism.

Dulles decided to visit Japan to explore the situation on the spot. He sensed that MacArthur would be a key figure in the treaty process and wanted at the same time to observe the Japanese. His trip was the first step in a new kind of diplomacy, involving frequent visits by the principal negotiator to the capitals of the nations with major interests in the negotiation. The participants had little or no contact with each other. The airplane was an essential instrument in the process, which in later years became known as "shuttle diplomacy." Dulles may have been its first practitioner.

After stopping briefly in Tokyo on June 17, 1950, Dulles flew on to Korea to talk to Syngman Rhee, who had become president of the new Republic of Korea two years earlier. Dulles wanted to play down the importance of his trip to Japan and to reassure South Korea of U.S. support.

Returning to Japan, he spent six days in a round of meetings with MacArthur, Yoshida, and SCAP officials. The general tended to be condescending toward most of his visitors from Washington because they knew little about Japan and often did not seem eager to learn. He placed Dulles in the category of those who knew little. MacArthur somewhat enigmatically told his political adviser that he did not want Dulles to have "any private meetings with Yoshida, as there is a grow-

ing wave of nationalism in Japan and he did not want to build up
Yoshida as a negotiator at this time." Nor did MacArthur want Dulles
to make any speeches.[27]

Before Dulles arrived in Japan, MacArthur prepared two memoranda: the "Peace Treaty Problem" and "Formosa."[28] Dated June 14, they
were probably prepared for Dulles and for Secretary of Defense Louis
Johnson and JCS chairman Omar Bradley, who were making a separate
visit to Tokyo at the time. MacArthur did not customarily engage in
intensive preparations for high-level meetings, let alone personally draft
papers for visiting officials. Instead, he relied on his almost theatrical
skill in person-to-person contact. He customarily displayed remarkable
command of facts and a flair for uttering authoritative pronouncements, as illustrated by three crucial meetings: his conference with President Roosevelt on war strategy in Honolulu in 1944, his meeting with
President Truman on the Korean War at Wake Island in 1950, and his
testimony before two Senate committees in 1951 after his relief.

In his first memorandum for Dulles, the supreme commander said he
was "deeply concerned over the psychologically adverse effect upon the
Japanese people of protracted delay" in moving toward a treaty. They
had faithfully fulfilled their surrender obligations and "had every moral
and legal right to the restoration of peace." The United States should
call a conference at once, work out just and proper terms, and invite all
nations concerned to ratify the agreed formula. The United States must
regain the initiative in the events stirring all of the Asian peoples, for "it
is the pattern of Oriental psychology to follow aggressive, resolute and
dynamic leadership but quickly turn away from a leadership characterized by timidity or vacillation."[29] This was MacArthur the Asian
expert speaking.

MacArthur had modified his position on the need for U.S. bases after
a peace treaty. Perhaps in deference to strong Pentagon views, he advocated a peace treaty provision making it possible that "points in
Japanese territory continue to be garrisoned by the Allied powers
. . . through the United States" until "irresponsible militarism" (the
term used in the Potsdam Declaration of 1945) ceased to exist as a
"threat to peace, security and justice" in Japan.[30]

MacArthur's memorandum on Formosa struck other familiar notes:
the island could be compared to "an unsinkable aircraft carrier and
submarine tender," and the United States "should initiate measures to
prevent the domination of Formosa by a communist power." He accordingly requested authorization to make a military survey of what was

needed to hold Formosa in event of a communist attack, reinforcing his earlier recommendation to Washington that the United States provide military aid to Chiang Kai-shek.[31] In MacArthur's eyes, Formosa equaled Okinawa in military importance; the United States should keep sovereign authority over Okinawa and guarantee the defense of Formosa.

The supreme commander and the Wall Street lawyer met for the first time on June 22, 1950. From the start, they hit it off well. They were not far apart in age, they were both conservative men who believed in a powerful world role for the United States, and both wanted an early treaty with Japan. Moreover, Dulles was a quick learner and a prodigious worker, qualities that no doubt impressed the general. Dulles sometimes spoke of MacArthur's "moral authority" in Japan, morality and authority being two qualities to which Dulles attached the highest value.

MacArthur and Dulles first discussed the general's memorandum on the security of Japan. Dulles asked MacArthur to prepare another, more detailed memo outlining his views on U.S. base rights and the defense of Japan, the two points that were at the heart of the Pentagon's concerns. The general wrote a follow-up memo the next day: "The entire area of Japan must be regarded as a potential base for defensive maneuver, with unrestricted freedom reserved" to the U.S. commander to move his forces in Japan where he thought best, subject to prior consultation with the prime minister, except in an emergency. On the second point the general asserted that Japan's right to self-defense "in case of predatory attack is implicit and inalienable," and in that event "Japan would muster all of its available human and material resources in support of the security forces committed to its defense."[32] MacArthur's thinking had advanced two steps: all Japan should be treated as a military base, and Japan could use everything available in its own defense.

The two men discussed MacArthur's follow-up memorandum at their second meeting on June 26. The general's modified position would clearly provide Dulles with room to maneuver in dealing with the Pentagon on base rights. Dulles also got the general's support for his idea that Japan would make arrangements with the United States as the representative of the Allied powers to maintain facilities in Japan pending its admission to the United Nations.[33]

Yoshida and Dulles also met for the first time on June 22. Yoshida said in his memoirs that the talks were "confined to general topics" but that Dulles made soundings "on the possibility of Japan's agreeing to a measure of rearmament." According to Dulles's report of their meeting, Yoshida was "vague as to what role he envisioned for Japan and would not commit himself on post-treaty security arrangements." He "talked at some length in a rather academic manner about how the nations of the Free World would come to the aid of Japan if Japan would prove that it had learned the lesson of the war and was firmly attached to democratic principles."[34]

MacArthur's political adviser, William J. Sebald, gave a revealing account of the meeting in his diary entry of June 22: "Yoshida, as usual, spoke in circles and parables—he refused to commit himself in any way. The most he would say was that security for Japan was possible providing the United States took care to preserve Japan's *amour propre.* Yoshida said Japan could have security if she demonstrated to the world that she is democratic, demilitarized, and peace-loving—then world public opinion would protect her. Dulles refused to follow this line of reasoning, but finally gave up trying to obtain a definite answer or commitment."[35]

Dulles wanted Japan to rearm. Yoshida was against it, believing that the nation could not afford rearmament, the people were opposed to it, and Japan's Asian neighbors would be alarmed by it. Dulles believed all U.S. friends and allies should do as much as possible to help defend themselves. This was the position the United States had adopted in dealing with its allies in the North Atlantic Treaty Organization (NATO), established the year before.

Dulles had a busy time in Japan meeting American and Japanese officials, seeing foreign diplomats and opposition politicians, making an important speech, and holding a press conference. His most curious contact was with an official of the imperial household, Matsudaira Yasumasa, a former marquis and scion of one of Japan's ancient families. The meeting had been arranged by the wheeling-and-dealing team of *Newsweek* magazine foreign editor Harry Kern and its Tokyo correspondent Compton Pakenham, himself from a distinguished English family and a former Coldstream Guards officer. Matsudaira later conveyed what was represented as an oral message from the emperor to Dulles through Kern to the effect that American visitors to Japan often did not meet experienced Japanese who could give valuable advice because most of them had been purged.[36]

Pakenham "prevailed" upon Matsudaira to put the emperor's views in writing. The resulting letter asserted that the emperor "feels that the action which would have the most beneficial effect on the interests of both America and Japan and do the most to foster good will would be the relaxation of the purge. While not suggesting its abolishment, it is certain that many useful, far-seeing and well-intentioned men could thus be freed to work for the general good." The emperor may have said this and may even have been willing to be quoted. But it seems more likely that the Matsudaira letter was another example of free-wheeling by a palace functionary or even that it was a fake.[37]

This visit enabled Dulles to carry out a careful probe of the all-important security issue. He started by "prodding" Yoshida but found him reluctant "to admit that Japan would have to contribute its share in some form or another" to its own protection.[38] Nevertheless, Dulles made good headway in his talks with MacArthur, and the vague outline of a security arrangement with Japan began to emerge. With Japan's consent, U.S. forces in Japan would have freedom of movement and could provide for Japan's defense for an interim period until more permanent security arrangements were made. Japan's right to take de-fensive measures in the event of an attack would be recognized. Dulles intended to go farther, however, and press Japan for a commitment to rearm. He flew out of Tokyo for Washington on June 27, 1950, two days after North Korea invaded the South.

CHAPTER 18

The Korean War

When John Foster Dulles visited Korea in the middle of June 1950, he went up to the Thirty-eighth Parallel, which divided North and South Korea, and was photographed staring toward the North with his usual grim mien. He also made a speech to the Korean National Assembly in which he assured its members that Korea "will never be alone so long as you continue to play worthily your part in the great design of human freedom." This brave phrasing, drafted in Washington, appealed to Dulles, who felt that Acheson had made a serious mistake because his Washington speech on Far Eastern policy delivered on January 12, 1950, failed to include Korea as an area of vital interest to the United States. No one expected Dulles's unequivocal words to be put to a test hours after he uttered them.[1]

No one in the Western camp knew much about North Korea. It had been only a bit player on the East Asian scene. Its leader, Kim Il Sung, had fought with the Soviet Army against the Japanese and gave every evidence of being a devout communist and a complete henchman of the Kremlin. North Korea's forces had skirmished frequently with those of South Korea in 1948 and 1949. But when 90,000 North Korean troops, spearheaded by Soviet T-34 tanks, swept into South Korea early in the morning of June 25, 1950, it came as a huge surprise to Tokyo, Washington, and possibly even to some communist capitals.[2]

The causes of the Korean War are in dispute. Some scholars assert that the evidence is compatible with an unprovoked invasion by the North *and* with retaliation by the North for earlier incursions by the

South. In either case the North was obviously far better prepared for war in June 1950 than the South was. How far Moscow and Beijing worked with Pyongyang in planning and carrying out the invasion remains a mystery, but almost certainly the Soviets and probably the Chinese knew in advance that Kim would attack. No doubt both countries would have been very happy to see the elimination of the anticommunist foothold on the Korean peninsula. Kim Il Sung may well have persuaded Stalin that an attack by North Korean forces would gain the support of dissident elements in the South and could win a quick victory. Stalin and Mao may have also felt that they had to act to forestall U.S. plans for an independent and revived Japan.[3]

U.S. forces in Japan and South Korea offered the only strong counterbalance to powerful communist armies in China, Siberia, and North Korea. In mainland Northeast Asia, South Korea was the only territory not under communist control. Right after the war ended in August 1945, the United States sent a Marine amphibious corps of 60,000 to North China under vague and ill-defined instructions to monitor the Japanese surrender and also to keep an eye on the Soviet and Chinese communist forces. MacArthur and other U.S. leaders did not think the Marines were necessary, and they were soon withdrawn.[4]

U.S. forces withdrew from South Korea in 1949 after the founding of the Republic of Korea, which had a small army force of its own assisted by American advisers. MacArthur several times expressed the opinion that South Korea was indefensible against an attack by Soviet or Chinese forces, and he did not favor large-scale military aid by the United States to the republic.[5]

Late in the day the North Koreans attacked, MacArthur speculated at a meeting in his office that the attack was a "reconnaissance in force." He was optimistic that everything was under control. "If Washington only will not hobble me, I can handle it with one arm tied behind my back." Dulles proposed immediate action: he sent a message to the State Department asserting that if the South Koreans did not repulse the attack, U.S. force should be used. "To sit by while Korea is overrun by unprovoked armed attack would start a disastrous chain of events leading most probably to world war."[6]

MacArthur remained confident the next day that the situation was in hand and somewhat reluctantly agreed with the U.S. ambassador in Seoul, John J. Muccio, that American women and children in Korea should be evacuated. During the day the South Korean Army retreated, and soon its line began to disintegrate.[7] On the following day, June 27, when Dulles was to board his plane for the return trip to Washington, he found MacArthur no longer the "jaunty, confident" commander of Sunday evening but a "dejected, completely despondent man." The general was even heard to say, "All Korea is lost." Dulles and Allison were dismayed by MacArthur's sudden loss of confidence. It was behavior of this kind that later caused Dulles to characterize the general as "high-strung."[8]

What MacArthur termed a "reconnaissance in force" by North Korea turned out to be a massive invasion. On June 27 President Truman authorized the use of U.S. air and naval forces to assist the ROK in combating the invasion. On June 30, in response to MacArthur's recommendation, he authorized the use of U.S. ground forces, and soon all four of the army divisions in Japan, more than 80,000 men, were transferred to Korea.

Planning by U.S. military experts had previously made no provision for action by the United States to defend South Korea in the event of an invasion by the North or other communist forces. Yet when the North Koreans invaded, and the ROK Army could not check them, the United States intervened. MacArthur and Dulles almost took it for granted that the United States should act to meet an "unprovoked, armed attack" on a friendly state. Little evidence can be adduced to show that they thought the security of Japan was a prime reason for the United States to move in, although officials in Washington did give thought to Japan's security in making their decision to send in U.S. forces. At a tense White House meeting soon after the invasion, Admiral Forrest Sherman, the chief of naval operations, mentioned "the strategic threat" to Japan, and Dean Acheson later reiterated this theme. Dulles, an eager student of Kremlinology, insisted that the North Koreans "did not do this purely on their own but as part of the world strategy of international communism."[9]

On June 25, 1950, the U.N. Security Council unanimously approved a resolution—the Soviets boycotted the meeting—condemning the aggression against South Korea; soon afterward it authorized the creation of a U.N. force under U.S. command to put down the invasion. In the summer of 1950 the U.N. forces were almost pushed out of the peninsula, but after a brilliant amphibious landing masterminded by General MacArthur at Inchon near Seoul, they swept north to the Yalu River, only to be hammered back to central Korea when large numbers of Chinese "volunteers" entered the fighting in November. Inside three months, Douglas MacArthur had won his most brilliant victory and suffered his most crushing defeat in a military career spanning a half century.

MacArthur told President Truman when they met at Wake Island in October 1950 that the Chinese communists would not intervene in Korea. But the general was not a good judge of the Chinese. Like many Americans of that era, he minimized the ability of the Chinese communists to conduct modern warfare; in September 1949 he told a congressional subcommittee that "their forces are grossly overrated." He stuck to the view that the Chinese Nationalists would have been a valuable asset with which to counter the communists, despite the record of Nationalist failure on the mainland. MacArthur was also an unabashed believer in air power and thought to the end that air strikes on Manchuria would destroy communist ability to carry on the war.[10]

Fighting went on in central Korea for more than two years until an armistice was reached on July 27, 1953. What the Japanese euphemistically called the "Korean disturbance" was in fact a full-scale war lasting three years and causing the death of 33,600 American servicemen as well as 4 million Koreans on both sides; an estimated 900,000 Chinese died or were wounded.

General MacArthur showed remarkable energy and resilience after the first uncertain days of the Korean War.[11] He gave most of his time to military operations in Korea but remained in full control of the occupation in Japan. He saw Prime Minister Yoshida regularly, met other senior Japanese officials, and kept abreast of treaty planning. Although the British ambassador complained that MacArthur no longer gave him any time, it is possible the general may have been glad for an excuse not to see persons he did not consider essential to his work. He even suggested that Sebald should meet with ambassadors in Tokyo, noting that the president of the United States, though head of state, did not regularly meet with foreign ambassadors in Washington.[12]

A surprising mood of calm and even apathy enveloped Tokyo and the rest of Japan during the war in Korea. The Japanese press carried detailed reports about the progress of the war, using exclusively foreign, usually American reports. No Japanese reporters or photographers were allowed in Korea. In line with SCAP censorship policy, no editorial commentary or speculation about the fighting was permitted. The Japanese, having experienced a similar situation during the Pacific War, could readily tell during the first months of the war that it was going badly.[13]

Throughout its modern history Japan's leaders had felt that a dependent Korea was essential to Japan's security. The metaphor of Korea as a "dagger pointed at Japan" had considerable appeal to Japanese during their early expansionist period. Thinking of this kind had led to Japan's invasion of Korea during the first Sino-Japanese War of 1894–1895 and its annexation of Korea in 1910. Japan did much to build up Korea economically and develop its industry, transportation, and schools. Koreans served in the Imperial Army, and some were even commissioned as officers. At the same time the Japanese sought to destroy the national identity and even the cultural heritage of the Korean people, causing Korean nationalism and hatred of Japan to swell when Korea became independent in 1945.

Yoshida was neither apathetic nor pessimistic about events in Korea. He had bet on the United States in the Pacific War, and he did the same in the Korean War. The British ambassador reported two weeks after the start of the fighting in Korea that Yoshida "did not seem displeased with, or anxious about, the Korean issue, which he appeared to think might assist Japan's economy on the short term." Two days later Yoshida made a ringing statement in the Diet supporting the United Nations in its defense of the ROK.[14]

Early in August Yoshida asked Gascoigne if he thought Red China would enter the war. The ambassador ducked by replying that he was optimistic about the conflict. Yoshida also turned out to be optimistic and "warmly praised the strong and speedy action taken by the United States and certain members of the United Nations against the communist aggression" in Korea. Two months later, after the Chinese had entered the war, the British minister in Tokyo commented somewhat snidely that there was no doubt of Japanese satisfaction that the Americans were being defeated by "mere Chinese," but he added that the Japanese still believed in an ultimate American victory.[15]

The emperor was reportedly grateful that the United States had acted promptly in the defense of Korea. The government turned down the suggestion that it might make a statement to this effect on the ground that such an action by a government under occupation might be misunderstood.[16]

Japanese communists were of course jubilant over North Korean successes in the fighting. Communist leaders no doubt hoped that a resounding military victory by the North would strengthen their position in Japan, but the purge of the party's central committee and the dislike of communism felt by the Japanese people resulted in a marked reduction of communist strength and influence in Japan.

The most far-reaching and immediate result of the Korean War was MacArthur's decision to order the limited rearmament of Japan. He sent a letter to the prime minister on July 8, 1950, stating that Japan's police force should be augmented by a "national police reserve of 75,000 men" and that its maritime safety force should add 8,000 men.[17] The regular police forces in Japan then totaled 125,000, consisting of separate forces in the big cities and a unified "rural" police headquartered in Tokyo with no central direction of all the police forces. The maritime safety agency, or coast guard, then consisted of 10,000 men.

The decision to rearm Japan was made by the supreme commander, who had in 1946 decreed that Japan should be permanently disarmed. U.S. policy had been moving in the direction of greatly strengthening Japan's internal security but not so far as to create even a disguised military force. MacArthur decided to take that extra step. The reason the general gave publicly was the need for "progressive development of law-enforcing agencies adequate to the maintenance of internal security and order and the safeguarding of Japan's coastlines."[18] He said nothing about the Korean War.

MacArthur had received suggestions from Washington several times that the "Japanese police establishment...should be strengthened" and "the presently centrally directed police organization" expanded. In May 1949 the State and Army departments told him that in their view U.S. policies directed him to improve police equipment and training, create a mobile reserve for handling disasters and organized violence, establish a national investigative bureau, and obtain better coordination among police units. In response SCAP took steps to improve the training and the equipment of the police but did not carry out the rest of the instruction. MacArthur turned down a request by Yoshida in 1949 to put the police under unified direction and to coordinate better the operations of the police and other government agencies.[19]

The prime minister went along enthusiastically with the new plan, thinking for some time he was getting a police force, not an army. In a remark to the British ambassador Yoshida said he was "naturally most grateful" for MacArthur's letter of July 8. He added that he would like "to model this new force upon the London Metropolitan Police."[20] It was some time before he realized the Americans looked upon the "police reserve" as an "embryonic army."

After receiving MacArthur's order to set up the police reserve, Yoshida tried for several days to see the supreme commander and finally got an appointment on July 11, their first meeting since the start of the war. Yoshida was told that detailed questions should be put to General Whitney. The author of the hard SCAP line on police for so many years, Whitney was now the maker of policy for the new force. At a meeting on July 13, Whitney told Chief Cabinet Secretary Okazaki that all measures to set up the new force including budgetary steps should be taken on the authority of the supreme commander's letter of July 8 and that this position should be made clear to the Diet, which began a special session that day.[21]

Whitney told the Japanese that the police reserve would be separate from the existing police. It would be directly under the control of the cabinet, would not be subject to existing legislative limitations, and would not require legislation for its establishment.[22] For more than a year SCAP had been trying to discourage Japanese use of cabinet ordinances because they were recognized to be an extralegal procedure of the kind widely used before the war. This fine distinction was disregarded in the emergency caused by the Korean War.

When the chief of staff of the U.S. Army, General J. Lawton Collins, was in Japan in mid-July 1950, he reported to Washington that "MacArthur plans to develop a quasi-military native force in Japan comprising a national police reserve which could eventually be made into the equivalent for home use of four light divisions. All military equipment would have to come from the U.S. This could be done by issuance to MacArthur for loan to the Japanese, thus avoiding political complications."[23]

At the start SCAP prepared a cover plan to disguise the military nature of the new force. But the U.S. officers working on the project made it clear that the reserve force was to be organized along military lines into four divisions. It was to have military equipment that would eventually include heavy weapons and tanks, and it was to be prepared for combat situations more serious than civil disorder and mob violence.[24]

Yoshida wrote in his memoirs that he told the Diet the new force "bore no relation to anything in the nature of rearmament," but, as he foresaw, this point increasingly came up for debate. Despite mounting evidence, Yoshida insisted to the end of his political career that the National Police Reserve (NPR) did not have "war potential," in the words of the constitution, and did not mean rearmament.[25] Because of the cloud of confusion surrounding the new force, public opinion did not coalesce into any opposition or even anxiety about the NPR.

Recruiting officers for the force and paying for it posed thorny issues.

The difficulty was not in getting volunteers, for 382,000 men applied right away, more than five for every opening. Times were still hard in Japan. But picking officers, especially for senior positions, forced a decision about the use of former personnel of the Imperial Army in the new unit. Ever distrustful of the military, Yoshida opposed commissioning former senior officers. Generals MacArthur and Whitney firmly supported his position. General Willoughby, however, pressed for recruitment of a number of former officers who had worked for him on intelligence activities during the occupation, including several who had served as military secretaries to General Tōjō Hideki, one being the notorious Colonel Hattori Takushirō. MacArthur rejected Willoughby's nominees.[26]

Finding funds for the NPR was initially easy. Thanks to the Dodge plan, Japan soon enjoyed a budget surplus. Funds that had originally been set aside for debt retirement became available for the new force. The only financial issue was the salary and benefits that the members of the reserve should receive. The Japanese government and G-2, which had created a special office to handle the organization of the NPR, favored a high salary level and a substantial bonus to attract good people, while GS opposed higher benefits on the ground that the morale of the regular police would be damaged if the new police received higher benefits. In the end, members of the NPR received a somewhat higher salary than the regular police and a smaller bonus on retirement than originally planned.[27]

The NPR legally came into being on August 10, 1950, one month after MacArthur ordered its establishment. The first unit of 7,000 men was organized on August 23. As units were formed, they took over barracks and buildings formerly used by U.S. forces or the old Japanese army. At the outset no former military officers were accepted, but in March 1951 about 300 younger officers of the former army were released from the purge and taken into the new force. In 1952 nine former colonels and one former navy captain were accepted. Senior officer positions in the new force were filled by nonmilitary outsiders. The civilian director of the new agency was Masuhara Keikichi, a career Home Ministry official who had won Yoshida's confidence early in the occupation.

Frank Kowalski, then a U.S. Army colonel attached to SCAP, a West Pointer, and later a congressman from Pennsylvania, wrote a fascinating account of the early days of the NPR. He described vividly both the determined effort and the hard work that went into the formation of the

NPR and the close cooperation that developed between U.S. military men and their Japanese counterparts. Kowalski called the new force "the disguise of a new Japanese army."[28]

No plans were made for the NPR to have an air arm. Although MacArthur was an enthusiastic advocate of air power, he seems to have felt that Japan should not have so potent an offensive capability. Sentiment existed in Washington and among the Allies that a peace treaty should prohibit Japan from developing peacetime civil aviation. It was this kind of thinking that led U.S. planners to stress ground forces for Japan. As a result , according to some observers, Japan has consistently had a disproportionately large and expensive army force, even though strong air and naval forces would afford a more effective first line of defense for an island country.

The United States did not pressure Japan to make a direct military contribution to the Korean War. But Japan did help in many indirect ways. The United States freely used bases and repair facilities in Japan to support Allied forces in Korea. Japanese not only manned ships to transport troops and supplies from Japan to Korea but also operated minesweepers to clear the waters off Korea, including the waters off Inchon and Wonsan before the landings in September and October 1950. Japanese received extra pay from U.S. forces for operating in a combat zone. One Japanese sailor was killed off Wonsan, and eight others were wounded. Japanese railway technicians were recruited to help out in Korea. Many Japanese contributed blood for soldiers wounded in Korea. There was no legal challenge—by Japanese or Americans—about the propriety of these activities in aid of an occupying power.[29]

The creation of the NPR, in effect a defense army, ranks with the writing of the 1946 constitution as one of the most momentous actions of the occupation. Both steps were the handiwork of General MacArthur. Initially, he had moved slowly in each case, but ultimaltely he acted with speed and firmness. The Japanese accepted both actions without serious demurrer.

The Korean War had other major consequences. In Washington the National Security Council, with the new head of the State Department's policy planning staff, Paul H. Nitze, playing an active role, formulated a drastic national policy, NSC 68, calling for "a rapid and sustained build-up of the political, economic and military strength of the free world." The policy's goal was "to frustrate the Kremlin design for world domination by creating a situation in the free world to which the

Kremlin will be compelled to adjust."[30] For Japan the Korean War made it much easier to accept a "peace treaty with many" of the Allied powers and to allow the United States to retain bases.

The Korean War led to the first big release of purgees. Yoshida had pressed MacArthur hard after reelection in January 1949 to permit an appeals board to review the purge. MacArthur consented, and the board examined 32,089 requests for review. For more than six months GS took no action and then in October 1950 approved all the 10,094 recommendations for release.[31]

War broke out in Korea at a time when the Dodge austerity program was taking hold in Japan. The national budget had a large surplus. Government spending had been sharply reduced by cutting subsidies to industry and by firing thousands of public workers. Unemployment and business failures were both up. Unsellable inventories of goods were accumulating. At the same time, the rate of inflation was going down, food and other commodities were more available, and exports showed some improvement.

The Korean War radically altered the situation. It brought a large surge in orders from U.S. forces for goods and services, leading to huge sales and causing a big export boom during the next few years. The U.S. military purchased myriad items, such as ammunition, barbed wire, trucks, tires, communications equipment, coal, textiles, and repair-and-rebuild services. Japanese inventories were wiped out. Hundreds of factories that had been closed as war industries were reopened to produce war-supporting items. The United States ordered $13 million worth of trucks in the first six months of the war.

This procurement, or *tokujū*, had a tremendous impact during the next few years:

—*Tokujū* to the end of the occupation in April 1952 amounted to nearly $1.4 billion. Total *tokujū* for the period of the Korean War, ending in 1953, was about $2.3 billion. Foreign exchange earnings reached $940 million by the end of 1951.

—Imports of essential raw materials, including cotton, wool, soybeans, wood, hemp, iron ore, salt, rayon pulp, petroleum, machinery, and chemicals, doubled after 1950, while exports nearly trebled.

—Industrial and mineral production increased by nearly 70 percent from 1949 to 1951, exceeding the prewar level for the first time in October 1950 and continuing to mount steadily. Soon production began to shift away from low value-added items such as textiles to the high value-added products of heavy and chemical industries, thereby reducing the foreign exchange needed for imports and increasing the earnings from exports. This shift in industrial structure meant that the ratio of imports to gross national product in the postwar period was only about one-half of that before the war.

—Investment in plant and equipment expanded. The increasing volume of imported foreign technology started to make up for ground lost in the wartime period. In 1950, 27 technical cooperation agreements were concluded with foreign firms; in 1951, 101; and in 1952, 133. Development focused on four industries: electric power, steel, marine transport, and coal. This policy, which echoed the priority production plan that Yoshida had adopted in 1947, was another key element in postwar reconstruction.

—Wages and employment rose. The demand for new workers caused the larger companies to add inducements, such as offers of lifetime employment.

—Legislative policies were devised to favor accumulation of capital and high earnings. The Japan Development Bank was set up in 1950 to take over the functions of the former Reconstruction Finance Bank in providing low-interest funds for investment in plant and equipment. The Export-Import Bank was established to promote exports. Tax benefits encouraged investment. The government used the foreign exchange allocation system, set up in 1949, to promote domestic industries such as the auto industry, which was able to develop virtually free of foreign competition.

—One month after the outbreak of war in Korea, an American engineer, W. Edwards Deming, lectured to a group of Japanese industrialists and persuaded them of the value of his statistical sampling technique to improve and control quality. His method has had a remarkable effect on the quality and efficiency of Japanese industrial production.

The economic boom caused by the Korean War was the first and probably the most important in Japan's postwar history because it gave the still-anemic economy a shot in the arm and a chance to test its ability to produce goods of quality in large volume. The boom also strengthened Japan's economic cooperation with the United States, reducing the need for Japan to look to Asia for markets and raw materials and ultimately enabling it to be a major exporter in world markets.

The year 1950 was epochal. Japan crossed a watershed in its political and economic revival by taking the first steps toward rearmament and self-sustaining economic growth and embarking on the path of partnership with the United States.[32] And to protect and defend the Pax Americana, the National Security Council decided that the United States should try to bring about the "recognition by this government, the American people, and all free peoples, that the cold war is in fact a real war in which the survival of the free world is at stake."[33]

CHAPTER 19

Shaping the Peace Settlement

After June 1950 the war in Korea occupied most of the time and energy of U.S. leaders in Washington and Tokyo. For nearly a year the military situation in Korea was extremely perilous. The United States was fighting a limited war, which had turned into a large-scale conflict with little prospect that it would end soon or favorably. It seemed unwise to engage in peace negotiations with Japan when bloody fighting on the Korean peninsula only a few hundred miles away posed a critical threat to the American position in East Asia.

Dulles was undaunted, however. After returning to Washington from Tokyo, he took the lead in urging action on a treaty. In a memorandum of July 19 to Secretary Acheson, he asserted that "the Korean attack makes it more important, rather than less important, to act" because the Japanese people were awakening from their "postwar stupor" and the United States might be able to "bring them an insight into the possibilities of the free world and their responsibility as a member of it."[1]

On July 24 Acheson raised the matter with the president, who agreed it was important to get on with the treaty. Acheson said State and Defense would send him detailed recommendations on how to proceed, and during the next month Acheson and Dulles waged a bitter bureaucratic battle to get a treaty. Only their heavy pressure persuaded the Pentagon to define its military requirements, which were extensive. Dulles reassured Secretary of Defense Johnson that MacArthur's views were being taken fully into account and that the draft treaty "gave the

United States the right to maintain in Japan as much force as we wanted, anywhere we wanted, for as long as we wanted." This seemed to mollify Johnson, who then thought he and Dulles could now "get together and go places."[2]

The two departments worked out a draft, thanks in good part to the skill of John Allison in winning the support of his defense counterpart, Major General Carter Magruder, a special assistant to the secretary of the army. The president approved the recommendations of the two departments on September 8, 1950. On the key security issue, this paper, NSC 60/1, provided that a treaty "must give the United States the right to maintain armed forces in Japan, where, for so long, and to such extent as it deems necessary." NSC 60/1 also provided that a treaty with Japan would not come into force until "after favorable resolution of the present United States military situation in Korea."[3]

As it turned out, many of the provisions in NSC 60/1 and most of its tough tone fell by the wayside in the course of the later discussions within the U.S. government and in negotiations with the Japanese for a security treaty and an administrative agreement. In final form those two documents contained several one-sided provisions, but they were nothing like the grab bag demands of NSC 60/1.

Dulles had meanwhile been laboring away on a short statement of seven principles to use as the basis for his talks with other nations. According to the statement, all nations at war with Japan could be parties to the treaty. Japan would seek membership in the United Nations. It would recognize the independence of Korea, agree to a U.N. trusteeship for the Ryukyu and Bonin Islands administered by the United States (this roundabout approach to the Okinawa problem was apparently Dulles's idea), and accept future big power decisions on the status of Formosa, South Sakhalin, and the Kuriles. "There would be continuing cooperative responsibility between Japanese facilities and U.S. and perhaps other forces" to maintain peace and security in the Japan area, pending satisfactory alternative security arrangements. Provision would also be made in a treaty for Japan to abide by multilateral political and commercial agreements and for settlement of claims and disputes.[4] Dulles's paper said nothing about occupation reforms, renunciation of war, or reparations.

On September 14 the president announced that he had authorized the State Department to open discussions with other nations regarding a peace treaty. Dulles told a press conference on September 15 that the United States did not intend to place any restrictions on Japanese rearmament. He commented that the treaty might be negotiated in a series of bilateral discussions, rather than at a general peace conference. He then began a round of diplomatic meetings with representatives of FEC nations attending the U.N. General Assembly in New York. The first reactions were especially cool toward his plans to waive reparations claims and to omit all restrictions on Japanese rearmament. The representatives countered with a variety of controls they wanted to impose on posttreaty Japan.[5]

The Soviets wanted the Big Four foreign ministers to negotiate the treaty. They objected to language that did not reaffirm their sovereignty over the Kuriles and South Sakhalin as well as Chinese title to Formosa. After the Australian representative read the seven-point memorandum, he told Dulles that "Australia would not, under any circumstances, accept such a treaty." Dulles clearly had a long way to go.[6]

The Chinese entry into the Korean War in October 1950 shocked the leaders in Washington far more than the setbacks had in the summer because the PRC could easily send "hordes of volunteers" to Korea, with unfathomable consequences. But no one regretted the decision to make peace with Japan. Some suggested unilateral U.S. measures such as restoring to Japan a large measure of autonomy in domestic affairs or enlisting Japanese personnel to fight alongside U.S. forces in Korea under some sort of U.N. aegis, but these stopgap measures won little support.[7]

Dulles next suggested that a mission be sent to Japan immediately to negotiate in cooperation with MacArthur an arrangement that would "commit Japan, spiritually and politically, to the cause of the free world." This arrangement might include a security pact linking Japan, Australia, New Zealand, the Philippines, the United States, and possibly Indonesia in a "Pacific Pact" somewhat like NATO in Europe. Secretary Acheson sent a memo to the new secretary of defense, George Marshall, recommending a joint approach to the president.[8]

After a meeting on January 8, 1951, the two secretaries sent a memo to the president, who approved it on January 10, 1951, and sent a letter to Dulles the same day naming him special representative to conduct the "negotiations necessary to bring a Japanese peace settlement to a satisfactory conclusion. . . . The principal purpose in the proposed settlement is to secure the adherence of the Japanese nation to the free nations of the world and to assure that it will play its full part in resisting the further expansion of communist imperialism." This wording went beyond the abortive 1949 treaty draft in that the United States officially espoused the goal of Japan's "adherence" to the free nations to play its "full part" in resisting communism. MacArthur had hoped since the end of the war that Japan would become a friend of the United States. But he never envisaged an active role for Japan in a worldwide anticommunist movement. Nor did George Kennan when he formulated the U.S. policy for Japan in 1948.[9]

Soon after the president made this pivotal decision, Dulles took off on his second trip to Japan. His first goal was "a United States–Japan understanding." To start negotiations for a peace settlement with the defeated nation without thoroughly canvassing the views of the other Allies was surely an unusual procedure. But Dulles was just as eager to obtain the full support of MacArthur, which he knew was essential to avoid attacks by the right-wing press in the United States and to win solid approval in the Senate.

For this mission Dulles had added two senior officials from the Department of Defense, Assistant Secretary of the Army Earl D. Johnson and General Magruder. By this time differences between State and Defense and within Defense had been all but eliminated. Dulles also added to his mission John D. Rockefeller III as an adviser on cultural matters. Rockefeller knew something about Japan because of his membership in the Institute of Pacific Relations and participation in military planning for Japan as a lieutenant commander in the navy. He took little part in the treaty discussions of the Dulles mission, however, although he did strike out on his own to see Japan and learn about the people. He retained a lifelong interest in Japan that was marked by significant philanthropic works.[10]

Following the first Dulles trip in June of 1950, a small group of Japanese Foreign Office experts had been canvassing the issues and the options open to Japan. They were assisted by two outside groups, one of former diplomats and academics and the other of former military men. These advisory groups came up with many different ideas, including "peace with all," which would mean peace with all the major powers including the Soviet Union and Communist China; "peace with many," which would be a settlement with most of the Allied powers; and even peace with the United States alone, which would provide for Japan's rearmament and the basing of U.S. forces in Japan. The former vice chief of the army general staff, General Kawabe Torashirō, argued that Japan should not rearm because it would be too dangerous but that Japan should agree to the basing of U.S. forces as a hedge in case of war.[11]

Again showing considerable acumen, Yoshida told the experts that he did not think war between the United States and the Soviet Union was likely but that there would be a long period of tension broken by periods of harmony. He recounted his remark to Dulles that it would be unwise for Japan to rearm before a peace treaty. Yet Yoshida told his experts, "In fact there will be rearmament." In the words of the perceptive diplomatic historian Hosoya Chihiro, Yoshida "perceived, because of the existing international circumstances, Japan would eventually have to proceed with rearmament. . . . But he believed that rearmament had to be postponed as long as possible so that Japan could have an adequate time to rebuild her war-devastated economy."[12]

To refine the general ideas they had been considering, Yoshida's staff worked up a series of alternative positions on the overriding security issue that ranged from a disarmed zone in East Asia to a peace treaty with the United States providing for U.S. bases in Japan. The sole issue Yoshida stood firm on was that he would not commit Japan to a rapid buildup of military forces. His goal was an immediate peace settlement, without any commitment to rearm. All else—the form of agreement, how many nations signed other than the United States, reparations, territory—was subordinate.

MacArthur had a "long talk" with Yoshida before Dulles arrived and thought he "had laid the groundwork for the mission's task,"[13] whereas Yoshida thought he had won the general's support for a go-slow position on rearmament. MacArthur told Dulles at their preliminary meeting on January 27 that the latest draft of a peace treaty was "a model document based on the highest principles of statesmanship." The general endorsed Dulles's determination to go ahead with a treaty, alone if necessary, commenting in the grand MacArthurian manner, "The United States thus far failed to appreciate that an essential attribute of world leadership is the capacity to act arbitrarily and even ruthlessly when the circumstances require," a lesson he felt the British had learned in their period of hegemony.[14]

Regarding Okinawa the general advised Dulles and his mission to be firm and tell the Japanese that this matter was "simply not open for discussion." A few days later he told Dulles that the Japanese understood the U.S. position on Okinawa and would not argue about it. Dulles had some reservations about being categorical on this score, but he played it tough and offered no compromise beyond his announced plan for a U.N. trusteeship administered by the United States, which would enable the Allied nations to decide "how they wished the island disposed of and administered." Ironically, the final version of the treaty did not strip Japan of sovereignty over Okinawa, but the road to that clever compromise was full of unhappiness for the Japanese, due in good part to the general's tough line.[15]

Yoshida and Dulles had their first meeting on January 29, 1951. The Americans had already given the Japanese a paper setting out the seven principles Dulles had formulated in Washington as well as a thirteen-point agenda for the talks. The prime minister began by reiterating what he had said to Dulles in June 1950 that virtually any agreement that did not wound the amour propre of the Japanese people would be accepted. He then gave the American negotiator a lecture on how the occupation forces had disregarded basic Japanese attitudes by abolishing the old family system; this was a subject of little interest to Dulles. Yoshida then suggested that Japanese businessmen could act as a kind of "fifth column for democracy" in dealing with the PRC. This suggestion did not catch the fancy of the sternly anticommunist Foster Dulles.[16]

Yoshida used an unusual negotiating tactic in discussing the treaty, commenting "that it would be a comparatively easy matter to conclude and that the United States was in a position to put through almost anything it desired." Dulles responded that "the treaty was a very serious matter." He wanted to know if opposition political parties would be hard to handle. Yoshida saw no problem there. Dulles tried to press Yoshida on what Japan would do for its own defense, prompting Yoshida to say that he did not want to bring back the militarists, who had gone "underground," and that building military forces would be a severe economic strain. Dulles felt "Japan should be willing to make at least a token contribution and a commitment to a general cause of collective security." Yoshida conceded "Japan would be willing to make some contribution" but stated that Japanese opinion did not support rearmament and that Japan had to recover its independence before it could consider how it might cooperate in security matters.[17]

Once again Dulles was unhappy about Yoshida's attitude. To Dulles's precise and businesslike mind, the prime minister was engaging in "a puff ball performance." Sebald surmised that Yoshida "was totally unprepared to discuss even broad principles" and was simply feeling Dulles out. Yoshida's principal expert said later, however, that Dulles had made an "unfavorable impression" on Yoshida in those early contacts. Whatever the reason, the proud and cagey prime minister was not going to lay his cards on the table so early in the game. Yoshida admired Dulles's skill and tenacity but later said that Dulles "accomplished the work he did with the aid of that fervour that comes from religious conviction."[18] Yoshida was not himself that moralistic a person. It took Yoshida some time to feel at ease with Dulles, whom he got to know well in the next few years. Yoshida may also have thought he held a high trump card in the person of MacArthur, whose distaste for Japanese rearmament was well known.

Right after this meeting, Yoshida and Dulles traveled in separate cars to see MacArthur. Dulles wanted the supreme commander to be fully involved and had hoped MacArthur would sit in on his talks with the Japanese. The general had not wanted to do this so that charges could not be made "that he, as SCAP, is attempting to impose on the Japanese the views of the United States government." But he was ready at all times to act as a "go-between" to assist in reconciling differences. [19]

This encounter, at 6 P.M. on January 29, 1951, was the sole occasion the Big Three met together, and it became famous in Japan. Only the three men were in the room, and no one kept a record of the conversation. According to the accounts Yoshida later gave to his staff or in his memoirs, he told the general that he was troubled by Dulles's "embarrassing question" about how Japan could contribute to the Free World. Reportedly the general smiled, looked at Dulles, and said, "What the Free World needs from Japan is not military power. That is not practical. Japan has capacity for military production. It has manpower for labor. These can be used to increase the strength of the Free World."[20]

Yoshida wrote in one of his reminiscences that he had asked MacArthur in advance to save him if Dulles raised the subject of rearmament. The general came through handsomely. The wily Yoshida called him a "lifeboat." To carry out MacArthur's suggestion, Yoshida's staff experts soon put together a list of unused factories and facilities that were available to produce items needed by the U.S. forces. The lack of any evidence to corroborate Yoshida's account of the Big Three meeting on January 29 is puzzling. Dulles, an acute observer and normally a meticulous record-keeper of significant events, described it the next day as "a purely courtesy call" in which the general wished them well and offered to help out if difficulties were encountered.[21]

More important, Dulles did not stop pressing Yoshida for a defense contribution. After all, the president's January 10 letter of instruction asserted that the United States "desires that Japan should increasingly acquire the ability to defend itself." As Dulles saw it, U.S. policy was embodied in the Vandenburg resolution approved by the Congress in

1949, which stated that nations entering into defense relationships with the United States should "take continuous and effective self-help measures" to provide for their own defense. If Japan would not take such steps, the United States would find it difficult to place forces in Japan committed to its defense.[22]

The Japanese made written comments on January 30 regarding some of the agenda items Dulles had proposed the day before. On January 31 Yoshida and Dulles discussed these points. Dulles firmly rejected a Japanese proposal that the U.N. trusteeship for the Ryukyu Islands be conducted jointly by the United States and Japan or that the United States occupy the islands on a lease basis, with Japan retaining sovereign rights. Dulles thought Yoshida had accepted his position, but the Japanese team found Dulles's attitude harsh and shocking.[23] Regarding security, Yoshida repeated Japan's standard reservations but added that Japan was "eager to play a positive role" and that he wanted to consult the Americans on the question of the specific contribution Japan might make to the common defense. Dulles and Sebald thought this was progress. Yoshida's advisers, notably Okazaki Katsuo and Iguchi Sadao from the Foreign Office, were obviously giving him the message that he must show at least an appearance of flexibility.[24]

The Japanese side felt that the discussions were at a low ebb. Yoshida and Dulles had found no common ground. Dulles even had trouble understanding Yoshida's English. The U.S. team kept asking the Japanese if Yoshida understood what Dulles was telling him and questioning whether the prime minister really had a good command of English. This hurt the feelings of the Japanese. Yoshida's ability to speak English was often the subject of debate by the English-speaking community in Japan and by the British when he was ambassador to the Court of St. James before the war. The record establishes that he was quite a good conversationalist in English and carried on much of his business with Americans and other English speakers with only occasional difficulty.[25]

On February 1, 1951, the atmosphere of the talks improved noticeably, not because of the efforts of the two protagonists, who were still feeling each other out, but because Yoshida and Dulles stayed out of the talks for several days and let their experts see what they could accomplish. The subordinates were less inhibited in searching for a compromise than the two principals had been.

Each side made concessions. With the approval of Yoshida, the Japanese submitted Plan B, "A Draft Agreement for Japanese-American

Security Cooperation," the plan most favorable to the United States. Its salient points were as follows:

1. The United States would guarantee Japan's security on behalf of the United Nations.
2. When the United Nations determined that aggressive actions had been taken against Japan, the United States would act to stop the aggression, and Japan would lend assistance to the extent its constitution permitted.
3. Japan agreed that U.S. forces could be stationed in Japan for this purpose. A joint Japan-U.S. committee would decide the conditions for the stationing of the U.S. forces.
4. Japan and the United States would consult whenever either country's territorial integrity or political independence was threatened.
5. The agreement would last ten years.

The Japanese reiterated that as their defense contribution they would make available industrial capacity, labor, and facilities. The Americans continued to press for a Japanese contribution of "ground forces."[26]

In addition, the Japanese submitted a second document on February 1 called "Items to Be Included in the Peace Treaty." It called for Japan and the United States to make security arrangements in accordance with the U.N. Charter, a point the Japanese considered important.[27] The next day the U.S. side, led by Johnson, submitted a counterproposal entitled "Agreement Concerning Japanese-American Cooperation for Their Mutual Security." This extensive draft, which had been under preparation in Washington for some time, contained general provisions, which had been modified somewhat to take account of the Japanese views submitted the day before, and detailed clauses regarding base rights and the legal status of the U.S. forces that might be stationed in Japan after the peace treaty went into effect. Detailed base arrangements of this sort were known as "status of forces" agreements. The Americans were wrestling with a knotty problem: they wanted an agreement including both a general security understanding and detailed base rights provisions, and they wanted this agreement to be drafted and accepted before the treaty came into force, when their bargaining leverage would be at its strongest.[28]

The Japanese did not like all the minutiae in the U.S. draft and suggested placing much of detail in a separate agreement. The U.S. side agreed. This meant that a separate executive agreement on security arrangements would have to be negotiated along with a more general security agreement and a treaty of peace. It was clear that both sides had hit on the form and general content of agreements they could accept, although they had not yet found precise phrasing for the crucial issue of Japan's defense.[29]

The U.S. negotiating strategy in the Tokyo talks was to get an acceptable security arrangement before tabling detailed views on the peace treaty. The Japanese, well aware that the price they would have to pay for a suitable peace treaty was a security arrangement the Americans could accept, hoped to strike a deal by which they would give the United States base rights but would avoid any undertaking to rearm. But on February 3 they became worried that they could not extract this kind of bargain from the Americans. They concluded that if they were going to get a peace treaty, they would have to agree to more definite steps toward rearmament.[30]

The Japanese negotiators proposed that the treaty establish a joint Japan-U.S. committee to develop plans for Japan's rearmament as well as measures for emergency action by the two governments in case of a threat of aggression. When the proposal did not satisfy the Americans, Yoshida decided on February 2 to prepare a plan for modified rearmament. The Japanese came up with a paper entitled "Initial Steps for Rearmament Program," which was given to Allison in the evening of February 3. The document bore no signature or initials. It provided:

(Tokyo) February 3, 1951

Simultaneously with the coming into force of the Peace Treaty and the Japanese-American Security Cooperation Agreement it will be necessary for Japan to embark upon a program of rearmament. The following are the principal features of this program contemplated by the Japanese Government.

(a) Security forces, land and sea, totalling 50,000 will be created apart from the existing police forces and the National Police Reserve. These security forces will be specially trained and more powerfully equipped, and placed under the proposed Ministry of National Security. The 50,000 men will mark the start of Japan's new democratic armed forces.

(b) What might be termed a "Security Planning Headquarters" will be set up in the National Security Ministry. Experts, conversant with American and British military affairs, will be assigned to this Headquarters; they will participate in the activities of the Joint Committee to be established under the Japanese-American Security Cooperation Agreement, and they will constitute the nucleus for the future General Staff of Japan's democratic armed forces. The government will seek the advice of American military experts (soldiers).[31]

Neither the United States nor Japan has published this document in full, although U.S. records make a cryptic reference to a Japanese paper on this subject and briefly describe the measures to be taken by Japan. In 1977 the *Tōkyō shimbun* published many of the details. Nishimura Kumao, one of Japan's principal treaty negotiators, confirmed the accuracy of the story, stating that he had taken down Prime Minister Yoshida's dictation of the document. Nishimura denied that there was a "secret promise" and pointed out that Yoshida had not negotiated the document with Dulles or made any agreement with him. Nishimura asserted that while Yoshida was prime minister Japan did in fact increase the size of its defense forces and did establish a security agency and later a self-defense agency. Yoshida thus did what he had agreed to do while staying within the limits of the Japanese constitution. To explain the silence of the official records, one can speculate that Yoshida might have extracted a promise from all involved not to reveal his plans for "rearmament." Whatever the explanation, it is hard to avoid the impression that the evanescent 1951 "rearmament plan" was but another piece in the scheme of confusion and deception that Article 9 of the 1947 constitution has generated.[32]

In view of the apparent progress at the staff level, Dulles concluded he should give the Japanese a clearer idea of the peace treaty terms he had developed. On February 5 Dulles's staff handed the Japanese negotiators a lengthy paraphrase of the treaty draft it had prepared in Washington, which in MacArthur's opinion reflected "the highest principles of statesmanship." Called a "provisional memorandum," this draft of six printed pages elaborated on the points Dulles had been refining for some months: no restrictions would be placed on Japan's peacetime activity, no provision would be made for reparations, Japan's right of self-defense would be recognized, and the Ryukyu and Bonin Islands would remain under U.S. control until the United Nations approved trusteeship arrangements. The Japanese were pleased with the proposals, which they considered "magnanimous and fair."[33]

It was in fact surprising that traditional peace treaty issues, such as property claims and economic rights, received so little attention in the entire peace negotiations with Japan. Several of the Allied powers emphatically disagreed with the U.S. insistence on a short and nonpunitive treaty, as Dulles was to find out. But during his talks in Tokyo in early 1951, security was the dominant issue, and the others were minor. Several technical issues were discussed, such as fisheries, war damage claims, and dumping of exports, and side agreements were reached on two of them. But they were considered to be of lesser importance.[34]

The security issue had not yet run its course. On February 3 the Japanese had given the Americans some comments on the U.S. draft of February 2, seeking to shorten it, tighten the U.S. commitment to defend Japan, and omit language about Japanese undertakings in case of emergency. Dulles did not like these changes and redrafted the entire security agreement; the redraft was remarkably like the treaty finally signed six months later in San Francisco. Dulles clearly had in mind a short, simple text for the collective defense agreement, relegating the rights and duties of U.S. forces stationed in Japan to a long, detailed document called an administrative agreement. On February 6 the Japanese accepted the U.S. proposals "practically without change." Thus, the basic approach for the security documents to be negotiated in the peace settlement was clearly laid out.[35]

On January 31 Dulles, who always maintained steady contact with the news media, held a press conference and on February 2 made a speech to the America-Japan Society of Tokyo. His speeches were invariably direct, unadorned, and tough-minded. He told the Japanese that if they wished they could "share collective protection against direct aggression. . . . The choice must be Japan's own choice." The peace sought by the United States would give Japan "the opportunity to share in collective security, to raise its standard of living and to achieve moral stature and respected leadership."[36]

Yoshida called on MacArthur on February 6. Japanese reports indicate the general was sympathetic with the prime minister's concern for the fate of Okinawa and with his desire to avoid all references in the treaty documents to the word *rearmament*. Yoshida seemed to rely on MacArthur almost as a confidant, and MacArthur responded with understanding, even when Yoshida's intentions went counter to U.S. policy. In a later remark to a U.S. senator, Yoshida said that he had a special arrangement for meetings with the general and that MacArthur was very useful to him and to Japan. The quality of this relationship was evident in Yoshida's resort to MacArthur in the meetings of January and February 1951. The general was in fact an invaluable go-between, certainly for the Japanese.[37]

Dulles had not been idle while the staff experts negotiated in early February. He saw the British ambassador twice to inform him in a general way of what the United States was doing and to consult him on the concept of a Pacific pact. The United States had picked this idea up from Australia and the Philippines, which were nervous, if not terrified, at the prospect of a rearmed Japan. The two countries were far less confident than the United States that Japan had become a peace-loving society only five years after World War II ended. To cope with this dilemma, they had conceived the idea of a multinational treaty in which all the members would agree to defend and protect one another against outside attack from any quarter. According to the usual formulation of the plan, the participants would include the United States, Australia, New Zealand, the Philippines, and possibly Indonesia and Japan. The Asian nations, fearing Japan at least as much as they feared the communist menace, would by this device receive protection and re-assurance.[38]

Dulles had explored the idea and found some support for it in Washington. He took it up with the British in Tokyo on January 29. Sir Alvary Gascoigne consulted London and on February 2 informed Dulles that London had serious reservations about the proposal for a Pacific defense council, noting that it did not include Hong Kong or Malaya and that the United Kingdom would not be a participant.[39] As a result, talk about a Pacific pact in connection with the Japanese peace treaty died out.

Yoshida and Dulles had a third and final meeting on February 7. This one went well. They talked briefly about several technical matters, and Yoshida restated his opposition to a military structure like the Prussian general staff.[40]

Dulles's visit culminated in the initialing on February 9, 1951, of five documents:

—A provisional memorandum describing in ten general paragraphs the provisions that might form the basis of a peace treaty

—A draft "collective self-defense agreement"

—A draft agreement by which Japan would permit the United Nations to use facilities in Japan to support U.N. forces in Korea

—A draft administrative agreement setting out the rights and privileges of U.S. forces in Japan after a peace treaty

—An understanding that the facilities and services to be provided by Japan at its expense pursuant to the administrative agreement would be similar to the arrangement between the United States and the United Kingdom[41]

Yoshida and Dulles also exchanged letters stating Japan would enter into negotiations with the United States for an agreement regarding fisheries conservation, another price Japan would have to pay for a peace treaty. As a final caveat, Dulles stressed to the Japanese that many differences of opinion existed among the Allies about the treaty and that there could be no assurances that the eventual treaty would be as free of restrictions as the U.S.- proposals were.[42]

Yoshida said later of his talks with Dulles in early 1951 that they reached understandings on several important matters: that occupation reforms would not be written into the peace treaty, that any reparations would be in the form of materiel and not money, and that no new war criminals would be implicated. A Japanese chronicler of Yoshida's political career claims there were other understandings as well: after the peace treaty Japan would propose an international collective security arrangement providing for close cooperation with the United States, rearmament would be decided by the people only after Japan achieved economic independence, and Japan would need U.S. economic aid to attain economic independence. Yoshida and Dulles discussed some of these points at length, such as rearmament and security, and others were touched on only lightly, if at all. But U.S. records do not reveal that any special agreements or "understandings" along the lines indicated by the Japanese were reached. These talks marked the beginning of the treaty negotiating process, and Dulles was in no position at the outset to make any commitments to the loser nation.[43]

The Dulles mission spent twelve days in Japan. He met with Yoshida three times and with MacArthur four times. His staff met regularly with Japanese experts. In addition, he saw several Allied ambassadors and met with a number of Diet members and private citizens. Dulles met briefly on February 6, 1951, with a group of Japanese conservatives, arranged by *Newsweek*'s Pakenham. Headed by Japan's leading purgee, Hatoyama Ichirō, and former Admiral Nomura Kichisaburō, who was ambassador to the United States when Pearl Harbor was attacked, the group gave Dulles a lengthy memo setting out measures it thought Japan should take, such as rearming and rebuilding the economy. At the end of his visit Dulles and his wife called on the emperor and empress.[44]

Dulles flew directly from Tokyo to Manila on February 11. He found the Filipinos bitter about the seven principles he had advanced for the Japanese treaty, especially the lack of any provision for reparations or restraints on Japan's future military activity. President Elpidio Quirino had particular reason to be bitter because his wife and daughter had been killed during the Japanese occupation. Dulles expressed sympathy for the Filipino position, as General MacArthur had done in the past, but they both felt that any obligation imposed on Japan to make reparation for war damage would mean only that the United States would have to increase its assistance to Japan in order to prevent economic collapse.[45]

Plunging down to Australasia, Dulles found that Canberra and Wellington would accept the kind of settlement with Japan that the United States had in mind if their security worries could be assuaged. Rarely nonplussed, Dulles suggested to Australia and New Zealand that a treaty linking them with the United States might be a solution to their concerns. He quickly sketched out an arrangement by which the three nations would agree to protect one another. This draft, which was later adopted by the three governments, became popularly known as the ANZUS (Australia–New Zealand–United States) Pact. It was understood that this agreement would be interdependent with the Japanese settlement: no government would be obliged to accept one without the other.[46]

After Dulles returned to Washington, he drafted the full text of the proposed treaty with Japan. This was much like the draft he had prepared before his trip to Tokyo, which had served as the basis of the provisional memorandum given the Japanese on February 5 and initialed on February 9. The full text of the new draft was given to the representatives in Washington of the fourteen principal Allied nations and to a representative of the Republic of Korea, which it was planned at that time would also be a signatory of the treaty.[47]

Dulles met with the representatives of the Allied powers and consulted with congressional committees. The Soviet representative to the United Nations, Jacob Malik, denied that he had had any talks with Dulles on the peace treaty, whereupon the State Department issued a press release describing four conversations with Malik and three written memoranda that had been exchanged. President Truman told Acheson that the U.S. note of May 19 to the Soviets was a "jewel."[48]

Within a year of taking on the job of negotiator, Dulles was well on the way to a peace treaty. He had unified the position of the U.S. government. The Japanese were enthusiastic about the draft treaty and ready to go along with the security arrangements. The Allies were grumbling but not mutinous, although the Soviet Union and India registered extreme discontent with the Dulles draft. The British were known to be drafting their own version of a treaty. Several key issues were yet to be fully addressed, such as reparations and who would sign for China. But with the Pentagon and the Japanese on board, Dulles had some reason to feel optimistic.

Dulles was scrupulous in keeping MacArthur informed. On March 2, 1951, he wrote the general about his trip around the western Pacific. In a letter of March 18 he wrote that the United Kingdom was causing problems and that "there are occasional signs of relapse in the Pentagon." At the end he said to MacArthur, "Your own position is central, dominating and indispensable."[49] This was surely Yoshida's view as well.

Three weeks later MacArthur was ordered out of Japan.

CHAPTER 20

The Firing of MacArthur

Early in the afternoon of April 11, 1951, General MacArthur was giving a luncheon at his embassy residence for visiting Senator Warren Magnuson, a Washington Democrat. MacArthur's wife whispered to him that a message had come from Washington stating that President Truman had relieved him of his commands, effective at once, and ordered him to return to the United States; General Matthew B. Ridgway, then serving in Korea, had been named successor. MacArthur said quietly, "Jeannie, we're going home at last." When the luncheon was finished, he returned to his office.[1]

Prime Minister Yoshida was host that day at a large midafternoon garden party at his official residence to view the cherry blossoms. Word about MacArthur's release spread rapidly, the news having already been announced in Washington. Yoshida asked Ambassador Sebald, who was present, if the report was true. Sebald said he would find out. He went to MacArthur's headquarters at the Dai Ichi building, where MacArthur's senior aide confirmed the report. By then Sebald's office had a telegram from the State Department asking him to advise the prime minister that MacArthur had been relieved and to assure Yoshida that there was no change in U.S. policy toward Japan or the peace treaty.[2]

Sebald called on Yoshida at 6:30 P.M. He found the prime minister attired in Japanese dress, looking more natural and dignified than in his usual Western-style dark suit and wing collar. Sebald conveyed the message from Washington, adding his personal hope that Yoshida and his cabinet would not resign in the Japanese traditional gesture of "responsibility" by a superior when something bad happened. "Visibly shaken," Yoshida was grateful for the message and said there would be no resignation. Sebald reported to Washington that Yoshida said MacArthur's departure would come as a "tremendous shock to the Japanese people." Yoshida also said he felt "personally indebted to MacArthur to whose guidance he attributes his political success and to whose influence he attributes preservation of the Emperor institution."[3]

Sebald then called on MacArthur, acting more in the role of adviser and confidant than of staff officer. He found the general in full control of himself, unlike Sebald, who could not hold back a tear. But MacArthur did vent the bitterness he felt in being "publicly humiliated after fifty-two years of service in the army." The general "intimated that his recall was a plot in Washington, that Formosa would be handed over to Red China, that our whole position in the Far East would crumble." MacArthur thought his successor, General Ridgway, was an "excellent soldier" but he doubted that he was "a good administrator." As Sebald noted in his diary, these were "bitter words, which may perhaps excuse them," but under the circumstances "they were understandable." MacArthur's memoirs reflect some of the same paranoia. Enemies in Washington and Allied capitals were out to get him. The Soviets had at last retaliated for his rejecting their request for a zone of occupation in Japan.[4]

The reasons for relieving MacArthur had nothing to do with his work in Japan as supreme commander for the Allied powers. Washington had in fact given some thought to allowing MacArthur to retain that position in order to finish the job there but had decided this would not be wise.[5] MacArthur's troubles stemmed from his differences with Washington on the conduct of the war in Korea, which had steadily grown more serious after the Chinese intervention. The situation came to a head over a letter MacArthur wrote on March 20 in reply to one from Representative Joseph W. Martin, a prominent Republican from Massachusetts. The general agreed with the congressman that Chinese Nationalist troops should be allowed to open a second front on the China mainland, even though MacArthur had stated some months before that Nationalist troops should not be used in the Korean War. Martin made the general's letter public on April 5 without asking for permission. MacArthur, despite his fabled memory, could not remember what he had said and had to pull the letter out of the files to refresh his recollection. MacArthur told Sebald it was a "personal letter." It was MacArthur's practice to write frequently to members of Congress without advising Washington.[6]

Dulles was routed out of bed on the night of April 10 to go to Secretary Acheson's home. Acheson said he and the president thought it imperative that Dulles go to Tokyo to confer with General Ridgway, who was unfamiliar with the treaty situation, and to reassure Japanese leaders that U.S. intentions were unchanged. Dulles agreed to think the matter over, commenting that MacArthur's dismissal could "have a very serious effect on Japanese public opinion" and on the goal of winning "the committal of the Japanese nation to the cause of the free world." Acheson was probably not pleased to hear Dulles assert that in his opinion MacArthur had been poorly handled by the administration and the JCS and that as a result the general felt his views were not given adequate consideration.[7]

Dulles then conferred with Republican leaders, once again asserting that the JCS were not able "to work with a high-strung person of great moral stature and sense of the dramatic such as General MacArthur." The Republican leaders, including Senator Robert A. Taft, agreed Dulles should try to retrieve the situation on condition the administration would not adopt a policy of appeasement in Asia and would proceed with the treaty along the lines concurred in by General MacArthur. Dulles decided to stay on the job and go to Japan. As he departed on April 13, Truman sent him a message reaffirming "the determination of the United States to work earnestly for prompt conclusion of the Japanese peace settlement."[8]

Most Japanese were confused by the recall of MacArthur. They had tremendous regard for him as a man who understood their plight and had helped guide them out of the dark valley of defeat. They had been confident that with the power of the United States behind him, MacArthur would win in Korea. Many of them were puzzled at the public airing by Americans in high places of differences over national policy.

MacArthur's departure from Tokyo on April 16 set off a huge outpouring of emotion, as thousands of Japanese lined the roads from the American Embassy to the suburban airport in Haneda to see the general off. In contrast to his arrival more than five years before, when only a few people watched him, he was now departing on a *hanamichi* many miles long under the most dramatic circumstances. He had become a "fallen hero," who had descended from the heights of success to the abyss of misfortune, the kind of person for whom the Japanese have always felt sympathy. Miyazawa Kiichi, then a senior Finance Ministry official and later a cabinet minister, was more cynical. "MacArthur's discharge," he thought, "did not really shake the Japanese minds. Those Japanese who know the background realize there is no change in U.S. policy. But most Japanese who do not know feel sorry for General MacArthur. It is generally realized the peace treaty is in the secure hands of Mr. Dulles. The emotional storm in Japan will subside."[9]

The two Japanese most profoundly affected were the emperor and the prime minister. Both asked to make farewell calls on the general, and when his staff demurred, they insisted. MacArthur took the narrow view that he had been deprived of all official status the moment he received the president's recall order and therefore could not perform official acts, such as receiving foreign officials or even saying farewell to his troops. He finally consented to short visits by the prime minister on April 14 and the emperor on April 15. Both Japanese realized they owed much to MacArthur, and they were deeply moved by the occasion.

An ironic lesson of the recall for the Japanese was the example it gave them in civilian control over the military as established in the United States. General MacArthur had carved out considerable autonomy for himself during the occupation of Japan and in the prosecution of the Korean War. His independence of Washington and his apparent desire to carry the war to Communist China in late 1950 bore certain parallels to the actions of Japanese officers in China who decided in 1931 to invade Manchuria and in 1937 to attack China. But MacArthur was not Caesar, and the Pacific was wider than the Rubicon. Washington stepped in, and MacArthur was stripped of his authority. The four members of the JCS agreed that he should be relieved. Senior State Department officials, including Dean Acheson, considered him irresponsible and threatening to U.S. interests.[10]

If MacArthur had been relieved much earlier—for example, in the summer of 1950 before agreement was reached by the State and Defense departments to go ahead with the treaties—the result might have been a lengthy delay in the peace settlement. But by the time he was recalled, the die had been cast in favor of prompt action. Indeed, MacArthur had played an indispensable role in overcoming Defense Deparment objections to the treaties with Japan.

General Ridgway arrived in Tokyo on April 14, three days after he received orders to replace MacArthur. He went immediately to see the retiring supreme commander. Ridgway reported in his memoirs that MacArthur "was entirely himself—composed, quiet, temperate, friendly and helpful to the man who was to succeed him." He was impressed by "the resilience of this great man" and wrote that MacArthur's "dismissal could have been handled with more grace."[11]

The fifty-six-year-old new supreme commander had risen to prominence in World War II in the fighting in Europe. A calm, businesslike, and purposeful man, he was a team player who made no pretense of being in the mold of MacArthur. Despite MacArthur's animadversions to Sebald, Ridgway was an excellent administrator as well as a brilliant combat officer. He was soon in full command of the occupation of Japan and the fighting in Korea.

His first contact with the Japanese was somewhat awkward. Ridgway went to the Tokyo airport on April 16 to greet Dulles a few hours after MacArthur had left. When he saw three Japanese there, he gave an order that they be turned away. Only after Sebald explained that they were senior officials who had also come for the purpose of greeting Dulles were they permitted to stay and be introduced to the new supreme commander.[12]

Sebald advised Ridgway to have official dealings only with the top level, although he might have informal contacts with other Japanese. GS also gave Ridgway detailed advice, generally to the effect that he follow the policies but not the style of MacArthur. Ridgway soon met with Yoshida, and a few weeks later the emperor called on him. The general made a point of saying in his memoirs that he had been advised that under no circumstances should he call on the Tennō.[13]

Dulles's purposes in Japan were to tell Ridgway where the treaty negotiations stood and to confer with Japanese leaders. Ridgway put it quaintly in his diary that Dulles "came, quite frankly, to look me over, to assure himself this impetuous, combat soldier wouldn't turn out to be a bull in the Japanese china shop."[14]

On April 18 Dulles met with Yoshida to reassure him that there had been no change in U.S. policy regarding the peace treaty. Ridgway was also present. In reporting on his recent meetings with representatives of other governments, Dulles said that the United Kingdom had submitted an alternative text of a treaty; his staff showed it to the Japanese, who said they preferred the U.S. draft.[15]

At a second meeting with Yoshida on the same day, Dulles listed the treaty problems as he saw them. The United Kingdom wanted Communist China to participate in making the treaty and proposed that the treaty should transfer Formosa to "China." The Philippines felt so strongly about reparations that Dulles began to consider a provision from the Italian peace treaty of 1947 to the effect that Japan might fabricate products from raw materials provided by the Philippines and turn over the finished products as reparations. He also mentioned the interest of some Allied nations in a provision that Japan would compensate Allied nationals whose property in Japan had been damaged during the war. MacArthur had opposed this. In the end, Dulles persuaded the Japanese to enact legislation to the same effect, thus obviating both the need for a treaty provision and the objection that the United States and the United Kingdom, whose nationals stood to benefit most, were "feathering their own nests."[16]

Dulles and Yoshida met again on April 23. Yoshida said that Japan would prefer that Korea, a liberated country and not one of the World War II Allies, not sign the treaty. This objection reflected concern that Korean nationals in Japan might benefit from the treaty's compensation clauses as well as Japanese antipathy for Koreans. The prime minister suggested that the draft treaty be made public to rebut charges by the opposition that he was engaging in "secret diplomacy." Only Yoshida and a few of his closest advisers knew the details of his treaty negotiations, and he was roundly criticized at the time and later for his failure to keep the Japanese public better informed. Dulles was against publicity, commenting testily that he was consulting the Japanese government "as a matter of good will and courtesy and not as a matter of right." But he added that confidential talks between Yoshida and the political leaders of Japan would be acceptable. Later on the Japanese presented several memoranda—on civil aviation, reparations claims, and the withdrawal of their objection to Korea's signing the treaty. The U.S. draft of the peace treaty was leaked to the press in Washington a few months later.[17]

The devolution of power from MacArthur to Ridgway took place with surprising ease. MacArthur's shadow over SCAP headquarters quickly faded. The glamour and magisterial quality vanished from the sixth floor of the Dai Ichi building, replaced by a more down-to-earth and businesslike way of operating.[18]

But MacArthur did not fade from the public scene. In May, a month after leaving Japan, he testified at length before two Senate committees in Washington on his recall and the military situation in the Far East. Events in Japan received almost no attention, other than a few simple questions and some favorable comment on what the general had done. MacArthur displayed a remarkable command of the facts, and as usual, he had ready answers, often very general or simplistic, to any question.

One of his offhand comments did much, unfortunately, to injure the amour propre of the Japanese people. In response to a question about the failure of democracy in Germany after World War I, the general observed, "If the Anglo-Saxon was, say, forty-five years of age in his development in the sciences, the arts, divinity, culture, the Germans were quite as mature. The Japanese, however . . . measured by the standards of modern civilization . . . would be like a boy of twelve as compared with our development of forty-five years."[19]

MacArthur was trying to say that Western concepts and institutions were still relatively new to Japan. The Japanese, however, interpreted these confusing remarks to mean they were like twelve-year-olds in mental and psychological development. This remark stung them and did great harm to the general's reputation. Appreciation for what MacArthur did in Japan remained strong, but admiration for him as a person rapidly faded.

The general had described the Japanese much the same way several years before but had added the saving language that they could be "molded, as distinct from the 45-year old nations who are 'unmoldable.'" Prime Minister Yoshida, who understood what the general intended, wrote in his memoirs that MacArthur meant the "Japanese people were still immature where liberalism and democratic government were concerned" and that MacArthur believed "there was much to be expected from Japan in the future."[20]

CHAPTER 21

Signing the Treaties and Ending the Occupation

For General Ridgway the task of dealing with Yoshida and Japan was more pressing than peace treaty matters, which were in the expert hands of John Foster Dulles. Yoshida was eager to test the new supreme commander on some occupation policies the prime minister considered unduly rigid. At one of his last meetings with General MacArthur, Yoshida had handed him an unsigned letter dated April 9, 1951, asking MacArthur's "advice" on proposed changes in eleven laws and nine ordinances or executive orders issued during the occupation. Yoshida presented the same letter to Dulles and Ridgway at a meeting on April 18, explaining that he had urged MacArthur to modify reforms that were "at variance with the actual needs of the country . . . and had obtained his consent in principle." This last assertion was hardly credible, given MacArthur's known reluctance to abandon policies he had been carrying out during the occupation. In fact GS reported, without citing its source, that the general's reaction to the Yoshida letter had been "unfavorable."[1]

Yoshida had got the impression somehow, perhaps from conversations with the general, that MacArthur did not personally support all the measures he had taken to carry out U.S. policy. Neither Ridgway nor Dulles commented on Yoshida's demarche, Ridgway because he was new on the job and Dulles because he did not concern himself with the rights and wrongs of the occupation. The Japanese gave Sebald a copy of the letter on April 20. The stated purpose of the letter was "to secure democracy more firmly by adapting the existing legislation to the actual conditions of the country." The items listed were all to be expected from a conservative like Yoshida, and except for omission of the purge, they were a catalogue of the occupation reforms he disliked most. Yoshida wanted to:

1. Increase political control over the national personnel agency and local public entities;
2. Readjust "the system for mutual assistance" between the national rural police and the urban police units and reduce the number of autonomous police forces;
3. Cut back such safeguards in criminal procedure as informing a suspect of the charges against him at the time of detention and the right of a defendant not to testify against himself;
4. Revise the 6-3-3-4 system in education and make boards of education advisory to local public entities;
5. Relax antimonopoly laws and labor standards legislation;
6. Revise the civil code to "recognize legally the head of the household as the center of family life";
7. Provide for primogeniture in the case of small farms and businesses.

Yoshida also wanted SCAP backing to keep in effect after the occupation cabinet ordinances dealing with price and rent controls, the National Police Reserve, and control of organizations that might be a threat to public order. It is quite understandable that MacArthur would have reacted unfavorably to Yoshida's letter.[2]

GS under new chief Frank Rizzo took the sensible position that because the occupation was governed by Allied policy decisions, it would be hard for SCAP to approve such sweeping changes. Moreover, even though the SCAP policy of advancing the turnover of responsibility to Japan would continue, it would be unfortunate if the impression were given that democratic reforms were to be abandoned. With Ridgway's approval, Rizzo notifed the chief cabinet secretary of these views on April 23. Nothing more was heard of the Yoshida scheme for wholesale change.[3]

Sebald sent the Yoshida paper to the State Department, adding that "we must recognize this fundamental conservatism not only as the underlying, predominant expression of contemporary Japanese thinking but also as the philosophy of those elements in Japan now most

inclined to cooperate with us and most capable of assisting in the implementation of our policies." The department suggested in reply that the
letter be treated with caution because of the effect it might have on the
Allied nations and on negotiations for the peace treaty.[4]

The Yoshida letter had no effect on relations between the prime
minister and the new supreme commander. Ridgway termed the prime
minister "frank, courageous, and completely trustworthy." Yoshida
found the new general "businesslike." They often met for several hours
alone, when Yoshida would tell the general candidly what the Japanese
thought about the actions the general wanted to take. One of their favorite subjects seems to have been China, about which Yoshida had some
unorthodox ideas regarding infiltration and use of Japan's commercial
skills. Ridgway evinced some interest in these schemes but not much
came of them. Ridgway said later the prime minister never failed to
carry out in detail anything the general asked him to do.[5]

The emperor called on the supreme commander soon after he arrived
and was happy to hear the general say he was sure the war in Korea
could be brought to a satisfactory close. The Tennō was hopeful Japan
and Korea could establish good relations. He was also pleased that the
purge directives would be revised and that Ridgway had supported the
Japanese government in banning use of the imperial plaza for a May
Day demonstration by labor unions. They ended the meeting by talking
about their families. Ridgway said he began to feel "a sense of
friendship for the polite little man who had to comport himself with
dignity in an extremely difficult situation." Ridgway met the emperor
five times during the next year.[6]

On May 3, 1951, the fourth anniversary of the postwar constitution,
Ridgway authorized the Japanese government to reexamine all laws
enacted pursuant to the Potsdam Declaration and to propose changes
based on its experience with them. Yoshida considered this action to be
in response to the unsigned letter he had given Ridgway two weeks
before asking for relaxation of many occupation reforms. He quickly
set up a committee of distinguished citizens of varying professional
backgrounds to serve as an advisory body to the government. During
the next year the committee made many recommendations for release of
persons from the purge orders and for revision of laws regarding labor,
agricultural reform, economic controls, and education. This Ordinance
Review Committee, or Seirei Shimon Iinkai, had a long and useful career
and continued to review the administrative actions of the government
for many years after the occupation ended.[7]

Ridgway had his own agenda for 1951. His two main goals were relaxation of the SCAP purge orders and stronger defense forces. Unlike MacArthur, who dragged his feet on the depurge of former officers in the Imperial Army and Navy in spite of instructions from Washington, Ridgway wanted to move quickly. On April 29, 1951, he decided that all career military officers commissioned after the China incident of 1937 should be depurged. The State Department thought he was going too far because the FEC had determined that all commissioned officers should be purged. When Ridgway countered with a proposal that officers commissioned after 1937 should not be considered career officers, State went along. Before the end of the occupation SCAP had released nearly 200,000 persons from the purge, mostly former military men.[8]

Several prominent political figures were depurged in the summer of 1951, notably Hatoyama Ichirō, Ishibashi Tanzan, and Kishi Nobu-suke, all of whom became prime ministers after the occupation. A few months before his depurge Hatoyama had a stroke that impaired the left side of his body but did not affect his mental powers or his ability to speak. Yoshida claimed that his friendship with Hatoyama was unchanged and that he had made strong representations to SCAP for the depurge of Hatoyama, but he refused to turn over the political reins to his afflicted friend because he felt Japan had to have a strong leader in the months before the peace conference.

The comeback of these old-guard figures strengthened the political opposition to Yoshida in the last months of the occupation. Forty-two percent of those elected to the lower house in October 1952, six months after the treaty came into force, were former purgees. Without the purge Yoshida would never have become prime minister of Japan, but he strongly opposed the purge and his memoirs are full of bitterness about its unfairness; he felt it was a form of retaliation by the victor nations and was particularly unjustified in the case of local government officials and those purged because of the economic positions they held.[9]

Strengthening the NPR in size and equipment was Ridgway's primary goal. The straitjacket into which MacArthur had crammed U.S. policy on the defense of Japan did not deter Ridgway from urging Washington and Yoshida to build up a sizable Japanese army with modern weapons. The new supreme commander believed that "the Japanese should take responsibility for their own defense." Ridgway asserted in his memoirs that he won Yoshida's agreement to build Japan's force to a level of 350,000 men by 1954. In fact, at a meeting in

February 1952 SCAP officials pressed for a force of 150,000, and the Japanese, speaking for Yoshida, insisted on a figure of 100,000.[10] This was the level Yoshida was willing to accept at the time the occupation ended.

U.S. pressure and Yoshida's evasive tactics combined in the late occupation period to create a lot of confusion about "rearmament" and force increases. Dulles was the first American to press Yoshida to rearm, and he continued to goad the prime minister until Yoshida left office. Dulles wanted Japan to "increasingly assume responsibility for its own defense against direct and indirect aggression," but he had no specific recommendations about either money or manpower.[11]

The United States did not have an approved policy for the level of Japan's defense forces until early 1952, shortly before the peace and security treaties went into effect. That policy, NSC 125/2, proposed that Japan build ground forces totaling ten divisions and appropriate naval and air forces; 300,000 was sometimes cited as the force level this would entail. Ridgway could have had this new policy in mind if indeed he suggested to Yoshida that Japan build a 350,000-man force. Yoshida's personal adviser confirmed that SCAP officers urged the Japanese government in January 1952 to increase the NPR to 325,000 men over the next few years. All these figures went way beyond Japanese thinking. Japan's total armed forces thirty-five years later were less than 300,000.[12]

Equipping Japan's forces also raised problems. The U.S. Defense Department wanted to supply the NPR with heavy armament and to arm the vessels of the Maritime Safety Agency. The State Department opposed these plans, largely because FEC policy decisions prohibited them but also out of concern that such actions might prejudice the treaty negotiations. State and Defense were able to resolve their differences during the summer of 1951. The president then instructed SCAP to take the necessary steps to implement the plans. Heavy equipment for four Japanese divisions was stockpiled but not delivered before the peace treaty went into effect, and planning for equipment to supply six more divisions was begun. Likewise, plans for strengthening the coastal safety force with necessary vessels and weapons leased from the United States and under the operational control of SCAP were made and put into effect after friendly Allies had been informed and the treaty signed.[13]

While Ridgway was winding up the business of the occupation in Japan, Dulles and his team were moving in Washington to line up the votes for the treaty and for a conference to sign it. In April 1951 British and U.S. experts met in Washington to reconcile the treaty drafts of their two countries, retaining much of the liberal and nonpunitive flavor of the American draft but adopting the technical precision and more comprehensive character of the British version.[14] They left the question of which government would represent China—the one on Taiwan or the one in Beijing—for solution by the top level.

Dulles and British foreign secretary Herbert Morrison, with the approval of the British cabinet, reached an agreement in London on June 12, 1951, that neither China would be invited to sign the treaty and that Japan would be free to determine which China to make peace with. Japan would be authorized to sign a similar treaty with any eligible nonsignatory state within three years after the peace treaty came into force. The two governments sidestepped another knotty issue by agreeing that Japan would renounce its sovereignty over Formosa, South Sakhalin, and the Kurile Islands without making any final disposition. By June 14 London and Washington had agreed on most of the other issues.[15]

When Allison visited Tokyo after the London talks, Yoshida expressed some unhappiness that Japan would have to decide which China it would sign a treaty with, but he knew the Allies were badly divided on this issue. He had great faith in the experience and sophistication of the British and often leaned their way, yet he knew the Americans had the might and the money that Japan needed more. Allison got Yoshida to issue two soothing statements regarding Japanese policy on shipbuilding and fisheries in order to calm the fears of the British and other Allies. Yoshida was also complaisant about another concession: he agreed to secure legislation that would enable Japanese assets in former neutral and enemy countries to be used to make a fund for compensating Allied prisoners of war the Japanese had held.[16]

Yoshida had asked Dulles earlier to put a clause in the draft treaty providing that the signatories would carry out the provision of the Potsdam Declaration obligating the Allies to permit Japanese military forces to return to their homes to lead peaceful lives. Dulles agreed. According to Japanese data, some 376,000 military personnel presumed to have been captured by the Soviets were still unaccounted for; Japanese and American experts estimate that most of them died in captivity. The Soviet Union returned about 1,000 Japanese prisoners of war in 1956, when the two countries resumed diplomatic relations. The Japanese are still bitter toward the Soviet Union because of its uncooperative attitude in refusing to return or account for prisoners and the bad treatment many of them suffered.[17]

The most significant and abrasive of the last-minute issues was the reparations article, which stirred resentment in the Philippines and several other badly damaged Asian nations. Dulles pushed the Japanese hard, and they finally consented in August 1951 to negotiate with nations they had occupied and damaged, "with a view to assisting to compensate those countries for the cost of repairing the damage done, by making available the services of the Japanese people in production, salvaging and other work." The Allied power involved would supply any necessary raw materials. Japan later made reparations agreements with most of the nations it had occupied during the war. These reparations arrangements, which turned out to be a good deal for Japan and for the recipient nations, consisted of various forms of assistance: goods and services (as provided by the treaty), technical assistance, and long-term credits. Total payments by Japan were $1.15 billion in reparations, mostly in the form of capital goods manufactured in Japan from raw materials provided by the recipient nations. In addition, Japan extended $707 million in loans, paying the largest amounts to the Philippines, Indonesia, and Burma. One result was that Japanese products got a foothold in various parts of Southeast Asia, thereby helping the Japanese economy and at the same time mitigating some of the wartime resentment against Japan.[18]

In the summer of 1951 the Americans proposed several changes in the draft security treaty initialed on February 11. The Japanese did not object. The title of the agreement was changed from "Agreement for Collective Self-Defense" to "Security Agreement" and then to its final form, "Security Treaty." The Japanese negotiators had tried hard to create an appearance of mutuality in the treaty, so they liked the reference to "collective self-defense." But they realized that Japan was making no commitment to defend the United States and that the title would therefore be a misnomer.[19]

Another U.S. change was more far-reaching. The draft had earlier provided that American forces "would be designed to contribute to the security of Japan against armed attack from without." The JCS wanted this clause amended to give the United States the right to use bases in Japan to support future military operations similar to the one in Korea. The wording was therefore modified to read: "Such forces may be utilized to contribute to the maintenance of international peace and security in the Far East and to the security of Japan against armed attack from without." This became known as the "Far East clause," which some Japanese critics felt went beyond U.N. Charter obligations and conferred exessive freedom on the United States to use bases in Japan to deploy its forces anywhere in the region. Japanese public opinion, especially in intellectual circles, opposed the security treaty because many felt it would implicate Japan in U.S. cold war operations in Asia. Nishimura Kumao, Japan's treaty expert, said later that this change should have been considered more carefully.[20]

The final draft of the security treaty gave the United States the right to use its forces to put down large-scale internal disturbances in Japan at the express request of the Japanese government. Dulles had inserted this U.S. proposal in his draft of February 5, and the Japanese had asked the next day that it be deleted. Discussion showed that the Japanese felt concern about their internal security after the treaty came into effect. In the end the clause was retained but qualified by reference to instigation "by an outside power." The security treaty received much criticism afterward because this clause seemed to confer on the United States an ill-defined right to interfere in Japan's internal affairs.[21]

The contents of the security treaty were known to but a few people. Even the United Kingdom and Australia received only general information, and the Japanese public knew very little. Prime Minister Yoshida was not informed until the day before when the signing would take place. The text of the treaty was released to the press at San Francisco on September 8 shortly before it was signed. The background and details of the treaty's negotiation remained obscure for years.[22]

Yoshida had many doubts about going himself to the peace conference. He was familiar with historical episodes, notably the signing of the Treaty of Portsmouth in 1905, engineered by Theodore Roosevelt to end the Russo-Japanese War, in which the Japanese peace negotiators came back to be greeted with public scorn and abuse because many people thought they had sacrificed Japanese interests to foreign pressure. Dulles personally urged Yoshida to attend. Finally, after an audience with the emperor, the prime minister decided to head his country's delegation.[23]

At Dulles's urging Yoshida tried to select a representative delegation to the conference. It included the minister of finance, Ikeda Hayato, Yoshida's favorite protégé; the president of the Bank of Japan, Ichimada Hisato; and former Marquis Tokugawa Muneyoshi, a direct descendant of the last of Japan's shoguns and a member of the House of

Councillors. One opposition leader, Tomabechi Gizō, of the conservative Democratic Party, was a delegate. It was hardly a broad-based delegation because it lacked anyone from the left-of-center parties, but it represented the groups that were even then emerging as the ruling elements in postwar Japan. The emperor attested the credentials of the Japanese delegation and gave its members an audience before they departed for the United States.[24]

What to do about General MacArthur turned out to be another prickly matter of protocol. Dulles very much wanted the former supreme commander to play a role in the signing ceremony. After getting the approval of the State Department and the White House, he phoned the invitation on August 11 to Colonel Bunker, who was still serving as aide to the general. The plan was for the president to speak at the opening session of September 4 and for the general to speak the next day at the first working session of the conference, presenting a review "based upon his five and one-half years' experience" in Japan. Dulles would then talk about the peace treaty.[25]

A few hours after Dulles's call to New York, General Whitney, who had also remained in loyal service to the general, called back to say in the best MacArthurian manner that the plan was "totally unacceptable" because it seemed to put MacArthur in the position of "an attendant to the U.S. delegation," a role incompatible with his position in Japan, where he had been the Allied commander, "not a United States official." MacArthur felt he could not attend the conference except "at the invitation of the Allied powers as a whole." As everyone realized, it would have run the risk of a divisive debate to propose that the conference delegates invite the general to give a talk. This risk was multiplied many times by word that the Soviets had accepted the invitation to attend the conference. And President Truman's offhand remark at a press conference that he would not object if MacArthur accepted the State Department's invitation to attend was not calculated to assuage the general's sensibilities. Dulles issued a cagey press release that the matter of the general's participation in the conference was under consideration but that "no arrangements . . . have been reached."[26]

At Sebald's urging Washington agreed that the Japanese delegation should be seated on the conference floor from the start of the meeting instead of being invited to come in later. The Japanese delegation was placed after the other delegations, but it was invited to all official receptions. These protocol concessions provided strong evidence that Japan had started on the road back to the comity of nations.[27]

Fifty-five nations, including Japan and the three associated states of Indochina but not the Republic of Korea, were expected to attend the conference. Three decided not to attend—India, Yugoslavia, and Burma. The Soviet Union accepted the invitation and stated it would have substantive proposals to make regarding the draft treaty. The Soviet presence in San Francisco converted what might have been a dreary conclave of the converted into one of the early diplomatic dramas of the cold war.

The meeting of fifty-two nations in the San Francisco Opera House from September 4 to September 8, 1951, was a unique peace conference. Called "The Conference for the Conclusion and Signing of the Treaty of Peace with Japan," it was not for negotiation. Everything had been arranged in advance, from the rules of procedure to the text of the document to be signed. The most careful precautions were taken against any surprises. And there were none. The conference put the stamp of international approval, and a degree of immortality, on the handiwork of John Foster Dulles, mightily abetted by Yoshida Shigeru, Dean Acheson, Harry S Truman, and Douglas MacArthur (in absentia), among others. That the United States could dominate such a star-studded conclave was surely a testament to its preeminent position in Japan and world politics in 1951.[28]

The most exciting event of the conference was the Soviet attempt, led by diplomatic veteran Andrei Gromyko, to open up the debate and radically alter the terms of the treaty. Dean Acheson, president of the conference, and Percy Spender of Australia, vice president, had the kind of majority parliamentarians dream about; it varied from 36 to 3 to 47 to 3 and enabled the conference to vote down all challenges to the rules of procedure carefully worked out in advance. Acheson's skill in outmaneuvering Gromyko in the opening wrangles over the conference's procedures won admiration from a nationwide audience.

President Truman's opening speech on September 4 was the first event in the United States to be carried on nationwide television. The remainder of the conference was also televised, including Acheson's near-wrestling match with Gromyko. News of the conference occupied headline attention in the American and Japanese press throughout the week. The president reviewed the achievements of the occupation and even paid tribute to the "outstanding leadership of General of the Army Douglas MacArthur." The general made a speech himself in Cleveland two days later, in another stop in the long series of homecoming visits around the nation, asserting that the treaty "while far from flawless embodies much of human justice and enlightenment."[29]

The San Francisco conference marked the debut of Yoshida Shigeru as an international figure, a role he came to enjoy and play well. Acheson and Dulles enjoined Yoshida in their first meeting to call upon the delegations of countries that might not sign the treaty to convince them that Japan would in good faith carry out all its provisions. As Asian nations emerging from colonialism, the Philippines and Indonesia were thought to be two of the most crucial to get on board. Pakistan and Ceylon were also unhappy about reparations. Australia, the Netherlands, and Norway had other grievances—over compensation for prisoners of war or fishing and whaling rights. Yoshida met with them all in an open, direct, and conciliatory way. In the end, all signed, largely because they felt Japan would do as Yoshida said and because they were reassured that the United States stood behind Japan to ensure that all went well.[30]

Once the initial wrangle over conference procedure had been decided, much of the conference was given over to speech-making. Gromyko proposed a number of amendments: the sovereign rights of the Soviet Union and the PRC to the territories they had claimed and taken over after the war should be recognized; the Ryukyu and Bonin Islands should be given back to Japan; no foreign troops should be based on Japanese territory after the treaty went into force; Japan should not enter into any alliance directed against a nation that had fought against Japan; and the straits in waters around Japan should be demilitarized. Acheson, who was presiding, ruled these proposed changes out of order, and the conference supported him. No one mentioned Dulles's earlier offer to the Soviets to support their claim to the Kuriles and South Sakhalin if the Soviet Union signed the treaty.[31]

After all the others had their say, Yoshida's turn came on the evening of September 7. It was the last item on the agenda, an "acceptance speech" by Japan before the vote and signing of the treaty. Yoshida had planned to speak in English. Sebald and State Department experts asked to see his text, thought "it was not good," and proceeded to rewrite much of the text. They also suggested that it would be more dignified if Yoshida spoke in his native tongue. Yoshida and his advisers accepted all of this somewhat overbearing advice. Yoshida spoke with candor and directness. "My people have been among those who have suffered greatly from the destruction and devastation of the recent war. Purged by that suffering of all untoward ambition, of all desire for the path of military conquest, my people burn with a passionate desire to live at peace with their neighbors in the East and in the entire world."[32]

He then spoke to points in the treaty that caused Japan "pain and anxiety." He reasserted Japan's historical claim dating back to 1875 to the Kurile Islands held by the Soviet Union. He said his people were glad the treaty would not deprive them of Okinawa and expressed the hope that all the southern islands would be returned soon. Some Japanese thought he should have taken a harder line about both the Kuriles and Okinawa. He said it was "too bad" a representative of China was not able to attend the conference. Yoshida assured his listeners that "this fair and generous treaty commands, I assure you, the overwhelming support of my nation." The prime minister made no mention of the occupation or of MacArthur. Acheson later called Yoshida's speech "simple, honest and brief."[33]

One of the historical curiosities of Yoshida's address was that he decided to cut down the length of his delivery as he went along. He wrote in his memoirs that he realized as he talked that almost no one in the audience understood what he was saying, and so he decided, in his whimsical way, to skip some of the text as he read it. His skilled interpreter, Shimanouchi Toshirō, later a distinguished ambassador, had experienced this kind of challenge before and neatly timed his version to coincide with the prime minister's. Yoshida's speech was inscribed on rice paper wound in scroll form, which fascinated observers. Reporters wrote the next day about the "toilet paper" his speech was written on.[34]

The representatives of forty-nine nations including Japan signed the treaty of peace on September 8. The Soviet Union, Poland, and Czechoslovakia did not sign, and Gromyko temporarily walked out of the conference. Acheson, Dulles, and two senators signed for the United States. All of the waverers—Indonesia, the Philippines, Ceylon, and Pakistan—signed. It was a moment of victory for Dulles and the United States, and a time of relief and pleasure for Yoshida and Japan. The day before the signing, Dulles sent a telegram to MacArthur saying, "You will be present in spirit for the signing."[35]

The treaty was brief, clear, and—reparations aside—almost entirely self-executing, thus avoiding future conflicts and entanglements. It did not contain a war-guilt clause and could fairly be described as nonpunitive. Yet it did sanction Japan's loss of half its prewar territory. It provided that Japan would pay reparations to nations it had damaged in war and that it would carry out the sentences imposed on war criminals by the Allied powers, although provision was made for possible parole if Japan requested it. It did not obligate Japan to retain reforms and changes carried out during the occupation. Nor did it impose restraints on economic activity. Japan declared its intention to abide by the principles of the U.N. Charter and to apply for admission to the United Nations.

At one point during the negotiations Acheson was prompted to say, "Never was so good a peace treaty so little loved by so many of its participants." Later he came to feel better about the treaty. He also became an admirer of Yoshida Shigeru, commenting that "his quick intelligence, delightful humor and complete integrity made him an unequalled colleague."[36]

After the signing ceremony, Acheson sent Yoshida a box of good cigars. Yoshida had sworn off cigars, one of his passions, some days before the peace conference so as to be in the best physical shape. The secretary of state felt the prime minister had earned the right to indulge once more. The next day Yoshida puffed away in an expansive mood and told his advisers at lunch that Japan, a loser, had done better at San Francisco than it had done thirty-two years before at Versailles, where it was among the victorious powers. Yoshida had been surprised at the good feeling displayed toward the Japanese delegation at San Francisco, contrasting it with the critical attitude toward Japan at Versailles, where he had been a junior member of his country's delegation.[37]

The companion piece to the peace treaty was the security treaty, signed the same day, September 8, late in the afternoon at the San Francisco Presidio. Acheson, Dulles, and two senators signed for the United States. Yoshida alone signed for Japan. He did not ask anyone else to sign because he "knew the security treaty was not popular in Japan." The treaty and the security tie to the United States remained controversial for almost two decades. The treaty was revised in 1960 as huge riots in the streets of Tokyo forced the cancellation of a visit to Japan by President Dwight Eisenhower. After that violent outburst, the treaty enjoyed almost universal acceptance in Japan.[38]

Acheson and Yoshida also signed and exchanged diplomatic notes stating that Japan would continue to provide facilities and support so long as needed for the U.N. forces operating in Korea. This agreement greatly reassured the United States and especially the Pentagon. It eliminated concern about bringing a peace treaty with Japan into force while the Korean War continued because Japan obligated itself to allow

U.N. forces fighting in Korea the continued use of its bases and logistic facilities.[39]

The peace and security treaties putting relations between Japan and the United States on a new footing were part of a larger security mosaic. The United States had a few days previously signed security treaties with Australia and New Zealand and with the Philippines. These three security treaties, linking the United States with Japan, the Philippines, Australia, and New Zealand, were designed to strengthen the offshore U.S. chain of defense in the western Pacific and to add to the protection of the four nations. Yoshida stated somewhat grandly on September 9 that the Japanese people were inspired "to shoulder their proper share of responsibility for the collective security of the Far East."[40]

The negotiation of the peace settlement was the high point of Yoshida's public career. Although criticized even now by some Japanese and Americans, usually on the ground that Yoshida gave away too much, especially in regard to China, few can disagree that the two treaties laid the basis for a close and rewarding relationship between the two nations for at least a generation after. (Yoshida brought back with him from San Francisco three terrier puppies. He named them San, Fran, and Cisco as a sign of his appreciation for the treaties.)[41]

The eminent historian Akira Iriye devised the term *San Francisco system* to describe the "new regime of American-Japanese relations that resulted from the San Francisco peace conference of 1951." This conceptual framework replaced the "internationalism" of the Yalta system in East Asia created by Roosevelt, Stalin, and Churchill in January 1945. The Yalta system had linked the great powers in a cooperative approach, primarily by establishing zones of influence, whereas the San Francisco system intensified competition among the major powers and heightened tensions between the United States and mainland China.[42] Yet the San Francisco system, based on a close relationship between the United States and Japan, surmounted the shocks posed by the Korean War and the rise of the PRC and eventually opened the way to a general reduction of violence and tensions in East Asia.

Japan acted quickly to ratify the peace and security treaties. A special session of the Diet convened in October, one month after the treaties were signed. Yoshida stoutly defended the accords, asserting that the peace treaty was one of reconciliation, a favorite Dulles description. According to Yoshida, the treaties would completely restore the nation's sovereignty. Japan had requested the security treaty to fill a vacuum. It had not committed itself to rearm; it would have a ground force only when its pacifism and democracy as well as its economic stability were solidly established.

By October 26 the two houses of the Diet had approved both treaties. The vote on the peace treaty was 307 to 47 in the lower house and 174 to 15 in the upper house. On the security treaty the vote was 284 to 71 in the House of Representatives and 147 to 76 in the House of Councillors. An unusually large number of members in both houses abstained. The Socialist Party was divided over the treaties, its right wing supporting the peace treaty but opposing the security treaty and its left wing voting against both, as did the Communist Party.[43]

Hardly had the treaties been signed when Dulles became concerned about opposition developing in the Senate to Japan's future relations with China. Fifty-six senators signed a letter to President Truman on September 12 stating that Japanese relations with the PRC would be adverse to the best interests of both Japan and the United States. This unwelcome intrusion and the risk that Yoshida was getting off the track were too much for Dulles. He decided to go to Tokyo and pin the Japanese down. Acheson also asked Dulles to consult with the British ambassador, Sir Esler Dening, in an effort to work out a common policy with the United Kingdom, despite Acheson's own inability to do this in London two weeks previously. It was increasingly evident that the British would oppose any action by Japan involving recognition of Nationalist China, although they would not object to trade relations between Japan and the ROC. One American historian has speculated that Dulles felt he could not trust Acheson to stand up to the British on the China issue and therefore decided to go to Tokyo and settle it himself. Accompanied by Senators John Sparkman, a Democrat from Alabama, and H. Alexander Smith, a Republican from New Jersey, Dulles arrived in Japan on December 10.[44]

On December 13 Dulles separately told both Yoshida and Dening that the issue was whether Japan's foreign policy would be "generally compatible" with that of the United States. He proposed to Yoshida that Japan negotiate a treaty with the Nationalist government that would establish relations along the lines of the San Francisco treaty and apply only to the territories under the actual control of the two parties. He conveyed this view to Dening. Yoshida said he did not object to this course but hoped the Americans and the British could agree on what to do.[45]

On December 18 Dulles handed Yoshida a draft letter for the prime minister to send him, stating in substance what Dulles had proposed on

December 13. The timing of the letter and its publication was discussed and left open. Yoshida said he saw no objection but would need to prepare public opinion in Japan.[46]

On December 20, while he was at the airport ready to leave for Washington, Dulles received five Japanese "observations" on his draft letter, including a reference to the Sino-Soviet treaty of 1950. These were in fact amendments, but Dulles readily accepted them. He took off just before a cable arrived in Tokyo describing a strong protest to the State Department by the British ambassador in Washington that Dulles was going "far beyond the scope of the Dulles-Morrison agreement." As soon as Dulles got to Washington he wrote a careful defense of his actions, asserting that "the purpose and spirit of the Morrison-Dulles memorandum would be violated if it were interpreted as preventing Japan from taking actions indispensable to her own self-interest."[47]

On January 7, 1952, Dulles received a signed letter from Yoshida dated December 24 that was all but identical with the draft Dulles had proposed on December 18. Japan would negotiate an agreement with the Nationalist government of China to establish normal relations "applicable to all territories which are now, or which may hereafter be, under the control of the National Government of the Republic of China. We will promptly explore this subject with the National Government of China." The only significant change from the original Dulles draft was the reference, suggested by the Japanese, to the Sino-Soviet treaty as a "military alliance aimed against Japan." In his covering letter Yoshida hit another of his pet themes: a loan to Japan by the United States "would produce a salutary psychological effect" in Japan and demonstrate dramatically "American intentions and policy toward Japan."[48]

The British and U.S. governments next tried to resolve their differences at the top. With the Conservative Party back in power for the first time since July 1945, Prime Minister Churchill and Foreign Secretary Anthony Eden visited Washington in early January 1952. Truman and Churchill decided to leave the issue of Japan and China to Eden and Acheson for solution. The two diplomatic chiefs reviewed the history of this knotty matter, with Dulles doing much of the talking for the United States. He told Eden of Yoshida's letter, which would have to be made "known during the course of the Senate's consideration of the peace treaty with Japan." Eden reiterated the British view that Japan should be able to act of its own free will in this matter.[49]

Eden was understandably not happy that on January 16, 1951, one day after his return from Washington, the famous "Yoshida letter" was released to the press. The Foreign Office complained to the State Department, which expressed regret and assured the British that it had not intended to convey any impression that the United Kingdom had concurred in the release. Acheson later termed the timing of the release of the letter an "inexcusable bungle." The opposition in Japan was critical of Yoshida's action. Even some conservatives argued that it had been a mistake for Japan to restrict its freedom of choice in dealing with the two Chinas. The prime minister, who had agreed in advance to releasing the letter, denied in the Diet that he had acted under U.S. pressure, although he admitted that the initiative had come from the Americans. Just as he had decided to stick with the United States on the peace and security issues, Yoshida had made up his mind to go along on the China question; this was one more element in his "look to America" policy.

The president submitted the peace and security treaties to the U.S. Senate for its advice and consent on January 19, 1952. In the hearings Dulles successfully parried a host of questions and pessimistic comments. The most serious threat was a series of nine reservations put forward by archconservative William Jenner of Indiana. Senators Sparkman and Smith and the Republican leader, William Knowland of California, led the defense and successfully beat down all the Jenner reservations on March 20.[50]

On the same day the Senate approved the peace treaty by a vote of 66 to 10 and the security treaty by 58 to 9. In London the House of Commons had approved the peace treaty bill by a vote of 382 to 33 on November 26, 1951, following the longest and most sustained debate on Japanese affairs during the occupation.[51] All the other signatory governments, including the Philippines and Indonesia, approved the peace treaty.

The final months of the occupation were taken up largely with the negotiation of several relatively minor agreements the United States considered essential. The United States felt that because it had been forthright in pushing through a peace settlement, it need not be bashful in asking Japan to make agreements it wanted for itself or for important Allies. Moreover, to make sure Japan did what was expected, it delayed bringing the peace treaty into force until these agreements had been signed. Yoshida probably did not like this kind of pressure, but he understood and cooperated.

Two of the agreements were treaties. The first was a treaty between Japan and the Republic of China. The Dulles letter from Yoshida at the end of 1951 committed Japan to establish relations with the Nationalist government and not to deal with Beijing. The negotiations, which began in Taipei on February 20, 1952, were not easy. The United States monitored them closely with advice to both sides. The key issue was whether the treaty would apply to all of China, as the Nationalists wanted, or only to the territory under the control of the parties, as the United States and Japan had agreed and as the Nationalist Chinese finally accepted. The two countries signed the treaty on April 28, 1952, the day the multilateral peace treaty came into effect.[52]

The second treaty was a fisheries agreement among the United States, Canada, and Japan applying to the waters of the North Pacific. Japan would have preferred to have negotiated this at greater leisure after the peace treaty took effect, but the two North American powers would not brook delay. After a short but tough negotiation, they reached an agreement.

A third negotiation of concern to the United States was the establishment of relations between Japan and the Republic of Korea. Simply persuading the two countries to come to the bargaining table was an enormous task. The suspicion, resentment, and even hatred between the two nations were intense and had not abated greatly in the years since the end of the war, even though the ROK maintained a diplomatic office in Tokyo through most of that period. The United States thought it crucial that the process of reconciliation at least begin. On February 15, 1952, in the office of the U.S. political adviser in Tokyo, representatives of the two governments sat down to talk. The negotiations went on intermittently for more than a decade. In 1965 a treaty establishing normal relations was finally signed.[53]

The most important negotiation was for an administrative agreement, which the United States and Japan signed on February 28, 1952, regarding the status of U.S. forces in Japan.[54] Reflecting the crucial importance of this matter, the two sides had top negotiators facing each other. The American was the highly articulate Georgian Dean Rusk, a future secretary of state, while the Japanese was Okazaki Katsuo, who played an important part throughout the occupation and became the foreign minister of Japan the day after the peace treaty came into force.

The security treaty committed Japan to make "facilities and areas" available to U.S. forces but did not mention such essential details as legal jurisdiction, customs procedures, taxes, claims, and movement of forces. The negotiators followed the model of a series of similar agreements between the United States and its NATO allies. The issue of legal jurisdiction was hard to resolve because the Defense Department wanted to retain more jurisdiction than the United States had granted the NATO nations, a position the Japanese strongly contested. It was finally agreed that after an interim period the NATO formula would be applied in Japan. The issue was much softened by an informal agreement with Japan that it would waive its primary jurisdiction in criminal cases except where the case was of "special importance" to Japan. Japan has faithfully carried out this understanding for nearly forty years.

The knottiest issue was posed by the U.S. desire for a provision that in the event of emergency all Japanese and U.S. forces in Japan would operate under an American commander. The Japanese refused to accept such a provision, and a compromise was finally reached on a vague formula that in an emergency the two governments would consult on the measures to take. Ironically, Washington had suggested virtually the same action to MacArthur soon after the Korean War started, and he had strongly opposed it on the ground that it was not militarily necessary and would undermine Japanese moral support and confidence in the United States.[55]

The last hours of the occupation on April 28, 1952, were surprisingly calm. There was no public ceremony, not even a parade. In fact, U.S. forces were not departing; most of them would remain in Japan under the new setup prescribed by the security treaty and administrative agreement. They would soon evacuate the ostentatious Dai Ichi Insurance building in downtown Tokyo and would eventually vacate most of the other buildings they had been using in the capital, with the prominent exception of a "rest hotel" that they maintained for thirty more years.

The new American ambassador, Robert Murphy, arrived on the night of April 28, but this event went largely unheralded. The only real excitement of the time was the May Day parade three days later. About 400,000 workers marched through the gardens of the Meiji Shrine. Several thousand broke away and marched downtown to Hibiya Park and the imperial plaza, which Prime Minister Yoshida and General Ridgway had forbidden to them. They set a few foreign cars on fire, tossed a couple of American servicemen into the imperial moat, and clashed with 5,000 police. In the ensuing melee several hundred persons were injured; shots were fired, allegedly into the air; at least one person was killed; and more than 1,200 marchers were arrested.[56]

Some people feared that the Hibiya riot was the harbinger of trouble in newly free Japan, but this was not the case. Order and discipline prevailed as the Japanese went ahead with reconstructing the nation their way, building on the foundation the Americans had given them.

PART VI

Aftermath

When the occupation ended, Yoshida's daughter, Asō Kazuko, and his close friend Shirasu thought the prime minister should retire from public life. After all, he had achieved his biggest goals: he had more than anyone else put the nation back on its feet, and he had won a good peace settlement. But he liked being prime minister, and so he stayed on for two and a half years longer, during a period of domestic political turbulence and stern pressure from the United States for rearmament.

For all his complaints about "occupation excesses," Yoshida did not actually make many changes after it was over. The police system was revised in 1954, over strong left-wing opposition, to put the National Public Safety Commission under the prime minister and to create a national police agency in charge of police administration throughout the country, except in the big cities. The fairly innocuous Law to Prevent Subversive Activities was passed in late 1952. In 1956 the boards of education were made appointive rather than elective. The anti-monopoly law was relaxed to authorize cartels for coping with depression or "rationalizing" industry and to permit more interlocking directorships and mergers. The last war criminals were not paroled until 1958. The constitution was not touched. It would be difficult to say that Japan embarked on a reverse course after 1952.

Yoshida survived two more elections—in the fall of 1952 and the spring of 1953. His well-known temper played a part in bringing on both of them. He was photographed in the act of throwing a glass of water at a photographer in September 1952, and in February 1953 he called a Socialist interrogator in the Diet a "damn fool." Opposition in his own party swelled with the return to political life of hundreds of purgees.

The most significant change in the early postwar era was the transition of the police reserve to a military force and the tightening of security ties between Japan and the United States. The NPR was converted in 1952 to a "public safety force" and in 1954 to a "self-defense force" with an authorized strength of 152,115. Intense U.S. pressure for a military force of some 300,000 men organized into thirteen divisions was fruitless, as Yoshida kept stalling on the ground that public opinion was hostile and the economy was too fragile to support heavy military expenditures.

Just before leaving office in late 1954, Yoshida made a grand tour of western Europe and the United States. This was his *hanamichi*. He met many leaders and prominent figures and was understandably much impressed by Adenauer, Churchill, and Eisenhower. Nor did Yoshida forget economic diplomacy, as he tried to sell the Americans on a "Marshall Plan" for Asia, but President Eisenhower was not interested. Shortly after Yoshida's return to Tokyo, he turned over the reins of office to Hatoyama and went back to Oiso to enjoy being a *genrō*, receiving visits from world leaders, senior politicians, junior diplomats, and old friends. He served as president of the Japan-America Society, wrote his memoirs, and occasionally went abroad. During the last years of his life he witnessed the takeoff of Japan's economic boom.

Like Yoshida, MacArthur lived a very active life for several years before settling down to enjoy the fruits of retirement. For more than a year after leaving Tokyo he mixed freely in the politics of the Republican Party; sought without avail to head off the presidential boom of his old subordinate from the Manila days, Dwight Eisenhower; and traveled around the country making speeches to celebrate patriotic virtues. As a general of the army, he remained on active duty and often wore his uniform when appearing as a public speaker.

When Eisenhower won the Republican nomination in 1952, MacArthur dropped out of the political limelight. He became the board chairman of a large corporation. He, too, saw many visiting dignitaries, including Yoshida in 1954 and other Japanese visitors, politicians, and youthful West Pointers. He continued to make speeches, receive honorary degrees, and hold reunions with old comrades. MacArthur was consulted by presidents. In 1952 he told President-elect

Eisenhower how to end the fighting in Korea, proposing among other rather farfetched ideas that both the Soviet Union and the United States should insert no-war clauses in their constitutions. MacArthur made a big impression on the young Jack Kennedy in 1961, although the general's advice not to build up U.S. forces on the Asian mainland was largely unheeded.

In 1961 the emperor awarded General MacArthur the Grand Cordon of the Order of the Rising Sun with Paulownia Flowers, Japan's highest honor for a foreigner other than a head of state. In 1961 MacArthur and his family made a nostalgic trip to the Philippines for the fifteenth anniversary of its independence. His *Reminiscences* appeared in 1964. Early that year, when Japan was already launched on its period of high economic growth, Yoshida invited MacArthur to Japan to "see with your own eyes how firmly your epochal reforms have taken root." But it was too late. He was diagnosed as suffering from a variety of ailments and underwent a series of operations in March. On April 5, 1964, he died.

Yoshida Shigeru, eighty-six years old and in failing health, traveled halfway around the world from Tokyo to attend the general's funeral at St. Paul's Episcopal church in Norfolk, Virginia, on April 11. His trip was more than a remarkable gesture of respect and friendship; it was the symbol of the new and fruitful relationship the United States and Japan had begun twelve years after the end of the occupation. Yoshida died in 1967 and, like MacArthur, was honored by a state funeral. Shortly before his death Yoshida was baptized by a Roman Catholic priest.[1]

Many years later—in 1983—four eminent scholars of the occupation period, two Japanese and two Americans, wrote about its significance.[2] The Japanese felt strongly that "there is really no question: the occupation reforms did exercise a decisive influence" and for the most part had a beneficial effect on postwar Japan, even if the occupation made some mistakes, as in the Red Purge of the labor movement, and slackened its reform efforts halfway through.

The Americans disagreed. One said that the occupation had changed little in Japan and that the "legacy of the occupation" was merely a cliché for a new conservative hegemony. The other asserted that "much if not most of what has developed within Japan during the past three decades would have come into being in broad outline without the interference or guidance of the occupation." He declared that even the security treaty "fits quite snugly into Japan's self-chosen role in the world."

A 1985 opinion poll consulted vox populi in the two countries about the effects of the occupation on the fortieth anniversary of the end of the war. The Americans thought its main achievement was to help Japan build its spectacularly successful economy. The Japanese thought the occupation's main legacy was freedom and democratic rights.[3]

Whatever historians say about "feudal survivals" or "reverse course," few people would disagree that Japan today is democratic, peaceful, and prosperous. This is the kind of Japan Americans wanted, and Japanese eagerly cooperated. Japan today is largely the result of its own efforts. But even though the basic cultural traits of its people have probably changed very little, the United States gave it an indispensable push in the right direction forty years ago. It is not too much to say—to borrow from the poet Milton—that the peace that followed the Pacific War in 1945 resulted in victory for both the United States and Japan.

Perhaps Yoshida should have the last word: "The Americans came into our country as our enemies, but after an occupation lasting little less than seven years, an understanding grew up between the two peoples which is remarkable in the history of the modern world."[4]

Chronology of Main Events

1945

July 26		Potsdam Declaration issued by the United States, the United Kingdom, and China
Aug.	6	Atomic bomb dropped on Hiroshima
	9	Atomic bomb dropped on Nagasaki
		Soviet Union declares war on Japan
	15	Emperor's speech accepting Potsdam terms
	17	Higashikuni cabinet formed
	19	Japanese delegation receives surrender plans at Manila
	26	Japanese set up the CLO
	30	MacArthur lands at Atsugi
Sept.	2	Surrender ceremony takes place aboard the *Missouri*
	3	Shigemitsu meets MacArthur re "direct occupation"
	10	SCAP orders free speech, press, and communications
	17	Yoshida named foreign minister
	20	MacArthur and Yoshida meet for first time
	22	U.S. initial policy for Japan made public
	27	First of eleven meetings of MacArthur and emperor
Oct.	4	SCAP "bill of rights" directive issued
	5	Higashikuni cabinet resigns
	9	Shidehara cabinet formed
	11	MacArthur asks Shidehara to make five major reforms
	16	SCAP announces Japanese demobilization completed
Nov.	3	U.S. basic policy directive sent to SCAP
	6	Four biggest zaibatsu companies dissolved
	8	SCAP "restricts" 354 zaibatsu companies

Dec.	9	SCAP ordered a liberal land reform program
	12	Pauley initial reparations report made public
	15	State Shintō disestablished
		Universal adult suffrage law enacted
	17	Trials of Class B and C war criminals begin
	21	Labor Union Law enacted
	26	FEC and ACJ set up

1946

Jan.	1	Emperor's declaration of humanity made public
	4	SCAP purge orders issued
	11	SWNCC 228 on political reform received by SCAP
	19	SCAP announces charter of IMTFE
	20	SCAP designates 389 factories for reparations
	25	MacArthur cables opinion discouraging trial of emperor
Feb.	3	MacArthur tells GS to draft new constitution
	13	Japanese government given draft
	19	Emperor begins series of visits around the country
	26	First meeting of the FEC
Mar.	6	Emperor publicly supports new constitution
	30	First shipment of food from the United States arrives
		Stoddard education report presented (6-3-3-4 system)
Apr.	1	Final report of Pauley reparations commission filed
	5	MacArthur addresses first meeting of ACJ
	10	Election of new lower house held; no majority winner
	20	HCLC set up
May	3	Trial of major war criminals begins
		Soviet forces evacuate Manchuria
	4	Hatoyama, head of Liberal Party, purged
	5	Hoover commission studying food shortages arrives
	19	May Day riots occur over food shortages
	22	Yoshida forms first cabinet
June	25	Revised constitution submitted to Diet
Aug.	12	ESB set up
Sept.	20	Labor relations adjustment law approved
Oct.	7	Revised constitution passes Diet
	21	Revised land reform bill approved
Nov.	3	Revised constitution officially promulgated
Dec.	27	Cabinet approves priority production plan

1947

Jan.	1	Yoshida calls labor leaders "lawless"
	4	Under SCAP pressure Japan orders purge of local officials, economic leaders, and media leaders
	18	Labor unions announce general strike for Feb. 1
	31	MacArthur press statement prohibits strike
Feb.	6	MacArthur orders general election
Mar.	19	MacArthur publicly calls for early peace treaty
	22	Fundamental law of education enacted
Apr.	4	United States orders interim reparations program
	14	Antimonopoly law goes into effect
	25	Socialists win majority in lower house election
May	1	Emperor holds his first press conference
	3	Revised constitution goes into effect
	12	United States sends FEC-230 deconcentration policy to FEC
June	1	Katayama forms three-party cabinet
July	3	SCAP orders breakup of Mitsui and Mitsubishi trading companies
Aug.	15	Limited foreign trade opened
	26	Diet begins investigation of wartime hoarded goods
Sept.	13	Ashida memo on defense policy given to Eichelberger
Nov.	12	Strike committee report for reduced reparations filed
Dec.	9	Law to bar excessive industrial concentrations passed
	17	Police reform law enacted, barring centralized force
	31	Home Ministry abolished, its functions dispersed

1948

Jan.	6	Secretary of Army Royall calls for self-supporting Japan
	16	First shipment of interim reparations sent to China
	21	United States notifies FEC of new U.S. focus on economic recovery
Feb.	10	Katayama cabinet resigns
Mar.	8	Police law goes into effect
	10	Ashida coalition cabinet formed without election
June	23	Arrests begin in Shōwa Denkō bribery scandal
July	22	MacArthur orders Ashida to revise public service law
	30	Exclusion of banks from deconcentration law announced
	31	Ashida cabinet issues ordinance 201 revising NPSL

Oct.	7	Ashida cabinet resigns because of Shōden scandal
	9	Truman approves NSC 13/2
	15	Yoshida forms second cabinet after party dissension
Nov.	12	Twenty-five major war criminals found guilty
Dec.	7	Ashida arrested in bribery scandal
	9	United States withdraws FEC-230 deconcentration plan
	19	Japan given nine-point directive calling for economic stabilization
Dec.	23	Tōjō and six other war criminals hanged
		Yoshida voted out of office by prearranged deal

1949

Jan.	1	MacArthur permits flying of Japanese flag
	23	Yoshida's Liberal Party wins overwhelming victory
Feb.	1	Dodge arrives to enforce economic austerity
	16	Third Yoshida cabinet formed
Apr.	23	Yen/dollar rate set at 360/1
May	12	United States announces end of Japan reparations program
	30	Start of campaign of violence by railway workers
June	18	Antimonopoly law amended
July	6	Shimoyama, president of National Railways, killed
Sept.	2	MacArthur states communism not a threat to Japan
Dec.	1	Foreign exchange and foreign trade control law passed

1950

Jan.	8	Cominform criticizes peace policy of Communist Party leader Nosaka
Feb.	9	Japanese government authorized to set up overseas offices
Apr.	24	Dulles advocates early peace for Japan
June	6	SCAP purges twenty-four members of Communist Party central committee
	21	Dulles arrives to explore peace treaty prospects
	25	War starts in Korea
July	8	MacArthur orders creation of 75,000-man police reserve
	24	Japanese private sector begins Red Purge of leftists
Oct.	13	Ten thousand Japanese released from 1946 purge

1951

Jan. 29	Dulles begins peace treaty talks with Yoshida
Feb. 9	Dulles and Yoshida approve five treaty documents
Apr. 11	Truman recalls MacArthur
14	Ridgway arrives in Tokyo to succeed MacArthur
16	Dulles arrives in Tokyo for third visit
Sept. 8	Peace and security treaties signed in San Francisco
Dec. 10	Dulles arrives in Tokyo to clarify China policy

1952

Jan. 16	Yoshida letter to Dulles on China policy made public
Feb. 28	U.S.-Japan administrative agreement signed
Apr. 28	Peace and security treaties come into force

List of Principal Actors

ASAKAI Kōichirō. Career diplomat who held important positions in the CLO dealing with the occupation forces; later ambassador to the United States.

ASHIDA Hitoshi. Prime minister from March to October 1948 and head of the conservative Democratic Party, which formed a coalition government with the Socialist Party in 1947.

ASŌ Kazuko. Daughter of Yoshida Shigeru, who often acted as his hostess and served him as adviser and confidante.

Joseph DODGE. Detroit banker who as a civilian adviser to General MacArthur beginning in 1949 supervised measures of budget and spending control—the "Dodge Line"—that significantly reduced inflation, helped stabilize Japan's economy, and prepared it for later economic growth.

William H. DRAPER, Jr. Under secretary of the army in 1947 and 1948 in charge of occupied areas; decided that the United States had to cut back the reparations and deconcentration programs in Japan and assist it to become self-supporting.

John Foster DULLES. Consultant to Secretary of State Dean Acheson in 1950–1952; played the leading part in negotiating a peace settlement with Japan; in 1953 became secretary of state in the Eisenhower administration.

Robert L. EICHELBERGER. Lieutenant general and commander of the Eighth U.S. Army from 1945 to 1947; had responsibility for the conduct of the occupation's civil affairs operations in Japan and for overseeing Japanese implementation of SCAP directives throughout the country.

HIGASHIKUNI Naruhiko. Imperial prince, general, and prime minister from August 17 to October 9, 1945.

IKEDA Hayato. Finance minister under Yoshida who survived a year of severe budgetary restraint imposed by the Dodge Line and served as prime minister from 1960 to 1964.

Charles L. KADES. Deputy chief of the SCAP GS from 1945 to 1948; the leading figure in the U.S. occupation effort to reform the constitutional and legal system of Japan along American lines.

George F. KENNAN. Eminent foreign policy planner and famous as author of the containment policy in 1946 for meeting worldwide communism; Kennan's policy paper for Japan, NSC 13/2, drafted in 1948, marked a significant turning point by emphasizing economic revival to help Japan achieve political stability and economic growth.

KONOE Fumimaro. Leading political figure who was three times prime minister before World War II; took poison in December 1945 before he was to be arrested as a Class A war criminal suspect.

Wolf J. LADEJINSKY. Russian-born agronomist; became a U.S. Department of Agriculture expert and later one of the principal architects of the highly successful occupation program for land reform in Japan.

Douglas MACARTHUR. Supreme commander for the Allied powers from 1945 to 1951 and the dominant figure of the occupation.

William F. MARQUAT. Career military officer and chief of ESS from late 1945 to the end of the occupation; dealt with one of the most important and difficult operations in SCAP, handling labor, reparations, foreign trade, and the breakup of the zaibatsu.

NISHIMURA Kumao. Foreign Office treaty expert with great knowledge of the law; Yoshida's main technical adviser for the negotiation of the peace and security treaties.

Donald R. NUGENT. Former schoolteacher and U.S. Marine Corps reserve officer; served as second chief of CIE from late 1945 to the end of the occupation.

OKAZAKI Katsuo. Career diplomat who served as operational chief of the Ministry of Foreign Affairs during most of the occupation; member of the Japanese delegation that went to Manila in August 1945 to discuss U.S. plans for the surrender; played a major role in the negotiations of the peace settlement and the administrative agreement.

Matthew B. RIDGWAY. Supreme commander for the Allied powers from April 1951 to the end of the occupation in April 1952.

William J. SEBALD. Longtime naval officer and later a lawyer in Japan who became the U.S. political adviser and chief of the SCAP DS in 1947 after George Atcheson, Jr., was killed in a plane crash; best known as the SCAP representative in the debates with the Soviet representative on the ACJ over Soviet failure to repatriate Japanese prisoners of war from Siberia.

SHIDEHARA Kijūrō. Career diplomat who was prime minister from October 1945 to May 1946; served when living conditions were at their worst and when the SCAP reform program was at its most active.

SHIRASU Jirō. British-educated and aristocratic in appearance and manner; adviser to Yoshida, negotiator with the Americans, and vice minister of MITI in 1949.

SUZUKI Kantarō. Naval hero of the Russo-Japanese War, admiral, and prime minister from April to August 1945, when Japan made its decision to surrender.

TŌJŌ Hideki. General and prime minister when Japan attacked Pearl Harbor; convicted of war crimes and hanged in 1948.

Courtney WHITNEY. Lawyer and MacArthur confidant; chief of GS during most of the occupation; played a key role in the purge and the revision of the constitution; adviser on MacArthur's political ambitions, Japanese rearmament, and aspects of the Korean War.

Charles A. WILLOUGHBY. Longtime intelligence officer who served with MacArthur throughout the Pacific War and in the occupation until MacArthur's relief in 1951; temperamental, strongly anticommunist, opposed to many of the reforms Whitney and others espoused, and widely criticized for his alleged failure to foresee the PRC invasion of Korea in October 1950.

Justin WILLIAMS, Sr. Historian and civil affairs officer; served in GS for almost the entire occupation; best known for his work in strengthening the role of the Diet in an effort to make it "the highest organ of state power."

YOSHIDA Shigeru. Prime minister four times, from May 1946 to May 1947 and from October 1948 to the end of the occupation; served a fifth term after the occupation; retired in December 1954; the dominant Japanese figure during the occupation.

Notes

Events are dated as of the place of occurrence.

Japanese personal names are rendered in accordance with Japanese custom, the family name preceding the personal name.

"SCAP" is used to refer to the staff of the supreme commander for the Allied powers, not to General MacArthur personally.

Macrons have been omitted from names of Japanese places in English usage.

Translations from Japanese are by the author, unless otherwise indicated.

INTRODUCTION

1. "Consider Japan."

2. Dower, "Yoshida in the Scales of History," 1; Sodei, *Senryō*, 164–174; Schaller, "MacArthur's Japan."

3. Sumimoto, *Senryō hiroku*, vol. 1, 119.

4. Sebald, *With MacArthur*, 98.

5. Ward and Sakamoto, "Introduction," in Ward and Sakamoto (eds.), *Democratizing Japan*, i; Ward, "Conclusion," in Ward and Sakamoto (eds.), *Democratizing Japan*, 401. Germany was also a major modern nation occupied after World War II, but it was initially divided into four zones and occupied by four powers; later it was formed into two zones, one occupied by the Soviet Union and the other by the three Western powers.

6. Dower, "Reform and Reconsolidation," 347.

PART I. ENEMIES FACE TO FACE

1. White, "Episode in Tokyo Bay."

2. Committee for the Compilation of Materials on Damage (ed.), *The Im-*

pact of the A-Bomb: Hiroshima and Nagasaki, 1945–1985, 19, 21, 46, 48, 59–60; S. Johnson, *The Japanese Through American Eyes,* 178, fn. 5. Widely varying statistics compiled by different agencies regarding A-bomb casualties can be partially reconciled by separating those who died at once or soon after the bombings from those whose later death could be attributed to the bomb. See also Bernstein, "Unravelling a Mystery"; Miles, "Hiroshima." The atomic bomb was successfully tested on July 16, 1945, two months after the surrender of Germany. There is no reason to believe the atomic bomb would not have been used against Germany if one had been ready in time.

3. Dower, *War Without Mercy;* DOS, *Occupation,* 53–55; Butow, *Japan's Decision,* 145–146; Editorials, *NYT,* July 30 and 31, 1945.

4. Butow, *Japan's Decision,* 42, 150–153; Takemi, "Remembrances of the War."

5. Butow, *Japan's Decision,* 166–174.

CHAPTER 1.   TENSE BEGINNINGS

1. Butow, *Japan's Decision,* 153, fn. 37, 175– 209; Arisue, *Shūsen hishi,* 39–46. Sigal, *Fighting to a Finish,* is a detailed account of Japan's decision to surrender based in large part on oral statements by Japanese leaders after the war. In Japanese practice the emperor did not "decide" policies; he approved decisions of his ministers, and in 1945 he expressed a "desire" or gave "advice" that the Allied terms be accepted, which the cabinet then adopted as its decision.

2. DOS, *Occupation,* 56–58; Butow, *Japan's Decision,* 207–208.

3. DOS, *Occupation,* 59–60.

4. Butow, *Japan's Decision,* 248.

5. "Voice of the crane" means a statement by the emperor.

6. Sumimoto, *Senryō hiroku,* vol. 1, 15–19; *Asahi shimbun,* Feb. 14. 1964, 8; *FRUS, 1945,* vol. 6, 702–708. See Pacific War Research Society (comp.), *Japan's Longest Day,* for a description of the events of August 14, 1945, in Tokyo.

7. *KJ,* vol. 4, 166–168.

8. Kōsaka, *One Hundred Million Japanese,* 22–23; Etō (ed.), *Senryō shiroku,* vol. 1, 70–97, 103; *FRUS, 1945,* vol. 6, 647–650; Mashbir, *I Was an American Spy,* 278–299; Sumimoto, *Senryō hiroku,* vol. 1, 2–14.

9. Etō (ed.), *Senryō shiroku,* vol. 1, 107; Morison, *Victory,* 359.

10. Arisue, *Shūsen hishi,* 76–79, 82; "Ichiban nori ga mita mono" (What the first plane saw), *Shūkan shinchō,* Aug. 24, 1968, 46.

11. Whitney, *MacArthur's Rendezvous,* 214; Willoughby (ed.), *The Reports of General MacArthur,* vol. 1, suppl. 31; MacArthur, *Reminiscences,* 270, fn.

12. Willoughby (ed.), *The Reports of General MacArthur,* vol. 1, 29.

13. Sodei, *Makkāsā no nisen nichi,* 76.

14. Kawai, *Japan's American Interlude,* 12–13. This remains a classic study of the U.S. occupation of Japan.

15. *PRJ,* 740. The two volumes of *PRJ* are consecutively numbered.

16. Amakawa, "Senryō seisaku," 215–218; Butow, *Japan's Decision*, 198; Etō (ed.), *Senryō shiroku*, vol. 1, 300–331; Matsumoto and Andō, "Daitōa sensō," vol. 25, 238–239. Amakawa's "Senryō seisaku" is a careful study of official Japanese reactions and plans in the early occupation period.

17. Morison, *Victory*, 362–368. See also James, *The Years of MacArthur*, vol. 2, 781–797; Kase, *Journey to the "Missouri."* James's three-volume life of MacArthur is thorough and scholarly. For an offbeat study of MacArthur, see Schaller, *Douglas MacArthur*.

18. James, *The Years of MacArthur*, vol. 2, 785.

19. Shigemitsu, *Japan and Her Destiny*, 372; Sumimoto, *Senryō hiroku*, vol. 1, 32–36. One reason advanced at the time to explain the willingness of Japanese leaders, especially military men, to go along with the surrender was the view that the United States and the Soviet Union would soon have a confrontation and Japan could "find a chance to regain its feet" (Hata, "The Postwar Period," 13–14).

20. *PRJ*, 736.

21. *NYT*, Sept. 3, 1945, 3; Murphy, *Diplomat*, 240–242. The crudely corrected copy of the Japanese-language text of the surrender instrument can be seen in the archives of the Foreign Office in Tokyo. The signing of the instrument of surrender by the Allied powers and Japan, according to the prevailing Japanese legal interpretation, made the surrender in 1945 one of a contractual nature, not an unconditional one (Taoka, "Sengo Nihon," English translation in author's possession).

22. *PRJ*, 737; DOS, *Occupation*, 65.

23. Statistics on Japanese casualties and damage vary widely. An authoritative study, made by the ESB and dated April 7, 1949, estimated Japan's war dead at 1,854,000 (1,555,000 military and 299,000 civilians). This report was summarized in POLAD desp. 249, "Transmission of Report on Losses Sustained by Japan as Result of the Pacific War," Apr. 22, 1949, 2, diplomatic file S 500, NRAS, RG 84, Box 2243. See also Dower, *War Without Mercy*, 297–298, 300.

U.S. combat deaths in the Pacific War were about 100,000, and about 292,000 troops were recorded as wounded or missing. The total cost of the Pacific War to the United States in money has been estimated at about $100 billion (Hadley, *Antitrust*, 134).

24. Tsuru, *Essays on Japanese Economic Development*, 160; Patrick, "The Phoenix Risen."

25. DOS, *Occupation*, 51.

26. Ibid., 52–53; Bohlen, *Witness to History*, 197–198; *FRUS, 1945*, vol. 6, 670.

27. Uchino, *Japan's Postwar Economy*, 17–18.

28. *FRUS, Conference of Berlin, 1945*, vol. 1, 908. One hundred fifty thousand Okinawan Japanese, or one-third of the island's population, were killed in the spring of 1945 (Dower, *War Without Mercy*, 298).

29. Shinobu, *Sengo Nihon seijishi*, vol. 1, 119–130.

30. Sodei, *Senryō*, 155–156.

CHAPTER 2. FIRST ENCOUNTERS

1. MacArthur, *Reminiscences*, 30–32.
2. Ziegler, *Mountbatten*, 296–297.
3. MacArthur, *Reminiscences*, 282–284; Sherwood, *Roosevelt and Hopkins*, 819.
4. Records of MacArthur, MMA, RG 5, Box 2. This is an office file of requests for appointments with the supreme commander. It is not a complete or fully accurate list of the meetings that actually took place, but it does provide useful reference material. James, *The Years of MacArthur*, vol. 3, 693–694, lists those who had frequent contact with MacArthur in 1945–1951; Yoshida is the only Japanese listed. James briefly described the contacts MacArthur had with Japanese prime ministers and the emperor (vol. 3, 309–325).
5. Sebald, Oral History Regarding Occupation Period, 528, NL, Special Collection; Bowers, "The Late General MacArthur," 168; Inumaru, "Ma Gensui," 209–211.
6. Willoughby, *Shirarezaru Nihon senryō*, 59. This book by MacArthur's intelligence chief is of interest not only as a sharp attack on many of the Americans who worked in GHQ SCAP, but also because it appeared only in Japan and in Japanese. See also Manchester, *American Caesar*, 633.
7. Etō (ed.), *Senryō shiroku*, vol. 1, 263–269; Williams, *Japan's Political Revolution*, 5; Bouterse, Taylor, and Maas, "American Military Government Experience," 330.
8. Etō (ed.), *Senryō shiroku*, vol. 1, 270–275; Inoki, *Hyōden Yoshida*, vol. 3, 219–220; Shigemitsu, *Japan and Her Destiny*, 375–377; Amakawa, "Senryō seisaku," 218–220; Maki, "The Role of the Bureaucracy," 391.
9. *FRUS, 1945*, vol. 6, 677, 712. The statement of September 20, 1945, was the closest the United States came to making an issue of "unconditional surrender." See *FRUS, 1944*, vol. 5, 1275–1285; Iokibe, "American Policy."
The only case of what might be called determined resistance to the orders of the occupation grew out of this SCAP order for the turnover of Japan's diplomatic records (*FRUS, 1945*, vol. 6, 473). The Japanese consul general in Dublin, Beppu Setsuya, rejected the orders of the Foreign Office and Allied representatives and remained at his post for three years after the surrender, with the tacit support of the government of Ireland, and finally came back to Japan in 1948. At the insistence of SCAP he was tried for violation of occupation orders and lightly penalized. He was later reinstated and had a successful diplomatic career (int. with Beppu). (See Etō [ed.], *Senryō shiroku*, vol. 2, 347–365.)
Regarding the knotty issue of who was sovereign during the occupation, Yoshida Shigeru told the Diet in 1946 that "Japan was a sovereign state but was limited by SCAP in the exercise of its sovereignty" (*SCAP Monthly Summation*, para. 37, July 1946). The Japanese also put it another way: the supreme commander had supreme authority, but Japan retained its sovereignty.
10. Masumi, *Postwar Politics*, 42; Morley, "The First Seven Weeks."
11. Masumi, *Postwar Politics*, 41–42; Etō (ed.), *Senryō shiroku*, vol. 3, 97–104; Morley, "The First Seven Weeks," 160–162; Inoki, *Hyōden Yoshida*, vol.

3, 89–90; Koseki, *Shinkempō no tanjō*, 8–13. See also Atcheson's comments in *FRUS, 1945*, vol. 6, 827, 841. Atcheson asserted the word *constitution* was used in error by the interpreter, but regardless of how it came up the record is clear that MacArthur did suggest Konoe might play a useful role in revising the constitution (*PRJ*, 91, fn.).

12. *FRUS, 1945*, vol. 6, 750, 757–758.

13. Suzuki, *Suzuki Tadakatsu-shi*, 106.

14. *YM*, 62–63; this is a frank and personal account based on Yoshida's four-volume *Kaisō jūnen* and elegantly rendered in English by his son. Yoshida kept the portfolio of foreign minister until 1952, except for one year in 1947–1948.

15. Two excellent biographies have been written about Yoshida. Dower, *Empire*, is a painstaking and in many respects brilliant study of Yoshida. Inoki's three-volume biography, *Hyōden Yoshida*, contains many important details but is less given to critical commentary.

16. Dower, *Empire*, 74; Yoshida, *Ōiso zuisō*, 86.

17. *YM*, 13; Shiroyama, *War Criminal*, 134–138.

18. Kōsaka, *Saishō Yoshida*, 17–21; Dower, *Empire*, contains a graphic description of the Konoe "memorial to the emperor" and the Yoshida antiwar movement (227–272). See also *FRUS, 1945*, vol. 6, 700–708.

19. Etō (ed.), *Senryō shiroku*, vol. 1, 290–292; "Yoshida genshushō no kaisō rokuon yōyaku" (Summary of recording containing recollections of former prime minister Yoshida), made in 1955, *Asahi shimbun*, Apr. 18, 1977. See also "Yoshida genshushō danwa yōshi" (Outline of talk with former prime minister Yoshida), Oct. 5, 1955, Shidehara Peace Collection, NDLT; Yoshida, *KJ*, vol. 1, 97.

20. The Japanese press at that time was carrying somewhat sensational reports of incidents such as thefts, rapes, and assaults by U.S. soldiers in Japan. SCAP quickly prohibited such reporting. Nevertheless, the Japanese press continued to report incidents without attributing them to Americans but in such a way that readers would readily understand—for example a theft by "a big man who did not speak Japanese."

21. *KJ*, vol. 1, 96; Asō Kazuko, "Kodomo no yō ni mujaki datta chichi" (My childlike father), *Shūkan Yomiuri*, Oct. 1, 1978, 42–43. See Harry Kern, "Yoshida's Special Credentials," *Yomiuri* (English ed.), Sept. 9, 1979, 7. Yoshida spoke some years later of MacArthur's habit of talking as he strode up and down his office and said, "I could understand him well when he was facing towards me, but when he turned his back I did not understand a single word of what he was saying. It used to make me so angry but there was nothing I could do" (Sebald oral history, 1053).

22. Kojima, "Tennō to Amerika," 115–119. Kojima, an expert chronicler of modern Japanese history, advised the author that he obtained this record from official Japanese sources. MacArthur said he offered the emperor a cigarette. The Tennō, who did not smoke, took it. His hand shook as the general lit it for him (*Reminiscences*, 287–288).

23. *Asahi shimbun*, Sept. 29, 1945, 1.

24. MacArthur, *Reminiscences*, 287; Diary of Iriye Sukemasa, at that time a chamberlain of the imperial household, entry of Sept. 27, 1945, *Asahi shimbun*, Jan. 26, 1989, 4.

25. *NYT*, Oct. 2, 1945, 5. MacArthur did not pay a call on the emperor at any time.

26. MacArthur, *Reminiscences*, 287–288. MacArthur told his political adviser on October 27, one month after meeting with the emperor, that the Tennō had said he did not seek "to escape responsibility" for the attack on Pearl Harbor because "he was the leader of the Japanese people and he was responsible for the actions of the Japanese people." Memo of conversation, Oct. 27, 1945, DOS diplomatic file 800, NRAW.

27. U.K. Public Records Office, F 1849/15/23, FO 371/63690, ltr. from Gascoigne to Dening, Jan. 22, 1947; Hirohito-Krisher int., *Newsweek*, Sept. 29, 1975, 7. Saionji Kimmochi, the last survivor of Japan's *genrō*, died in 1940. Regarding Hirohito's knowledge and support of plans for the attack on Pearl Harbor, see Bergamini, *Japan's Imperial Conspiracy*, 830; Sugiyama, *Sugiyama memo*, vol. 1, 370; Kido, *Kido Kōichi nikki*, vol. 2, 928. Titus, *Palace and Politics*, offers a persuasive explanation of the way in which imperial will was used to make basic national decisions in prewar Japan (316–321).

28. One Japanese authority has described the modern emperor institution as dualist in nature—absolutist/authoritarian versus liberal/democratic—and has argued that Shōwa was liberal in his outlook and hopeful of somehow merging the two strands. Takeda Kiyoko, "Shōwa no gekidōki to Hirohito tennō" (Emperor Hirohito and the Shōwa upheaval), *Asahi shimbun*, Jan. 8, 1989, 11.

29. Titus, *Palace and Politics*, 328; Ike (ed.), *Japan's Decision for War*, 151, fn. 36, 283; ltr. of Dec. 24, 1990, to author from N. Kojima.

30. K. Sansom, *Sir George Sansom*, 166.

31. MacArthur, *Reminiscences*, 288; K. Sansom, *Sir George Sansom*, 166. Of the eleven meetings between MacArthur and the emperor, only the first and the third have been reported in some detail. A partial report of the fourth meeting on May 6, 1947, quotes MacArthur as saying "the basic idea of the United States is to ensure the security of Japan" but not to "defend Japan as it would California," as has sometimes been attributed to MacArthur. Kojima, *Nihon senryō*, vol. 3, 25–30; *PRJ*, 769. (See Hata, *Hirohito*, 190–193.)

32. Inoki, *Hyōden Yoshida*, vol. 3, 78; Fearey memo to Atcheson, Oct. 13, 1945, POLAD Tokyo, DS 800 01, NRAS, RG 84, Box 2275.

CHAPTER 3.   PLANNING AND ORGANIZING
THE OCCUPATION

1. James, *The Years of MacArthur*, vol. 2, 775; *FRUS, 1945*, vol. 6, 648; U.K. Public Records Office F 5735/631/23, FO 371/46455, FO memo, Aug. 25, 1945; *FRUS, 1946*, vol. 8, 150–151.

2. U.S. Senate, *Military Situation*, part 1, 54; SCAP, *History of the Non-Military Activities*, monograph 2.

3. MacArthur, *Reminiscences*, 282–283.

4. DOS, *Occupation*, 53–55; Borton, "The Allied Occupation," 34, fn. 3.

5. *FRUS, The Conference of Berlin, 1945*, vol. 1, 894–897, 900–901; vol. 2, 68–69, 1268; Wolfe (ed.), *Americans as Proconsuls*, 42–44. The provision regarding possible retention of the emperor system was modified several days later by the State Department. See Masumi, *Postwar Politics*, 17–19. General MacArthur thought this provision should have been retained (James, *The Years of MacArthur*, vol. 2, 775).

6. DOS, *Occupation*, 56–58; Matsumoto and Andō, "Daitōa sensō," 237–238; Amakawa, "Senryō seisaku," 217–222.

7. *PRJ*, 423–426; Takemae, *Senryō sengoshi*, 30. Much of the presurrender U.S. planning was done by a small group of experts on Japan led by George H. Blakeslee and Hugh Borton. Former ambassador to Japan Joseph C. Grew had a minor advisory role. See Borton, "American Presurrender Planning," 22–23. A considerable degree of consensus existed in planning for postwar Japan, with little evidence of factionalism between so-called Japan hands and China hands in the State Department, although this categorization seems embedded in much occupation historiography.

8. Whitney, *MacArthur's Rendezvous*, 246–247.

9. *FRUS, 1945*, vol. 6, 581–584.

10. *YM*, 127; Reischauer, *Japan*, 222; *PRJ*, 774. Masumi termed the Potsdam Declaration and initial policy "ambiguous and contradiction-laden" (*Postwar Politics*, 41).

11. DOS, *Activities of the FEC*, 49–58; *PRJ*, 774.

12. *PRJ*, 428–439; letter from Hull of War Department to Sutherland, SCAP chief of staff, OPD 381, Aug. 22, 1945, NRAW, Sutherland file; MacArthur message to Marshall, CA 51630, Sept. 3, 1945, NRAW, Sutherland file.

13. War Dept. message to MacArthur, WX 59245, Sept. 4, 1945, NRAW, Sutherland file; int. with Borton, who served in the Office of Japanese Affairs in the State Department for several years after the war.

14. *FRUS, 1945*, vol. 3, 483–503. Named after Roosevelt's last secretary of treasury, the "Morgenthau concept" proposed the breakup of large industries and the "pastoralization" of Germany after the war.

15. T. Cohen, *Remaking Japan*, 4. Cohen was an important official in the ESS and headed the labor division for a year.

16. Memo of conversation between Bishop of POLAD and Chamberlain, DCOS, SCAP, Feb. 11, 1946, NRAS, DS file 500.

17. Ōkita, *Japan's Challenging Years*, 25–29; Ōkita, *Watakushi no rire-kisho*, 51–65.

18. Inoki, *Hyōden Yoshida*, vol. 3, 61–63; Kōsaka, *Saishō Yoshida*, 19–20.

19. James, *The Years of MacArthur*, vol. 1, 564.

20. Letter from Compton to Truman, Oct. 4, 1945, 6, NRAW, RG 59, Box 3812; "Japan's Fanatics Are MacArthur's Number One Problem," *NYT*, Aug. 26, 1945, E3; Truman, *Memoirs*, vol. 2, 520–521.

21. *PRJ*, 742. MacArthur's gesture in permitting the Japanese to disarm their forces was much appreciated by the Japanese military leaders. SCAP had initially opposed this (*FRUS, 1945*, vol. 6, 666–669, 671).

22. Bowers, "The Late General MacArthur," 164. Bowers served as a military aide to the general in 1945–1946 and has continued to be a great admirer of

MacArthur, even if this irreverent article presents more "warts" than do most accounts about the supreme commander (int. with Bowers).

23. SCAP, *Selected Data*, contains charts, and descriptions of the SCAP/FEC organization (2, 6, 8, and 9).

24. Int. with Sackton, former chief of joint staff, GHQ, SCAP/FEC, Tokyo.

25. CLO memo,to SCAP, Sept. 8, 1945, MMA, RG 9, Box 41; Hata (ed.), *Amerika no tai-nichi*, 530, 532; Nanto, "The United States Role," 66, 145. The best information seems to be that depending on the method of calculation, Japan paid between $4.23 and $4.98 billion in occupation costs, while it received $1.95 billion in U.S. economic assistance.

26. *FRUS, 1945*, vol. 6, 655–656; *FRUS, 1946*, vol. 8, 95–98; Atcheson memo to MacArthur, Sept. 24, 1945, regarding POLAD status, NRAS, RG 84, Box 2275. POLAD had a limited operational role for much of the occupation. In 1950 it was permitted to establish direct telegraphic communications with the State Department, thus acquiring independence and a degree of freedom from the watchful eye of SCAP officials.

27. See Mason, "The Liaison Offices."

28. *PRJ*, 192–193; Oppler, *Legal Reform*, 42, 330–331; McNelly, *Politics and Government*, 28. Imperial ordinances issued to carry out the instrument of surrender were popularly known as Potsdam ordinances.

29. Inoki, *Hyōden Yoshida*, vol. 3, 80–82; *NYT*, Oct. 7, 1945, 29; Sebald, *With MacArthur*, 98–99.

30. *FRUS, 1945*, vol. 6, 741; Amakawa, "Senryō seisaku," 226– 227.

31. Inoki, *Hyōden Yoshida*, vol. 3, 85; Uchino, *Japan's Postwar Economy*, 253.

32. Kojima, *Nihon senryō*, vol. 1, 158; *PRJ*, 741; FO 371/46450, Sansom ltr. to FO, Oct. 12, 1945. MacArthur, *Reminiscences*, 293–294, gives a somewhat different version of the list, omitting any reference to the constitutional issue and putting some stress on "full employment in useful work of everyone."

33. Etō (ed.), *Senryō shiroku*, vol. 3, 105–111; *YM*, 7.

34. Masumi, *Postwar Politics*, 19; "The Japanese Constitution," *NYT*, Oct. 28, 1945, E6; Editorial, *New York Herald Tribune*, Oct. 31, 1945; *FRUS, 1945*, vol. 6, 841, 969; J. Williams, *Japan's Political Revolution*, 272; Etō (ed.), *Senryō shiroku*, vol. 3, 114–115; Koseki, *Shinkempō no tanjō*, 8–29. See Emmerson, *The Japanese Thread*, 264–267.

35. J. Williams, *Japan's Political Revolution*, 101–102, 175–177; Masumi, *Postwar Politics*, 139; McNelly, "Limited Voting," 2–5.

36. Masumi, *Postwar Politics*, 133–138; Inoki, *Hyōden Yoshida*, vol. 3, 99–100; Emmerson, *The Japanese Thread*, 270; "Political Parties' Situation," desp. 17 from POLAD Tokyo to DOS, Oct. 15, 1945, NRAS, DOS file 800.

PART II. MACARTHUR'S TWO HUNDRED DAYS

1. By 1940 Japan had experienced constitutional government for a half century, with no less success than some Western European countries had achieved. Japan had also some success in experimenting with political parties. See Watkins, "Prospects of Constitutional Democracy." "The Japanese had

also made their transition to being an industrialized nation, a fully educated nation, and a modernized nation in the nineteenth century" (Reischauer, "Two Harvard Luminaries," 12).

2. Report of presidential envoy Locke to Truman, Oct. 19, 1945, president's secretary file, HSTL.

3. MacArthur, *Reminiscences*, 305–306, fn.

CHAPTER 4.   FIRST WAVE OF REFORM

1. *PRJ*, 460; James, *The Years of MacArthur*, vol. 3, 300–301.

2. Coughlin, *Conquered Press*, 21–22, 47; F 15685/2/23, FO 371/54109, Gascoigne ltr. to FO, Oct. 2, 1946; Mayo, "Civil Censorship"; Etō, "Genron tōsei."

3. *NYT*, Sept. 14, 1945, 8; *PRJ*, 739.

4. *NYT*, Sept. 15, 1945, 4; Kojima, *Nihon senryō*, vol. 1, 100–102; *PRJ*, 740; S. Johnson, *The Japanese Through American Eyes*, 39–54.

5. *FRUS, 1945*, vol. 6, 715–719; *NYT*, Sept. 18, 1945, 3, and Sept. 23, 1945, 1, E3; Kojima, *Nihon senryō*, vol. 1, 113; Feis, *Contest over Japan*, 28–29.

6. RLED, Oct. 20, 1945.

7. *PRJ*, 463–465; Bouterse, Taylor, and Mass, "American Military Government Experience," 332.

8. Takemae, *Senryō sengoshi*, 99–107. The concept of *kokutai* referred to "the harmonious unity of the ruler and the people, the whole nation as one family under the rule of the emperor, his line unbroken for ages eternal" (Irokawa, *The Culture of the Meiji Period*, 247). When Japanese hear the word *kokutai* now, more than a generation later, they probably think of a national athletic contest, the acronyn for which is pronounced the same way.

9. Takemae, *Senryō sengoshi*, 156; SCAP, *History of the Non-Military Activities*, monograph 14, 8. Sixty percent of the senior officials of the Home Ministry were removed from office (C. Johnson, "Japan: Who Governs?" 20).

10. Etō (ed.), *Senryō shiroku*, vol. 1, 356–357; Sone, *Watakushi no memoāru*, 127.

11. Takemae, *Senryō sengoshi*, 125–128; desp. 200. 7, POLAD file 850, Oct. 10, 1945, NRAS, RG 84, Box 2275; Emmerson, *The Japanese Thread*, 70–71. Emmerson, one of the outstanding foreign service officers of his time, was never promoted to ambassador. Norman, who had taken part in Communist Party activities while a student at Cambridge University in the 1930s and who later rose to posts of great distinction in the foreign service of Canada, committed suicide in Cairo in 1957, a few days before a U.S. congressional committee began a lengthy investigation into communist activities in occupied Japan. See Dower, "Introduction," 98–101.

12. Uchino, *Japan's Postwar Economy*, 15–18; Patrick, "The Phoenix Risen," 306–307. See also J. Cohen, *Japan's Economy*, 417, 459; Gordon, *Evolution of Labor Relations*, 363.

13. T. Cohen, *Remaking Japan*, 344–345, gave an estimate of ¥35 billion (about $2.5 billion). SCAP had issued an order earlier forbidding the Japanese

to dispose of government property, but it was ignored. The Diet conducted an investigation of hoarded and stolen property in 1947, but little came of it, despite the huge sums that may have been involved.

It is difficult to estimate the value of the Japanese yen in dollars during the occupation because there was heavy and rapid inflation during its early years and no unitary exchange rate was set until 1949. An approximate yen value is used in this book based on a dollar/yen comparative formula devised by Theodore Cohen, who served in the SCAP ESS. These yen equivalents were based on the wholesale price index up to September 1946 and thereafter on the consumer price indexes, until an official rate was established in April 1949. The "Cohen formula" is set out in *Remaking Japan* (465):

1945	August	¥13.6	1947	September	190
	December	31		December	200
1946	March	40	1948	March	231
	June	55		June	248
	September	67		September	304
	December	71		December	324
1947	January	80	1949	March	355
	March	99		June	360 (official rate)
	June	142			

14. See Uchino, *Japan's Postwar Economy*, 254; *YM*, 80; Reischauer, *The Japanese*, 222; Arisawa, *Shōwa keizaishi*, vol. 2, 4–5. Statistics on Japanese caloric intake in the early occupation period vary widely. In one famous episode in 1947 Tokyo district court judge Yamaguchi Yoshitada allegedly starved to death because he refused to eat food other than official rations (C. Johnson, *MITI*, 185).

15. MacArthur, *Reminiscences*, 313; SCAP, *History of Non-Military Activities*, monograph 4, 97–98.

16. Nakamura, *The Postwar Japanese Economy*, 18–20; Lincoln, "Shōwa Economic Experience," 194.

17. Allen, *Japan's Economic Recovery*, 17–18; int. with Watanabe Takeshi. An intelligent and hard-working Ministry of Finance official who spoke excellent English, Watanabe was a conservative who seemed to feel that New Dealers had great influence during the occupation. SCAP did have a number of New Dealers, some of whom were highly effective, but it probably had at least as many conservatives and many more politically inert participants. Very few U.S. generals were New Dealers.

18. Levine, "Labor Laws," vol. 4, 351.

19. Tsurumi, *Japanese Business*, 82, 85; J. Cohen, *Japan's Economy*, 436.

20. *PRJ*, 58; Coughlin, *Conquered Press*, 80–110; T. Cohen, "Labor Democratization," 187–188; J. Moore, "Production Control," 2–26; Gordon, *The Evolution of Labor*, 480, fn. 18.

21. Takemae, *Sengo rōdō kaikaku*, 79–81; Garon, *The State and Labor*, 236–237; T. Cohen, *Remaking Japan*, 214–218.

22. Tsurumi, *Japanese Business*, 81; Gordon, *The Evolution of Labor*, 331; T. Cohen, *Remaking Japan*, 199.

23. T. Cohen, "Labor Democratization," 176–177; Tsurumi, *Japanese Business*, 78. Japan's auto workers formed an industrywide union in 1947, but it broke up shortly after the occupation ended (Cusumano, *The Japanese Automobile*, 142–164).

24. "Notes on MacArthur-Townsend Conference," Mar. 18, 1947, MMA, RG 5, official correspondence, file 2.

25. T. Cohen, "Labor Democratization," 187–188.

26. Peter Frost, "Land Reforms of 1946," *Kodansha Encyclopedia of Japan*, vol. 4, 364–365; Dore, *Land Reform*, 23–53; Takemae, *GHQ*, 128–130; Patrick, "The Phoenix Risen,"302–303.

27. Dore, *Land Reform*, 114–125; Nakamura, *The Postwar Japanese Economy*, 170; Masumi, *Postwar Politics*, 250–252.

28. MacArthur, *Reminiscences*, 313; Dore, *Land Reform*, 131–132. See also T. Cohen, *Remaking Japan*, 37–39.

29. Dore, *Land Reform*, 134–135; Masumi, *Postwar Politics*, 251; YM, 198–199; Nakamura, *The Postwar Japanese Economy*, 170. Land reform was a matter upon which the Japanese took an independent initiative in 1945, but the occupation soon intervened to demand stronger measures. (See Amakawa, "Senryō seisaku," 223.)

30. *PRJ*, 425.

31. Hadley, *Antitrust*, 439. Eleanor Hadley has won great respect in Japan and the United States for her authoritative studies of the zaibatsu.

32. Cohen, *Japan's Economy*, 426.

33. F 8263/364/23, FO 371/46429/135, U.K. Economic and Industrial Planning Staff paper, Oct. 23, 1945; Lockwood, "Industrial Development." One general active in economic planning, Suzuki Teiichi, and two bureaucrats active in finance, Kaya Okinori and Hoshino Naoki, all of whom were connected with operations in China, were indicted and convicted as Class A war criminals.

34. MacArthur, *Reminiscences*, 308; *FRUS, 1948*, vol. 6, 702.

35. J. Cohen, *Japan's Economy*, 102; Hadley, "Zaibatsu Dissolution," *Kodansha Encyclopedia of Japan*, vol. 8, 364. See Bisson, *Zaibatsu Dissolution in Japan*, 6–32, for a description of zaibatsu history and organization.

36. Bisson, *Zaibatsu Dissolution in Japan*, 24–25.

37. *NYT*, Oct. 20. 1945, 6; YM, 150–151; Hadley, *Antitrust*, 43–44; Bisson, *Zaibatsu Dissolution in Japan*, 70–71.

38. Bisson, *Zaibatsu Dissolution in Japan*, 73–74, 81, 241–244; SCAPIN 249, Nov. 6, 1945; DOS, *Occupation*, 166–168.

39. Locke letter to Truman, Oct. 4, 1945, 5–6, HSTL.

40. Nishi, *Unconditional Democracy*, 18.

41. *PRJ*, 433.

42. Hall, *Education for a New Japan*, 2; MacArthur message to War Dept., Jan. 4, 1946, War Dept. file 894.42 A/1-1446, NRAW.

43. Nishi, *Unconditional Democracy*, 164–165, 173; Suzuki E., *Nihon senryō*, 68–71. Twenty-two percent of all teachers and school officials either resigned or were removed. See Maeda, "The Direction of Postwar Education."

44. MacArthur, *Reminiscences*, 286–287; Nishi, *Unconditional Democra-*

cy, 51; Coleman, "Harry Kelly"; DOS, *Activities of the FEC*, 109.

45. Nishi, *Unconditional Democracy*, 189, 193; Suzuki, *Nihon senryō*, 153.

46. DOS, *Report of the First U.S. Education Mission*.

47. Royall to Truman, Apr. 27, 1949, Truman correspondence, subject file, HSTL. Ray Moore of Amherst College has done extensive research on this subject and is the source of this reference.

48. Woodward, *The Allied Occupation*, 245; James, *The Years of MacArthur*, vol. 2, 291–292.

49. MacArthur, *Reminiscences*, 310–311; Hall, *Education for a New Japan*, 75.

50. SCAPIN 448, *PRJ*, 467–469; Takemae, *Senryō sengoshi*, 269.

51. *PRJ*, 470; Woodward, *The Allied Occupation*, 317–321.

52. Int. with Fukushima, who helped Shidehara with both the English and Japanese texts; Murata, *Japan*, 388–391.

53. Ltr. of Dec. 31, 1945, MMA, RG 10, Box 2, VIP file—Yoshida.

54. *PRJ*, 471; MacArthur, *Reminiscences*, 311.

55. Kawai, *Japan's American Interlude*, 74; Masumi, *Postwar Politics*, 58.

56. F 1849/18442, FO 371/63690, Gascoigne ltr. to Dening, Jan. 22, 1947; Mainichi (ed.), *Ichiokunin no shōwashi*, vol. 5, 147–177. After the occupation the emperor did not make extensive trips of this kind.

57. Cary (ed.), *War-Wasted Asia*, 280–288.

58. Yoshida ltr. to MacArthur, Dec. 22, 1945, and Bunker reply, Dec. 27, 1945, MMA, RG 5, Box 1-A, VIP file—Yoshida.

CHAPTER 5. THE ALLIES: THEIR ROLE AND REPARATIONS

1. DOS, *Occupation*, 75.

2. *FRUS, 1945*, vol. 6, 630–631. On his own initiative Harriman turned down the Soviet proposal. John McCloy said later it was fortunate Harriman had done so because Washington "was so keen to get the fighting stopped that it would have accepted about anything the Russians came back with" (Harriman and Abel, *Special Envoy*, 501).

3. *FRUS, 1945*, vol. 6, 683–685; Blakeslee, *The FEC*, 2–11.

4. *FRUS, 1945*, vol. 6, 813.

5. Ibid., 765–773.

6. MacArthur message to War Dept., CA 53682, Oct. 22, 1945, Leahy file, NRAW.

7. DOS, *Occupation*, 69–73; *PRJ*, 421–422. See Feis, *Contest over Japan*, 31–118, for study of negotiations leading to agreement on the FEC and the ACJ.

8. *PRJ*, 740; MacArthur, *Reminsicences*, 292; SCAP message to DA, C-65957, Dec. 4, 1948, NSC 13/2 file, MMA, RG 5; Whitney, *MacArthur's Rendezvous*, 247.

9. MacArthur, *Reminiscences*, 293. For a frank and authoritative account by a ranking member of its secretariat of a useful and much misunderstood international body, see Stratton, "The Far Eastern Commission."

10. *FRUS, 1946*, vol. 8, 124.

11. *FRUS, 1945*, vol. 6, 744–746, 762–765; *PRJ*, 440–441.

12. *FRUS, 1945*, vol. 6, 667–668, 670. Truman's reply to Stalin (670) seemed to constitute recognition of the Soviet claim to all the Kurile Islands. See desp. 416, June 27, 1949, RG 84, B. 229, DOS file, NRAS.

13. MacArthur, *Reminiscences*, 285

14. *FRUS, 1945*, vol. 6, 785. Stalin complained to Harriman that the Soviet representative in Japan was being treated "like a piece of extra furniture" by General MacArthur's headquarters (*FRUS, 1945*, vol. 6, 791).

15. Harriman and Abel, *Special Envoy*, 531; *YM*, 52–53; Stephan, "Soviet Policy," 74. See *FRUS, 1946*, vol. 8, 285–286, 337–339.

16. DOS, *Occupation*, 55, 80.

17. Borton, "The Allied Occupation," 401.

18. Pauley, *Report on Japanese Reparations*, 6–7.

19. Kōsaka, *One Hundred Million Japanese*, 88.

20. *FRUS, 1946*, vol. 8, 124.

21. Asakai, *Shoki tainichi senryō seisaku*; Gordon, "The United States and Japan," 24.

22. SCAP, *Summation of Non-Military Activities*, 68.

23. Fearey memo to Atcheson, Oct 13, 1945, NRAS, RG 84, Box 2275.

24. WX 85811, JCS to CINCAFPAC, Nov. 30, 1945, NRAW, Leahy file; *FRUS*, vol. 8, 87–92. Ambassador Grew expressed the opinion in May 1945 that "the best we can hope for in Japan is the development of a constitutional monarchy, experience having shown that democracy in Japan would never work" (*FRUS, 1945*, vol. 6, 546). See G. Sansom, "Can Japan Be Reformed?"

25. Arisue, *Shūsen hishi*, 212.

26. CA 57235, MacArthur message to Eisenhower, Jan. 25, 1946, *FRUS, 1946*, vol. 8, 395–397; Masumi, *Postwar Politics*, 59–60. This message bears traces of the thinking of MacArthur's psychological warfare expert, Brigadier General Bonner F. Fellers, about the role of the emperor. (See Fellers memo to CINC, Oct. 2, 1945, MMA, RG 5, Box 1-A.) SCAP records reflect only a perfunctory investigation of the emperor's prewar role in policymaking; the file consists mainly of letters to MacArthur sent by Japanese individuals after the war (IPS case no. 254, NRAS, RG 331).

27. *FRUS, 1946*, vol. 8, 401.

28. Ibid., 423–428.

29. Ibid., 199–201. Edwin O. Reischauer asserted that in December 1945 while on military duty in Washington he drafted SWNNC 209, "Treatment of the Institution of the Emperor of Japan" (see *FRUS, 1946*, vol. 8, 199–201), which advocated retention of the emperor institution as a constitutional monarchy. This position eventually became U.S. and Allied policy (*My Life*, 106–107). The catalytic action, however, was without doubt the MacArthur telegram of January 25, 1946.

30. F 1826/2/23, FO 371/54082, Gascoigne tels. to London from Sansom, no. 95 and 101, Jan. 31, 1946; F 1849/18442, FO 371/63690, Gascoigne ltr. to Dening, Jan. 22, 1947.

31. Gluck, "'Dokuhaku' kara miete," 63; Kojima, *Tennō*, 141–151; Hata, *Hirohito*, 177–214.

CHAPTER 6. WAR CRIMES AND PUNISHMENT BY PURGE

1. Minear, *Victors' Justice*, 8–9, 49–50; Keenan and Brown, *Crimes*, 16.
2. Smith, *The Road*, 3, 45–47.
3. Montgomery, *Forced to Be Free*, 150–151.
4. MacArthur, *Reminiscences*, 318, 298.
5. *FRUS, 1945*, vol. 6, 921–923.
6. WX 62612, JCS to MacArthur, Sept. 12, 1945, GS file (B), NDLT; *NYT*, Sept. 12, 1945, 3; *FRUS, 1945*, vol. 6, 960–961.
7. *FRUS, 1945*, vol. 6, 932–936.
8. *PRJ*, 431–432.
9. The IRAA was organized in 1940 to bring all political groups into one body that would "assist imperial rule" in fighting the war against China. Although sometimes compared with the Nazi Party in Hitler's Germany, the IRAA was never well organized or particularly effective even as a political association.
10. *FRUS, 1945*, vol. 6, 952–953, 962–963, 984–985.
11. Ibid., 963–966, 967–970, 977–978.
12. Ibid., 971–973, gives a brief description of the two memoranda, which were transmitted to the State Department. For Konoe's remark, see Emmerson, *The Japanese Thread*, 267.
13. DOS, *Occupation*, 147–153. See Horwitz, "The Tokyo Trial," 483–493.
14. Horwitz, "The Tokyo Trial," 498.
15. Ibid., 495–496; Hata, *Nankin jiken*, 32. Horwitz stated (495) that an executive committee of the prosecutors selected the suspects to be indicted.
16. FU 6078/5/73, FO 371/57428, Gascoigne tel. 699 to London, June 24, 1946; Minear, *Victors' Justice*, 111, fns. 74, 75. Keenan told a news conference on June 17, 1946, that a decision was made "on high political levels" not to try the emperor and that although some prosecutors disagreed with this decision, Keenan personally felt the emperor was "a figurehead and fraud perpetrated on the Japanese people" (*NYT*, June 18, 1946, 1). MacArthur reportedly once told Keenan that if the emperor had been put on trial, he would have taken "all the responsibility" for Japan's entry into the war, presumably to shield others from punishment (POLAD desp. 782, Dec. 14, 1948, NRAW, RG 84, Box 2289).
17. MacArthur, *Reminiscences*, 288.
18. Horwitz, "The Tokyo Trial," 496.
19. Ibid., 496. Two other defendants, Hoshino Naoki and Kaya Okinori, were bureaucrats who had held important financial positions in Manchuria before the war.
20. Kido, *Kido Kōichi nikki*, vol. 2, for Dec. 10, 1945. See also Kojima, "Sempan risuto," 283–284.
21. Horwitz, "The Tokyo Trial," 494; Liu, "The Tokyo Trial," 168–170.
22. *In Re Yamashita*, 327 U.S. 1 (1946), 28; Manchester, *American Caesar*, 487.
23. MacArthur, *Reminiscences*, 295–296. Lt. Samuel S. Stratton, a naval language officer who participated in the defense of Yamashita and later became

a congressman from upstate New York, told MacArthur on October 28, 1945, that Yamashita had done his best to prevent atrocities by his forces. MacArthur said, "Let history decide" (int. with Stratton).

24. *Homma v. Steyer*, 327 U.S. 759 (1946); MacArthur, *Reminiscences*, 296–298; James, *The Years of MacArthur*, vol. 3, 94–102.

25. Harriman and Abel, *Special Envoy*, 544; Harry Kern, "Harry Kern's Story," *Yomiuri shimbun* (English ed.), Sept. 4, 1978, 7. MacArthur did not mention in his official review of the Homma case or in his *Reminiscences* that Homma had rejected Wainwright's offer to surrender.

26. Minear, *Victors' Justice*, 168, fn. 16; Kennan, *Memoirs*, 370; Weiner, "MacArthur Unjustifiably Accused." I am indebted to Charles Kades for giving me the Weiner article.

27. *PRJ*, 8–81, 482–488.

28. *PRJ*, 413.

29. *PRJ*, 431, Part I, para. 5 (b).

30. CINCAFPAC message to War Dept., CA 52394, Sept. 24, 1945, NRAW, Sutherland file; F 13031/2/23, FO 371/54105, Gascoigne ltr. no. 177 to Bevin, Sept. 9, 1946.

31. GS memo to chief of staff, "Removal and Exclusion of Undesirable Personnel from Public Office," Dec. 7, 1945, NRAS, RG 331, Box 2053.

32. CofS Marshall memo to chief, GS, Dec. 30, 1945, NRAS, RG 331, Box 2152; J. Williams, *Japan's Political Revolution*, 38–39; Baerwald, *The Purge*, 80; int. with Kades.

33. *PRJ*, 489.

34. Kades ltr. to Williams, July 17, 1974, JWC; Montgomery, *Forced to Be Free*, 26; *PRJ*, 42–44.

35. Int. with Kades; Borton, *Japan's Modern Century*, 412. Borton asserted the purge "went far beyond its original purpose. . . . Its arbitrary classifications brought unjust treatment to many." Reischauer, who was an army officer dealing with Japanese affairs during and after the war, said the purge affected many more Japanese than U.S. planners had anticipated (int. with Reischauer).

SCAP might have tried more Japanese as war crimes suspects under the broad language of its directives from Washington but concluded that an "extensive exclusion from influential positions" was preferable (CLKL).

36. Morita, *Made in Japan*, 48–49.

37. Inoki, *Hyōden Yoshida*, vol. 3, 103; Whitney, *MacArthur's Rendezvous*, 245–246. Yoshida asserted in his memoirs (*YM*, 68) that he never had such a meeting with MacArthur, but as Inoki said, Yoshida was almost certainly wrong.

38. *PRJ*, 17.

39. Whitney memo to supreme commander, Jan. 28, 1946, NRAS, RG 331, Box 2055. In an amicable meeting, Shidehara tried to get Whitney's agreement to a narrower interpretation of the purge order, but Whitney did not budge (CLKL).

40. Whitney memo to CINC, Feb. 11 1946, NRAS, RG 331, Box 2055.

41. Whitney memo to SC, Feb. 12, 1946, NRAS, RG 331, Box 2055. Whitney was indignant at this attempt to undercut purge policy, attributing it to a

conservative cabal in headquarters (CLKL). Those who think SCAP was dominated by New Dealers do not realize that conservatives such as Willoughby and Bunker also had a lot of influence.

42. Sebald, Oral History, NL, Special Collection, 551–552; see J. Williams, *Japan's Political Revolution*, 74–97, for a sympathetic portrait of Whitney.

43. Sone, *Watakushi no memoarū*, 132; J. Williams, *Japan's Political Revolution*, 33–51.

44. GS memo to CofS, Jan. 16, 1946, and GS memo to G-3, Jan. 25, 1946, NRAS, GS file, RG 331, Box 2187.

45. General Order no. 10, June 23, 1947, *PRJ*, 801.

46. Whitney memo to CINC, Feb. 11, 1946, NRAS, RG 331, Box 2055.

CHAPTER 7. THE NEW CONSTITUTION

1. MacArthur, *Reminiscences*, 302.

2. *KJ*, vol. 2. 60. The Japanese was Satō Tatsuō, former head of the Cabinet Legislative Bureau and author of one of the best works in Japanese on the 1946 constitution: Satō, *Nihonkoku kempō*.

3. J. Williams, *Japan's Political Revolution*, 40, 87, 284, fn. 14.

4. Atcheson memo to supreme commander, Oct. 4, 1945, NRAW, RG 84, Box 2276.

5. *FRUS, 1945*, vol. 6, 739–740, 757–758.

Shidehara may not have understood on October 11, 1945, that the supreme commander had "directed . . . the prime minister to initiate a constitutional revision" (*FRUS, 1945*, vol. 6, 841).

6. Ibid., 854–856. The basis for the supreme commander's optimism was not explained.

7. Ibid., 882–884. The text of SWNCC 228, which was not a directive to the supreme commander, is given in *FRUS, 1946*, vol. 8, 99–103. A careful study of SWNCC 228 by Williams of GS seemed to indicate that the drafters of the constitution knew of its existence and made some, but not extensive, use of it (Williams ltr. to Kades, Mar. 20, 1964, and Kades reply to Williams, Mar. 25, 1964, JWC).

8. Blakeslee, *The FEC*, 65–66.

9. *FRUS, 1945*, vol. 6, 855; *FRUS, 1946*, vol. 8, 169–172; J. Williams, *Japan's Political Revolution*, 23.

10. J. Williams, *Japan's Political Revolution*, 102–103; *FRUS, 1946*, vol. 8, 124; Etō (ed.), *Senryō shiroku*, vol. 3, 12. A specialist on the GS staff, Milo Rowell, was at the time making a study of constitutional issues. Kades got the impression from the questions asked by the Philippine representative and to some extent by the French member that they thought SCAP should be doing more about revising the constitution. His memo on the meeting was read by Whitney and MacArthur, and MacArthur "may have thought there was an implied criticism of him in the interchange" (CLKL). Two weeks later MacArthur decided to act on the constitution.

11. *PRJ*, 622–623. Kades was assisted in drafting the study by two other GS

attorneys, Alfred R. Hussey, Jr., and Milo Rowell. Kades said that he later had a long argument with his good friend, Ben Cohen, a prominent New Deal lawyer and postwar adviser to Secretary of State Byrnes, about the merits of the memo.

12. MacArthur, *Reminiscences*, 302; Whitney, *MacArthur's Rendezvous*, 247.

13. *Mainichi*, Feb. 1, 1946, 1; *PRJ*, 611–618; Masumi, *Postwar Politics*, 53; Inoki, *Hyōden Yoshida*, vol. 3, 108; Koseki, *Shinkempō no tanjō*, 73–80. Whitney thought the *Mainichi* article might have been a trial balloon floated by Yoshida to test U.S. reactions.

14. Whitney memo to supreme commander, Feb. 2, 1946, Hussey Papers no. 2, NDLT.

15. Whitney memo to CINC, Feb. 19, 1946, Hussey Papers no. 2, NDLT.

16. More has been written in the United States and Japan about the constitution than about any other occupation subject. There are many good accounts: *PRJ*, 101–111; McNelly, "'Induced Revolution,'" 76–106; J. Williams, *Japan's Political Revolution*, 107–118; Takayanagi Kenzō, "Making the Japanese Constitution: What Really Happened," *Japan Times*, Mar. 16, 1959. One of the most authoritative accounts is contained in the documents prepared by one of the main participants, Alfred R. Hussey, and now filed as the Hussey Papers, Library of the University of Michigan, and a copy in the Shidehara Peace Collection, NDLT. The account of the making of the constitution by Satō, *Nihon koku kempō*, is more complete and analytical than those in English. Two important contributions appeared in 1989: Koseki's scholarly *Shinkempō no tanjō*, and Kades's authoritative "The American Role." If Japan's constitution could be said to have a father, Kades would have a strong claim.

17. Hussey Papers, undated memo, NDLT, listing the GS personnel who wrote the draft; Rizzo ltr. to Hellegers, June 7, 1974, JWC. Among the political party drafts of a new constitution were one prepared by the Social Democratic Party and another by Takano Iwasaburō of the University of Tokyo. (See Koseki, "Shōchō tennōsei.")

18. Whitney's statement about the use of force appears in the record of the meeting with the Japanese made by GS. But several of the GS participants including Kades do not recall it, and one wrote an affidavit challenging the accuracy of the GS record (CLKL).

19. *PRJ*, 102. Why MacArthur suggested a unicameral legislature is not known. It may have been because the membership and function of the upper house in a restructured Diet would not be much different than that of the lower house, particularly because the peerage had been abolished, or possibly because MacArthur was impressed by the unicameral system in states such as Nebraska and Nevada (Rizzo ltr. to Hellegers, June 7, 1974, JWC).

20. Whitney memo to CINC, Feb. 6, 1946, Hussey Papers, NDLT; Kades memo for record, Mar. 12, 1946, Hussey Papers, NDLT; Borton, *Japan's Modern Century*, 424, fn 7.

21. James Michener, "The Secret of America," *Parade Magazine*, Sept. 15, 1985, 6.

22. The first draft of this provision, prepared by two young reserve officers, Richard A. Poole and George Nelson, stated that "an Imperial Throne shall be the symbol of the State, and an Emperor shall be the symbolic personification thereof." The word *symbol* in reference to the future role of the emperor seems to have been in the minds of several leading figures in Washington and Tokyo, as was the concept of a pacifist Japan. Prince Takamatsu, the emperor's brother, once asked Whitney and Kades what "symbol" meant, and they replied that for Americans it was something like the American flag (CLKL).

23. See Kawashima, "The Americanization."

24. *PRJ*, 104; Kades, "Revisiting." Kades, "The American Role," contains much of the same material.

25. Account based on Hussey Papers, NDLT. "Aghast" is the adjective used by Masumi, *Postwar Politics*, 55.

26. Hussey Papers, NDLT.

27. Whitney, *MacArthur's Rendezvous*, 252; Hussey Papers, NDLT.

28. *YM*, 133.

29. Whitney, *MacArthur's Rendezvous*, 251; Etō (ed.), *Senryō shiroku*, vol. 3, 41–42. Shirasu told the author that the GS account was all a "lie" and that no B-29 flew over at any time during the meeting (int. with Shirasu).

30. *PRJ*, 624; Etō (ed.), *Senryō shiroku*, vol. 3, 219–223.

31. GS memo for record, Feb. 18, 1946, Hussey Papers, NDLT; Etō (ed.), *Senryō shiroku*, vol. 3, 204–210.

32. Ashida Hitoshi, "Nikki," *Tōkyō shimbun*, entry of Mar. 12, 1979, 8. Ashida was welfare minister in the Shidehara cabinet.

33. Whitney memos to MacArthur, February 19 and 21, 1946, Hussey Papers, NDLT.

34. Ashida, "Nikki."

35. Masumi, *Postwar Politics*, 61; Hata, *Hirohito*, 216.

36. *PRJ*, 106, states the emperor fully supported the SCAP draft. Yoshida's views are contained in a recording of his recollections published in *Asahi shimbun*, Apr. 18, 1977, 2, and in *YM*, 135.

37. Memo of conversation between Narahashi and several GS officers, Feb. 25, 1946, Hussey Papers, NDLT.

38. Memo of meeting, Feb. 22, 1946, Hussey Papers, NDLT. The GS drafters opposed an amendment procedure requiring a two-thirds vote of all members of each house of the Diet and favored a two-thirds vote of the members of each house present and voting. Kades was at a loss to explain how the final version of the constitution came out with the more stringent provision and thought that General Whitney must have decided to go along with the Meiji Constitution version and Matsumoto Jōji's position (CLKL). At the meeting with Matsumoto on February 22, 1946, Whitney had seemed amenable to compromise on this issue.

39. *PRJ*, 625–630; int. with Kades. The Americans claimed that the Japanese used translation devices to change the meanings of Japanese words. For example, they tried and failed to substitute the word *seiji*, meaning "politics," for the word *seifu*, meaning "government," and *shikō*, meaning "supremacy," for *shuken*, meaning "sovereignty." (See Koseki, "Japaniz-

ing the Constitution," 239.)

40. Etō (ed.), *Senryō shiroku*, vol. 3, 236; ints. with Kades and Poole; CLKL. The first part of the thirty-hour session on March 4–5 was stormy. Not only did Matsumoto walk out of the meeting after his quarrel with Kades about translation points, but they had a curious tiff earlier over an unusual provision in the SCAP draft providing that "the ultimate fee to the land and to all natural resources reposes in the state as the collective responsibility of the people." Matsumoto opposed this. Williams called it the "Red Clause." The Americans agreed to delete the clause. (J. Williams, *Japan's Political Revolution*, 115–116.) In land-short Japan, especially in urban areas, this provision might have helped control large private holdings of real estate and exorbitant prices. See comment of Tsuru, "Nihon senryō," 208.

41. *FRUS, 1946*, vol. 8, 174; *PRJ*, 657; Etō (ed.), *Senryō shiroku*, vol. 3, 259–279, 279–288. When Shidehara showed the Tennō the final draft, he expressed the hope that the peerage could be retained, and Shidehara replied that would be quite impossible (int. with Etō). SCAP's original plan had been that the peerage would disappear as living peers died off, but when the Japanese side proposed immediate abolition, SCAP agreed (Takemae, "Kades Memoir," 284–285).

42. Borton, *Japan's Modern Century*, 424, fn. 7.

43. Blakeslee, *The FEC*, 48–55.

44. Ibid., 49.

45. Ibid., 50–51.

46. Ibid., 52.

47. Etō (ed.), *Senyō shiroku*, vol. 3, 43.

48. MacArthur, *Reminiscences*, 302–303; McNelly, "The Renunciation of War."

49. MacArthur, *Reminiscences*, 411; U.S. Congress, *Selected Speeches—Douglas MacArthur*, 86; McNelly, "General MacArthur's Pacifism."

50. Borton, *Japan's Modern Century*, 419–421; *FRUS, 1946*, vol. 8, 153–155; *FRUS, 1947*, vol. 6, 221.

51. Williams ltr. to author, Nov. 17, 1983; int. with Shirasu.

CHAPTER 8.   THE EMERGENCE OF YOSHIDA SHIGERU

1. DOS, *Occupation*, 136; Blakeslee, *The FEC*, 58, 59–63.

2. SCAPIN 677, *PRJ*, 477; Reischauer, *My Life*, 107–108. General MacArthur assumed all powers of government over Korea south of the Thirty-eighth Parallel on September 7, 1945, as commander of U.S. Army forces in the Far East but delegated operational command to Lieutenant General John R. Hodge, the commanding general of U.S. Army forces in Korea. All Japanese administrative authority there was terminated by a SCAP order of October 2, 1945, following a storm of protest in Korea that Japanese officials were being permitted to continue administrative functions. Nevertheless, both GS and POLAD in Tokyo were for some months involved in advising on policy for Korea. U.S. military government was established in the Ryukyus (Okinawa)

soon after the surrender of Japan; the Ryukyus were administered by the United States separately from Japan until 1972.

3. *PRJ*, 719–720.

4. Sone, *Watakushi no memoāru*, 138.

5. Ltrs. of May 4, 1947, JWC; *PRJ*, 494–495. The outstanding authority on the purge program in occupied Japan, Hans Baerwald, who served in GS, wrote that the purge of Hatoyama seemed to exemplify the view the "a case could be made supporting the purge of almost anyone" on the basis of the broad definitions in the January 4, 1946, purge directive (*The Purge*, 24).

6. *YM*, 72.

7. Inoki, *Hyōden Yoshida*, vol. 3, 144–152; *YM*, 72–74. Yoshida suggested several other possible candidates. One of these was Kojima Kazuo, an old-guard politician, who rejected the offer because of his age. The other was Matsudaira Tsuneo, a well-born former ambassador to the United States and minister of the imperial household, whom Hatoyama rejected. Some machine politicans in the Liberal Party opposed Yoshida as a political neophyte too old to be an effective leader.

8. Inoki, *Hyōden Yoshida*, vol. 3, 149–150; *YM*, 72–74.

9. Inoki, *Hyōden Yoshida*, vol. 3, 150–151; Masumi, *Postwar Politics*, 105–106; Takemi, *Nihon ishakai*, 12–14; *YM*, 75; Kōsaka, *One Hundred Million Japanese*, 87; int. with Asō Kazuko.

10. *YM*, 75; Inoki, *Hyōden Yoshida*, vol. 3, 105–106; Masumi, *Postwar Politics*, 106.

11. Yoshida ltr., May 15, 1946, MMA, RG 10, VIP file—Yoshida.

12. For the Japanese, the occupation was "primarily a MacArthur operation, secondarily an American operation, and only remotely an Allied operation" (Kawai, *Japan's American Interlude*, 18).

13. Yoshida's service as prime minister in five cabinets: May 22, 1946–May 24, 1947; October 19, 1948–February 16, 1949; February 16, 1949–October 30, 1952; October 30, 1952–May 21, 1953; May 21, 1953–December 10, 1954. He also served concurrently as foreign minister to the end of April 1952, when the San Francisco peace treaty came into force.

14. Inoki, *Hyōden Yoshida*, vol. 3, 186.

15. *YM*, 205; Masumi, *Postwar Politics*, 108; Iriye Sukemasa, Diary, entry of May 19, 1946, *Asahi shimbun*, Jan. 27, 1989, 4.

16. Sodei, *Makkāsā*, 97–122; *YM*, 200–201.

17. Inoki, *Hyōden Yoshida*, vol. 3, 165; Masumi, *Postwar Politics*, 110–111; Inoki, *Hyōden Yoshida*, vol. 3, 166.

18. Gayn, *Japan Diary*, 223.

19. Blakeslee, *The FEC*, 176.

20. Blakeslee, *The FEC*, 178; *PRJ*, 749; Draper ltr. to secretary of agriculture, Oct. 22, 1947, NRAS, Draper file, RG 335, Box 54; POLAD desp. 403, July 1, 1948, NRAS, RG 84, Box 2290; SCAP, *History of the Non-Military Activities*, monograph 4, 89; T. Cohen, *Remaking Japan*, 143–146.

21. Ladejinsky, "The Occupation and Japanese Agriculture, Oct. 1945 to Apr. 1952," desp. 164, June 3, 1952, NRAW, DOS file 894.20/6-352; Ball, *Japan*, 87–90. According to Nanto, "The United States' Role," U.S. aid in the

form not only of food but also of grains and agricultural supplies and fertilizer during the occupation totaled about $1.8 billion.

22. Kōsaka, *One Hundred Million Japanese*, 92.

23. *PRJ*, 750.

24. MacArthur, *Reminiscences*, 301; Maki (trans. and ed.), *Japan's Commission*, 80; *PRJ*, 110–111; Inoki, *Hyōden Yoshida*, vol. 3, 188; Koseki, *Shinkempō no tanjō*, 166–172.

25. Inoki, *Hyōden Yoshida*, vol. 3, 191, 195–197.

26. Ibid., 198–199; *YM*, 140.

27. Koseki, "Japanizing the Constitution," 236–238, states that recent research has established that Kanamori Tokujirō, not Ashida, was the author of the revised language approved by the House Subcommittee on the Constitution. Kades was certain, however, that Ashida, who was chairman of the subcommittee, brought the revision to him for approval, which he readily gave (int. with Kades). Earlier writers had all ascribed the concept and wording to Ashida. (See Inoki, *Hyōden Yoshida*, vol. 3, 200–202; Hata, *Nihon saigumbi*, 71–74.)

28. Int. with Hata; Koseki, "Japanizing the Constitution," 236–238.

29. Kades, "The American Role," 238.

30. Koseki, "Japanizing the Constitution," 235–236. See Takemae, "Kedeisu Nihon," 276. Kades later explained that because aliens in the United States did not in all cases in 1946 receive equal treatment with that of citizens, SCAP felt it would have been hypocritical to oppose the Japanese amendment (Kades ltr. of July 5, 1989, to author).

31. Whitney memo to MacArthur, July 17, 1946, Hussey Papers, NDLT; J. Williams, "Making the Japanese Constitution," 677. Williams staunchly defends the role of MacArthur and GS and lauds Yoshida's contribution; he makes only passing reference to the FEC.

32. Oppler, *Legal Reform*, 50.

33. DOS, *Activities of the FEC*, 65–67; Blakeslee, *The FEC*, 52–54; *PRJ*, 660.

34. DOS, *Activities of the FEC*, 65–66; Blakeslee, *The FEC*, 54–55.

35. DOS, *Activities of the FEC*, 65–66; Blakeslee, *The FEC*, 57; Koseki, "Japanizing the Constitution," 238; Kades, "The American Role," 30.

36. DOS, *Activities of the FEC*, 67; Blakeslee, *The FEC*, 58–61.

37. *YM*, 144–145; *FRUS, 1949*, vol. 7, 626–627. The Ashida government, which was in office when SCAP suggested the constitution be reviewed, started an examination but soon left office. The incoming Yoshida cabinet did not pursue the matter.

38. Etō (ed.), *Senryō shiroku*, vol. 3, 143; Bisson, *Nihon senryō*, 239.

39. J. Williams, "Making the Japanese Constitution," 676–678; *PRJ*, 111; Oppler, *Legal Reform*, 48.

40. *SCAP Monthly Summation* (Nov. 1946): 22–23.

41. *PRJ*, 682–683.

42. Maki (trans. and ed.), *Japan's Commission*; Ward, "The Commission."

43. MacArthur's letter is quoted in an article by commission chairman Takayanagi Kenzō in the *Japan Times*, Mar. 16, 1959, 8.

44. Yoshida ltr. to commission, "Kempō chōsakai daihachi-kai sōkai giji-

roku" (Commission on the constitution, minutes of 8th plenary meeting), Dec. 17, 1957, 1–11.

45. Maki (trans. and ed.), *Japan's Commission*, 85–86.

46. Kawashima T., *Nihonjin no hōishiki*, 39.

47. "Emperor Vows to Remain 'At One with the People,'" *Japan Times* (Weekly overseas ed.), Jan. 28, 1989.

CHAPTER 9. THE SECOND REFORM WAVE

1. Yoshida-MacArthur ltrs., Sept. 27, 1947, MMA, RG 10, Box 11.

2. *KJ*, vol. 1, 114–116; memo by Yamada, Sept. 17, 1946, Ministry of Foreign Affairs Records Office, reel 0226, Tokyo; *YM*, 54.

3. MacArthur said in *Reminiscences* (294), no doubt speaking for the record, that "the whole occupation would fail if we did not proceed from this one basic assumption—the reform had to come from the Japanese."

4. Sodei and Fukushima (eds.), *Makkāsā no kiroku*, 176; Hussey/Tilton memo to Whitney, Feb. 14, 1947, Hussey Papers, NDLT; Sodei, *Senryō*, 200.

5. Int. with Kades.

6. G-2 memo to chief of staff, June 7, 1947, "Leftist Personnel in GHQ," MMA, RG 23, Box 18, describes the background and activities of eleven alleged leftists in SCAP. Some of them were foreign born, and most reportedly had some connection with the Institute of Pacific Relations. Suspicion was also aroused because some were said to be friendly with American newsmen thought to be leftists. The memos were drafted by C. Nelson Spinks, a Stanford University Ph.D. and specialist in extremist movements in prewar Japan, who was then serving in G-2 and later became a senior officer in the State Department. Interestingly, Sir George Sansom remarked in his notes on his trip to Japan in 1946 that "many of . . . the younger men in SCAP drawn from civilian life have communistic leanings" and "these are visible in their work" (F 3595/2/23, FO 371/54086, Mar. 9, 1946). Only in very few cases was hard evidence produced that there were communists in SCAP.

7. Ozaki Shinae, the daughter of the famed octagenarian liberal and Diet member, Ozaki Yukio, once called Bunker to ask if her father could ride in the passenger car set aside for occupation personnel on Japanese trains when he traveled back and forth from his home in the country to Tokyo for Diet sessions. Bunker fixed this up (Bunker memo to MacArthur, Feb. 5, 1947, MMA, RG 5, Box 63).

8. *PRJ*, 30–31, 48, 435; Bisson, *Nihon senryō*, 122.

9. See Sodei and Fukushima (eds.), *Makkāsā no kiroku*, 191–202; Sodei, *Haikei makkāsā Gensui-sama*, an analysis of letters to MacArthur from Japanese. MacArthur received about one thousand letters a day, which the G-2 translation section scanned and sometimes translated (Mainichi [ed.], *Ichioku-nin no shōwashi*, vol. 2, 106).

10. Yoshida ltr. to the supreme commander, Oct. 22, 1946, MMA, RG 10, VIP file—Yoshida.

11. Whitney memo to CINC, Nov. 8, 1946, GS file, NRAS, RG 331, Box 2055.

12. *PRJ*, 496–498.

13. *YM*, 155–156; Yamada, *Beranme gaikōkan*, 86–89.

14. *PRJ*, 499, 500.

15. F 17621, FO 371/54163, Gascoigne ltr. to FO, Nov. 14, 1946. MacArthur also told Gascoigne he was planning to order a new election in the spring.

16. Ibid.

17. *PRJ*, 501–548; Baerwald, *The Purge*, 92, 94.

18. FJ 1017/44, FO 371/83807, Gascoigne desp. no. 162, June 7, 1950.

19. J. Cohen, *Japan's Economy*, 429; Yoshida-MacArthur ltrs., July 16, 19, and 25, 1946, MMA, RG 10, VIP file—Yoshida. The two tax laws enacted in October and November 1946 were the Wartime Indemnity Special Measures Law and the Capital Levy Law.

20. *PRJ*, 40; GS memo for record, Apr. 30, 1947, NRAS, GS file, RG 331, Box 2151; memo from Kades to Whitney, Oct. 25, 1947, Ishibashi file, GS (B) 03110, NDLT; Nolte, *Liberalism*, 305–320.

21. DOS, *Report of the Mission on Japanese Combines*, part 1. (Edwards Report)

22. T. Cohen, *Remaking Japan*, 368–369, 364. FEC-230 was sent to SCAP "for information" but not as an "interim directive" from the U.S. government. For various SCAP reservations about the Edwards report, see Hadley, *Antitrust*, 126–127.

23. Hadley, *Antitrust*, 163–165; remarks by Tristan Beplat, in Redford (ed.), *The Occupation*, 236–244; C. Johnson, *MITI*, 174–175.

24. Ball, *Japan*, 113–120.

25. *PRJ*, 753; *YM*, 200.

26. *YM*, 200.

27. *PRJ*, 577; Dore, *Land Reform*, 172–173. See Dore, *Shinohata*, 57–61, for a case study of the land reform program.

28. *PRJ*, 760; *YM*, 201–203; int. with Kades.

29. Inoki, *Hyōden Yoshida*, vol. 3, 215; F 3595/2/23, FO 371/54086, Mar. 9, 1946, Sansom diary, 34; *YM*, 168.

30. "6-3-3 System Not Imposed," *Japan Times Weekly* (International ed.), Oct. 4, 1986.

31. Wray, "The Trilateral Relationship"; Inoki, *Hyōden Yoshida*, vol. 3, 214–219; Kōsaka, *One Hundred Million Japanese*, 91; *YM*, 168=169.

32. Atcheson ltr. to Hilldring, Dec. 14, 1946, DOS file 840.2, NRAW. According to Reischauer, use of Chinese ideographs "is likely to fade slowly into primarily scholarly and official use," but even so language barriers contribute to making Japan "an isolated, inward-looking country beneath its cosmopolitan sheen," thus helping to create a psychological problem that "is probably the most significant fact about Japan today" (*The Japanese Today*, 384, 394).

33. Nishi, *Unconditional Democracy*, 196–198. In June 1948, at the instigation of GS, the Diet passed a resolution declaring that the imperial rescript on education was without effect and should be withdrawn from the education system, which would thereafter be governed by the concepts of the fundamental Law of Education (J. Williams, *Japan's Political Revolution*, 49).

34. *YM*, 167–175.

35. MacArthur, *Reminiscences*, 279; ltr. of Aug. 15, 1946, MMA, RG 10, VIP file—Yoshida; *KJ*, vol. 1, 117. When American newsmen later criticized Yoshida for opposing MacArthur and his reforms, Yoshida reportedly denied the charge and stated that he followed Admiral Suzuki's advice—namely, go along with the general (Matsumoto, "Kaisō").

36. Naganuma, "Tennō-Makkāsā," 27–30.

37. Toyoshita, "Tennō-Makkāsā."

38. F 13031/2/23, FO 371/54105, Gascoigne tel. 177 to Bevin, Sept. 9, 1946.

CHAPTER 10.   THE 1947 LABOR CRISIS AND THE
DEFEAT OF YOSHIDA

1. See Takemae, *Sengo rōdō kaikaku*, 157–177; Masumi, *Postwar Politics*, 115–135, for accounts of the 1947 strike threat.

2. *PRJ*, 762; T. Cohen, *Remaking Japan*, 294. Although Cohen claimed he and Marquat wrote MacArthur's statement (286), MacArthur did it himself, according to Frank Sackton, then a colonel who was secretary of the joint SCAP/FEC staff (int. with Sackton).

3. Borton, "The Allied Occupation," 397–398; Farley, *Aspects*, 39, 190.

4. DOS, *Activities of the FEC*, vol. 1, 91–93; Takemae, "GHQ Labor Policy," 102.

5. Masumi, *Postwar Politics*, 113–115; Takemae, *Sengo rōdō kaikaku*, 158; J. Moore, *Japanese Workers*, 229–233.

6. Inoki, *Hyōden Yoshida*, vol. 3, 271–272; F 15640 G, FO 317/54109, Gascoigne tel. to FO, Oct. 25, 1946; Farley, *Aspects*, 186.

7. Takemae, *Sengo rōdō kaikaku*, 161–162.

8. T. Cohen, "Labor Democratization," 187.

9. The unions were asking for a ¥1,800 monthly wage, about equal to $22.50; Masumi, *Postwar Politics*, 119.

10. RLED, Jan. 26, 29, and 30, 1947, May 10, 1947.

11. Masumi, *Postwar Politics*, 130–132; Asahi Shimbun (ed.), *The Pacific Rivals*, 174–177; J. Moore, *Japanese Workers*, 239.

12. *PRJ*, 424, 436, 433; Bisson, *Nihon senryō*, 174; Garon, "The Imperial Bureaucracy," 450.

13. Inoki, *Hyōden Yoshida*, vol. 3, 273.

14. *KJ*, vol. 1, 146; Shinobu, *Sengo Nihon seiji-shi*, vol. 2, 458; int. with Inoki; Farley, *Aspects*, 154.

15. F 1618, FO 371/63690, Gascoigne tel. to FO, Feb. 6, 1947; Inoki, *Hyōden Yoshida*, vol. 3, 268.

16. J. Moore, *Japanese Workers*, 241–243.

17. Gluck, "Entangling Illusions," 206. "Reverse course" has various meanings for students of the occupation. Interpreted narrowly, its meaning is generally accepted as emphasis on economic recovery over reform, beginning in about 1947. The extreme interpretation by some scholars—Japanese and American—is that the occupation began in about 1947 to abandon reform, or even cancel some reforms, and increasingly sought to involve Japan in cold war

politics as a partner of the United States and its allies. See Dower, "Rethinking World War II," 166, for a moderate revisionist interpretation of shifting trends during the occupation.

18. Whitney, *MacArthur's Rendezvous*, 246–247. See Ōhtake, "Postwar Politics"; J. Moore, "Production Control," 2–3; J. Moore, *Japanese Workers*, 101–108.

19. Garon, *The State and Labor*, 237.

20. *PRJ*, 721.

21. F 15640, FO 371/54109, Gascoigne tel. to FO, Oct. 25, 1946; F 17576, FO 371/54163, Gascoigne tel. 1454. to FO, Dec. 7, 1946.

22. F 1618, FO 371/63696, Gascoigne tel. 163, Feb. 9, 1947; Yoshida ltr. to MacArthur, Feb. 10, 1947, JWC.

23. Williams, *Japan's Political Revolution*, 175–177; Inoki, *Hyōden Yoshida*, vol. 3, 281–282. The view in SCAP, and probably that of General MacArthur, seemed to be that neither of the two electoral systems the Japanese had used could be said to be clearly more democratic than the other (Takemae, "Kedeisu Nihon," 286–288).

24. *KJ*, vol. 1, 151–152; Inoki, *Hyōden Yoshida*, vol. 3, 283–284.

25. GS files states that Yoshida was "screened and passed" on Mar. 12, 1947, because he had retired to private life in 1938 and was not drawn into any wartime or nationalist activities "that might compromise his present position" as president of the Democratic Liberal Party (GS name file, NDLT).

26. Kawashima T., *Nihonjin no hōishiki*, 39.

27. Blakeslee, *The FEC*, 61–63; James, *The Years of MacArthur*, vol. 3, 139–141.

28. *PRJ*, 196–198, 679, 680, 724–725; Oppler, *Legal Reform*, 75, 165–168; Oppler memo to Whitney, Apr. 30, 1947, NRAS, GS file, RG 331, Box 2142; J. Williams, *Japan's Political Revolution*, 273–279; *Kodansha Encyclopedia of Japan*, vol. 5, 65–66; Yamada, *Beranme gaikōkan*, 102–105.

29. MacArthur ltr. to Yoshida, Mar. 22, 1947, MMA, RG 10, VIP file—Yoshida; Inoki, *Hyōden Yoshida*, vol. 3, 296.

30. Int. with Tsuru; Yoshida ltr. to MacArthur, Mar. 28, 1947, MMA, RG 10, VIP file—Yoshida.

31. C. Johnson, *MITI*, 181–183; J. Cohen, *Japan's Economy*, 448; Patrick, "The Phoenix Risen," 306.

32. Yoshida ltr. to MacArthur, Dec. 3, 1946, MMA, RG 10, Box 11; Arisawa (ed.), *Shōwa keizaishi*, vol. 2, 55–59; Uchino, *Japan's Postwar Economy*, 36–37; Ōkita, *Watakushi no rirekisho*, 70–74; Yoshida ltr. to MacArthur, Dec. 11, 1946, MMA, RG 10, Box 11.

33. J. Cohen, *Japan's Economy*, 470; Yoshida ltr. to MacArthur, Dec. 11, 1946, MMA, RG 10, VIP file—Yoshida; C. Johnson, *MITI*, 185.

34. Dickover letter to McCoy, file of U.S. delegation to FEC, NRAW, RG 43, Box 239; Schonberger, *Aftermath of War*, 99–102; Tsurumi, *Japanese Business*, 84–85.

35. Takemae, *Sengo rōdō kaikaku*, 343.

36. *PRJ*, 323–337; Inoki, *Hyōden Yoshida*, vol. 3, 289–290; Masumi, *Postwar Politics*, 139–141.

37. *PRJ*, 767.

38. Ibid., 348–349; YM, 85–86.

39. Masumi, *Postwar Politics*, 141–146; Inoki, *Hyōden Yoshida*, vol. 3, 291–292; Katayama Naikaku, *Katayama Tetsu*, 222–223.

40. Yoshida ltr. to MacArthur, May 24, 1947, MMA, RG 5, Box 62, military secretary correspondence.

41. Yoshida-Whitney exchange, JWC.

42. YM, 83–84.

43. Borton, "Proposals," 19.

CHAPTER 11.   MACARTHUR, THE ALLIES,
AND WASHINGTON

1. *PRJ*, 422, 746–748. The supreme commander instructed that all directives to the Japanese government on substantive matters be sent in advance to the ACJ for comment or concurrence (CofS memo, Apr. 19, 1946, CIE file, RG 84, Box 5148, NDLT). The Australian member of the ACJ also represented the United Kingdom, New Zealand, and India.

2. Early in the occupation MacArthur considered that he held the protocol rank of "semi-sovereign," equal to that of a viceroy (MacArthur tel. to Steyer, June, 26, 1946, MMA, RG 5, Box 2). In remarks to the political adviser in 1950, MacArthur gave himself a promotion; he said he did not see why he should meet with the chiefs of foreign diplomatic missions in Tokyo. "And why, as a sovereign, should I? President Truman doesn't do so, nor does the King of England" (Sebald, *With MacArthur*, 119).

3. F 13031/2/23, FO 371/54105, Gascoigne ltr. 177 to Bevin, Sept. 9, 1946. Malik was a Japan specialist in the Soviet diplomatic service. He played a key role in negotiations at the United Nations in 1949 to end the Berlin airlift.

4. Minutes of second ACJ meeting, NRAW, RG 59, Box 3815; Ball, *Japan*, 25–26; memo entitled "Allied Council—General Whitney," Apr. 25, 1946, JWC.

5. POLAD cable 3353 to Washington, Apr. 5, 1946, NRAW, file 740.0019—Japan.

6. See Sebald, *With MacArthur*, 126–150, for an authoritative account of ACJ proceedings.

7. Ibid., 136–137. The Soviet government stated on May 20, 1949, that only 594,000 Japanese military personnel were taken prisoner at the end of the war. The Soviets added that 70,880 were immediately freed, 418,166 were repatriated to Japan between December 1, 1946, and May 1, 1949, and the remaining 95,000 [*sic*] would be returned by November 1949, except for a few war crimes suspects still under investigation (*FRUS, 1949*, vol. 7, 754). In 1990 a Soviet official stated that 60,000 Japanese prisoners of war had died in captivity and that the USSR would give Japan a list of their names and gravesites (*Japan Times* [Weekly international ed.], Dec. 3–9, 1990, 4).

8. *FRUS, 1947*, vol. 7, 177–179.

9. Ibid., 323–325.

10. Tucker, "Gen. S. M. Chu"; Dingman, "The View"; Atcheson ltr. to Acheson, Dec. 6, 1946, NRAW, file 740.00119 Control (Japan)/12-646; Atche-

son letter to Penfield, NRAW, 740.00119 Control (Japan)/12-1046; *FRUS, 1946*, vol. 8, 354–356.

11. MacArthur, *Reminiscences*, 292. MacArthur thought the United States should have used its veto power freely to prevent undesirable FEC actions. U.S. representatives wished to avoid use of the veto as far as was practical.

12. Asakai, *Shoki tainichi*, vol. 1, 211–252.

13. *FRUS, 1945*, vol. 6, 603–609; DOS, *Occupation*, 89–94; Willoughby (ed.), *The Reports of General MacArthur*, vol. 1, supplement, 62–63.

14. DOS memo for record by Green, Jan. 25, 1949, NRAW, RG 84, Box 2293.

15. *FRUS, 1946*, vol. 8, 329–332; War Dept. memo to DOS, May 23, 1946, DOS general file.

16. Harriman and Abel, *Special Envoy*, 533–534; Blakeslee, *The FEC*, 132.

17. DOS, *Activities of the FEC*, vol. 1, 68–76; ltrs. of Oct. 23 and Nov. 10, 1946, MMA, RG 10, VIP file—Yoshida.

18. Blakeslee, *The FEC*, 135–141. The United States used its authority under the terms of reference of the FEC to issue interim directives only a few times.

19. *PRJ*, 765–767; Sebald, *With MacArthur*, 244.

20. F 15640 G, FO 371/54109, tel. 1257 to London, Oct. 26, 1946.

21. F 3970/1/23, FO 371/63646, tel. 364 to London, Mar. 20, 1947.

22. "Washington Deaf to MacArthur Plan," *NYT*, Mar. 19, 1947; Hilldring memo to Peterson, May 31, 1947, DOS files, RG 59, 740.0011, Peace, NRAW; *FRUS, 1947*, vol. 6, 453.

23. Borton, "The Allied Occupation," 422.

24. Dunn, *Peace-Making*, 56, fn.

25. Murphy, *Diplomat*, 307.

26. *YM*, 136.

27. See Manchester, *American Caesar*, 308–312, 353–363. Schonberger, "The General," gives a detailed account of MacArthur's presidential efforts.

28. RLED, Oct. 20, 1945; Millis (ed.), *The Forrestal Diaries*, 325; RLED, July 26 and Sept. 11, 1947; Clifton Daniel, *NYT Magazine*, June 3, 1984, 17. MacArthur also told the representative of the British prime minister in Tokyo in late 1947 that he thought it unlikely Eisenhower could get the Republican nomination "as he was not considered a good Republican and as he had Jewish blood in his veins" (F 16902/23G, FO 371/63830, UKLM 1645, Dec. 26, 1947). MacArthur wrote in *Reminiscences* (96) that FDR once told him, "I think you are our best general, but I believe you would be our worst politician."

29. MacArthur ltr. to MacNider, Oct. 14, 1947, GS files, NRAS, RG 331, box 2155.

30. *NYT*, Jan. 24, 1948, 2; CLM desp. 110, Apr. 13, 1948, Ottawa file 521-2

31. Manchester, *American Caesar*, 521–522.

32. John Osborne, "My Dear General," *Life*, Nov. 27, 1950, 127–141.

33. Sebald, *With MacArthur*, 106.

34. MacArthur, *Reminiscences*, 319.

35. Two senior staff officers who saw MacArthur frequently, Sebald and

Bunker, said they did not hear any talk about American politics around head-quarters at that time (ints. with Sebald and Bunker).

36. *Newsweek*, Dec. 1, 1947, 36–38; Schonberger, "Zaibatsu Dissolution," 327–359. See *Fortune* (Sept. 1948), 6, 10; U.S. Senate, *Congressional Record*, 80th Cong., 2nd sess. (1947–1948), 94, pt. 1, 116–119, 299–301.

37. *PRJ*, 780, 783.

38. Ibid., 783. By 1948 MacArthur had become equivocal on the zaibatsu issue. W. R. Herod, an American businessman, on Jan. 12, 1948, rephrased the general as saying, "Thank God he had stopped FEC-230 by putting it in his desk. He said that neither Lovett nor Marshall had even read it." "Harry Kern's Story (5)," *Yomiuri* (English ed.), Sept. 8, 1979, 7.

39. *Newsweek*, Jan. 27, 1947, 40; *PRJ*, 549; *Newsweek*, June 23, 1947, 37–42.

40. "American Council on Japan Formed," *Yomiuri* (English ed.), Sept. 5, 1979; Schonberger, "The Japanese Lobby," 327–359; Millis (ed.), *The Forrestal Diaries*, 328. Little hard evidence has been unearthed, despite considerable scholarly activity, to show that American policies toward Japan were much influenced by the American Council. For example, Kennan said in 1981 that he knew little about Kern or the American Council (int. with Kennan). Sebald said much the same thing (int. with Sebald). Kern, however, felt that some decisions in Washington had been influenced by his reports, including the decision in 1951 to relieve MacArthur (int. with Kern). Kern's articles in *Newsweek* probably had more influence than the work of the American Council on Japan.

41. James, *The Years of MacArthur*, vol. 3, 304. On one occasion MacArthur was so incensed by an article in the *Times* of London that he had the British ambassador called out of a reception celebrating the king's birthday, at which the ambassador was host, to demand a retraction by the correspondent, Frank Hawley, who was a frequent target of complaint by both MacArthur and Yoshida (FJ 1611/5, FO 371/84037, Gascoigne tel. 382, June 8, 1950).

42. Coughlin, *Conquered Press*, 51–52.

43. Baldwin, Oral History, No. 159A, Columbia University Library, 1961; "Trial Balance," *Time*, July 14, 1947, 11–12. In response to Baldwin's criticisms, MacArthur wrote Draper on July 29, 1948, that he was reducing controls (precensorship of the press and media may have been one of these) but could not eliminate them completely (Draper file, NRAS, RG 335, Box 53). G-2 SCAP considered Baldwin "favorable to communism" (G-2 memo of July 15, 1950, to CIE, NRAS, RG 331, Box 509). It is noteworthy that MacArthur maintained a large and active intelligence organization throughout the occupation (SCAP, *History of the Non-Military Activities*, monograph 8, 231–267).

CHAPTER 12. THE FAILURE OF COALITION POLITICS

1. *PRJ*, 770; Ball, *Japan*, 73–75.

2. *SCAP Monthly Summation* (May 1947), 28; Sodei and Fukushima, *Makkāsā no kiroku*, 214.

3. Masumi, *Postwar Politics*, 147; *PRJ*, 726.

4. Katayama ltr. of Sept. 4, 1947, MMA, RG 10, VIP file—Katayama.
5. War tel. 91108 from Royall to MacArthur, Nov. 25, 1947, and tel. from MacArthur to Royall, Dec. 9, 1947, both in Draper file, NRAS, RG 335, Box 18; Watanabe T., *Senryōka*, 74.
6. Amakawa, *Senryō seisaku*, 225–227.
7. *PRJ*, 291–304; Pulliam memo, Aug. 18, 1947, NRAS, RG 331, Box 277; memo from Willoughby to Bratton, Aug. 24, 1947, NRAS, RG 331, Box 277.
8. *PRJ*, 703–704, 705–706. MacArthur met with his experts on September 5 and instructed them to work out their differences (Pulliam memo, Dec. 1. 1947, NRAS, RG 331, Box 278).
9. *PRJ*, 297.
10. Fifty-eighth special meeting of the ACJ, Apr. 28, 1948, NRAW, RG 59, Box 3825; Auer, *The Postwar Rearmament*, 4.
11. Int. with Shirasu; Garon, *The State and Labor*, 244–245.
12. Pharr, "The Politics of Women's Rights," 234–245; Upham, *Law and Social Change*, 156–165, 214–218.
13. *PRJ*, 215; Oppler, *Legal Reform*, 119.
14. *PRJ*, 770.
15. Nugent memo to supreme commander, Oct. 7, 1947, MMA, RG 5, Box 11.
16. Memo of Jan. 26, 1948, GS (B) file 01287, RG 5, Box 2152, NDLT; Nishi, *Unconditional Democracy*, 44–45.
17. Int. with Nichols; Bowers, "The Late General MacArthur," 164; James, *The Years of MacArthur*, vol. 3, 292; Gunther, *The Riddle*, 75; F 1416/1015/23, FO 371/76179, Gascoigne tel. 11 of Jan. 8, 1949, enclosing ltr. of CLM reporting on talk with MacArthur.
18. Masumi, *Postwar Politics*, 149–151; Baerwald, *The Purge*, 54–57; Inoki, *Hyōden Yoshida*, vol. 3, 302–303; Oppler, *Legal Reform*, 227–229; memo for record, Kades's conference with prime minister, Oct. 25, 1947, NRAS, GS file, RG 331; memo for record, Oppler's conference with Chief Justice Tanaka, June 19, 1950, NRAS, GS—Napier file, RG 331.
19. Masumi, *Postwar Politics*, 151–155; *PRJ*, 714.
20. F 3588, FO 371/69519, desp. 36 to London, Feb. 13, 1948.
21. 1947 constitution, Art. 7, *Kodansha Encyclopedia of Japan*, vol. 2, 10.
22. F 4984, FO 371/69820, desp. 67 to London, Mar. 19, 1948.
23. Katayama Naikaku, *Katayama Tetsu*, 397–399; Morito, "Katayama naikaku," vol. 6, 127.
24. F 3588, FO 371/69519, desp. 36 to London, Feb. 13, 1948.
25. Masumi, *Postwar Politics*, 157; GS/CIE press statement of Feb. 24, 1948, GS file, NRAS, RG 331, Box 272; Bunker memo to CINC, Feb. 27, 1948, MMA, RG 5, Box 63.
26. Baerwald, *The Purge*, 95–96.
27. CLM desp. no. 110 to Ottawa, Apr. 13, 1948, 40 50061 v. 4; F 14233/5129/23, UKLM quarterly report, Oct. 1, 1947.
28. *PRJ*, 734; CLM desp. no. 176 to Ottawa, May 27, 1947, 40 50061 v. 4.
29. Memo on Ashida, Draper conference, Mar. 24, 1948, Draper/Dupuy file, NRAS, RG 319, Box 19; *PRJ*, 581–583; J. Williams, *Japan's Political Revolu-*

tion, 217. See Takemae, *Sengo rōdō kaikaku*, 209–250, for an account of the revision of the NPSL.

30. *PRJ*, 258; MacArthur appointment schedule, July 6, 1948, MMA, RG 5, Box 65; Takemae, *Sengo rōdō kaikaku*, 231. Kades letter to Williams, June 3, 1974, JWC. Some confusion exists in the records as to whether the Mac-Arthur meeting was on July 6 or July 21, but the latter date seems probable (T. Cohen, *Remaking Japan*, 390).

31. *PRJ*, 581–583.

32. Takemae, *Sengo rōdō kaikaku*, 236–237.

33. *SD*, Aug. 9 and July 30, 1948.

34. Blakeslee, *The FEC*, 172–175; CLM desp. no. 383 to Ottawa, Sept. 13, 1948, 40 50061, v. 4; F 14472, F 14107/144/25, FO 371/69824, Gascoigne tel. to London 1172, Oct. 16, 1948.

35. C 63093, SCAP tel. to Draper, Aug. 18, 1948, MMA, RG 9, Blue Binder series, Labor; Z 21291, SCAP to DA, Aug. 29, 1948, MMA, RG 9, Blue Binder series, Labor. The State Department, presumably through the Department of the Army, sent General MacArthur a long and closely reasoned telegram in early October commending his handling of the issues but recommending clearer separation of employees of the Japanese government engaged in industrial activities from other civil servants and further refinement of the types of industrial employees involved (*FRUS, 1948*, vol. 6, 866–870). Speaking through General Whitney, MacArthur replied that there was no policy statement applicable to public servants; therefore, he had discretion to act as the sole executive authority of the Allied powers, implying that he was free to act as he saw fit. This of course begged the key question, which was whether the FEC policy applied to all workers or only to those in private sector–type activities (C-64458, SCAP tel. to Draper, Oct. 12, 1948, MMA, RG 9, Blue Binder series, Labor).

36. Farley, *Aspects*, 205–207; C. Johnson, *Japan's Public Policy Companies*, 28–30. As part of this reorganization, the government obtained passage of the Public Coporations and National Enterprises Labor Relations Law.

37. Memos of conversations between Whitney and chief cabinet secretary Masuda, Nov. 19 and 25, 1949, reel 0046,0048, Japanese FO files. See also GS memo, "Reply to Aide Memoire Dated Dec. 2, 1949," Dec. 6, 1949, GS file, NDLT.

38. Whitney-Masuda coversations, reel 0046,0048, Japanese FO file; Watanabe T., *Watanabe Takeshi nikki*, 688–689; int. with Suzuki G.; SCAP, *History of the Non-Military Activities*, monograph 13, 66; Pempel, "The Tar Baby Target," 179; C. Johnson, *MITI*, 43.

39. Baerwald, *The Purge*, 80; Shimoda, *Sengo Nihon gaikō*, vol. 1, 39; Suzuki E., *Nihon senryō*, 68–71. A GS report in 1946 stated, "The Japanese bureaucrat . . . has been nurtured on the idea that the government is supreme, that the authority of the state is unchallengeable by the people and that the government knows what is good for the people and does what it wills toward the people" (Maki memo to Whitney, "The Japanese Bureaucracy," July 18, 1946, GS [B], NDLT). See Pempel, "The Tar Baby Target," 165–167; Wolferen, *The Enigma of Japanese Power*, 348. Of the 1,809 purged government employees, two-thirds were members of the Dai Nihon Butokukai (Japan Mili-

tary Virtue Society), a government-supported society that promoted martial arts (*PRJ*, 67–72).

40. Masumi, *Postwar Politics*, 158–161; Inoki, *Hyōden Yoshida*, vol. 3, 316–318.

41. *PRJ*, 307–313; J. Williams, *Japan's Political Revolution*, 45–47; T. Cohen, *Remaking Japan*, 334–350.

42. Masumi, *Postwar Politics*, 159–161; Inoki, *Hyoden Yoshida*, vol. 3, 318–319. Kades was rumored to have been involved, but no credible evidence was produced to implicate him.

CHAPTER 13. END OF THE WAR CRIMES TRIALS:
THE EMPEROR DECIDES NOT TO ABDICATE

1. *FRUS, 1948*, vol. 6, 898–907. Harries and Harries, *Sheathing the Sword*, 95–182, gives a good account of the Tokyo trial.

2. Röling and Rüter (eds.), *The Tokyo Judgment*, vol. 1, 22. This book contains in two volumes the counts of the indictment, the judgment, the concurring and dissenting opinions, and the sentences.

3. *NYT*, Oct. 2, 1946, 1, 20; Sebald, *With MacArthur*, 167–169.

4. *FRUS, 1948*, vol. 6, 908.

5. MacArthur, *Reminiscences*, 328–329; Hata, *Nankin jiken*, 25. General MacArthur told President Truman at their conference on Wake Island on Oct. 15, 1950, that "war crimes trials don't work, they don't deter" (MMA, RG 5, Box 1B).

6. Brackman, *The Other Nuremberg*, 350: Ball, *Japan*, 110. Colonel J. Stanton Babcock, who had served in Japan before the war as an army attaché and who went there in early 1946 with the FEAC, reported on the basis of talks with many Japanese that "there was no feeling of guilt; not even that they had made a mistake. The attitude was that of men who had taken a desperate but necessary gamble, done everything possible to ensure success, but had lost. . . . They had had to go to war. They knew that their only chance lay in prolonging the war to the point where we would tire and give up. They failed" (*FRUS, 1946*, vol. 8, 162).

7. Minear, *Victors' Justice*, 114–115.

8. Röling and Rüter (eds.), *The Tokyo Judgment*, vol. 1, 380. The Japanese note could be interpreted as an ultimatum and therefore constituted adequate notice to the United States of Japan's intention to commence hostilities.

9. F 2130/48/23, FO 371/69831, Gascoigne desp. 19 to London, Jan. 25, 1948; Brackman, *The Other Nuremberg*, 154–162.

10. U 8295/5/73, FO 371/57428, FO minute, Jan. 7, 1947.

11. Sebald, *With MacArthur*, 157; F 14947/12434/23, FO 371/63820, Nov. 10, 1947, Gascoigne tel. 1492; CLM desp. to Ottawa, no. 185, July 2, 1948, 40 50061 v. 4.

12. Röling and Rüter (eds.), *The Tokyo Judgment*, vol. 1, 27–43, 439–442; Comyns-Carr, "The Tokyo War Crimes Trial," 109–110.

13. Ibid., 514, 496; Sebald, *With MacArthur*, 164. See Bergamini, *Japan's Imperial Conspiracy*, ix–xv.

14. Piccigallo, *The Japanese on Trial*, 29–31; Röling and Rüter (eds.), *The Tokyo Judgment*, vol. 2, 517–1148.

15. 338 *U.S. Reports* 197, June 29, 1949; *FRUS, 1948*, vol. 6, 937.

16. This account including the Tōjō poem is from Sebald, *With MacArthur*, 172–176.

17. MacArthur, *Reminiscences*, 318–319. MacArthur was ordered by Royall, with the agreement of Truman, to permit photographers at the executions (War tel. 80163, Nov. 25, 1948, Draper file, NRAS, RG 335, Box 18). MacArthur objected and proposed that the issue be taken to the FEC (SCAP tel. 65707, Nov. 26, 1948, Draper file, NRAS, RG 335, Box 18). Royall backed down and authorized MacArthur to handle the matter (personal unnumbered tel. from Royall to MacArthur, Nov. 26, 1948, Draper file, NRAS, RG 335, Box 18). This was one of only two occasions during the occupation where the supreme commander opposed direct orders by his superiors in Washington. The other was War tel. 91108 of Nov. 25, 1947, Draper file, NRAS, RG 335, Box 18, regarding deconcentration.

18. Sanmonji, "Tōkyō gunji saiban," vol. 5, 302–308; *Washington Post*, Apr. 21, 1979, 3.

19. *FRUS, 1948*, vol. 6, 936–937. SCAP wanted to try seventeen of them as Class B and C war criminals, but Washington said this would require the approval of the FEC. After studying the IMTFE judgment, SCAP lawyers decided against trial of all but two, both former admirals, who were then tried for Class B and C war crimes. Some observers have claimed that failure to try important suspects like Kishi and Kodama reflected a reversal in U.S. war crimes policy. A more realistic view is that Washington and SCAP felt that one Class A trial was enough.

20. Mainichi (ed.), *Ichiokunin no shōwashi*, vol. 2, 192–193, 202.

21. Yoshida request, Dec. 8, 1948, MMA, RG 5, Box 63; Inoki, *Hyōden Yoshida*, vol. 3, 384–386. This action won Yoshida considerable goodwill from former Japanese military men. Yoshida also submitted a deposition in Shigemitsu's defense in the Class A trial.

22. Mainchi (ed.), *Ichiokunin no shōwashi*, vol. 2, 192; Reischauer, *The United States and Japan*, 242–243.

23. CINCFE tel. C 53663, June 27, 1947, MMA, RG 9, Box 155; Brackman, *The Other Nuremberg*, 196–197.

24. CINCFE tel. C 52423, May 6, 1947, MMA, RG 9, Box 155; SWNCC 351/3, Mar. 11, 1948, NRAW, Military Records, Taylor biological warfare file; OSD historian Goldberg memo to Oldaker, Apr. 14, 1977, NRAW, Military Records, Taylor biological warfare file.

25. *Japan Times*, Aug. 29, 1982, 12; CINCFE tel. C 52423, May 6, 1947, MMA, RG 9, WC 147; Piccigallo, *The Japanese on Trial*, 150–154; *Japan Times*, Sept. 5, 1982, 10. See F 18863/1661/23, FO 371/76254, Gascoigne tel. 1358, Dec. 15, 1949.

26. *DOSB*, Feb. 13, 1950, 244; DA tel. W 99564, Feb. 15, 1950, MMA, RG 9, WC 307; SCAP tel. C 55407, Mar. 15, 1950, MMA, RG 9, WC 312.

27. Brackman, *The Other Nuremberg*, 200; U.S. House, *The Treatment*, 3–5, 9, 16–18, 33, 63. The Japanese involved allegedly told American interro-

gators that no experiments were performed on Americans for fear of possible retaliation by the United States (*NYT*, Mar. 22, 1983, A2).

28. Gomer, Powell, and Röling, "Japan's Biological Weapons"; Morimura, *Akuma no hōshoku*.

29. P. Williams and Wallace, *Unit 731*, xiv, 130, 133, 207.

30. Takeyama, "Questions"; Onuma, "Beyond Victor's Justice."

31. See Smith, *Road*, 132–151.

32. MacArthur, *Reminiscences*, 319; Kawai, *Japan's American Interlude*, 23–24.

33. Shiroyama, *War Criminal*, 290.

34. CLM desp. to Ottawa, no. 196, June 17, 1948, file 104-C(S).

35. Ibid.

36. Sebald, *With MacArthur*, 162; *SD*, Oct. 8, 1948, and Oct. 28, 1948; Sebald ltr. to Benninghoff, Oct. 29, 1948, NRAW, DOS file, 894.001/10.2948.

37. Tajima ltr. to supreme commander, Nov. 12, 1948, MMA, RG 5, Box 27; *Yomiuri shimbun*, Aug. 15, 1978, 1; Reuters ticker, R 940, Dec. 4, 1979; Iriye Sukemasa, Diary entry of Nov. 12, 1948, *Asahi shimbun*, Feb. 1, 1989, 4; F 1380, FO 371/70256, Gascoigne ltr. no. 11, Jan. 13, 1949. Sebald asserted that by late 1948 "the throne . . . was established as an invaluable adjunct of SCAP" (*With MacArthur*, 164).

38. F 1380, FO 371/70256, Gascoigne ltr. no. 11 to FO, Jan. 13, 1949.

39. FJ 10111/34, FO 371/83815, Gascoigne desp. no. 148, May 22, 1950; FJ 10111/39, FO 371/83815, Gascoigne desp. no. 158, May 31, 1950. The English tutor would presumably have taken the place of Elizabeth Gray Vining, an American Quaker, who served as tutor to the crown prince from 1946 to 1950. MacArthur arranged a meeting between the emperor and Henry R. Luce, the editor of *Time*, on Nov. 6, 1946. Luce said that he asked the emperor how it felt to be a mortal after having been a god for so long, but the interpreter politely reworded the question into something innocuous (Swanberg, *Luce*, 249). The general also arranged for Lord and Lady Killearn to call on their majesties, who obviously enjoyed hobnobbing with British nobility (F 2024/2023/23, FO 371/69912, en clair tel. to London, Feb. 6, 1948).

CHAPTER 14.   WASHINGTON INTERVENES:
DRAPER AND KENNAN

1. Sherwood Fine, "Summary and Evaluation of Japan's Economic Recovery Under the Occupation," Briefings presented to the supreme commander for the Allied powers, JWC, Apr. 1952, 3. Fine was the well-trained economic adviser to SCAP who played a key part in the execution of its policies and plans.

2. *DOSB*, May 8, 1947, vol. 16, 991–994; *DOSB*, vol. 16, June 15, 1947, 1159–1160.

3. Minutes of meeting of secretaries of state, war and navy, Apr. 16, 1947, DOS files, 740.00119/9-1947.285, NRAW, RG 59, Box 3820; *FRUS, 1947*, vol. 6, 200–201, 265–266; F 3970/1/23, FO 371/63646, Gascoigne tel. no. 364, Mar. 20. 1947.

4. Draper memo to Royall, Oct. 1, 1947, Draper file, NRAS, RG 335, Box

53. See Schonberger, *Aftermath of War*, 161–163.

5. T. Cohen, *Remaking Japan*, 361; Hadley, *Antitrust*, 147–165. In 1982 the U.S. Congress, with the Japanese model in mind, enacted a trading company act to promote U.S. trade; more than one hundred companies have been certified under the act, but it has yet to produce significant results.

6. *FRUS, 1948*, vol. 6, 654–656; Royall "Speech, January 6, 1948," 117.

7. Fine, "Summary and Evaluation," 3–4; Schonberger, *Aftermath of War*, 163–165.

8. Blakeslee, *The FEC*, 123; *FRUS, 1949*, vol. 7, 609–614.

9. *FRUS, 1948*, vol. 6, 710–711; Reuters ticker from Tokyo, no. 0342, July 31, 1980.

10. J. Cohen, *Japan's Economy*, 425.

11. *FRUS, 1948*, vol. 6, 985.

12. *FRUS, 1949*, vol. 7, 735–736, 744; Morishima, *Why Has Japan 'Succeeded'?* 163–164; Blakeslee, *The FEC*, 158.

13. *FRUS, 1948*, vol. 6, 1056–1059; T. Cohen, *Remaking Japan*, 372.

14. Bisson, *Zaibatsu Dissolution*, 145–146; *FRUS, 1948*, vol. 6, 1017–1019, 1054–1056; Royall tel. to MacArthur, War 80376, Apr. 25, 1948, Draper file, NRAS, RG 335, Box 53.

15. Hata (ed.), *Amerika*, 368.

16. Bisson, *Zaibatsu Dissolution*, 154–156. ESS trustbusters developed a plan to divide Japan into three banking districts with banking operations limited to one of the three. This was another American model and probably an impractical one. The finance division in ESS successfully opposed this plan. The banking system was the only industry in Japan that SCAP did not break up. It is a strong and intensively competitive system today. Tristan Beplat, a former finance division officer, discussed this issue in the panel dicussion on Deconcentration in Post-war Japan, in the proceedings of the symposium The Occupation of Japan: Economic Policy and Reform, MMA, Apr. 13–15, 1978, 236–245.

17. CLM to Ottawa no. 110, Apr. 7, 1948, file 104-C, 50061, v. 4, Canadian FO; CLM to Ottawa no. 109, Apr. 28, 1948, file 104-C, 50061, v. 4, Canadian FO; Hadley, *Antitrust*, 445–453; McCraw (ed.), *America Versus Japan*, 20–21; Shirai, "A Supplement," 370. The statement about the success of zaibatu dissolution was attributed to Uemura Kogorō, president of Keidanren (*Kodansha Encyclopedia of Japan*, vol. 8, 366).

18. *FRUS, 1948*, vol. 6, 857–862.

19. Kennan, *Memoirs*, 368–369, 375–377.

20. Ibid., 373, 376.

21. MacArthur, *Reminiscences*, 322; Kennan, *Memoirs*, 382.

22. Kennan, *Memoirs*, 384; *FRUS, 1948*, vol. 6, 697–699.

23. *FRUS, 1948*, vol. 6, 699–706.

24. Ibid., 700–701.

25. Ibid., 702–703.

26. Ibid., 703–706.

27. Ibid., 706–712.

28. PPS no. 28, "Recommendations on U.S. Policy," Mar. 28, 1948, DOS file, NRAW, 740, 00119 control Japan; *FRUS, 1948*, vol. 6, 689–690, 716–

719; Kennan ltrs. to Butterworth, Mar. 9, 14, and 16, 1948, NRAW, PPS file, Box 19.

29. *FRUS, 1948*, vol. 6, 691; Kennan, *Memoirs*, 386–387.

30. *FRUS, 1948*, vol. 6, 691–696. Commodore Perry had recommended in 1853 that the United States take control of Okinawa if his mission to open Japan to international intercourse failed. In 1943 Franklin Roosevelt thought Okinawa should be turned over to Nationalist China (Borton, *Japan's Modern Century*, 36; FRUS, *Conferences at Cairo and Teheran, 1943*, 324, 869).

31. Kennan, *Memoirs*, 390; int. with Kennan; Dupuy memo of Mar. 24, 1948, Draper file, NRAS, RG 335, Box 53; Paul memo to Schuyler, Apr. 30, 1948, Plans and Operations Division, Army staff, NRAS, RG 319, Box 19. Some writers have claimed that Kennan recommended an increase in the size of Japan's police forces, but he did not do so.

32. *FRUS, 1948*, vol. 6, 819–823.

33. SCAP message C-65997 to DA, Dec. 4, 1948, MMA, RG 5, NSC 13/2 file; SCAP message C-66402 to DA, Dec. 18, 1948, MMA, RG 5, NSC 13/2 file; SCAP message C-67296 to DA, Jan. 23, 1949, MMA, RG 5, NSC 13/2 file; *FRUS, 1948*, vol. 6, 932–934.

34. *FRUS, 1948*, vol. 6, 938–942; SCAP message C-66402 to DA, Dec. 18, 1948, Draper file, NRAS, RG 335, Box 53.

35. *FRUS, 1949*, vol. 7, 724–727. The final text of NSC 13/3 was adopted on May 6, 1949 (*FRUS, 1949*, vol. 7, 730–736).

36. POLAD desp. no. 298, "Launching of Program to Effect Relaxation of Occupation Controls in Japan," May 10, 1949, File 360/125.4, NRAW; *FRUS, 1949*, vol. 7, 743–744.

37. J. Williams, *Japan's Political Revolution*, 216, commenting that "these and other moves were already in the works."

38. Kennan, *Memoirs*, 393. Kennan made clear (358–359) that his concept did not mean "containment by military means of a military threat, but the political containment of a political threat."

39. *FRUS, 1948*, vol. 6, 713.

40. Kennan, *Memoirs*, 393.

41. Kennan talk on "The Current Situation," at the CIA, Oct. 13, 1949, Kennan Papers, Box 17, Princeton University Library.

42. *FRUS, 1949*, vol. 7, 831; Kennan, *Memoirs*, 392–393.

CHAPTER 15.   NEW LIFE IN TOKYO:
YOSHIDA AND DODGE

1. *KJ*, vol. 1, 156; YM, 88.

2. J. Williams, *Japan's Political Revolution*, 50; Inoki, *Hyōden Yoshida*, vol. 3, 319. The Williams papers in the East Asia collection, University of Maryland (JWC), contain a series of memos from Williams to Whitney on the political maneuverings during October and November 1948.

3. *YM*, 88.

4. *YM*, 88; Yoshida, *Sekai to Nihon*, 90; Uchida, "Kokunai seijika, 163.

5. The following account is based on Miki ltr. to author, Mar. 18, 1981.

6. Inoki, *Hyōden Yoshida*, vol. 3, 319–321; Masumi, *Postwar Politics*, 166; Williams memo to Whitney, Oct. 14, 1948, JWC.

7. F 14563/44/23, FO 371/69824, Gascoigne tel. no. 1176 to London, Oct. 16, 1948.

8. Inoki, *Hyōden Yoshida*, vol. 3, 321; Masumi, *Postwar Politics*, 164.

9. Inoki, *Hyōden Yoshida*, vol. 3, 322; Bunker memo to MacArthur, Oct. 19, 1948, MMA, RG 5, Box 64; Takeuchi (ed.), *Yoshida naikaku*, 550.

10. J. Williams, *Japan's Political Revolution*, 217–218.

11. Watanabe T., *Senryōka*, 177–178; J. Williams, *Japan's Political Revolution*, 68.

12. Katayama's resignation in February 1948 automatically brought about the resignation of his cabinet but did not dissolve the lower house. In November Yoshida "insisted on the right of the government to dissolve the Diet under Article 7" (*YM*, 89). GS, which had carefully drafted the dissolution provisions of the constitution to make dissolution dependent on Diet authorization, vigorously opposed this interpretation.

13. Williams memo to Whitney, Nov. 26, 1948, JWC; J. Williams, *Japan's Political Revolution*, 218–219; Inoki, *Hyōden Yoshida*, vol. 3, 332–333; *YM*, 89. MacArthur wobbled on the timing of dissolution; at first he seemed to accept Yoshida's proposal for a dissolution called by the prime minister after the NPSL amendments were enacted, but "later he had to renege on his commitment" (Williams memo to author, Nov. 3, 1978).

14. Kades memo for record, Nov. 29, 1948, JWC; Inoki, *Hyōden Yoshida*, vol. 3, 334; J. Williams, *Japan's Political Revolution*, 220–221.

15. Yoshida ltr. to MacArthur, Nov. 28, 1948, JWC.

16. Ibid.

17. J. Williams, *Japan's Political Revolution*, 221; Watanbe T., *Senryōka*, 178–179; *KJ*, vol. 3, 198.

18. J. Williams, *Japan's Political Revolution*, 91–92; T. Cohen, *Remaking Japan*, 430.

19. Inoki, *Hyōden Yoshida*, vol. 3, 338; *FRUS, 1948*, vol. 6, 605–607.

20. Inoki, *Hyōden Yoshida*, vol. 3, 339–340.

21. Masumi, *Postwar Politics*, 180.

22. F 19974, FO 371/76203, Gascoigne desp. no. 24, Jan. 27, 1949.

23. Ibid.; Dower, "Yoshida in the Scales of History," 5.

24. F 2420/1015/23, FO 371/76179, Gascoigne desp. no. 30, Feb. 2, 1949.

25. MacArthur and GS explained the election results in terms of left and right: the combined vote for the Democratic Liberals and the Democrats on the right and for the Socialists and Communists on the left was not greatly different from the previous election in 1947. Therefore, GS felt no great cause for concern about the results. See POLAD desp. no. 114, Feb. 21, 1949, NRAW, 894.00/2-2149.

26. Inoki, *Hyōden Yoshida*, vol. 3, 338. Of those elected in 1949, 18.2 percent were former officials. This level has held fairly constant since then (C. Johnson, *MITI*, 46). Many of these politicians have brought technical expertise and sophistication to Japanese politics even if they had been trained in prewar Japan.

27. *FRUS, 1945*, vol. 6, 460–468; Yoshida ltr. to Sebald, Apr. 6, 1949, MMA, VIP file—Yoshida; Sebald, *With MacArthur*, 72–74, 301–302; DOS, *TIAS* Series 1911, "*Awa Maru* Claim," signed at Tokyo, Apr. 11, 1949.

28. CLM desp. no. 48 to Ottawa, Feb. 14, 1949, file 104-C 50061, v. 4; POLAD desp. 314, May 16, 1949, NRAW, DOS file 894.00/5-1649.

29. *FRUS, 1949*, vol. 7, 660, 663.

30. Int. with Kades; Shūkan Shinchō Henshūbu (ed.), "Kadeisu taisa," 335–336; Masumi, *Postwar Politics*, 167. Kades's departure from Japan in late 1948 is sometimes regarded as a significant turning point in American policy. His unpublished speech to the Council on Foreign Relations in New York on May 10, 1949, was approved by MacArthur and presented what might be termed an official SCAP view on occupation goals and policies; copy in author's file.

31. MacArthur ltr., Dec. 19, 1948, MMA, RG 10, VIP file—Yoshida; *FRUS, 1948*, vol. 6, 1066–1067.

32. Marquat memo of July 15, 1948, MMA, RG 10, VIP file—Yoshida; Yoshida ltr., Dec. 19, 1948, MMA, RG 10, VIP file—Yoshida; Watanabe T., *Senryōka*, 152–153.

33. Saltzman memo to Acheson, Jan. 26, 1949, DOS file, RG 59, Box 3825, NRAW.

34. SCAP message C 66236 to DA, Dec. 12, 1948, MMA, RG 10, Box 11; CLM desp. no. 183 to Ottawa, Mar. 18, 1949, file 104-C 50061, v. 4. MacArthur did not like to be given orders or advice from outside his own camp. On the wall of his office in Tokyo he had placed a quotation from the Roman historian Livy, citing a speech by the Roman general, Lucius Aemilius Paulus, who fought the Macedonians in 168 B.C. It ended with the words "Rest assured that we shall pay no attention to any councils but such as shall be framed within our own camp." At the bottom of the quotation MacArthur had written the words "Amen. Douglas MacArthur" (Gunther, *The Riddle*, 55–56).

35. T. Cohen, *Remaking Japan*, 431–435; Watanabe T., *Senryōka*, 189–195; Halberstam, *The Reckoning*, 125–130.

36. Hunsberger, *Japan and the United States*, 106; Hata (ed.), *Amerika*, 391–395; J. Cohen, *Japan's Economy*, 84–86. To promote trade SCAP developed a large office in ESS. This office worked closely with MITI. Some Japanese believe this large staff in ESS had the long-term effect of imposing tight governmental control over the economy (see Yoshino, "A Private Matter," 13).

37. *KJ*, vol. 3, 204–211; Inoki, *Hyōden Yoshida*, vol. 3, 342.

38. Watanabe T., *Senryōka*, 190; Miyazawa, *Tōkyō-Washinton*, 14.

39. Miyazawa, *Tōkyō-Washinton*, 21–22.

40. Uchino, *Japan's Postwar Economy*, 48–51; Watanabe T., *Senryōka*, 189–190.

41. Inoki, *Hyōden Yoshida*, vol. 3, 350.

42. Suzuki G., "Impact of the Korean War: A Memoir," and "Impact of the Korean War: An Overview."

43. See McDiarmid, "The Japanese Exchange Rate"; Suzuki G., "Japan's Experience," 2–6.

44. Suzuki G., "Japan's Experience," 6; Dick K. Nanto, "Shoup Mission,"

Kodansha Encyclopedia of Japan, vol. 7, 172–173; Inoki, *Hyōden Yoshida*, vol. 3, 360.

45. Ints. with Shirasu and Takeuchi Ryūji. See C. Johnson, *MITI*, 191–194; this book contains a thorough study of twentieth-century Japanese trade and industrial policy. Yoshida, who had a particular interest in commercial policy throughout his diplomatic career, was careful to provide MITI with some top-drawer diplomatic talent (McCraw [ed.], *America Versus Japan*, 122).

46. C. Johnson, *MITI*, 194–195; Watanabe T., *Senryōka*, 257–263.

47. *FRUS, 1950*, vol. 6, 1134; Schaller, *The American Occupation*, viii; Borden, *The Pacific Alliance*, 191–222; James, *The Years of MacArthur*, vol. 3, 234–235.

48. *FRUS, 1949*, vol. 7, 1215–1220; *FRUS, 1951*, vol. 6, 33–63; Acheson speech, "Crisis in Asia—An Examination of U.S. Policy," *DOSB*, Jan. 23, 1950, 111–118; Watanabe A., "Southeast Asia," 80–95; Hunsberger, *Japan and the United States*, 184–185. See Yamamoto, "The Cold War." The term *great crescent* was used in the early draft of a State Department policy planning staff paper, PPS 51 (*FRUS, 1949*, vol. 7, 1128–113), but was omitted in later versions, which became the NSC 48 series. Hayes, *The Beginning of American Aid*, 3–58, gives a careful summary of U.S. aid to Southeast Asia up to June 1951: the total programmed for Indochina, Burma, Thailand, and Indonesia amounted to $49 million in various forms of technical assistance; deliveries to recipient countries lagged between one and three years after the programs were authorized (46–51). Indonesia also received a $100 million credit from the U.S. Export-Import Bank in 1950 (49).

49. Suzuki G., "Impact of the Korean War: A Memoir," 7–11; int. with Nagano.

50. F 6745/1615/23, FO 371/76182, Pink letter to FO, Apr. 30, 1949.

51. Int. with Asō Kazuko; CLM desp. no. 183 to Ottawa, Mar. 18, 1949, 104-C, 50061 v. 4; *KJ*, vol. 4, 67–69.

52. Nakamura, *The Postwar Japanese Economy*, 38–39; "Consider Japan," Sept. 1, 1962, 795; Tsutsui, *Banking Policy*, 105–106.

53. Comment of Bronfenbrenner, proceedings of the symposium The Occupation of Japan: Economic Policy and Reform, MMA, Apr. 13–15, 1978, 77; T. Cohen, *Remaking Japan*, 442.

CHAPTER 16.   UNREST AND VIOLENCE ON THE LEFT

1. CLM desp. no. 183 to Ottawa, enclosure entitled "Notes on Talk with General MacArthur," Mar. 18. 1949, file 104 C 50061, v. 4.

2. Yoshida ltr. of Apr. 19, 1949, to MacArthur, JWC; Suzuki G., "Japan's Experience," 6.

3. Farley, *Aspects*, 215, 226, fn. 17; Takemae, *GHQ*, 201; Takemae, *Sengo rōdō kaikaku*, 351.

4. C. Johnson, *Conspiracy*, 79–81. The government's criteria for discharging workers were uncooperativeness, unfitness as a public service employee,

inferiority in technical knowledge and physical condition, short period of service, and poor performance (Farley, *Aspects*, 52–53, 228–230).

5. C. Johnson, *Conspiracy*, 46–107, summarizes the three incidents.

6. *YM*, 177; Yoshida ltr. to MacArthur, Aug. 6, 1949, MMA, RG 10, VIP file—Yoshida. In 1951 Yoshida told Dulles that the government had determined that a Korean had assassinated Shimoyama but had been unable to catch him (*FRUS, 1951*, vol. 6, no. 1, 1008); little evidence has been produced to support Yoshida's assertion.

7. The popular book was by Matsumoto, *Nihon no kuroi kiri*, 7–96.

8. Inoki, *Hyōden Yoshida*, vol. 3, 352–353.

9. Dynaword, "A Brief History," 9.

10. Sullivan memo to Rusk, Apr. 27, 1950, DOS files, NRAW, RG 59, Box 5655.

11. SCAP, "Selected Data," 11; Fearey, *The Occupation*, 206; F 2626/44/23, FO 69819, Gascoigne ltr. to London, Jan. 29, 1948.

12. *YM*, 233–235; Yoshida ltr. to MacArthur, June 8, 1950, MMA, RG 5, VIP file—Yoshida; Yoshida statement of July 15, 1949, MMA, RG 5.

13. Swearingen, *The Soviet Union*, 64.

14. Gunther, *The Riddle*, 162; Yoshida statement, June 4, 1950, MMA, RG 10, VIP file—Yoshida.

15. MacArthur ltrs. to Yoshida, June 6, 7, and 26, 1950, MMA, RG 10, VIP file—Yoshida.

16. *FRUS, 1950*, vol. 6, 1221–1222.

17. MacArthur ltr. of June 6, 1950, MMA, RG 5, VIP file—Yoshida.

18. Takemae, *GHQ*, 201–202; Takemae, *Senryō sengoshi*, 186–201; MacArthur ltr. of July 18, 1950, MMA, RG 5, VIP file—Yoshida; C. Johnson, *Conspiracy*, 79. Yoshida's ltr. of August 9, 1949 (JWC), listed many steps he thought necessary for "national reconstruction," including "elimination of communist influence from government service and educational institutions." The Red Purge was conducted without legal procedure or other recourse. Those purged did receive all compensation and pension payments due them, and improving economic conditions helped many of them find new employment. In 1949–1950 about 12,480 persons were discharged in the Red Purge, and about 600,000 were discharged under administrative retrenchment, according to Shinobu (*Sengo Nihon seijishi*, vol. 4, 1184) and Takemae (*Sengo rōdō kaikaku*, 351).

19. *YM*, 241.

20. Enclosure to CLM desp. no. 183 to Ottawa, March 18, 1949, file no. 104 C, 50061, v. 4.

21. *YM*, 211–231; Garon, *The State and Labor*, 243.

22. Schonberger, *Aftermath of War*, 128–133; Takemae, "Sōhyō."

23. Takemae, *Sengo rōdō kaikaku*, 306–307.

24. Garon, *The State and Labor*, 242–248; Shirai, "A Supplement," 369–384; *Japan Times Weekly* (Overseas ed.), Dec. 9, 1989, 4.

25. Nishi, *Unconditional Democracy*, 258–261.

26. *YM*, 174, 175; *Japan Times Weekly* (Overseas ed.), May 27, 1989, 6.

27. RLED, Apr. 25, 1948; *YM*, 177.

28. DS staff study, "Status and Treatment of Koreans in Japan," Aug. 15, 1949, MMA, RG 84, Box 2291; *SD*, Aug. 8, 1949.

29. Yoshida undated ltr. to MacArthur, MMA RG 5, Box 3, Folder 2; Sebald memo to MacArthur, Sept. 9, 1949, MMA, RG 5, Box 3, Folder 2; *FRUS, 1951*, vol. 6, no. 1, 1007–1008.

30. Robert Ricketts, who has carefully studied the status of Koreans in Japan, has provided the author with useful information and documents.

PART V.   PEACE SETTLEMENT

1. Kennan, *Memoirs*, 395.

CHAPTER 17.   THE SEARCH FOR PEACE

1. Byrnes, *Speaking Frankly*, 173, 214; *FRUS, 1946*, vol. 8, 152–155; Borton, "The Allied Occupation," 421; *FRUS, 1947*, vol. 6, 473–474, 491–492, 509–511. Burma and Pakistan became members of the FEC in November 1949, raising its membership to thirteen (*FRUS, 1949*, vol. 6, 900–901).

2. Draft peace treaty, Aug. 5, 1947, State Department file 740.0011 (PW Peace) 8-647, NRAW; draft peace treaty, Jan. 8, 1948, State Department FE file (peace treaty), NRAW; *FRUS, 1948*, vol. 6, 656–660; Dunn, *Peace-Making*, 70.

3. *FRUS, 1947*, vol. 6, 454–456, 512–515.

4. Nishimura, "Kōwa jōyaku," 217; J. Williams, *Japan's Political Revolution*, 248–250; Nishimura, *Sanfuranshisuko heiwa*, 32–34, 43; *KJ*, vol. 3, 25–26, 35. Ashida also gave the memo to several other foreign representatives, including Macmahon Ball, the Australian representative on the Allied Council. See also *World Report*, Dec. 11, 1947; *Yomiuri shimbun*, Dec. 11, 1947, 1, based on Associated Press despatch from Washington of Dec. 5, 1947; POLAD airgram A-130, Dec. 9, 1947, NRAW, State Dept file 500, Jap treaty; Nishimura, *Sanfuranshisuko heiwa*, 45–47, lists the thirty-six documents prepared by the Foreign Office.

5. In 1949 a German "basic law" or constitution came into effect in the three western zones, and an occupation statute was agreed upon by the three Western Allies and the German government to govern their relations (Gimbel, *The American Occupation*, 253–257). C. J. Friedrich of Harvard University played a key role in advising German leaders regarding the drafting of the German constitution (Wolfe [ed.], *Americans as Proconsuls*, 110).

6. Acheson, *Present at the Creation*, 338.

7. *FRUS, 1949*, vol. 7, 877–878; draft peace treaty, Oct. 13, 1949, DOS file 740.0011 (PW peace) 10-1449, NRAW; Dunn, *Peace-Making*, 83–86.

8. Butterworth ltr. to Sebald, Nov. 4, 1949, NRAW, dipl. file 320.1, RG 84, Box 2292; Dunn, *Peace-Making*, 85–86.

9. Dunn, *Peace-Making*, 648–649; Sebald desp. to DOS, "Secretary of the Army's Off-the-Record Press Conference," Feb. 15, 1949, NRAW, DOS file, RG 59, 740.00119 Japan, 2-1549; F 14488/1015/23, FO 371/76210, Tokyo to

London, report of MacArthur interview with G. Ward Price of *Daily Mail*, Mar. 2, 1949.

10. See *YM*, 246–248; Inoki, *Hyōden Yoshida*, vol. 3, 369; Tamamoto, "Unwanted Peace."

11. *FRUS, 1950*, vol. 6, 1166–1167.

12. Miyazawa, *Tōkyō-Washinton*, 56–59. See Inoki, *Hyōden Yoshida*, vol. 3, 358–362; Nishimura, "Kōwa jōyaku," 227–229.

13. Miyazawa, *Tōkyō-Washinton*, 40–41

14. Inoki, *Hyōden Yoshida*, vol. 3, 362.

15. *FRUS, 1950*, vol. 6, 1195–1196; Miyazawa, *Tōkyō-Washinton*, 58–59.

16. *FRUS, 1950*, vol. 6, 1198, fn. 5.

17. RLED, July 28 and Sept. 18, 1947; *YM*, 265; *KJ*, vol. 3, 23–26, 108–114; Nishimura, "Sanfuranshisuko heiwa," 37–38; Kojima, *Nihon senryō*, vol. 3, 28. The "Ashida memo" was also given subsequently to the Australian foreign minister, H. V. Evatt, and on September 13, 1947, to General Eichelberger.

18. Miyazawa, *Tōkyō-Washinton*, 64–67.

19. Acheson, *Present at the Creation*, 556.

20. *FRUS, 1950*, vol. 6, 1175–1176, 1178.

21. Acheson, *Present at the Creation*, 432.

22. Pruessen, *John Foster Dulles*, 443–448; Beal, *John Foster Dulles, 1888–1959*, 116.

23. Oral History interview with Babcock, Mar. 5, 1965, 2, John Foster Dulles Papers, Princeton University Library. See *FRUS, 1949*, vol. 7, 890–894.

24. *FRUS, 1950*, vol. 6, 1207–1212; Hoopes, *The Devil*, 113.

25. Dunn, *Peace-Making*, 98–102.

26. *FRUS, 1950*, vol. 6, 1209.

27. *SD*, June 6, 1950; *FRUS, 1950*, vol. 6, 1231.

28. MacArthur memos on the Japanese peace treaty and Formosa, MMA, RG 5, Box 1, Folder 5; *FRUS, 1950*, vol. 6, 1213–1221.

29. *FRUS, 1950*, vol. 6, 1215.

30. Ibid., 1218; see also 1205–1207.

31. FJ 19111/13, FO 371/83814, Tokyo desp. 53, Feb. 18, 1950; Hosoya, "The Road to San Francisco."

32. *FRUS, 1950*, vol. 6, 1227–1228.

33. Ibid., 1229–1230.

34. Ibid., 1231–1232.

35. *SD*, June 22, 1950.

36. *FRUS, 1950*, vol. 6, 1230–1237. In a meeting with the British ambassador, Dulles confided that he was aiming for a peace conference in June 1951 (FT 1021, FO 371/8383, Tokyo desp. to London, June 26, 1950).

37. *Asahi shimbun*, Aug. 12, 1979, 3; Kern letter to Dulles, Aug. 19, 1950, John Foster Dulles Papers, Princeton University Library. A Japanese who was at Dulles's meeting with Kern, Matsudaira, and others on June 22, 1950, thought the "Matsudaira letter" was a fake (int. with Watanabe Takeshi).

38. *FRUS, 1950*, vol. 6, 1232.

CHAPTER 18. THE KOREAN WAR

1. U.S. Senate, *Military Situation*, 2020; *DOSB*, vol. 23, July 3, 1950, 12–13; *DOSB*, vol. 22, January 23, 1950, 116; Lowe, *The Origins of the Korean War*, examines how the war started.

2. Schnabel, *Policy and Direction*, 63–65.

3. Stephan, "Soviet Policy," 87; Halliday and Cumings, *Korea*, 71–74; Talbot (trans. and ed.), *Khrushchev Remembers*, 367–368, recounts how Kim Il Sung persuaded Stalin to support a North Korean attack on the South, which Kim was confident would quickly succeed and produce a revolt in the South against the government of Syngman Rhee; nothing appears in the Khrushchev account about the possibility of a U.S. peace treaty with Japan.

4. Gallicchio, *The Cold War*, 95–101, 116–119; Morison, *Victory*, vol. 14, 354–355. Morison said that the "best prophet was Gen. A. C. Wedemeyer, USA, commanding the China Theater . . . [who] urgently demanded priority for occupation of Manchuria and the Chinese seaports, in order to prevent the Chinese Reds from taking over." Dean Acheson also believed that the U.S. Marines should have been kept there (*Present at the Creation*, 140).

5. Blair, *MacArthur*, 284–289; James, *The Years of MacArthur*, vol. 3, 387–418. Both describe MacArthur's shifting views before June 1950 on the defense of Korea.

6. Allison, *Ambassador*, 129–131.

7. Allison reported that the evening after the attack MacArthur appeared to be surprised when Dulles phoned him to say the South Korean Army was in full retreat. Actually, MacArthur had been receiving reports since a few hours after the attack and had ordered ammunition to be sent to Korea (James, *The Years of MacArthur*, vol. 3, 420).

8. Allison, *Ambassador*, 137. According to one account, Dulles advised President Truman a few days later that MacArthur should be "hauled back to the United States" (Diary of Eben A. Ayres, entry of July 1, 1950, 106–107, HSTL). But no other evidence supports this statement, which would seem to have been out of character for Dulles, a conservative Republican who had established good relations with MacArthur. (See *FRUS, 1951*, vol. 6, 972–976, for Dulles's reaction to the relief of MacArthur in 1951.)

9. Bernstein, "The Week We Went to War"; *DOSB*, vol. 23, July 10, 1950, 23–57, 49–50; Pruessen, *John Foster Dulles*, 414–418.

10. Wake Island conference, MMA, RG 5, Box 1B. MacArthur went to Formosa on July 31, 1950, for two days to discuss with Chiang Kai-shek "military coordination" between Nationalist Chinese and U.S. forces. MacArthur considered that as theater commander he had general authorization to do this (Sebald, *With MacArthur*, 122–125).

11. MacArthur initially felt that Japanese treaty planning had been "entirely eclipsed by events in Korea," but he soon got back in stride on treaty issues (*SD*, July 7, 1950).

12. Sebald, *With MacArthur*, 119.

13. In the first days of the war, Marquat confidentially asked Suzuki Gengo, an official of the Japanese Finance Ministry, if Japan could duplicate and print a

large amount of Bank of Korea banknotes. When told it would take a month, Marquat said U.S. forces could not wait that long. Suzuki asked if U.S. forces were going to Korea. Marquat said, not entirely in jest, that Suzuki would be shot if anything about this leaked out. Suzuki got quick delivery of nearly ¥25 billion worth of Koreans banknotes (int. with Suzuki).

14. FJ 10111/50, FO 371/83816, Gascoigne desp. 224 to London, July 13, 1950; Yoshida statement, Aug. 3, 1950, MMA, RG 10, Box 11. Yoshida reportedly called the war "a Gift of the Gods" (Shinobu, *Sengo Nihon seijishi*, vol. 4, 1151). MacArthur is said to have called it "Mars' last gift to an old warrior" (Rovere and Schlesinger, *The General*, 104). Neither Yoshida nor MacArthur was a particularly strong believer in divinity.

15. FJ 10111/53, FO 371/83816, Gascoigne desp. 249 to London, August 2, 1950; FJ 1025/2, FO 371/83842, Tokyo tel. 1661 to London, December 13, 1950.

16. POLAD tel. 40 to DOS, July 6, 1950, MMA, RG 9, Box 83.

17. Ltr. of July 8, 1950, MMA, RG 5, VIP file—Yoshida.

18. Ibid.

19. *FRUS, 1948*, vol. 6, 859; *FRUS, 1949*, vol. 7, 671–673, 725; Yoshida-MacArthur exchange of letters, Aug. 6 and Aug. 8, 1949, MMA, RG 10, VIP file—Yoshida.

20. FJ 10111/50, FO 371/83816, UKLM desp. 224 to London, July 13, 1950.

21. Rizzo memos for record, "Conference Regarding SCAP Police Letter of July 8, 1950," and July 13, 1950, Japanese FO file, reel A0048-0102.

22. Ibid.

23. Message C 57814, CINCFE to DA, July 14, 1950, MMA, RG 5, Box 1.

24. GHQ FEC staff study, July 10, 1950, MMA, RG 6, Box 100.

25. *YM*, 182–195; *KJ*, vol. 2, 165–171; Inoki, *Hyōden Yoshida*, vol. 3, 377.

26. Inoki, *Hyōden Yoshida*, vol. 3, 381; Dower, "The Eye of the Beholder," 16.

27. Okazaki memo to Marquat, Sept. 20, 1950, NRAS, RG 331, Box 2187; Dodge memo to Marquat, "National Police Reserve," Nov. 30, 1950, NRAS, ESS file.

28. Kowalski, *Nihon saigunbi*, 24–36. This book has been published only in Japanese. An English version is available in the NDLT.

29. Murphy, *Diplomat*, 347–348; Drifte, "Japan's Involvement," 128–130.

30. NSC 68, *FRUS, 1950*, vol. 1, 291; Gaddis, *Strategies*.

31. Baerwald, *The Purge*, 59.

32. Sakeda, "Kōwa to kokunai seiji," 108.

33. NSC 68, *FRUS, 1950*, vol. 1, 292.

CHAPTER 19.   SHAPING THE PEACE SETTLEMENT

1. *FRUS, 1950*, vol. 6, 1243–1244. Dulles was suggesting to the State Department at the same time, in a "think piece," that Japanese might be recruited

to take part individually in an international force to serve in Korea (ibid., 1246–1248). Nothing came of this idea; it was not too different from the Chinese idea of a volunteer force, which the PRC sent into Korea in November.

2. Ibid., 1255, 1264–1265.

3. Ibid., 1288–1296. One senior State Department official described the provisions of NSC 60/1 as "brutally frank" (ibid., 1304).

4. Ibid., 1196–1297. "Trusteeship" meant that the United States did not acquire sovereign rights. The emperor had reportedly suggested earlier that Japan agree to a fifty-year lease of Okinawa to the United States (POLAD desp. 1293, Sept. 22, 1947, DOS file 801, NRAW); Iriye Sukemasa, "Nikki," *Asahi shimbun*, February 23, 1989, 4; Toyoshita, "Tennō-Makkāsā," part 2, 110–114.

5. Fearey, "Summary of the Negotiations," 281. This concise summary of the peace treaty negotiations by an insider does not deal with security treaty.

6. *FRUS, 1950*, vol. 6, 1332–1336, 1308.

7. Ibid., 1356–1358.

8. Ibid., 1359–1360, 1363–1367.

9. *FRUS, 1951*, vol. 6, no. 1, 788–789. Dean Acheson told a press conference on February 8, 1950, that a "theme" of the U.S. response to the Soviet threat was "the transformation of our two former enemies into allies and their attachment by firm bonds of security and economic interest to the free nations in Europe and Asia" (*Present at the Creation*, 378).

10. Rockefeller was instrumental in creating the Japan Society in New York and the International House in Tokyo, both of which became influential in promoting cultural interchange.

11. Nishimura, *Sanfuranshisuko heiwa*, 65, 81–86; Inoki, *Hyōden Yoshida*, vol. 3; 389–397; Nishimura, "Kōwa jōyaku," 230–231.

12. Inoki, *Hyōden Yoshida*, vol. 3, 397; Hosoya, "Japan's Response," 20.

13. *FRUS, 1951*, vol. 6, no. 1, 812.

14. Ibid., 818–820.

15. Ibid., 821–822, 836.

16. Ibid., 827–828.

17. Ibid., 828–830; *KJ*, vol. 2, 160–162; Nishimura, *Sanfuranshisuko heiwa*, 87–88.

18. *FRUS, 1951*, vol. 6, no. 1, 832; *YM*, 277. Yoshida's principal expert was Nishimura Kumao.

19. *FRUS, 1951*, vol. 6, no. 1, 800, 818.

20. Ibid., 832–834; Nishimura, *Sanfuranshisuko heiwa*, 88–89.

21. Kosaka, *Saishō Yoshida*, 58–59; *Asahi shimbun*, Feb. 14, 1964, 8; *FRUS, 1951*, vol. 6, no. 1, 832.

22. *FRUS, 1951*, vol. 6, no. 1, 789; Nishimura, *Sanfuranshisuko heiwa*, 94, note.

23. *FRUS, 1951*, vol. 6, no. 1, 833–838, 839; Nishimura, "Sanfuranshisuko kōwa," 30–31; Nishimura, *Sanfuranshisuko heiwa*, 90.

24. Nishimura, *Sanfuranshisuko heiwa*, 90–91; *FRUS, 1951*, vol. 6, no. 1, 833–834, 839; *SD*, Jan. 31, 1951.

25. Nishimura, "Kōwa jōyaku," 237; Nishimura, "Sanfuranshisuko kōwa," 31. This appraisal of Yoshida's ability to speak and understand English

is based on interviews with several who knew Yoshida well, such as Sebald and Matsui Akira, and on several personal conversations.

26. Nishimura, "Kōwa jōyaku," 239–241; Hosoya, "Japan's Response," 23.

27. Nishimura, "Kōwa jōyaku," 238–239.

28. *FRUS, 1951*, vol. 6, no. 1, 843–849.

29. Nishimura, *Sanfuranshisuko heiwa*, 82, 89–90; Nishimura, "Sanfuranshisuko kōwa," 30; Hosoya, "Japan's Response," 23.

30. Hosoya, "Japan's Response," 24.

31. *Tōkyō shimbun*, May 13, 1977, 3, gives an account of the contents of the Japanese rearmament plan (Hosoya, "Japan's Response," 25). Nishimura later confirmed the accuracy of this report ("Sanfuranshisuko kōwa," 33). Inoki stated he had seen the document given Allison on Feb. 3 and confirmed the general accuracy of the press report (int. with Inoki). The document is evidently in the State Department historical files but was not made public, probably because the Japanese government so requested.

32. *FRUS, 1951*, vol. 6, no. 1, 849, editorial note. Johnson's report of Feb. 8, 1951, to Secretary of Defense Marshall on the Yoshida-Dulles talks makes no reference to the Yoshida rearmament plan (MMA, RG 5, Box 68).

Yoshida had told his advisers on Jan. 1, 1950, evidently in a pessimistic mood, that Japan might have to agree in the forthcoming negotiations to a 200,000-man army (Watanabe A., "Kōwa mondai," 47). Perhaps he decided to try out a figure of 50,000 to get agreement in the February negotiations. Dower perceptively commented that "the issue, in Yoshida's view, was no longer rearmament *per se* but the pace and appearance of rearmament" (*Empire*, 400). The appearance was more significant for him than the pace, as Americans were to find out in dealing with him for the next several years. Speculating that Yoshida may have cooked up the plan for a 50,000-man army as an "instantaneous idea," Hosoya noted that "improvisation was a characteristic of his diplomatic style" (Hosoya, "Japan's Response," 25).

33. *FRUS, 1951*, vol. 6, no. 1, 849–855, 860–861; Hosoya, "Japan's Response," 26; Nishimura, "Sanfuranshisuko kōwa," 32–33.

34. *FRUS, 1951*, vol. 6, no. 1, 866–869; Nishimura, *Sanfuranshisuko heiwa*, 94–95.

35. *FRUS, 1951*, vol. 6, no. 1, 856–857, 863.

36. *DOSB*, vol. 24, Feb. 12, 1951, 252–255.

37. Inoki, *Hyōden Yoshida*, vol. 3, 405; Nishimura, *Sanfuranshisuko heiwa*, 94; H. Alexander Smith Oral History, Dulles Papers, Princeton University Library; *FRUS, 1951*, vol. 6, no. 1, 1326–1328.

38. *FRUS, 1950*, vol. 6, 26–27, 45, 81–83, 121–123, 214–219, 223–227; *FRUS, 1951*, vol. 6, no. 1, 143–144, 825–827, 830–832, 842–843.

39. *FRUS, 1951*, vol. 6, no. 1, 825–827, 830–832, 842–843.

40. *FRUS, 1951*, vol. 6, no. 1, 866–867.

41. *FRUS, 1951*, vol. 6, no. 1, 874–880.

42. Ibid., 866–869.

43. YM, 250–251; Curtis, "The Dulles-Yoshida Negotiations," 50–52; Takeuchi (ed.), *Yoshida naikaku*, 380–385.

44. *DOSB*, vol. 24, Feb. 26, 1951, 351; Hatoyama, *Hatoyama Ichirō*, 85–

92; Masumi, *Postwar Politics*, 280; Auer, *The Postwar Rearmament*, 76; *FRUS, 1951*, vol. 6, no. 1, 873–874.

45. *FRUS, 1951*, vol. 6, no. 1, 880–883; Fearey, "Summary of the Negotiations," 284.

46. *FRUS, 1951*, vol. 6, no. 1, 885–887, 169–179; Fearey, "Summary of Negotiations," 284.

47. *FRUS, 1951*, vol. 6, no. 1, 944–950.

48. *DOSB*, vol. 24, May 28, 1951, 852–858. See *DOSB*, vol. 24, July 23, 1951, 138–143.

49. *FRUS, 1951*, vol. 6, no. 1, 900–903, 931.

CHAPTER 20.   THE FIRING OF MACARTHUR

1. James, *The Years of MacArthur*, vol. 3, 600; MacArthur, *Reminiscences*, 395.

2. Sebald, *With MacArthur*, 227–228. Sebald was accorded the personal rank of ambassador on October 11, 1950, after strong endorsement by MacArthur and in spite of considerable State Department reluctance to so honor a relative newcomer to the diplomatic service.

3. Ibid., 228–230; *FRUS, 1951*, vol. 6, no. 1, 968–969.

4. *SD*, Apr. 11, 1951; MacArthur, *Reminiscences*, 285, 395.

5. U. Johnson, *The Right Hand*, 117.

6. Sebald, *With MacArthur*, 230.

7. *FRUS, 1951*, vol. 6, no. 1, 972–973.

8. Ibid., 973–975, 975–976.

9. Sebald, *With MacArthur*, 234; Hara, "Makkāsā Kainin," vol. 5, 219–227; Miyazawa letter to Reid, Apr. 19, 1951, Kolko Papers, Box 3, Dodge file, London School of Economics Library.

10. Acheson, *Present at the Creation*, 526–528; U. Johnson, *The Right Hand*, 106–109.

11. Ridgway, *Soldier*, 223.

12. Sebald, *With MacArthur*, 236.

13. Ibid., 237, 240; memo from Rizzo to Fox, Apr. 20, 1951, NRAS, GS file.

14. Ridgway, *Soldier*, 224.

15. Fearey, "Summary of the Negotiations," 285; Nishimura, *Sanfuranshisuko heiwa*, 112–114; *FRUS, 1951*, vol. 6, no. 1, 986, 1003.

16. *FRUS, 1951*, vol. 6, no. 1, 985–989; Nishimura, *Sanfuranshisuko heiwa*, 114–121.

17. *FRUS, 1951*, vol. 6, no. 1, 1006–1009, 1011. Nishimura later commented somewhat bitterly that the Americans took the position that they had not come to negotiate a peace treaty, since Japan had surrendered unconditionally, but only to consult ("Sanfuranshisuko no omoide," 75). Both sides considered the negotiation of the security treaty as one between equals.

18. FJ 1202/10/025677, FO 371/92655, Clutton desp. 142 to London, Apr. 30, 1951.

19. U.S. Senate, *Military Situation*, 312.

20. *YM*, 49; F 328/23, FO 371/69858, Jan. 2, 1948, report of meeting on Dec, 19, 1947, of U.K. parliamentary delegation with MacArthur.

CHAPTER 21. SIGNING THE TREATIES AND ENDING THE OCCUPATION

1. *YM*, 46; GS memo to chief of staff, "Letter from Prime Minister to General MacArthur," Apr. 19, 1951, NRAS, GS file, RG 331, Box 2187. Yoshida asserted in his memoirs that he did not actually have the opportunity to give the letter to MacArthur before the general's recall but did discuss the subject with him (*YM*, 252).

2. Unsigned ltr. from Yoshida to MacArthur, Apr. 9, 1951, NRAS, GS file, RG 331, Box 2187. Yoshida later told a trusted official that MacArthur did not agree with all the things he had been instructed to do during the occupation (Watanabe T., *Watanabe Takeshi nikki*, 666). Yoshida's daughter thought that her father wrote the letter because he wanted to rescue the general from some of the "excesses" committed during the occupation (int. with Asō Kazuko).

3. GS memo to chief of staff, Apr. 23, 1951, NRAS, GS file, RG 331, Box 2187. Sodei described at length Yoshida's "last attempt to mutilate MacArthur's reforms" (*Senryō*, 215–218) and observed that MacArthur made no concession other than to "fade away."

4. Sebald ltr. to Johnson, Aug. 3, 1951, DOS file 794.00/8-351, NRAW; Johnson ltr. to Sebald, June 16, 1951, DOS file 794.00/8-351, NRAW.

5. Ridgway, *Soldier*, 225; Ridgway memo of conversation with Yoshida, Jan. 1, 1952, Ridgway file, Army War College Library, Carlisle Barracks, Pa.

6. Ridgway, *Soldier*, 226–228.

7. *FRUS, 1951*, vol. 6, no. 1, 1022–1023; *YM*, 46–47; Dower, *Empire*, 559, fn. 105.

8. *FRUS, 1951*, vol. 6, no. 1, 1045–1049, 1138–1141, 1328–1329; Baerwald, *The Purge*, 79.

9. *YM*, 147–166; Masumi, *Postwar Politics*, 274–276, 279–281; Montgomery, *Forced to Be Free*, 48.

10. Ridgway, *Soldier*, 226; *KJ*, vol. 2, 180; Dower, *Empire*, 432. Yoshida told his staff he would not consider any specific plans and budgets for force increases of more than 50,000 a year (CAS memo to CofS, Feb. 23, 1952, with memo for record by Kowalski, file GS [B] 04394, NDLT; *FRUS, 1952–1954*, vol. 14, no. 2, 1232). It was characteristic of Yoshida that he did not shrink from entering into vague understandings that required action in the future. By playing the artful dodger, he could get past the immediate hurdle.

11. Dower, *Empire*, 386; Weinstein, "Defense Policy," 167; Rusk-Okazaki memo, Feb. 11, 1952, NRAW, DOS file, 794.5/2-1152; Welfield, *An Empire*, 70.

12. NSC 125/2, Feb. 21, 1952, *FRUS, 1952*, vol. 14, no. 2, 1300–1308.

13. *FRUS, 1951*, vol. 6, no. 1, 888–895, 898–900, 1001–1002, 1208–1215, 1330–1331.

14. *FRUS, 1951*, vol. 6, no. 1, 1021–1022.

15. Ibid., 1024–1037, 1119–1133; Fearey, "Summary of the Negotiations," 287–289. Several issues, mostly technical, were still unsettled: fisheries, shipping, Japanese assets in Thailand, compensation for Allied wartime property losses, and reparations.

16. *FRUS, 1951*, vol. 6, no. 1, 1171–1174; Fearey, "Summary of the Negotiations," 289.

17. *FRUS, 1951*, vol. 6, no. 1, 1274; Sebald, *With MacArthur*, 136–149; Reischauer, *The United States and Japan*, 242–243.

18. *FRUS, 1951*, vol. 6, no. 1, 1251, 1255–1256; Andrew Gordon, "Reparations for Southeast Asia," *Kodansha Encyclopedia of Japan*, vol. 6, 302.

19. *FRUS, 1951*, vol. 6, no. 1, 1153–1155.

20. Nishimura, "Sanfuranshisuko kōwa," 34; Takemae, *GHQ*, 202–204; *FRUS, 1951*, vol. 6, no. 1, 857–858, 1227. The Japanese believed the security treaty should conform closely with the international obligations set out in the U.N. Charter and that the United States was imposing obligations in excess of charter requirements (Nishimura, "Ampo jōyaku kaitei," 27).

21. *FRUS, 1951*, vol. 6, no. 1, 860, 863. This provision was eliminated from the revised security treaty signed in 1960.

22. Sebald, *With MacArthur*, 280; Kosaka, *Saishō Yoshida*, 55–59, 69–71.

23. *FRUS, 1951*, vol. 6, no. 1, 1207–1208.

24. Ibid., 873–874, 1235, 1242, 1248–1249, 1274; Sebald, *With MacArthur*, 271–272.

25. *FRUS, 1951*, vol. 6, no. 1, 1275–1277.

26. Ibid.

27. Ibid., 1229–1230, 1299–1300.

28. Sebald, *With MacArthur*, 269; Fearey, "Summary of the Negotiations," 294–295.

29. Truman speech, *DOSB*, vol. 25, Sept. 17, 1951, 447–450; see U.S. Congress, *Selected Speeches—Douglas MacArthur*, 33–38, in which he reviewed the achievements of the occupation.

30. *FRUS, 1951*, vol. 6, no. 1, 1315–1318.

31. Multilateral Japan Peace Treaty, signed Sept. 8, 1951, *TIAS*, vol. 3, part 3 (1952), 3169–3325; Dunn, *Peace-Making*, 183–184. Dulles told the Soviets that the United States would support Soviet claims to the Kuriles and South Sakhalin if the USSR became a party to the Japanese peace treaty (*FRUS, 1951*, vol. 6, no. 1, 886).

32. Sebald, *With MacArthur*, 278–280; Nishimura, "Sanfuranshisuko kōwa," 36.

33. *FRUS, 1951*, vol. 6, no. 1, 1343–1344; Nishimura, *Sanfuranshisuko heiwa*, 272–278; Acheson, *Present at the Creation*, 547; Takemae, *Senryō sengoshi*, 17.

34. Nishimura, "Sanfuranshisuko kōwa," 36; Inoki, *Hyōden Yoshida*, vol. 3, 418.

35. *FRUS, 1951*, vol. 6, no. 1, 1339; James, *The Years of MacArthur*, vol. 3, 352; Dulles message to MacArthur, Sept. 6, 1951, MMA, RG 21.

36. Acheson, *Present at the Creation*, 544, 551; United States–Japan Secu-

rity Treaty, signed Sept. 8, 1951, *TIAS*, vol. 3, part 3 (1952), 3329–3341.

37. *KJ*, vol. 3, 48–50; Inoki, *Hyōden Yoshida*, vol. 3, 418; Kosaka, *Saishō Yoshida*, 4. A year later Yoshida told the American ambassador that the emperor had advised him to give up cigars; Yoshida said in reply he had no intention of doing so (Murphy desp., Sept. 13, 1952, NRAW, DOS file, RG 59, Box 4246).

38. Nishimura, "Sanfuranshisuko kōwa," 37. (See Packard, *Protest*, 252–302.)

39. *DOSB*, vol. 25, Sept. 17, 1951, 465.

40. *FRUS, 1951*, vol. 6, no. 1, 250–251; *NYT*, Sept. 9, 1951, 1, 22, 25, 28.

41. *Yomiuri*, Aug. 13, 1979, 10.

42. Iriye, *The Cold War*, 93–97, 182–191.

43. Igarashi, "Peace Making," 11, no. 2 (Summer 1985), 323–356; Masumi, *Postwar Politics*, 218. See Williams, "Diet Interpellations on the Peace and Security Treaties," memos dated Oct. 19 and Oct. 28, 1951, JWC.

44. *FRUS, 1951*, vol. 6, no. 1, 1416–1418, 1347, editorial note; Nishimura, *Sanfuranshisuko heiwa*, 312–326; W. Cohen, "China," 40.

45. *FRUS, 1951*, vol. 6, no. 1, 1437–1439.

46. Ibid., 1443–1446. As early as May 1951 Yoshida had indicated that Japan would not make a treaty with the PRC but would make peace with the ROC (*FRUS, 1951*, vol. 6, no. 1, 1050). On December 13, 1951, Yoshida handed Dulles a short draft treaty Japan proposed to negotiate with the Nationalist government after the multilateral treaty came into force, but Dulles paid little attention to it (ibid., 1436–1437; *SD*, Dec. 13, 1951). Nevertheless, the impression remains strong in Japan and among foreign scholars that the United States pressured Yoshida into agreeing to make a treaty with the ROC (Masumi, *Postwar Politics*, 217–218). Dower pointed out that Yoshida may have been ambivalent about the China issue (*Empire*, 404).

47. *FRUS, 1951*, vol. 6, no. 1, 1446–1447, 1467–1470.

48. Ibid., 1465–1467. Yoshida remained worried about his letter. He wrote to Dulles on Dec. 27 urging that the United States and the United Kingdom reach agreement on China policy, with which Japan would go along for the sake of a common front of the free nations (ibid., 1471–1472; *SD*, Dec. 27, 1951).

49. *FRUS, 1952*, vol. 14, no. 2, 1077–1080, memo of Jan. 10, 1952, Eden-Dulles meeting.

50. Acheson, *Present at the Creation*, 772; Schonberger, *Aftermath of War*, 275–276; *SD*, Jan. 15, 1952.

51. Buckley, *Occupation Diplomacy*, 181.

52. *FRUS, 1952–1954*, vol. 14, no. 2, 1248; Usui, "Postwar Japan-China Relations," *Kodansha Encyclopedia of Japan*, vol. 1, 290.

53. *FRUS, 1952–1954*, vol. 14, no. 2, 1251–1252, 1259–1262; Owada Hisashi, "Korea-Japan Treaty of 1965," and Soon Sung Cho, "Korea-Japan Treaty of 1965, Supplementary Agreements," *Kodansha Encyclopedia of Japan*, vol. 4, 287–288.

54. Text of administrative agreement, *TIAS*, vol. 3, part 4 (1952), 3341–3419; *FRUS, 1952–1954*, vol. 14, no. 2, 1197–1206.

55. DA tel. W 87569 to CINCFE, Aug. 1, 1950, MMA, RG 9, radiograms;

CINCFE tel. 021209 to DA, Aug. 2, 1950, MMA, RG 9; J. Williams, *Japan's Political Revolution*, 278–279.

56. *NYT*, May 2, 1952, 1, 3; *Asahi shimbun*, May 2, 1952, 1; Shinobu, *Sengo Nihon seijishi*, vol. 4, 1432.

AFTERMATH

1. *Asahi shimbun*, Oct. 21, 1967, 15, and Oct. 23, 1967, 14; Horie, "Yoshida-san no senrei," 251–252.

2. Wray and Conroy (eds.), *Japan Examined*, 335–364.

3. *NYT*, Aug. 8, 1985, 1, 3. I am indebted to Carol Gluck for this reference.

4. *YM*, 60.

Bibliography

Acheson, Dean. *Present at the Creation: My Years in the State Department.* New York: Norton, 1969.

Adams, T. F. M., and Hoshii Iwao. *A Financial History of the New Japan.* Tokyo: Kodansha, 1972.

Aduard, E. J. Lewe van. *Japan: From Surrender to Peace.* The Hague: Martinus Nijhoff, 1953.

Allen, G. C. *Japan's Economic Recovery.* London: Oxford University Press, 1958.

Allinson, Gary. "Japan's Second Bureaucracy: Civil Service Reforms and the Allied Occupation." In *The Occupation of Japan: Educational and Social Reform,* edited by Thomas W. Burkman, 471–497. Norfolk, Va.: Mac-Arthur Memorial Foundation, 1982.

Allison, John M. *Ambassador from the Prairie, or Allison Wonderland.* Tokyo: Charles E. Tuttle, 1975.

Amakawa Akira. "Senryō seisaku to kanryō no taiō" (Occupation policy and the bureaucratic response). In *Shisō no kagaku kenkyūkaihen,* 215–246. Tokyo: Gendaishi Shuppankai, 1978.

Arisawa Hiromi (ed.). *Shōwa keizaishi* (Economic history of the Shōwa period). 2 vols. Tokyo: Nikkei Shinsho, 1980.

Arisue Seizō. *Shūsen hishi, Arisue kikanchō no shuki* (Memoir of group leader Arisue). Tokyo: Fuyō Shobō, 1976.

Asahi Shimbun (ed.). *The Pacific Rivals.* Tokyo: Weatherhill/Asahi, 1972.

Asakai Kōichirō. *Shoki tainichi senryō seisaku* (Early occupation policy). 2 vols. Tokyo: Mainichi Shimbunsha, 1978.

Ashida Hitoshi. *Ashida Hitoshi nikki* (Diary of Ashida Hitoshi). Tokyo: Iwanami Shoten, 1986.

Auer, James E. *The Postwar Rearmament of Japanese Maritime Forces, 1945–*

71. New York: Praeger, 1973. (First published in Japanese as *Yomigaeru Nihon kaigun*. 2 vols. [Tokyo: Jiji Tsūshinsha, 1972.])

Baerwald, Hans H. "Occupation Purge." *Kodansha Encyclopedia of Japan*, vol. 6, 58. Tokyo: Kodansha, 1983.

———. *The Purge of Japanese Leaders Under the Occupation*. Berkeley and Los Angeles: University of California Press, 1959.

Ball, W. Macmahon. *Japan—Enemy or Ally?* New York: John Day, 1949.

Barnet, Richard J. *The Alliance: America-Europe-Japan, Makers of the Postwar World*. New York: Simon and Schuster, 1983.

Beal, John R. *John Foster Dulles, 1888–1959: A Biography*. New York: Harper & Brothers, 1959.

Beer, Lawrence Ward (ed.). *Constitutionalism in Asia: Asian Views of the American Influence*. Berkeley and Los Angeles: University of California Press, 1979.

Bergamini, David. *Japan's Imperial Conspiracy*. New York: Pocket Books, 1972.

Bernstein, Barton J. "Unravelling a Mystery: American Prisoners of War Killed at Hiroshima." *American Foreign Service Journal* (Oct. 1979): 17 ff.

———. "The Week We Went to War: American Intervention in the Korean Civil War, Part II." *American Foreign Service Journal* (Feb. 1977): 8–9.

Bisson, T. A. *Nihon senryō kaisōki* (An occupation memoir). Tokyo: Sanseido, 1983.

———. *Prospects for Democracy in Japan*. New York: Macmillan, 1949.

———. *Zaibatsu Dissolution in Japan*. Berkeley and Los Angeles: University of California Press, 1976.

Blair, Clay, Jr. *MacArthur*. New York: Pocket Books, 1977.

Blakeslee, George H. *The Far Eastern Commission: A Study in International Cooperation, 1945 to 1952*. DOS Publication 5138, Far Eastern Series 60. Washington, D.C.: GPO, 1953.

Blum, Robert M. *Drawing the Line: The Origin of the American Containment Policy in East Asia*. New York: Norton, 1982.

Bohlen, Charles E. *Witness to History, 1929–1969*. New York: Norton, 1973.

Borden, William S. *The Pacific Alliance*. Madison: University of Wisconsin Press, 1984.

Borg, Dorothy, and Shumpei Okamoto (eds.). *Pearl Harbor as History: Japanese-American Relations, 1931–1941*. Studies of the East Asia Institute. New York: Columbia University Press, 1972.

Borton, Hugh. "The Administration and Structure of the Japanese Government." *DOSB*, vol. 11, Dec. 24, 1944, 817–833.

———. "The Allied Occupation of Japan, 1945–1947." In *The Far East, 1942–1946*, edited by F. J. Jones, Hugh Borton, and B. R. Pearn, 307–428. London: Oxford University Press, 1955.

———. "American Presurrender Planning for Postwar Japan." Occasional Papers of the East Asia Institute. New York: Columbia University, 1967.

——— (ed.). *Japan*. Ithaca: Cornell University Press, 1951.

———. *Japan's Modern Century*. New York: Ronald Press, 1955.

———. "Proposals for an Early Peace Treaty and Extended Visit to Japan."

New York: 1983, unpublished ms.

Bouterse, Arthur D., Philip H. Taylor, and Arthur A. Maas. "American Military Government Experience in Japan." In *American Experiences in Military Government in World War II,* edited by C. J. Friedrich, 318–354. New York: Rinehart, 1948.

Bowers, Faubion. "How Japan Won the War: 25 Years Ago." *New York Times Magazine,* Aug. 30, 1970.

―――. "The Late General MacArthur, Warts and All." *Esquire* (Jan. 1967): 91 ff.

Brackman, Arnold C. *The Other Nuremberg: The Untold Story of the Tokyo War Crimes Trials.* New York: Quill/William Morrow, 1987.

Buckley, Roger. *Japan Today.* 2nd ed. Cambridge: Cambridge University Press, 1990.

―――. *Occupation Diplomacy: Britain, the United States and Japan, 1945–1952.* Cambridge: Cambridge University Press, 1982.

Butow, Robert J. C. *Japan's Decision to Surrender.* Stanford: Stanford University Press, 1954.

―――. *Tōjō and the Coming of the War.* Stanford: Stanford University Press, 1961.

Byrnes, James F. *All in One Lifetime.* New York: Harper & Brothers, 1958.

―――. *Speaking Frankly.* New York: Harper & Brothers, 1947.

Cary, Otis (ed.). *War-Wasted Asia, Letters, 1945–1946.* Tokyo: Kodansha, 1975.

Cohen, Bernard. *The Political Process and Foreign Policy: The Making of the Japanese Peace Settlement.* Princeton: Princeton University Press, 1957.

Cohen, Jerome B. *Japan's Economy in War and Reconstruction.* Minneapolis: University of Minnesota Press, 1949.

―――. *Japan's Postwar Economy.* Bloomington: Indiana University Press, 1958.

Cohen, Theodore. "Labor Democratization in Japan: The First Years." In *The Occupation of Japan: Economic Policy and Reform,* edited by Lawrence H. Redford, 162–173. Norfolk, Va.: MacArthur Memorial Foundation, 1978.

―――. *Remaking Japan: The American Occupation as New Deal,* edited by Herbert Passin. New York: Free Press, 1987.

Cohen, Warren I. "China in Japanese-American Relations." In *The United States and Japan in the Postwar World,* edited by Akira Iriye and Warren I. Cohen, 36–60. Lexington: University of Kentucky Press, 1989.

Coleman, Samuel. "Harry Kelly and the Early Years of Japanese Science Research Under the Occupation." Paper prepared for the Washington and Southeast region seminar on Japan, College Park, Maryland, Apr. 20, 1985.

Colton, Kenneth. "Prewar Political Influences in Postwar Conservative Parties (Japan)." *American Political Science Review* 42, no. 5 (Oct. 1948): 940–957.

Committee for the Compilation of Materials on Damage Caused by the Atomic Bombs in Hiroshima and Nagasaki (ed.). *The Impact of the A-Bomb: Hiroshima and Nagasaki, 1945–1985.* Tokyo: Iwanami Shoten, 1985.

Comyns-Carr, A. S. "The Tokyo War Crimes Trial." *Far Eastern Survey,* May

18, 1949, 109–114.

"Consider Japan." *The Economist*, Sept. 1, 1962, 793–819; Sept. 8, 1962, 913–932.

Costello, William. *Democracy vs. Feudalism in Postwar Japan*. Tokyo: Itagaki Shoten, 1949.

Coughlin, William J. *Conquered Press*. Palo Alto: Pacific Books, 1952.

Curtis, Gerald L. "The Dulles-Yoshida Negotiations on the San Francisco Peace Treaty." In *Columbia Essays in International Affairs, the Dean's Papers*, edited by Andrew W. Cordier, vol. 2, 37–61. New York: Columbia University Press, 1966.

Cusumano, Michael. *The Japanese Automobile Industry*. Cambridge, Mass.: Council on East Asian Studies, Harvard University, 1985.

Dingman, Roger. "Reconsiderations: The United States–Japan Security Treaty." *Pacific Community* 7, no. 4 (July 1976): 471–493.

———. "The View from Down Under." In *The Occupation of Japan: The International Context*, edited by Thomas Burkman, 91–115. Norfolk, Va.: MacArthur Memorial Foundation, 1984.

Doi Takeo. *The Anatomy of Dependence*. Tokyo: Kodansha, 1973.

Dore, Ronald P. *City Life in Japan: A Study of a Tokyo Ward*. Berkeley and Los Angeles: University of California Press, 1958.

———. *Land Reform in Japan*. London: Oxford University Press, 1959.

———. *Shinohata: A Portrait of a Japanese Village*. New York: Pantheon, 1978.

Dower, John W. *Empire and Aftermath: Yoshida Shigeru and the Japanese Experience, 1878–1954*. Cambridge, Mass.: Council on East Asian Studies, Harvard University, 1979.

———. "The Eye of the Beholder: Background Notes on the U.S.–Japan Military Relationship." *Bulletin of Concerned Asian Scholars* 2, no. 1 (Oct. 1969): 15–31.

———. "Introduction." In *Origins of the Modern Japanese State, Selected Writings of E. H. Norman*, 1–100. New York: Pantheon, 1975.

———. "Occupied Japan as History and Occupation History as Politics." *Journal of Asian Studies* 34, no. 2 (Feb. 1975): 485–504.

———. "Occupied Japan in the American Lake, 1949–1950." In *America's Asia: Dissenting Essays on Asian-American Relations*, edited by Edward Friedman and Mark Selden, 146–206. New York: Pantheon, 1971.

———. "Reform and Reconsolidation." In *Japan Examined: Perspectives on Modern Japanese History*, edited by Harry Wray and Hilary Conroy, 343–351. Honolulu: University of Hawaii Press, 1983.

———. "Rethinking World War II in Asia." *Reviews in American History* 12, no. 2 (June 1984): 155–169.

———. "The Superdomino in Postwar Asia: Japan In and Out of the Pentagon Papers." In *The Senator Gravel Edition of the Pentagon Papers*, edited by Noam Chomsky and Howard Zinn, vol. 5, 101–142. Boston: Beacon Press, 1972.

———. *War Without Mercy: Race and Power in the Pacific War*. New York: Pantheon, 1986.

———. "Yoshida in the Scales of History." Paper prepared for Hōsei University Symposium on "The Allied Occupation of Japan in World History," 1983. (Published in Japanese as "Yoshida Shigeru no shiteki ichi." In *Sekaishi no naka no Nihon senryō*, edited by Sodei Rinjirō, 142–156.) Tokyo: Nihon Hyōronsha, 1985.

Drifte, Reinhard. "Japan's Involvement in the Korean War." In *The Korean War in History*, edited by James Cotton and Ian Neary, 120–134. Manchester: Manchester University Press, 1988.

Dunn, Frederick S. *Peace-Making and the Settlement with Japan*. Princeton: Princeton University Press, 1963.

Duus, Peter. *The Rise of Modern Japan*. Boston: Houghton Mifflin, 1976.

Dynaword, Inc. (ed.). "A Brief History." Tokyo: Toyota Motor Corp., 1982.

Emmerson, John K. *The Japanese Thread: A Life in the U.S. Foreign Service*. New York: Holt, Rinehart and Winston, 1978.

Etō Jun. "Genron tōsei—senryōka Nihon ni okeru kenetsu" (Free speech—occupation censorship). In *Tennō ga baiburu yonda hi*, edited by Ray Moore, 115–154. Tokyo: Kodansha, 1982.

———. *Mo hitotsu no sengoshi* (Another postwar history). Tokyo: Kodansha, 1978.

——— (ed.). *Senryō shiroku* (Occupation records). 4 vols. Tokyo: Kodansha, 1981.

———. "The Severed Tie with the Past: Literature and Occupation Censorship, the Case of Yoshida Mitsuru and 'The Last of the Battleship *Yamato*.'" Paper prepared for the Wilson Center for Scholars Seminar, Washington, D.C., Nov. 13, 1979.

———. *Wasureta koto to wasuresaserareta koto* (Things we forgot and things we were made to forget). Tokyo: Bungei Shunjū, 1979.

Farley, Miriam S. *Aspects of Japan's Labor Problems*. New York: John Day, 1950.

Fearey, Robert A. *The Occupation of Japan, Second Phase: 1948–1950*. New York: Macmillan, 1950.

———. "Summary of the Negotiations Leading Up to the Conclusion of the Treaty of Peace with Japan." In *The Occupation of Japan: The International Context*, edited by Thomas W. Burkman, 279–295. Norfolk, Va.: MacArthur Memorial Foundation, 1984.

FEC-230. "U.S. Policy with Respect to Excessive Concentrations of Economic Power in Japan." In *Antitrust in Japan*, by Eleanor M. Hadley, 495–514. Princeton: Princeton University Press, 1970.

Feis, Herbert. *The Atomic Bomb and the End of World War II*. Princeton: Princeton University Press, 1970.

———. *Contest over Japan*. New York: Norton, 1967.

Fine, Sherwood. *Japan's Postwar Industrial Recovery*. Tokyo: Foreign Affairs Association of Japan, 1953.

Gaddis, John Lewis. *Strategies of Containment*, 89–126. New York: Oxford University Press, 1982.

Gaimushō (Foreign Ministry) (ed.). *Shūsen shiroku* (Records of the end of the war). Tokyo: Shimbun Gekkansha, 1952.

Gallicchio, Mark. *The Cold War Begins in Asia: American East Asian Policy and the Fall of the Japanese Empire.* New York: Columbia University Press, 1988.

Garon, Sheldon. "The Imperial Bureaucracy and Labor Policy in Postwar Japan." *Journal of Asian Studies* 43, no. 3 (May 1984): 441–457.

——. *The State and Labor in Modern Japan.* Berkeley and Los Angeles: University of California Press, 1987.

Gayn, Mark. *Japan Diary.* New York: William Sloane, 1948.

Gibney, Frank. *Japan: The Fragile Superpower.* New York: Norton, 1975.

Gilmartin, William M., and Wolf J. Ladejinsky. "The Promise of Agrarian Reform in Japan." *Foreign Affairs* 26, no. 2 (Jan. 1948): 313–324.

Gimbel, John. *The American Occupation of Germany.* Stanford: Stanford University Press, 1968.

Gluck, Carol. "'Dokuhaku' kara miete kuru Shōwa Tennō no mitsu no kao" (The three faces of Emperor Hirohito as seen from the "Soliloquy"). *Newsweek* (Japanese edition), Dec. 6, 1990, 62–63.

——. "Entangling Illusions—Japanese and American Views of the Occupation." In *New Frontiers in American–East Asian Relations: Essays Presented to Dorothy Borg*, edited by Warren Cohen, 169–236. New York: Columbia University Press, 1983.

Gomer, Robert, John W. Powell, and Bert V. A. Röling. "Japan's Biological Weapons, 1930–1945." *The Bulletin of Atomic Scientists*, Oct. 1981, 43–53.

Goodman, Grant (ed.). *The American Occupation of Japan: A Retrospective View.* Lawrence: University of Kansas Press, 1968.

Gordon, Andrew D. *The Evolution of Labor Relations in Japan: Heavy Industry, 1853–1955.* Cambridge, Mass.: Council on East Asian Studies, Harvard University, 1988.

——. "The United States and Japan in Postwar Asia: Japanese War Reparations, 1945–1960." Honors thesis, Harvard University, Jan. 6, 1975.

Grew, Joseph C. *Turbulent Era: A Diplomatic Record of Forty Years.* 2 vols. Cambridge, Mass.: Riverside Press, 1952.

Gunther, John. *The Riddle of MacArthur: Japan, Korea and the Far East.* New York: Harper & Brothers, 1974.

Hadley, Eleanor M. *Antitrust in Japan.* Princeton: Princeton University Press, 1970.

——. "Zaibatsu, Zaibatsu Dissolution." *Kodansha Encyclopedia of Japan*, vol. 8, 361–366. Tokyo: Kodansha, 1983.

Halberstam, David. *The Reckoning.* New York: William Morrow, 1986.

Hall, Robert King. *Education for a New Japan.* New Haven: Yale University Press, 1949.

Halliday, Jon. *A Political History of Japanese Capitalism.* New York: Pantheon, 1975.

Halliday, Jon, and Bruce Cumings. *Korea, The Unknown War.* New York: Pantheon, 1988.

Hara Fumio. "Makkāsā kainin no isshūkan" (The week MacArthur was relieved). *Ichiokunin no Shōwa-shi—Senryō kara kōwa made*, no. 5 (Nov. 1975): 219–217.

Harries, Meirion, and Susie Harries. *Sheathing the Sword: The Demilitarization of Postwar Japan*. New York: Macmillan, 1987.

Harriman, W. Averell, and Elie Abel. *Special Envoy to Churchill and Stalin, 1941–1946*. New York: Random House, 1975.

Hata Ikuhiko (ed.). *Amerika no tai-nichi senryō seisaku* (U.S. occupation policy toward Japan). Vol. 3 of *Shōwa zaiseishi: Shūsen kara kōwa made*. Tokyo: Tōyō Keizai Shimpōsha, 1976.

———. *Hirohito Tennō itsutsu no ketsudan* (The emperor's five decisions). Tokyo: Kodansha, 1984.

———. "Japan Under the Occupation." *Japan Interpreter* 10, nos. 3–4 (Winter 1976): 361–380.

———. *Nankin jiken* (The Nanjing incident). Tokyo: Chūō Kōron, 1986.

———. *Nihon saigunbi* (Japanese rearmament). Tokyo: Bungei Shunjū, 1976.

———. "The Postwar Period in Retrospect." *Japan Echo*, no. 11 (1984): 12–21.

Hatoyama Ichirō. *Hatoyama Ichirō kaikoroku* (Memoirs of Hatoyama Ichirō). Tokyo: Bungei Shunju, 1957.

Havens, Thomas. *Valley of Darkness: The Japanese People and World War Two*. New York: Norton, 1978.

Hayes, Samuel P. *The Beginning of American Aid to Southeast Asia: The Griffin Mission to Southeast Asia of 1950*. Lexington, Mass.: D. C. Heath, 1971.

Heinrichs, Waldo H., Jr. *American Ambassador: Joseph C. Grew and the Development of the United States Diplomatic Tradition*. Boston: Little, Brown, 1966.

Henderson, Dan Fenno. *The Constitution of Japan: Its First Twenty Years, 1947–67*. Seattle: University of Washington Press, 1968.

Hoopes, Townsend. *The Devil and John Foster Dulles*. Boston: Atlantic Monthly Press, 1973.

Horie Shigeo. "Yoshida-san no senrei" (Yoshida's baptism). *Chūō kōron* 83, no. 2 (Feb. 1968): 251–252.

Horwitz, Solis. "The Tokyo Trial." *International Conciliation*, no. 465 (Nov. 1950): 474–584.

Hosoya Chihiro (ed.). *Japan's Postwar Diplomacy in the Asian-Pacific Region*. Occasional Paper, no. 1. Urasa: International University of Japan, 1984.

———. "Japan's Response to U.S. Policy on the Japanese Peace Treaty: The Dulles-Yoshida Talks of January–February 1951." *Hitotsubashi Journal of Law and Economics* 10 (Dec. 1981): 15–27.

———. "Retrogression in Japan's Foreign Policy Decision-Making Process." In *Dilemmas of Growth in Prewar Japan*, edited by James W. Morley, 81–105. Princeton: Princeton University Press, 1971.

———. "The Road to San Francisco." *Japanese Journal of American Studies*, no. 1 (1981): 87–117.

Hosoya Chihiro and Homma Nageyo (eds.). *Nichibei kankeishi* (History of Japanese-U.S. relations). Tokyo: Yuikaku Sensho, 1982.

Hunsberger, Warren. *Japan and the United States in World Trade*. New York: Harper & Row, 1964.

Ienaga Saburō. *Taiheiyō sensō* (The Pacific War). Tokyo: Iwanami Shoten, 1978.

Igarashi Takeshi. "American-Japanese Peace-Making and the Cold War, 1947–1951." *Amerika kenkyū* 15 (1978): 166–187.

———. "George Kennan and the Change in Occupation Policy Toward Japan, NSC 13/2." Paper prepared for a conference at Amherst College, Amherst, Massachusetts, Aug. 1980.

———. "Peace-Making and Party Politics: The Formation of the Domestic Foreign-Policy System in Postwar Japan." *Journal of Japanese Studies* 11, no. 2 (Summer 1985): 323–356.

Ike, Nobutaka (ed.). *Japan's Decision for War: Records of the 1941 Policy Conferences*. Stanford: Stanford University Press, 1967.

Inamaru Keizō. "Ma Gensui to no yonjippun" (Forty minutes with General MacArthur). In *Makkāsā no kiroku, sengo Nihon no genten*, edited by Sodei Rinjirō and Fukushima Jūrō, 209–211. Tokyo: Nippon Hōsō Shuppan Kyōkai, 1981.

Inoki Masamichi. *Hyōden Yoshida Shigeru* (Yoshida Shigeru: A critical biography). 3 vols. Tokyo: Yomiuri Shimbunsha, 1981.

Iokibe Makoto. "American Policy Toward Japan's 'Unconditional Surrender.'" *Japanese Journal of American Studies* 1, no. 1 (1981): 19–54.

———. *Beikoku no Nihon senryō seisaku* (American occupation policy for Japan). 2 vols. Tokyo: Chūō Kōron, 1985.

Iriye, Akira. *Across the Pacific: An Inner History of American–East Asian Relations*. New York: Harcourt, Brace & World, 1967.

———. *The Cold War in Asia*. Englewood Cliffs, N.J.: Prentice-Hall, 1974.

———. *Power and Culture: The Japanese-American War, 1941–1945*. Cambridge, Mass.: Harvard University Press, 1981.

Iriye, Akira, and Warren I. Cohen (eds.). *The United States and Japan in the Postwar World*. Lexington: University of Kentucky Press, 1989.

Irokawa Daikichi. *The Culture of the Meiji Period*, edited by Marius B. Jansen. Princeton: Princeton University Press, 1985.

Ishibashi Tanzan. *Tanzan kaisō* (Recollections of Tanzan). Tokyo: Mainichi Shimbunsha, 1951.

Ishida Takeshi, and Ellis S. Krauss (eds.). *Democracy in Japan*. Pittsburgh: University of Pittsburgh Press, 1989.

James, D. Clayton. *The Years of MacArthur*. 3 vols. Boston: Houghton Mifflin, 1970–1985.

Johnson, Chalmers. *Conspiracy at Matsukawa*. Berkeley and Los Angeles: University of California Press, 1972.

———. *An Instance of Treason: Ozaki Hotsumi and the Sorge Spy Ring*. Stanford: Stanford University Press, 1964.

———. "Japan: Who Governs? An Essay on Official Bureaucracy." *Journal of Japanese Studies* 2, no. 1 (Autumn 1975): 1–28.

———. *Japan's Public Policy Companies*. AEI-Hoover Policies Studies 24. Washington, D.C.: American Enterprise Institute, 1978.

————. *MITI and the Japanese Miracle: The Growth of Industrial Policy, 1925–1975*. Stanford: Stanford University Press, 1982.

Johnson, Paul. *Modern Times: The World from the Twenties to the Eighties*. New York: Harper & Row, 1983.

Johnson, Sheila K. *The Japanese Through American Eyes*. Stanford: Stanford University Press, 1988.

Johnson, U. Alexis. *The Right Hand of Power*. Englewood Cliffs, N.J.: Prentice-Hall, 1984.

"Jūnen no ayumi" (Journey of ten years). *Mainichi shimbunsha*, 15 parts, Aug. 5 to Aug. 20, 1955.

Kades, Charles L. "The American Role in Revising Japan's Imperial Constitution." *Political Science Quarterly* (Summer 1989): 215–247.

————. "Current Issues Confronting SCAP." Statement made to the Council on Foreign Relations, New York City, May 10, 1949.

————. "Revisiting Revising the Imperial Constitution of Japan." New York, 1988, unpublished ms.

Kaplan, David E., and Alex Dubro. *Yakuza: The Explosive Account of Japan's Criminal Underworld*. Reading, Mass.: Addison-Wesley, 1986.

Kase Toshikazu. *Journey to the Missouri*, edited by David N. Rowe. New Haven: Yale University Press, 1950.

————. "Kōen—Yoshida Shigeru o kataru" (A discussion about Yoshida Shigeru). *Kasekikai kaihō* 281 (July 1989): 12–16; 282 (Aug. 1989): 11–15.

————. *Yoshida Shigeru no yuigon* (The legacy of Yoshida Shigeru). Tokyo: Yomiuri Shimbunsha, 1967.

Katayama Naikaku Kiroku Kankōkai. *Katayama Tetsu to sengo no seiji* (Katayama Tetsu and postwar politics). Tokyo: Jiji Tsūshinsha, 1980.

Kawai, Kazuo. *Japan's American Interlude*. Chicago: University of Chicago Press, 1960.

Kawashima Takayoshi. *Nihonjin no hōishiki* (Japanese perceptions of law). Tokyo: Iwanami Shoten, 1967.

Kawashima Yasuhide. "The Americanization of Japanese Family Law, 1945–1975." *Law in Japan* 16 (1983): 54–68.

Keenan, Joseph B., and Brendan F. Brown. *Crimes Against International Law*. Washington, D.C.: Public Affairs Press, 1950.

Kennan, George F. *Memoirs, 1925–1950*. Boston: Little, Brown, 1967.

Kennedy, Paul. *The Rise and Fall of the Great Powers: Economic Change and Military Conflict from 1500 to 2000*. New York: Random House, 1987.

Kenney, George C. *The MacArthur I Know*. New York: Duell, Sloan and Pearce, 1951.

Kennoki Toshihiro. *Ushi no ayumi, kyōiku ni waga michi o mitomete* (At a snail's pace—finding our way in education). Tokyo: Shōgakkan, 1973.

Kern, Harry. "Harry Kern's Story." *Yomiuri shimbun* (English ed.), 12 parts, Sept. 1, 1979–Sept. 19, 1979.

Kido Kōichi. *Kido Kōichi nikki* (Kido Kōichi diary). 2 vols. Tokyo: Tokyo Daigaku Shuppankai, 1966.

Kodansha Encyclopedia of Japan. 9 vols. Tokyo: Kodansha, 1983.

Kojima Noboru. *Nihon senryō* (Occupation of Japan). 3 vols. Tokyo: Bungei Shunjū, 1978.

———. "Sempan risuto no naka no Tennō" (The emperor on a war criminal list). *Bungei shunjū* (Dec. 1975): 278–299.

———. "Tennō to Amerika to taiheiyō sensō" (The emperor, the United States and the Pacific War). *Bungei shunjū* (Nov. 1975): 94–127.

———. *Tennō to sensō sekinin* (The emperor and war responsibility). Tokyo: Bungei Shunjū, 1988.

Kolko, Gabriel, and Joyce Kolko. *The Limits of Power*. New York: Pantheon, 1972.

Kon Hidemi. *Yoshida Shigeru*. Tokyo: Kodansha, 1967.

Kōsaka Masataka. *One Hundred Million Japanese: The Postwar Experience*. Tokyo: Kodansha, 1972.

———. *Saishō Yoshida Shigeru* (Premier Yoshida Shigeru). Tokyo: Chūō Kōron, 1968.

Koseki Shōichi. "Japanizing the Constitution." *Japan Quarterly* 35, no. 3 (July–Sept. 1988): 234–241.

———. *Shinkempō no tanjō* (The birth of the new constitution). Tokyo: Chūō Kōron, 1989.

———. "Shōchō tennōsei no seiritsu katei" (The process of creating the symbolic emperor). *Hōritsu Jihō* 52, no. 7 (1980), 92–99; no. 8, 95–191; no. 10, 78–83; no. 11, 81–87.

Kowalski, Frank. *Nihon saigumbi: Watakushi wa Nihon o saibusō shita* (The rearmament of Japan: How I rearmed Japan). Tokyo: Saimaru Shuppankai, 1969.

Ladejinsky, Wolf J. "Agriculture." In *Japan*, edited by Hugh Borton, 46–50. Ithaca: Cornell University Press, 1951.

Lehmann, Jean-Pierre. *The Roots of Modern Japan*. New York: St Martin's Press, 1982.

Lincoln, Edward J. "The Shōwa Economic Experience." *Daedalus* 119, no. 3 (1990): 191–208.

Liu, James. "The Tokyo Trial: Source Materials." *Far Eastern Survey*, July 28, 1948, 168–170.

Livingston, Jon, Joe Moore, and Felicia Oldfather. *Postwar Japan—1945 to the Present*, vol. 2. New York: Pantheon, 1973.

Lockwood, William W. "Industrial Development." In *Japan*, edited by Hugh Borton, 64–80. Ithaca: Cornell University Press, 1951.

Long, Gavin. *MacArthur as Military Commander*. London: B. T. Batsford, 1969.

Lowe, Peter. *The Origins of the Korean War*. London: Longman, 1986.

MacArthur, Douglas. *Reminiscences*. New York: McGraw-Hill, 1964.

McCraw, Thomas K. (ed.). *America Versus Japan*. Boston: Harvard Business School Press, 1986.

McDiarmid, Orville J. "The Japanese Exchange Rate." *Far Eastern Survey* 18, no. 12 (July 15, 1949): 133–135.

McNelly, Theodore H. "General MacArthur's Pacifism." *International Journal on World Peace* 6, no. 1 (Jan.–Mar. 1989): 41–59.

———. "'Induced Revolution': The Policy and Process of Constitutional Reform in Occupied Japan." In *Democratizing Japan: The Allied Occupation*, edited by Robert E. Ward and Sakamoto Yoshikazu, 76–106. Honolulu: University of Hawaii Press, 1987.

———. "Limited Voting in Japanese Parliamentary Elections." Paper prepared for the annual meeting of the American Political Science Association, Denver, Colorado, Sept. 2 to Sept. 5, 1982.

———. "Military Occupations and Social Revolutions: The Cases of Germany and Japan." Paper presented at the eleventh World Congress of Sociology, New Delhi, Aug. 18–22, 1986.

———. *Politics and Government in Japan.* 3rd ed. Lanham, Md.: University Press of America, 1984.

———. "The Renunciation of War in the Japanese Constitution." *Armed Forces and Society* 13, no. 1 (Fall 1986): 81–106.

Maeda Tamon. "The Direction of Postwar Education in Japan." *Japan Quarterly* 3, no. 4 (1956): 414–425.

Mainichi Shimbunsha (ed.). *Ichiokunin no shōwashi* (The story of 100 million people in the Shōwa era). 5 vols. Tokyo: Mainichi Shimbunsha, 1975–1980.

Maki, John M. (trans. and ed.). *Japan's Commission on the Constitution: The Final Report.* Seattle: University of Washington Press, 1980.

———. "The Role of the Bureaucracy in Japan." *Pacific Affairs*, no. 20 (1947): 391.

Manchester, William. *American Caesar: Douglas MacArthur, 1880–1964.* Boston: Little, Brown, 1978.

Martin, Edwin M. *The Allied Occupation of Japan.* Stanford: Stanford University Press, 1948.

Maruyama Masao. *Thought and Behavior in Modern Japanese Politics*, edited by Ivan Morris. London: Oxford University Press, 1963.

Mashbir, Sidney F. *I Was an American Spy.* New York: Vantage Press, 1953.

Mason, Mark. "The Liaison Offices in the Occupation of Japan." Cambridge, Mass.: Harvard University, Jan. 9, 1984, unpublished course paper.

Masumi Junnosuke. *Postwar Politics in Japan, 1945–1955.* Berkeley: Institute of East Asian Studies, University of California, 1985.

Matsumoto Seichō. *Nihon no kuroi kiri* (Black mist over Japan). Tokyo: Bungei Shunjū, 1974.

Matsumoto Shigeharu. "Kaisō no Yoshida Shigeru" (Yoshida Shigeru remembered). *Chūō Kōron* (Dec. 1967): 193.

Matsumoto Shunichi and Andō Yoshirō. "Daitōa sensō: Shūsen gaikō" (The Great East Asia war: End of war diplomacy). In *Nihon Gaikōshi*, vol. 25. Tokyo: Kajima Kenkyūjo Shuppankai, 1972.

Mayo, Marleen. "Civil Censorship and Media Control in Early Occupied Japan." In *Americans as Proconsuls: United States Military Government in Germany and Japan, 1944–1952*, edited by Robert Wolfe, 263–320. Carbondale: Southern Illinois University Press, 1984.

———. "Popularizing Japan's Postwar Constitution." *Japan Society Newsletter* (Oct. 1987): 2–7.

Miles, Rufus E., Jr. "Hiroshima—The Strange Myth of Half a Million American Lives Saved." *International Security* (Fall 1985): 121–140.

Millis, Walter (ed.). *The Forrestal Diaries*. New York: Viking Press, 1951.

Minear, Richard H. *Victors' Justice: The Tokyo War Crimes Trial*. Tokyo: Charles E. Tuttle, 1971.

Miyashita Akitoshi. "The Origins of the Pacific Alliance: U.S. Containment Strategy and Japan, 1947–1952." *American University Journal of International Affairs* 1, no. 1 (Fall 1990): 57–109.

Miyazawa Kiichi. *Tōkyō-Washinton no mitsudan* (Washington-Tokyo secret talks). Tokyo: Bigokai, 1975.

Montgomery, John D. *Aftermath: Tarnished Outcomes of American Foreign Policy*. Dover, Mass.: Auburn House, 1986.

———. *Forced to Be Free: Artificial Revolution in Germany and Japan*. Chicago: University of Chicago Press, 1957.

Moore, Barrington, Jr. *Social Origins of Dictatorship and Democracy: Lord and Peasant in the Making of the Modern World*. Boston: Beacon, 1966.

Moore, Joe. *Japanese Workers and the Struggle for Power, 1945–1947*. Madison: University of Wisconsin Press, 1983.

———. "Production Control: Workers Control in Early Postwar Japan." *Bulletin of Concerned Asian Scholars* 17, no. 4 (Oct.–Dec. 1985): 2–26.

Moore, Ray. "Reflections on the Occupation of Japan." *Journal of Asian Studies*, no. 38 (Aug. 1979): 721–734.

——— (ed.). *Tennō ga baiburu o yonda hi* (The day the emperor read the Bible). Tokyo: Kodansha, 1982.

Morimura Seiichi. *Akuma no hōshoku* (The devil's gluttony). Tokyo: Kōbunsha, 1981.

Morishima Michio. *Why Has Japan 'Succeeded'? Western Technology and the Japanese Ethos*. Cambridge: Cambridge University Press, 1982.

Morison, Samuel Eliot. *Victory in the Pacific*. Vol. 14 of *History of United States Naval Operations in World War II*. Boston: Little, Brown, 1960.

Morita Akio. *Made in Japan—Akio Morita and Sony*. New York: Dutton, 1986.

Morito Tatsuo. "Katayama naikaku no koro" (The time of the Katayama cabinet). In *Kataritsugu shōwashi*, vol. 6, 99–143. Tokyo: Asahi Shimbunsha, 1977.

Morley, James W. (ed.). *Dilemmas of Growth in Prewar Japan*. Princeton: Princeton University Press, 1971.

———. "The First Seven Weeks." *Japan Interpreter* 6, no. 2 (Sept. 1970): 151–164.

Morris, Ivan I. *Nationalism and the Right Wing in Japan: A Study of Postwar Trends*. London: Oxford University Press, 1960.

Murata Kiyoaki. *Japan: The State of the Nation*. Tokyo: Japan Press, 1979.

Murphy, Robert. *Diplomat Among Warriors*. Garden City, N.Y.: Doubleday, 1964.

Nagai Yōnosuke and Akira Iriye (eds.). *The Origins of the Cold War in Asia*. New York: Columbia University Press, 1977.

Naganuma Setsuo. "Tennō-Makkāsā daisankai kaiken no zembō" (Story of the third emperor-MacArthur meeting). *Asahi Jiyānaru* (March 1984): 26–30.

Nakamura Takafusa. *The Postwar Japanese Economy*. Tokyo: University of Tokyo Press, 1981.

Nanto, Dick K. "The United States Role in the Postwar Economic Recovery of Japan." Ph.D. diss., Harvard University, 1977.

Nishi Toshio. *Unconditional Democracy: Education and Politics in Occupied Japan, 1945–1952*. Stanford: Hoover Institution Press, 1982.

Nishimura Kumao. "Ampo jōyaku kaitei no rekishi" (History of the revision of the security treaty). *Kokusaihō gaikō zasshi* 59, nos. 1–2 (July 1960): 1–27.

———. "Kōwa jōyaku" (Peace treaties). In *Kataritsugu Shōwashi*, vol. 6, 209–254. Tokyo: Asahi Shimbunsha, 1977.

———. *Sanfuranshisuko heiwa jōyaku* (San Francisco peace treaty). Vol. 27 of *Nihon gaikōshi*. Tokyo: Kajima Kenkyūjo Shuppankai, 1971.

———. "Sanfuranshisuko kōwa jōyaku ni tsuite" (The San Francisco peace treaties). *Kasumigaseki-kai kaihō*, no. 400 (Dec. 5, 1978): 23–37.

———. "Sanfuranshisuko no Omoide" (Memories of San Francisco). *Chūō Kōron* (May 1957): 74–80.

Nixon, Richard M. *Leaders*. New York: Warner Books, 1982.

Nolte, Sharon. *Liberalism in Modern Japan: Ishibashi Tanzan and His Teachers, 1905–1960*. Berkeley: University of California Press, 1987.

Ohtake Hideo. "Postwar Politics: Liberalism Versus Social Democracy." *Japan Echo*, no. 2 (1983): 43–53.

Ōkita Saburō. *Japan's Challenging Years: Reflections on My Lifetime*. Canberra: Australia-Japan Research Centre, 1983.

———. *Watakushi no rirekisho* (My resume). Tokyo: Nihon Keizai Shimbunsha, 1977.

Olson, Lawrence. *Japan in Postwar Asia*. New York: Praeger, 1970.

Ōnuma Yasuaki. "Beyond Victors' Justice." *Japan Echo* 11, Special Issue (1984): 62–72.

Oppler, Alfred C. *Legal Reform in Occupied Japan: A Participant Looks Back*. Princeton: Princeton University Press, 1976.

Osborne, John. "My Dear General." *Life*, Nov. 27, 1950, 127–141.

Pacific War Research Society (comp.). *Japan's Longest Day*. Tokyo: Kodansha, 1973. (Originally published in Japanese as *Nihon no ichiban nagai hi* [Tokyo: Bungei Shunjū, 1965]).

Packard, George R. *Protest in Tokyo: The Security Treaty Crisis of 1960*. Princeton: Princeton University Press, 1966.

Passin, Herbert. "The Legacy of the Occupation—Japan." East Asian Institute Occasional Paper. New York: Columbia University Press, 1968.

Patrick, Hugh. "The Phoenix Risen from the Ashes: Postwar Japan." In *Modern East Asia: Essays in Interpretation*, edited by James B. Crowley, 298–336. New York: Harcourt, Brace and World, 1970.

Pauley, Edwin W. *Report on Japanese Reparations to the President of the United States, November 1945 to April 1946*. DOS publication 3174, Far Eastern Series 25. Washington, D.C.: GPO, 1946.

Pempel, T. J. "The Tar Baby Target: 'Reform' of the Japanese Bureaucracy." In *Democratizing Japan: The Allied Occupation*, edited by Robert E. Ward and Sakamoto Yoshikazu, 157–187. Honolulu: University of Hawaii Press, 1987.

Perry, John Curtis. *Beneath the Eagle's Wings: Americans in Occupied Japan.* New York: Dodd, Mead, 1980.

Peterson, Edward N. *The American Occupation of Germany—Retreat to Victory.* Detroit: Wayne State University Press, 1977.

Pharr, Susan J. "The Politics of Women's Rights." In *Democratizing Japan: The Allied Occupation*, edited by Robert E. Ward and Sakamoto Yoshikazu, 221–252. Honolulu: University of Hawaii Press, 1987.

Piccigallo, Philip R. *The Japanese on Trial: Allied War Crimes Operations in the East, 1945–1951.* Austin: University of Texas Press, 1979.

Powell, John W. "Japan's Biological Weapons: A Hidden Chapter in History." *Bulletin of Atomic Scientists* 37, no. 8 (Oct. 1981): 44–53.

Pruessen, Ronald W. *John Foster Dulles: The Road to Power.* New York: Free Press, 1982.

Quigley, Harold S., and John E. Turner. *The New Japan: Government and Politics.* Minneapolis: University of Minnesota Press, 1956.

Redford, Lawrence H. (ed.). *The Occupation of Japan: Economic Policy and Reform.* Norfolk, Va.: MacArthur Memorial Foundation, 1978.

Reischauer, Edwin O. *Japan: The Story of a Nation.* New York: Knopf, 1974.

———. *The Japanese.* Cambridge, Mass.: Belknap Press, 1977.

———. *The Japanese Today.* Cambridge, Mass.: Belknap Press, 1988.

———. *My Life Between Japan and America.* New York: Harper & Row, 1986.

———. "Two Harvard Luminaries Bid Farewell." *Harvard Independent* (Commencement 1981): 11, 13.

———. *The United States and Japan.* Cambridge, Mass.: Harvard University Press, 1950.

Reitzel, William, Morton A. Kaplan, and Constance G. Coblenz. *United States Foreign Policy, 1945–1955.* Washington, D.C.: Brookings Institution, 1956.

Rhodes, Richard. *The Making of the Atomic Bomb.* New York: Simon and Schuster, 1986.

Ridgway, Matthew B. *Soldier: The Memoirs of Matthew B. Ridgway.* New York: Harper & Brothers, 1956.

Roberts, John G. *Mitsui: Three Centuries of Japanese Business.* Tokyo: Weatherhill, 1973.

Röling, B. V. A., and C. F. Rüter (eds.). *The Tokyo Judgment: The International Military Tribunal for the Far East, 29 April 1946 to 12 November 1948.* 2 vols. Amsterdam: APA Amsterdam Press, 1977.

Rovere, Richard, and Arthur M. Schlesinger, Jr. *The General and the President.* New York: Farrar, Straus and Young, 1951.

Royall, Kenneth C. "Speech, January 6, 1948." In *Postwar Japan—1945 to the Present*, edited by Jon Livingston, Joe Moore, and Felicia Oldfather, vol. 2. New York: Pantheon, 1973.

Sakeda Masatoshi. "Kōwa to kokunai seiji" (Peace settlement and domestic politics). In *Sanfuranshisuko kōwa*, edited by Watanabe Akio and Miyazato Seigen, 87–112. Tokyo: Tōkyō Daigaku Shuppankai, 1986.

Sanmonji Shōhei. "Tōkyō gunji saiban" (Tokyo court). In *Kataritsugu shōwashi*, vol. 5, 281–314. Tokyo: Asahi Shimbunsha, 1977.

Sansom, George. "Can Japan Be Reformed?" *Far Eastern Survey*, Nov. 2, 1949, 258–259.

———. "Conflicting Purposes in Japan." *Foreign Affairs* 26, no. 2 (Jan. 1948): 302–311.

Sansom, Katherine. *Sir George Sansom and Japan: A Memoir*. Tallahasee, Fla.: Diplomatic Press, 1972.

Satō Tatsuō. *Nihon koku kempō no seiritsushi* (History of the enactment of Japan's national constitution). Tokyo: Yuhikaku, 1962.

Scalapino, Robert A. "The American Occupation of Japan—Perspectives After Three Decades." *Annals, American Association of Political and Social Science*, no. 428 (Nov. 1976): 104–113.

Schaller, Michael. *The American Occupation of Japan: The Origins of the Cold War in Asia*. New York: Oxford University Press, 1985.

———. *Douglas MacArthur: The Far Eastern General*. New York: Oxford University Press, 1988.

———. "MacArthur's Japan: The View from Washington." *Diplomatic History* 10, no. 1 (Winter 1986): 1–23.

———. "Securing the Great Crescent: Occupied Japan and the Origins of Containment in Southeast Asia." *Journal of American History* 69, no. 2 (Sept. 1982): 392–414.

Schonberger, Howard B. *Aftermath of War: Americans and the Remaking of Japan, 1945–1952*. Kent, Ohio: Kent State University Press, 1989.

———. "The General and the Presidency: Douglas MacArthur and the Election of 1948." *Wisconsin Magazine of History*, no. 57 (Spring 1974): 201–219.

———. "The Japanese Lobby in American Diplomacy, 1947–1952." *Pacific Historical Review* 46, no. 3 (Aug. 1977): 327–359.

———. "Zaibatsu Dissolution and the American Restoration of Japan." *Bulletin of Concerned Asian Scholars* 5, no. 2 (Sept. 1973): 16–31.

Schnabel, James F. *Policy and Direction: The First Year*. Vol 1 of *The U.S. Army and the Korean War*. Washington, D.C.: GPO, 1972.

Schurmann, Franz. *The Logic of World Power: An Inquiry into the Origins, Currents and Contradictions of World Politics*. New York: Pantheon, 1974.

Sebald, William J. *With MacArthur in Japan: A Personal History of the Occupation*. New York: Norton, 1965.

Sherwood, Robert E. *Roosevelt and Hopkins: An Intimate History*. New York: Harper & Brothers, 1948.

Shigemitsu Mamoru. *Japan and Her Destiny: My Struggle for Peace*. New York: Dutton, 1958. (Originally published in Japanese as *Shōwa no dōran* [Tokyo: Chūō Kōron, 1952].)

Shimoda Takesō. *Sengo Nihon gaikō no shōgen: Nihon wa kōshite saisei shita* (Witness of Japan's postwar diplomacy: Japan's revival). 2 vols. Tokyo: Gyōsei Mondai Kenkyūjo, 1984.

Shindō Eiichi. "Bunkatsu sareta ryōdo" (Divided territory). *Sekai* (Apr. 1979): 31–51.

Shinobu Seizaburō. *Sengo Nihon seijishi, 1945–1952* (A history of postwar politics). 4 vols. Tokyo: Keisō Shobō, 1965.

Shirai Taishirō (ed.). *Contemporary Industrial Relations in Japan*. Madison: University of Wisconsin Press, 1983.

———. "A Supplement: Characteristics of Japanese Management and Their Personnel Policies." In *Contemporary Industrial Relations in Japan*, edited by Shirai Taishirō, 369–384. Madison: University of Wisconsin Press, 1983.

Shiroyama, Saburō. *War Criminal: The Life and Death of Hirota Kōki*. Tokyo: Kodansha, 1974. (Originally published in Japanese as *Rakujitsu moyu* [Tokyo: Shinchosha, 1974].)

Shūkan Shinchō Henshūbu (ed.). "Kadeisu Kaisa no jōnetsu to zasetsu" (The zeal and chagrin of Colonel Kades). In *Makkāsā no Nihon*, 335–336. Tokyo: Shūkan Shinchō, 1970.

———. *Makkāsā no Nihon* (MacArthur's Japan). Tokyo: Shūkan Shinchō, 1970.

Sigal, Leon V. *Fighting to a Finish: The Politics of War Termination in the United States and Japan, 1945*. Ithaca: Cornell University Press, 1988.

Smith, Bradley F. *The Road to Nuremberg*. New York: Basic Books, 1981.

Sodei Rinjirō. *Haikei makkāsā gensui-sama: Senryōka no Nihonjin no tegami* (Dear General MacArthur: Letters from Japanese during the occupation). Tokyo: Ōtsuki Shoten, 1985.

———. *Makkāsā no nisen nichi* (MacArthur's two thousand days). Tokyo: Chūkō Bunkō, 1976.

——— (ed.). *Sekaishi no naka no Nihon senryō* (The occupation of Japan in world history). Tokyo: Nihon Hyōronsha, 1985.

———. *Senryō shita mono sareta mono: Nichibei kankei no genten o kangaeru* (The occupier and the occupied: Thoughts on the U.S.-Japan nexus). Tokyo: Simul Press, 1986.

Sodei Rinjirō and Fukushima Jūrō. *Makkāsā no kiroku: Sengo Nihon no genten* (A MacArthur encyclopedia: The origins of postwar Japan). Tokyo: Nippon Hōsō Shuppan Kyōkai, 1981.

Sone, Eki. *Watakushi no memoāru: Kasumigaseki kara Nagatachō e* (My Memoirs: From the Foreign Office to the Diet). Tokyo: Nikkan Kōgyō Shimbunsha, 1975.

Steiner, Kurt. *Local Government in Japan*. Stanford: Stanford University Press, 1965.

Stephan, John J. "Soviet Policy in Asia, 1945–1951: An Overview." In *Japan and Postwar Diplomacy in the Asian-Pacific Region*, edited by Hosoya Chihirō, 59–99. Occasional Paper, no. 1. Urasa: International University of Japan, 1984.

Stimson, Henry L., and McGeorge Bundy. *On Active Service*. New York: Harper & Brothers, 1948.

Stratton, Samuel S. "The Far Eastern Commission." *International Organization* 2, no. 1 (Feb. 1948): 1–18.

Strike, Clifford S. *Report on Industrial Reparations Survey of Japan to the*

United States of America. New York: Overseas Consultants, February 1948.

Sugiyama Gen. *Sugiyama memo.* 2 vols. Tokyo: Hara Shobō, 1967.

Sulzberger, Cyrus. *Long Row of Candles: Memoirs and Diaries, 1934–1954.* New York: Macmillan, 1969.

Sumimoto Toshio. *Senryō hiroku* (Secret records of the occupation). 2 vols. Tokyo: Mainichi Shimbunsha, 1952.

Supreme Commander for the Allied Powers. *History of the Non-Military Activities of the Occupation of Japan.* 55 monographs. Tokyo: SCAP, 1950–1951.

———. *Monthly Summation of Non-Military Activities in Japan.* Tokyo: SCAP Historical Section, Sept. 1945–Aug. 1948.

———. *SCAPINS.* 2 vols. Tokyo: SCAP, Sept. 4, 1945–Mar. 8, 1952.

———. *Selected Data on the Occupation of Japan.* Tokyo: SCAP, 1950.

Supreme Commander for the Allied Powers. Government Section. *Political Reorientation of Japan: September 1945 to September 1948.* 2 vols. Washington, D.C.: GPO, 1949.

Suzuki Eiichi. *Nihon senryō to kyōiku kaikaku* (The occupation of Japan and education reform). Tokyo: Keisō Shobō, 1985.

Suzuki Gengo. "Impact of the Korean War: A Memoir." Paper prepared for a conference at the MacArthur Memorial Foundation, Norfolk, Virginia, Oct. 16, 1986.

———. "Impact of the Korean War: An Overview." Paper prepared for a conference at the MacArthur Memorial Foundation, Norfolk, Virginia, Oct. 16, 1986.

———. "Japan's Experience of Stabilizing Its Economy." *Japan Society of London Bulletin,* no. 97 (July 1982): 2–6.

Suzuki Tadakatsu. "Suzuki Tadakatsu-shi danwa sokkiroku" (Transcript of talks with Suzuki Tadakatsu). *Naiseishi kenkyūkai,* 5 interviews, Mar. 5, 1974–May 7, 1974.

Swanberg, W. A. *Luce and His Empire.* New York: Charles Scribners' Sons, 1972.

Swearingen, Rodger. *The Soviet Union and Postwar Japan.* Stanford: Hoover Institution Press, 1978.

Swearingen, Rodger, and Paul Langer. *Red Flag in Japan: International Communism in Action, 1919–1951.* Cambridge, Mass.: Harvard University Press, 1952.

Takemae Eiji. *GHQ.* Tokyo: Iwanami Shinsho, 1983.

———. "GHQ Labor Policy During the Period of Democratization, 1946–1948: Second Interview [with Theodore Cohen]." *Journal of the Tokyo Keizai University,* no. 122 (1981): 91–150. (In Japanese and English.)

———. "Kedeisu Nihon senryō kaikōroku" (Kades's occupation memoir). *Tokyo Keizai Daigaku,* no. 148 (Nov. 1986): 243–327. (In Japanese and English.)

———. "Koen-Takemae intabiyū, senkyūhyaku nanajū shichinen shichigatsu nanoka" (Cohen-Takemae interview, July 7, 1977). *Nihon Rōdō Kyōkai Zasshi,* no. 255 (June 1980). (In Japanese and English.)

———. *Sengo rōdō kaikaku: GHQ rōdō seisakushi* (Postwar labor reform in

Japan: A history of GHQ labor policy). Tokyo: Tokyo Daigaku Shuppan-kai, 1985.

———. *Senryō sengoshi—Tainichi kanri seisaku no zenyō* (A history of the postwar occupation—A full picture of the control policies of Japan). Tokyo: Soshisha, 1980.

———. "Senryō shuketsu-ki no rōdō seisaku: GHQ saigo no rōdō kachō Ēmisu ni kiku" (Labor policy at the end of the occupation: Interview with Amis, the last chief of the Labor Division). *Tokyo Keizai Daigaku*, nos. 116–117 (Sept. 1980): 195–218. (In Japanese and English.)

———. "Sōhyō and U.S. Occupation Labor Policy: An Interview with Valery Burati." *Tokyo College of Economics*, nos. 97–98 (1976): 253–294. (In Japanese and English.)

Takemi Tarō. *Nihon Ishakai* (The Japan Medical Association). Tokyo: Asahi Shimbunsha, 1983.

———. "Remembrances of the War and the Bomb." *Journal of the American Medical Association* (Aug. 5, 1983): 618–619.

Takeuchi Iwao (ed.). *Yoshida naikaku* (The Yoshida cabinets). Tokyo: Yoshida Naikaku Kankōkai, 1954.

Takeyama Michio. "Questions on the Tokyo Trial." *Japan Echo*, vol. 11, special issue, 1984, 55–62.

Talbot, Strobe (trans. and ed.). *Khrushchev Remembers*. Boston: Little, Brown, 1970.

Tamamoto Masaru. "Unwanted Peace—Japanese Intellectual Thought in American-occupied Japan, 1948–1952." Ph.D. diss. School of Advanced International studies, Johns Hopkins University, 1988.

Taoka Ryōichi. "Sengo Nihon no hōritsuteki ichi" (The legal status of Japan after the war). In *Shūsen shiroku*, edited by Gaimushō, 154–180. Tokyo: Shimbun Gekkansha, 1952.

Thorne, Christopher. *Allies of a Kind: The United States, Britain, and the War Against Japan, 1941–1945*. London: Hamish Hamilton, 1978.

Titus, Daivd A. *Palace and Politics in Prewar Japan*. New York: Columbia University Press, 1974.

Tōgō Fumihiko. *Nichibei gaikō sanjūnen* (Thirty years of Japan-U.S. diplomacy). Tokyo: Sekai no Ugokisha, 1982.

Toland, John. *The Rising Sun: The Decline and Fall of the Japanese Empire, 1936–1945*. New York: Random House, 1970.

Toyoshita Narahiko. "Tennō-Makkāsā kaiken no rekishiteki ichi" (The historical place of the emperor-MacArthur meeting). *Sekai*, part 1, "Tennō wa nani o katatta ka" (What did the emperor say?), Feb. 1990, 232–251; part 2, "Kūhaku no sengoshi" (The postwar vacuum), Mar. 1990, 105–117.

Truman, Harry S. *Memoirs*. 2 vols. Garden City: Doubleday, 1955–1956.

Tsuru Shigeto. *Essays on Japanese Economic Development*. Tokyo: Kinokuniya Shobō, 1958.

———. "Nihon senryō no baransu shiito" (Balance sheet of the occupation of Japan). In *Sekaishi no naka no Nihon senryō*, edited by Sodei Rinjirō, 203–209. Tokyo: Nihon Hyōronsha, 1985.

Tsurumi, Yoshi. *Japanese Business*. Tokyo: Praeger, 1978.

Tsutsui, William M. *Banking Policy in Japan: American Efforts at Reform During the Occupation*. London: Routledge, 1988.

Tucker, Nancy (discussant). "Gen. S. M. Chu on the Allied Council and Sino-Japanese Relations." In *The Occupation of Japan: The International Context*, edited by Thomas Burkman, 41–44. Norfolk, Va.: MacArthur Memorial Foundation, 1984.

Uchida Kenzō. "Kokunai Seijika to shite no Yoshida no genkai" (Yoshida's limitations in domestic politics). In *Sekaishi no naka no Nihon senryō*, edited by Sodei Rinjirō, 160–165. Tokyo: Nihon Hyōronsha, 1985.

Uchino Tatsurō. *Japan's Postwar Economy*. Tokyo: Kōdansha, 1978.

U.S. Congress. House of Representatives. Committee on Veterans' Affairs. *The Treatment of American Prisoners of War in Manchuria*, 99th Cong., 2nd sess. Sept. 17, 1986, no. 99–61.

———. Legislative Reference Service. *Selected Speeches—Douglas MacArthur*. 88th Cong., 2nd sess. Washington, D.C.: GPO, 1984.

———. Senate Committee on Armed Services and Committee on Foreign Relations. *Military Situation in the Far East*. 82nd Cong., 1st sess, Part 1. Washington, D.C.: GPO, May 3–May 14, 1951.

———. Senate Committee on Foreign Relations. *Japanese Peace Treaty and Other Treaties Pertaining to Security in the Pacific*. 82nd Cong., 2nd sess. Washington, D.C.: GPO, 1952.

U.S. Department of the Army. *Report on the Economic Position and Prospects of Japan and Korea and the Measures Required to Improve Them* (Johnston Report). Washington, D.C.: GPO, Apr. 26, 1948.

———. Adjutant General Corps. *Report of the Second U.S. Education Mission to Japan, 1950*. Washington, D.C.: GPO, 1950.

U.S. Department of State. *Activities of the Far Eastern Commission—Report by the Secretary General*. 3 vols. Washington, D.C.: GPO, 1947–1950.

———. *Foreign Relations of the United States*. Washington, D.C.: GPO, annual.

———. *Occupation of Japan: Policy and Progress*, Publication 267, Far Eastern Series 17. Washington, D.C.: GPO, 1946.

———. *Report of the First U.S. Education Mission to Japan* (Stoddard Report). DOS publication 2579, Far Eastern Series 11. Washington, D.C.: GPO, 1946.

———. *Report of the Mission on Japanese Combines* (Edwards Report). DOS publication 2628, Far Eastern Series 14. Washington, D.C.: GPO, 1946.

Upham, Frank K. *Law and Social Change in Postwar Japan*. Cambridge, Mass.: Harvard University Press, 1987.

Vining, Elizabeth Gray. *Windows for the Crown Prince*. Philadephia: Lippincott, 1970.

Ward, Robert E. "The Commission on the Constitution and Prospects for Constitutional Change in Japan." *Journal of Asian Studies* (Sept. 1965): 401–429.

———. "Reflections on the Allied Occupation and Planned Political Change in Japan." In *Political Development in Modern Japan*, edited by Robert E. Ward, 477–535. Princeton: Princeton University Press, 1973.

Ward, Robert E., and Sakamoto Yoshikazu (eds.). *Democratizing Japan: The Allied Occupation.* Honolulu: University of Hawaii Press, 1987.

Ward, Robert E., and Frank Joseph Shulman (eds.). *The Allied Occupation of Japan, 1945–1952: An Annotated Bibliography of Western-Language Materials.* Chicago: American Library Association, 1974.

Watanabe Akio. "Kōwa mondai to Nihon no sentaku" (Peace settlement issues and Japan's options). In *Sanfuranshisuko kōwa,* edited by Watanabe Akio and Miyazato Seigen, 11–56. Tokyo: Tōkyō Daigaku Shuppankai, 1986.

———. "Southeast Asia in U.S.-Japanese Relations." In *The United States and Japan in the Postwar World,* edited by Akira Iriye and Warren I. Cohen, 80–95. Lexington: University of Kentucky Press, 1989.

Watanabe Akio and Miyazato Seigen. *Sanfuranshisuko kōwa* (San Francisco peace settlement). Tokyo: Tōkyō Daigaku Shuppankai, 1986.

Watanabe Takeshi. *Senryōka no Nihon zaisei oboegaki* (A memorandum on Japan's finance during the occupation). Tokyo: Nihon Keizai Shimbunsha, 1966.

———. *Watanabe Takeshi nikki* (The diary of Watanabe Takeshi). Tokyo: Tōyō Keizai Shimpōsha, 1983.

Watkins, Frederick M. "Prospects of Constitutional Democracy." In *Japan's Prospect,* edited by Douglas H. Haring, 305–331. Cambridge, Mass.: Harvard University Press, 1946.

Weiner, F. B. "MacArthur Unjustifiably Accused of Meting Out 'Victors' Justice' in War Crimes Cases." *Military Law Review* 113 (1986): 203–211.

Weinstein, Martin E. "Defense Policy and the Self-Defense Forces." *Japan Interpreter* 2, no. 6 (Summer 1970): 165–181.

———. *Japan's Postwar Defense Policy, 1947–1968.* New York: Columbia University Press, 1971.

Welfield, John. *An Empire in Eclipse.* London: Athlone Press, 1988.

White, Theodore H. "Episode in Tokyo Bay." *The Atlantic* (Aug. 1970): 53–59.

Whitney, Courtney. *MacArthur's Rendezvous with History.* New York: Knopf, 1956.

Wildes, Harry Emerson. *Typhoon in Tokyo: The Occupation and Its Aftermath.* New York: Macmillan, 1954.

Williams, Justin. "A Forum—American Democratization Policy in Occupied Japan: Correcting the Revisionist Version." *Pacific Historical Review* (May 1988): 179–202, with "A Rejoinder" by John W. Dower, 202–209, and Howard B. Schonberger, 209–218.

———. *Japan's Political Revolution Under MacArthur: A Participant's Account.* Athens: University of Georgia Press, 1979.

———. "Making the Japanese Constitution: A Further Look." *American Political Science Review* 59, no. 3 (Sept. 1965): 665–679.

Williams, Peter, and David Wallace. *Unit 731—The Japanese Army's Secret of Secrets.* London: Hodder and Stoughton, 1989.

Willoughby, Charles A. (ed.). *The Reports of General MacArthur.* 2 vols. Washington: GPO, 1966.

———. *Shirarezaru Nihon senryō—Kaikōroku.* (The unknown occupation of

Japan—a memoir). Tokyo: Bancho Shobō, 1973.

Willoughby, Charles A., and John Chamberlain. *MacArthur, 1941–1951.* New York: McGraw-Hill, 1954.

Wittner, Lawrence S. (ed.). *MacArthur.* Englewood Cliffs, N.J.: Prentice-Hall, 1971.

Woodward, William P. *The Allied Occupation of Japan, 1945–1952, and Japanese Religions.* Leiden: Brill, 1972.

Wolfe, Robert (ed.). *Americans as Proconsuls: United States Military Government in Germany and Japan, 1944–1952.* Carbondale: Southern Illinois University Press, 1984.

Wolferen, Karel van. *The Enigma of Japanese Power.* New York: Knopf, 1989.

Wray, Harry. "The Trilateral Relationship of the Ministry of Education, the Japanese Education Reform Committee, and the Education Division of CIE." Paper prepared for the Amherst College conference, The Allied Occupation of Japan, Amherst, Massachusetts, Aug. 20–23, 1980.

Wray, Harry, and Hilary Conroy (eds.). *Japan Examined: Perspectives on Modern Japanese History.* Honolulu: University of Hawaii Press, 1983.

Yamada Hisanori. *Beranme gaikōkan* (Outspoken diplomat). Tokyo: Kongō Shuppan, 1966.

Yamamoto Mitsuru. "The Cold War and U.S.-Japan Economic Cooperation." In *The Origins of the Cold War in Asia,* edited by Nagai Yōnosuke and Akira Iriye, 408–425. New York: Columbia University Press, 1977.

Yamamura, Kozo. *Economic Policy in Postwar Japan: Growth Versus Economic Democracy.* Berkeley and Los Angeles: University of California Press, 1967.

Yanaga, Chitoshi. *Japanese People and Politics.* New York: Wiley, 1956.

Yoda Seiichi. "Postwar Social Reforms." Paper prepared for the Amherst College conference, The Allied Occupation of Japan, Amherst, Massachusetts, Aug. 20–23, 1980.

Yoshida Shigeru. "Japan and the Crisis in Asia." *Foreign Affairs* 29, no. 2 (Jan. 1951): 171–181.

———. *Japan's Decisive Century, 1867–1967.* New York: Praeger, 1967.

———. *Kaisō jūnen* (Memories of ten years). 4 vols. Tokyo: Shinchōsha, 1957.

———. Letters exchanged with Makino Nobuaki, NDLT.

———. *Ōiso seidan* (Oiso conversations). Tokyo: Okakura Shobō Shinsha, 1952.

———. *Ōiso zuisō* (Random thoughts from Ōiso). Tokyo: Sekkasha, 1962.

———. *Sekai to Nihon* (The world and Japan). Tokyo: Banchō Shobō, 1963.

———. *The Yoshida Memoirs,* translated by Yoshida Kenichi. Boston: Houghton Mifflin, 1962.

Yoshino Bunroku. "A Private Matter: Japanese Investment and Trade Strategies." In *Speaking of Japan,* 4–37. Tokyo: Keizai Kōhō Center, Jan. 1984.

Yoshitsu, Michael. *Japan and the San Francisco Peace Settlement.* New York: Columbia University Press, 1983.

Ziegler, Philip. *Mountbatten: A Biography.* New York: Knopf, 1985.

Interviews

Asakai Kōichirō, Japanese diplomat, 10/27/80.

Asō Kazuko, Yoshida's daughter, 9/23/82.

Asō Tarō, Yoshida's grandson and Diet member, 9/8/82.

Beppu Setsuya, Japanese diplomat, 6/28/80.

Borton, Hugh, professor, 3/19/80.

Bowers, Faubion, aide to MacArthur, 3/7/81.

Bronfenbrenner, Martin, SCAP economist, 10/17/80.

Bunce, W. Kenneth, SCAP religions officer, 8/24/80.

Bunker, Laurence E., MacArthur aide, 4/15/77.

Cohen, Ben V., lawyer, 8/29/80.

De la Mare, Arthur, U.K. diplomat, 8/11/83.

Doba Hajime, journalist, 10/25/80.

Egeberg, Roger, SCAP doctor, 5/23/79.

Emmerson, John K., U.S. diplomat, 3/16/80.

Etō Jun, writer, 9/28/82.

Fearey, Robert A., U.S. diplomat, 4/14/78.

Fine, Sherwood, SCAP economist, 12/18/79.

Fox, Alonzo P., Jr., SCAP officer, 4/10/82.

Fujisaki Masato, Japanese diplomat, 9/7/82.

Fujiyama Naraichi, Japanese diplomat, 9/17/82.

Fukushima Shintarō, Japanese diplomat and journalist, 8/29/80.

Furness, George, SCAP lawyer, 9/20/82.

Hadley, Eleanor, SCAP economist, 11/9/86.

Hata Ikuhiko, historian, 10/22/80.

Hattori Masaya, Finance Ministry, 6/13/84.

Hosoya Chihiro, historian, 9/30/80.

Igarashi Takeshi, historian, 1/8/80, 3/18/80, 1/8/81.

Inoki Masamichi, professor, 11/13/80.

Janow, Seymour, SCAP economist, 10/9/80.

Kades, Charles L., GS officer, 8/19/79, 9/27/79, 3/6/81.

Kaihara Osamu, Japan Defense Agency, 11/15/80.

Kanō Masanao, professor, 10/22/81.

Kase Toshikazu, ambassador, 7/13/80.

Kennan, George F., diplomat and writer, 12/11/80.

Kennoki Toshihiro, Education Ministry, 11/12/80.

Kern, Harry, journalist, 6/23/88.

Kitazawa Naokichi, aide to Yoshida, 11/2/80.

Kojima Noboru, writer and historian, 6/13/80.

Kōsaka Masataka, professor, 11/2/80.

Matsui Akira, ambassador, 10/22/82.

Matsumoto Shigeharu, journalist, 9/23/82.

Meyers, Howard, GS, 7/31/80, 12/13/80.

Miyazawa Kiichi, Finance Ministry, 3/27/86.

Munson, Frederick, Japan military specialist, 10/3/79.

Nagai Yōnosuke, professor, 8/16/83.

Nagano Shigeo, industrialist, 3/17/79.

Nakajima Kazuo, Japanese diplomat, 10/14/80.

Nakasone Yasuhiro, political leader, 10/2/80.

Nichols, Walter, SCAP religions expert, 4/16/84.

Nishimura Kumao, diplomat, 9/14/80, 4/7/83.

Ogata Shijurō, finance specialist, 11/14/80.

Ono Katsumi, Japanese diplomat, 10/29/80.

Poole, Richard A., GS, 8/17/19.

Reischauer, Edwin O., U.S. ambassador, 10/19/79.

Ryder, William S., ESS, 3/8/81.

Sackton, Frank J., SCAP staff aide, 10/22/82.

Sakurada Takeshi, textile businessman, 3/14/79.

Sebald, W. J., ambassador and MacArthur adviser, 3/14/79.

Shidehara Michitarō, son of former prime minister, 11/14/80.

Shima Shigenobu, ambassador, 11/7/80.

Shimanouchi Toshirō, ambassador, 11/12/80.

Shimoda Takesō, ambassador, 10/21/80.

Shindō Eiichi, occupation historian, 8/30/78.

Shirasu Jirō, Yoshida confidant, 9/29/82.

Sodei Rinjirō, occupation historian, 4/15/77, 10/12/86.

Stratton, Samuel S., naval officer and congressman, 6/14/82.

Suzuki Gengo, Finance Ministry, 11/4/81, 10/6/87.

Suzuki Tadakatsu, ambassador, 10/16/80.

Takemae Eiji, occupation historian, 9/25/82.

Takeuchi Harumi, ambassador, 4/17/84.

Takeuchi Ryūji, ambassador, 11/7/80, 11/11/80.

Takeyama Yasuo, journalist, 8/19/82.

Tōgō Fumihiko, ambassador, 2/8/80.

Tsuru Shigeto, economist, 9/19/77, 11/8/80.

Watanabe Takeshi, Finance Ministry, 10/39/80, 9/30/82.

Watanabe Tsuneo, journalist, 10/25/80.

Williams, Justin, Sr., GS, 11/3/78.

Index

Abe Yoshishige, 61
Acheson, Dean G., 61, 76; and Dulles, 242, 251–252, 253; and emperor's role, 72; European trips of, 201–202, 372–373; and Higashikuni, 48; and Japan as "workshop," 195; and MacArthur's dismissal, 288, 289; on early policy for Japan, 38; on Japan and Korean War, 260, 270; and peace treaty, 156, 242, 246, 251, 253, 272, 305; press club speech on Asia, 225, 229, 258; and San Francisco peace conference, 302, 303, 304; as secretary of state, 192, 246; and U.S. forces, 48; and Yoshida letter on China policy, 307, 308, 309
Adenauer, Konrad, 246
Administrative agreement, 278–279, 281, 310–311; and joint military command, 311
Agricultural cooperatives, 132. See also Food shortages; Land reform
Akahata ("Red Flag"), 42, 233, 234
Akihito: as crown prince, 16, 190; as emperor, 122
Allen, G. C., 52
Allied Council for Japan, 130, 151, 152, 153, 166, 175, 183, 205; established, 68; and Japanese awareness, 154; and land reform, 130; and 1947 election, 153; powers, 68; and repatriation of Japanese prisoners, 152–153. See also Far Eastern Commission

Allied powers, 9, 27, 29, 35, 44, 56–57, 66–67, 154, 246, 248; and control council, 67; and emperor, 71–74, 97; and FEC/ACJ, 67, 68, 152, 248, 282; and occupation forces, 69, 154; and MacArthur, 67
Allison, John M., 252, 260, 271, 279, 298
Amano Teiyū, 237
American Council on Japan, 161
Anti-Comintern Pact of 1936, 21
Antitrust, 40. See also Deconcentration
ANZUS (Australia–New Zealand–United States) Pact, 284, 306
Arisawa Hiromi, 146
Asahi, 53, 113
Asakai Kōichirō, 37, 71, 154
Ashida Hitoshi, 148, 159, 177, 178; and constitution, 116, 118, 119; and Draper, 172; memo on security, 248, 250; and NPSL, 172, 174; and peace treaty, 246; as prime minister, 171, 172–173, 189, 213, 220
Asō Kazuko, 20, 22, 110, 125, 226–227, 313
Associated Press, 48
Atcheson, George, Jr., 38, 39, 41, 78, 90, 152, 153, 156; on emperor, 72
Atomic bomb, 28; and Higashikuni interview, 48; Hiroshima, 1; Japanese reaction to, 48; MacArthur's reaction to, 1; Nagasaki, 1–2; and second bomb, 2
Atsugi air base, 7

Attlee, Clement L., 246
Australia, 15, 61, 93, 98, 99, 104, 130,
    151, 153, 166, 175, 186, 221, 235,
    302, 306; and emperor, 71, 72, 73,
    79, 91; and Pacific pact, 272, 282,
    303; and peace treaty, 272, 284; role
    in occupation, 67
Awa Maru, 218

Babcock, C. Stanton, 252
Bacon, Ruth, 156
Baldwin, Roger, 162, 352n. 43
Ball, W. Macmahon, 130, 153–154
Basic directive of November 1945, 31–
    33, 77, 83; amendment, 206; eco-
    nomic clauses, 32–33; MacArthur's,
    reaction to, 31–32; main points, 32–
    33; and New Deal, 33
Bataan (MacArthur's airplane), 7
Bataan: and "Bataan crowd," 17, 87;
    "death march," 81–82, 184
Beppu Setsuya, 328n. 9
Bevin, Ernest, 175, 247
Big Three meeting, 276–277
"Bill of rights" directive of 1945, 49–50
Bishop, Max W., 218
Bisson, T. A., 141
Blyth, R. H., 63
Bonin Islands, 107, 271, 280, 303,
Borton, Hugh, 80, 90, 150, 156–157, 158
Bradley, Omar, 254
British Commonwealth Occupation
    Forces (BCOF), 35–36, 154–155
Bunce, W. Kenneth, 60
Bunker, Laurence E., 65, 125, 171, 213,
    301
Burakumin (eta), 239
Burati, Valery, 236
Bureaucracy system, 18, 166–167, 173,
    217–218, 228–229; and SCAP re-
    forms, 176–177; and social bureau-
    crats, 49, 53, 141
Burma, 156, 299, 302
Bushidō (way of the warrior), 212
Butterworth, W. Walton, 250
Byrnes, James F., 67, 68, 102, 104

Canada, 10, 50, 78, 189–190, 200, 218,
    310
Cary, Otis, 65
Castle, William R., 161
Casualties: Hiroshima, 1; Japanese deaths
    in World War II, 11; Nagasaki, 1;
    statistics, 325–326n. 2
Censorship during occupation, 47, 162,
    205, 207

Central Liaison Office (CLO), 38–39, 71,
    97, 123
Ceylon (Sri Lanka), 303, 304
Charter Oath of 1868, 64
Chiang Kai-shek, 155, 168, 242
China, 9, 12, 20, 151, 153, 155, 187, 298,
    304, 307–309. *See also* People's Re-
    public of China (PRC); Republic of
    China (ROC)
Christianity, 16, 62–63, 163, 167–169,
    189
Churchill, Winston, 306; and China, 308;
    and MacArthur, 7; and war crimes
    trials, 75, 203
Civil Information and Education Section
    (CIE), 37, 133, 168–169
Civil Intelligence Section (CIS), 109
Civil procedure, Japanese code of, 145,
    167; equality of sexes, 167; family
    system, 96, 167, 294
Clay, Lucius D., 196, 221
Coal industry, legislation to nationalize,
    164
Cohen, Theodore, 138, 139, 142
Cold war, 192
Collins, General J. Lawton, 264
Communism, 219; alleged communists in
    SCAP, 316n. 6; communist political
    prisoners released, 49–50; influence in
    labor movement, 137; and MacAr-
    thur's views, 163, 216, 232–233, 235;
    and Yoshida's views, 217, 233
Communist Party, 41–42, 108, 143, 148,
    163, 216, 217, 229, 230–231; attack
    by Cominform, 233; illegalization,
    232–233, 234–235; and labor, 137,
    138, 229, 233; and MacArthur's
    views, 234–235; and Organization
    Control Law, 232; size, 232
Compton, Karl T., 34
Comyns-Carr, Arthur, 79, 181
Constantino, Anthony, 139
Constitution of 1889 (Meiji Constitu-
    tion), 26
Constitution of 1947, 19, 40–41, 89–
    104; as amendment to 1889 constitu-
    tion, 100, 117–118; approval by
    Japan, 101, 119–120; Article 9, 94,
    95, 96, 98, 99, 100, 103–104, 115–
    117, 121; Ashida amendment, 116–
    117; basic principles, 95; "a beautiful
    jewel," 89; *bunmin* (civilian), 118;
    changes in GS draft, 119; commission
    on the constitution, 120–121; Diet de-
    bate, 115–117; and Diet dissolution,
    214; drafting of, 93–96; and emperor,
    14, 95, 96, 97, 98, 99, 101, 115, 119–

120; emperor-Shidehara meeting, 99–100; and family system, 96, 115, 121, 167, 294; and FEC, 89, 91, 101–103, 118–119; implementing legislation, 144–145, 167, 294; and Japanese reaction to, 89, 97, 98, 104, 108, 114–115, 122; and MacArthur, 89, 90, 92, 96, 101, 328–329n. 11; MacArthur-Shidehara meeting, 99; main points of GS draft, 95–96; March 4–5 meeting, 101; nationality provision, 117; preamble, 95, 100; promulgation, 120; review of, 119; revisions by Diet and FEC, 119; Sansom's views of, 90; and Shirasu's role, 98, 100, 101, 104; and sovereignty, 95, 115, 117, 118; and unicameral legislature, 94, 96, 98, 100; U.K. view of, 90; and U.S. guidance (SWNCC 228), 90–91, 95, 118; and U.S. pressure, 92, 104; and Whitney's role, 89, 90, 92–93, 94, 96, 97, 98–99, 100, 102, 104, 117; and Yoshida, 97, 98, 100, 119, 120, 121
Containment, 182, 201, 208
Cramer, Myron C., 181
Criminal procedure, Japanese code of, 145, 167, 294
Czechoslovakia, 192, 304

Dai Ichi building, 17, 19, 37, 286, 291, 311
Dan, Takuma, 57
"Declaration of humanity" (*ningen sengen*), by emperor, 63–64
Deconcentration, 30, 40, 129, 199, 200; antimonopoly law, 224; deconcentration law, 164–165; fair trade commission, 129; financial institutions, 129–130, 200; Review Board, 199, 200; trading companies, 196. *See also* Economic developments, in Japan; Zaibatsu
Deming, W. Edwards, 268
Democratic Liberal Party, 178, 212, 213, 216, 217, 218, 223
Democratic Party (Japan), 121, 148, 162, 169, 171, 213, 215, 216, 217
Democratization leagues (*mindō*), 139, 231
Demokurashii ("democracy"), 23, 27, 40–41, 44, 124, 135, 211; Japan's preparation for, 43–44
Dening, Esler, 307
Derevyanko, Kuzma, 130, 131, 151–152
Dewey, Thomas E., 160

Diet, 55, 130–131, 164, 172, 307; "collusive" dissolution in 1948, 213, 214–215, 216
Diplomatic Section (DS), 37, 152
Direct military government, 17–18, 38, 88
Disarmament and demilitarization, 29, 48, 71, 83, 197; and MacArthur's statement, 35; U.S. draft treaty of, 103–104, 245
Dobashi Kazuyoshi, 137
Dodge, Joseph M., 192, 221, 222; achievements of, 226–227; criticisms of, 221, 227; and exchange rate, 223–224; and FY 1949 budget, 223; and Ikeda, 222–223, 249–250; and Japanese, 226; and Korean War, 227, 267; and MacArthur, 226; opinion of Yoshida, 227
Dōmei (labor confederation), 237
Draper, William H., Jr., 161, 172, 191, 195–196, 203; and deconcentration, 196, 199–200; and Japanese cooperation, 196; and MacArthur, 200; and rearmament, 203, 205; and reparations, 197–199; and U.S. economic policy, 192, 196–197, 201, 221
Dulles, John Foster, 241; background, 251–252; and Allies, 272, 284; America-Japan Society of Tokyo speech, 281; and ANZUS Pact, 284, 306; and basic treaty principles, 271, 280; on communist world strategy, 260; early trips to Japan (1950 and 1951), 241, 253–257, 273–284, 288, 290–291; goal for Japan, 242; and Japanese, 253, 283; and Korea, 253, 258, 259–260, 270; and MacArthur, 253, 255, 257, 274–275, 285, 288, 289, 301, 304; meeting with MacArthur and Yoshida, 276; negotiating strategy, 253, 271–272, 273, 279; and Okinawa, 271, 274–275; and Pacific pact, 281–282; and rearmament, 242, 276–277, 297; and reparations, 284, 290–291; and San Francisco peace conference, 302, 303, 305, 306; and security treaty, 277–280, 281, 299, 300, 305; shuttle diplomacy, 253, 272; and treaty documents, 282–283; as treaty negotiator, 251, 252–253, 272–273; trip to Philippines, Australia, and New Zealand, 283–284; and U.K. draft peace treaty, 298; and Yoshida, 255–256, 275, 277, 283, 290–291; and Yoshida's letter on China, 307–309

Dunn, Frederick S., 247
Dyke, Kermit R., 60, 64

Economic aid to Japan, by U.S., 195, 197,
332n.25
Economic and Scientific Section (ESS), 35,
54, 58, 59, 125, 128, 130, 146, 215
Economic developments, in Japan: in
1945, 50–51; in 1947, 146; in 1949,
221–222; in 1950, 267; potential of,
59
Economic Stabilization Board (ESB), 145,
172
The Economist, 227
Economy, Japan: economic policies, 52,
195; economic purge, 126, 127–128;
effects of World War II on, 51; exchange rates, 223–224, 333–
334n.13; impact of Korean War
(*tokujū*), 267–269; priority production, 146–147, 268; stabilization
program, 145, 219–224, 226; and
U.S. economic policy, 32, 50, 52, 195,
197, 198. *See also* Dodge, Joseph M.;
Draper, William H.; Korean War
Eden, Anthony, 308
Education, 40, 59–62, 313; basic laws,
133–134; CIE organization, 69; condition of schools in 1945, 59, 60;
cyclotrons, 61; early reforms, 60; Education Ministry, 54, 61, 132–133;
and Eells, 237; JERC, 62, 132, 133;
Japan Teachers Union (*Nikkyōso*),
61; language reform, 133; leftists, 237;
number of universities, 133; purge,
60, 177; reforms, 132–134; 6-3-3
system, 62, 132–133, 294; technical
schools (*semmon gakkō*), 4–59; textbooks, 61; U.S. policy, 60; U.S. (Stoddard) mission to Japan, 61–62, 132;
Yoshida views, 134, 237–238
Edwards, Corwin, 128–129
Eells, Walter C., 237
Eichelberger, Robert L., 35, 38, 48, 76,
140, 158, 161–162, 250
Eisenhower, Dwight D., 305; and Mac-
Arthur, 34, 103, 158, 159, 314
Elections, 40, 43–44, 86, 143–144; 1946
election, 107–108; 1947 election,
106, 143, 144, 147–149; 1949 elec-
tion, 215–217
Emmerson, John K., 50, 78
Emperor. *See* Akihito; Hirohito
Emperor system, 30, 91, 92, 94, 95–96,
98, 118, 145, 287; Diet debate, 115
Eta (*burakumin*), 239
Evatt, H. Vere, 67, 154

The Face of the World (Hatoyama), 109
Fair Trade Commission (FTC), 129
Far Eastern Advisory Commission, 67,
73, 92; trip to Japan, 69, 73
Far Eastern Commission (FEC), 31, 68,
78, 107, 113, 154, 180, 186, 202,
203, 205, 245, 272, 296, 297; and
constitution, 91, 92, 101–103, 118–
119; and FEC-230, 129, 161, 164,
199–200; Japanese knowledge of,
154; and labor policy, 138, 175; and
MacArthur, 101–103, 202, 203; and
reparations, 155–156, 198, 199–200
Fearey, Robert A., 55, 78, 252
Federation of Economic Organizations
(*keidanren*), 147
Fisheries treaty (Canada–Japan–United
States), 310
Food shortages, 50–51, 134; and FEC,
113; "Food May Day," 112; and U.S.
assistance, 113–114
Foreign Affairs, 201
Foreign diplomatic missions, 151, 153–
154
Formosa. *See* Taiwan
Forrestal, James V., 161, 196
Fraternization, 17
Fuchu prison, 50
Fukuda, Takeo, 177
Fundamental Law of Education, 133

G-2, SCAP Intelligence Section, 37, 165,
235, 265
G-3, SCAP Planning Section, 87
Gairdner, Charles, 142
Garon, Sheldon, 143
Gascoigne, Alvary; meetings with
MacArthur and Yoshida, 73–74, 127,
135, 139, 143, 171, 175, 190, 212,
216–217, 261, 262, 263; Pacific pact,
287, 282
Gayn, Mark, 113
General Headquarters (GHQ), 35
Genrō, 26, 314, 330n.27
Germ warfare, and trials, 185–187;
MacArthur involvement in, 185, 187;
U.S. congressional investigation, 187
Germany, 11, 43, 78, 83, 126, 127, 192,
196, 199, 205, 221, 242, 246, 292,
325n.5, 364n.5
Goering, Hermann, 76–77
Government Section (GS), 35, 41, 87–88,
132, 210; and Communist Party, 234;
and constitution, 89, 90, 91, 92, 93,
100, 104, 116, 117, 167; gift from
emperor, 104; and Home Ministry,
166–167; and Japanese, 100, 123,

212; and NPR, 264, 265; and police reform, 165–166; and *Political Reorientation of Japan*, 33, 92, 98; primacy in SCAP, 87–88; and purge, 83–86, 104, 125, 128; and Red Purge, 234; and Yoshida, 99, 100, 111, 123, 171, 212, 215, 294

Gozen kaigi (cabinet meetings with emperor), 5

Graham, Billy, and emperor's interest in Christianity, 62–63

"Greater East Asia War," 63

Grew, Joseph C., 161; and democracy in Japan, 337n. 24; and emperor, 72

Gromyko, Andrei, 302, 303, 304

Habomai and Shikotan islands, 12, 107

Hall, Robert K., 60, 133

Harriman, W. Averell, 69–70, 82

Hatoyama Ichirō: background, 108, 109–111; and organized Liberal Party, 42, 44; as political leader, 44, 107, 108, 139, 283; and purge/depurge, 108–111, 296, 314

Hattori Takushirō, 265

Heisei ("achieving peace"), 122

Henderson, Harold, 60, 63, 64

Hi no maru (Japanese flag), 238

Higashikuni Naruhiko, 9, 38, 48; and MacArthur, 18–19; as prime minister, 6; and Yoshida, 19

Higgins, John P., 181

Hirano Rikizō, 169

Hirohito, emperor, 16, 44, 48, 171–172, 283, 301; abdication rumors, 188–190; and alleged letter on purge, 256–257, 365n. 37; and attack on Pearl Harbor, 26; and Christianity, 62–63, 189; and constitution, 98, 99–100; declaration of humanity, 64; and Diet dissolution, 170, 214; and end of war, 2, 5–6, 326n. 1; and food crisis, 112; and gift to GS staff, 104; "imperial will," 26, 330n. 27; and MacArthur, 23–25, 49, 65, 134–135, 189–190, 250, 289; political philosophy, 26; as prewar constitutional monarch, 26–27; as "puppet," 73, 74; and Ridgway, 295; and Shidehara meeting, 99–100; as "symbol" of Japan, 170, 190; and Tōjō, 26–27; and trips in Japan, 64–65; and tutor for crown prince, 190; and war crimes, 71–74, 80, 97, 180, 186; and war responsibility, 24, 25–27, 74, 180, 330n. 26, 338n. 16; and Yoshida, 22, 64, 113

Hiroshima, 1, 2, 182

Hirota Kōki, 20–21, 78, 179, 188

Hoarded goods, 51, 178, 333–334n. 13

Hokkaido, 69, 206

Holding Company Liquidation Commission (HCLC), 58, 129

Home Ministry, 165, 166–167, 177

Homma Masaharu, 81–82

Hong Kong, 282

Hoover, Blaine, 173–175, 176, 213

Hoover, Herbert C., 113

Hosoya Chihiro, 274

ICFTU (International Confederation of Free Trade Unions), 236

Ichikawa Fusae, 84

Ichimada Hisato, 300

Iguchi Sadao, 277

Ii Yashirō, 137, 140

Ikeda Hayato, 217, 222, 223, 300; meeting with Dodge in Washington, 249–250

Ikeda Seihin, 79

Imperial Rule Assistance Association (IRAA), 77, 338n. 9

India, 284–285, 302

Indochina, 225, 242

Indonesia, 225, 242, 282, 299, 303

Initial policy for occupation, 29; FEC approval, 31; main points, 30–31; and public reaction, 31

Inoki Masamichi, 132

Institute of Pacific Relations, 273

International Military Tribunal for the Far East (IMTFE). *See* War crimes trials

International Prosecution Section (SCAP), 77–78, 80, 186–187

Iriye, Akira, and San Francisco system, 306

Ishibashi Tanzan, 112, 127–128, 296

Ishii Shirō, 185, 186

Itō Ritsu, 233

Iwo Jima, 12

Izumiyama Sanroku, 215

Japan: and Asia, 242; cabinet (formerly imperial) ordinances, 39, 264; central liaison office, 38, 123; Export-Import Bank, 268; fisheries treaty with U.S. and Canada, 310; Home Ministry, 165, 166; Japan Development Bank, 268; and Korea (ROK), 310; and Korea (annexation), 261–262; and Korean War, 260, 261; Labor Ministry, 167; and MacArthur's dimissal, 288–289; national anthem (*Kimi ga yo*), 238; national flag (*Hi no maru*),

Japan (*continued*)
  238; and Pacific pact, 272, 282; plan-
  ning for occupation, 33–34, 38; and
  Potsdam Declaration acceptance, 5, 6;
  Supreme Council for the Direction of
  the War, 2, 5; territory of, 12, 107;
  and U.S. before war, 14; wartime
  morale and resistance, 12–13
Japan Management Association (Nik-
  keiren), 147
Japan Teachers Union (Nikkyōso), 61
Japan Times (*Nippon Times/Japan Times
  & Mail*), 162, 172
"Japanizing" the constitution, 117
Jenner, William E., 309
Johnson, Chalmers, 224
Johnson, Earl D., 273, 278
Johnson, Louis A., 251, 270–271
Johnston, Percy, 198
Joint Chiefs of Staff, 32, 91, 92, 94, 186,
  288, 289; and JCS 1067, 32, 33

Kades, Charles L., 83, 87, 169, 174, 178;
  and constitution, 92, 94, 95, 97–98,
  100, 101, 103, 116; and MacArthur,
  219; and Yoshida, 124, 210, 214
Kanamori Tokujirō, 115, 116, 119
Katayama Tetsu, 41, 108, 149, 163–167,
  216; and coal bill, 164; and constitution implementing legislation, 167;
  and deconcentration, 164–165; and
  Diet dissolution, 170; forms coalition
  government, 149–150, 163; and four-
  party agreement, 149–150; and labor,
  173, 236; and MacArthur, 163, 164,
  169–170, 170–171; and NPSL, 173;
  and police reform, 165–166; and
  rearmament, 170–171; and religion,
  163, 167–168; resignation, 169; and
  SCAP reforms, 166–167; and Shōwa
  Denkō scandal, 177; and Socialist
  Party, 163, 169, 171
Katō Kanju, 216
Katō Shizue, 216
Kauffman, James L., 161
Kawabe Torashirō, 273
Kawai Kazuo, 8, 188
Keenan, Joseph B., 77–78, 79, 80, 158,
  180, 181, 185
Keidanren (Federation of Economic
  Organizations), 147
Kellogg-Briand Pact of 1928, 182
Kelly, Harry, 61
Kennan, George F., 82, 192, 246; back-
  ground, 201–202; on future of Japan,
  209, 242, 273; and Korean War, 241;
  and MacArthur, 202–203, 205–206,
  209; and NSC 13/2, 204–205, 206,

207, 208–209; and occupation, 203,
  204, 205, 208; and police, 204–205;
  on rearmament, 203, 208, 242; and
  reverse course, 207–208; and U.S.
  policy, 192, 201, 202–203
Kern, Harry, 82, 161, 256
Kido Kōichi, 19, 26–27, 39, 78, 180;
  diary of, 80
Kikugorō, 8
Kikunami Katsumi, 137
Killen, James S., 174, 175
Kim Il Sung, 258, 259
Kimi ga yo (national anthem), 238
Kishi Nobusuke, 184, 296
Knowland, William F., 161, 309
Kodama Yoshiō, 184
Kokutai ("national polity"), 49, 115, 117
Konoe Fumimaro, 7, 78; and constitution, 19, 41; "Konoe Memorial," 21;
  and MacArthur, 19, 328–329n. 11
Korea, 107, 238, 239; Dulles's visit to,
  253, 258; and Japanese peace treaty,
  271, 291, 302; negotiations with
  Japan, 310; and North Korean attack,
  258–259; and U.S. post-surrender
  control, 343–344n. 2
Korean War, 226, 241, 258–262, 311,
  366n. 11; effect on Japanese economy,
  197, 227, 267–269; Japanese contribution to, 266; Japanese reaction
  to, 261–262; and MacArthur's dismissal, 287–288; and NSC-68, 266–
  267; PRC intervention, 260–261,
  262, 272, 287; and ROC forces, 261,
  287; as threat to Japan, 260; as threat
  to U.S., 270; U.N. forces in, 260, 305–
  306; U.S. forces in, 260
Koreans, in Japan, 1, 12, 204, 291; treatment and problems, 238–239
Kōsha (government corporation), 176
Kowalski, Frank, 265–266
Kramer, Raymond C., 58–59
Krueger, Walter, 35
Kurile Islands, 12, 69, 107, 271, 272,
  298, 303, 304
Kurusu Saburō, 34

Labor, 30, 40, 52–53; administrative
  retrenchment in 1949, 228–229;
  amendments, 232; "anti-capitalist
  radicalism," 142; "democratization
  leagues" (*mindō*), 139; Dōmei, 237; as
  dynamic movement, 50, 52–53, 54,
  105, 112, 237; enterprise unions, 54;
  FEC policy, 138; general strike threat,
  136–140; government enterprise
  unions, 228–229; ICFTU, 236; Japan
  Congress of Industrial Unions (JCIU),

136–137, 138; Japan Federation of
Labor (JFL), 137, 138; Japanese attitudes about, 141, 142, 143; Labor
Relations Adjustment Law, 137,
173; Labor Standards Law, 147, 294;
Labor Union Law, 53–54; labor unrest, 173–174, 229; "lawless gangs"
(*futei no yakara*), 138; and MacArthur, 54, 139–140; MacArthur strike
ban, 136, 140–141, 173–174, 229;
production control, 53; "reverse
course," 142–143; Shin Rengō, 237;
Sōhyō, 236–237; and Toyota strike,
231; U.S. policy, 30, 32, 141, 237;
wages, 137, 140, 142, 173, 213, 215,
231–232; World Federation of Trade
Unions, 236; Yoshida'a attitude about,
138, 141–142. *See also* National
Public Service Law (NPSL)
Labor Ministry, 165, 167, 177
Ladejinsky, Wolf, 55
LaFollette, Philip, 159, 167
Land reform, 50, 54–56, 113, 130–132;
Japanese initiatives, 56; legislation,
130–131; MacArthur's interest in, 55,
131; prewar conditions, 54–55; re-
sults of, 131–132
Language, reform of Japanese writing,
133
Law for the Elimination of Excessive Con-
centrations of Economic Power, 164–
165, 200. *See also* Deconcentration
Law for Prohibition of Private Monopoly,
129
Leftists, in SCAP, 124–125, 203
Letters, exchanged by MacArthur and
Yoshida, 124
Liberal Democratic Party, 112, 217
Liberal Party, 42, 91, 108, 110, 112, 121,
143, 148, 169, 211
"Liberation army," 112, 114
Lippmann, Walter, 192

MacArthur, Arthur (father of Douglas),
15–16, 131
MacArthur, Arthur (son of Douglas), 15–
16, 65
MacArthur, Douglas: and ACJ, 68, 151–
153; and Allies, 67–69, 154, 246;
arrival in Japan, 6–8; and atomic
bomb, 1; background of, 14–17, 151;
and "big business," 59, 200; and communism, 216, 232–233, 235; and
constitution, 89, 90, 92–97, 99–104,
115–121, 328–329n. 11; criticisms
of, 47–49, 140, 161, 162, 219; and
cyclotrons' destruction, 61; and defense of Japan, 247–248, 254, 255;

and demobilization, 23, 35; and
democracy, 23; and Diet dissolution
of 1948, 214–215; and economic
policy, 195–196, 200; and economic
stabilization, 219–221, 223; and
education, 60, 61, 133; and elections
in Japan, 108, 143, 148, 149, 216;
and the emperor, 16, 22–29, 44, 49,
62–65, 72–74, 79, 97, 134–135,
189–190, 330n. 31; and end of war, 6,
9–11, 13, 28, 29; dismissal of, 286–
289, 291; and FEC, 68, 101–103,
107, 118–119, 154; and food crisis,
51, 113–114; and Japanese germ warfare, 185–187; and Japanese personnel system, 228–229; and Japanese
writing reform, 133; and Koreans in
Japan, 239; and labor, 54, 136, 141–
143, 213, 236; and land reform, 55,
130, 131; and NPR, 263–266; and
NSC 13/2, 206–209; and NPSL, 171–
176, 215; and *Newsweek,* 160–161,
352n. 40; and occupation policy, 16,
28–29, 40, 135, 202–203, 207, 211–
212; and Pax Americana, 13; and
peace treaty, 156–158, 241–246, 254,
276, 289, 302, 304; personality and
style of, 28, 29, 33, 35, 37, 44–45, 51,
66–67, 124, 160, 350n. 2; and police
reform, 165–66, 263; post-occupation
activities, 314–315; and press conference of 1947,156; press relations of,
47–48, 160–162; and purge, 82, 86,
109, 125–128, 152, 161, 234, 235;
and rearmament, 170–171, 203, 242,
263–266; and religion, 62–63, 167–
169; and reparations, 71, 155, 198;
resignation threat of, 134; and San
Francisco conference, 301–304;
"sermons" of, 22–24, 202; and State
Department, 37–38, 201–202; testimony to U.S. Senate, 291–292; and
threat of guerrilla warfare, 34; and
U.S. goals for Japan, 29, 31–33, 135,
273; and U.S. military policy in Asia,
259; and U.S. presidential politics,
106, 142, 157–160, 163; and violent
demonstrations, 114, 141–143; and
war crimes, 76–79, 179–183,
355n. 5; and zaibatsu, 57, 160–161,
202, 352n. 38. *See also* SCAP
MacArthur, Jean (wife of Douglas), 15,
24, 65, 286
Magruder, Carter, 271, 273
Mainichi, 53, 93
Makino Nobuaki, 20, 110
Malaya, 80, 156, 282
Malik, Jacob, 152, 284

Manchuria, 1, 11, 57, 63, 69, 80, 157, 185, 261
Manila, 7, 8, 283
Mao Zedong (Mao Tse-tung), 157, 192, 235, 242, 252, 259
Maritime Safety Agency, 166, 297
Marquat, William F., 59, 128, 139–140, 146, 173, 215, 220, 250
Marshall, George C., 272; and MacArthur, 201; Marshall Plan, 195, 209; and "Marshall Plan" for Asia, 314
Marshall, Richard J., 72–73
Martin, Joseph W., 287
Masuhara Keikichi, 265
Matsudaira Yasumasa, 189, 256, 365n.37
Matsukawa incident, 230–231
Matsumoto Jōji, 40, 91, 97, 98, 100, 101
"Meiji, Men of," 20
Meiji Constitution, 26, 100, 101, 117–118
Memoirs (George F. Kennan), 208
Miki Takeo, 211, 212
Military currency, 17, 18
Military government teams, 37
Missouri, 9, 10, 11, 66
Mitaka incident, 230
MITI (Ministry of International Trade and Industry), 177, 224
Mitsubishi, 57, 58, 196
Mitsui, 57, 58, 80, 196
Miyazawa Kiichi, 222; on MacArthur, 249, 288–289
Mokusatsu (ignore), 2
Morgenthau, Henry, Jr., 32
Morita Akio, 85
Morrison, Herbert, 298, 308
Mountbatten, Louis, 15
Muccio, John J., 259
Murphy, Frank, 81
Murphy, Robert, 311

Nagasaki, 1–2, 182
Nakasone Yasuhiro, 121
Nambara Shigeru, 62, 115, 132
Nanjing, 188
Narahashi Wataru, 100
National Advisory Council (NAC), 220
"National penitence," 13
National Public Service Law (NPSL), 172–176; amendments, 174, 176, 213, 215; bureaucratic examinations, 176; cabinet order 201, 174; and MacArthur's letter to, 174; national personnel authority, 173, 213, 294; opposition to decision, 175; reform of bureaucracy, 176–177, 354n.35
National Security Council (NSC): U.S.

Policy Toward Japan (NSC 13/2), 201, 203–209, 246; NSC 13/3, 198; U.S. Policy in Asia (NSC 48/2), 225; Japanese Peace Treaty (NSC 60/1), 271; U.S. Objectives and Programs for National Security (NSC 68), 266–267, 269; U.S. Policy for Japan (NSC 125/2), 297
NATO (North Atlantic Treaty Organization), 256, 310–311
NPR (National Police Reserve): Collins report, 264; cover plan, 264; creation, 263–266; equipment, 264, 266, 297; former imperial officers, 265; funding, 265; Kowalski book, 265–266; legal basis of, 264, 294; MacArthur role, 266; organization, 265, 266; post-occupation, 314; Ridgway policy, 296–297; size, 296–297, 314; and U.S. policy, 263, 297; "war potential," 264; Yoshida views, 263, 264, 294
Netherlands, 156, 303
Neutral nations, diplomatic records, 18
"New Deal," 33, 43, 52, 56, 87, 139, 160, 167, 222, 339–340n.41
New York Herald Tribune, 41
New York Times, 2, 41, 47–48
New Zealand, 272, 282, 284, 306; and emperor, 71, 79
Newsweek, 82, 160, 256, 283
Nimitz, Chester W., 9
Ningen sengen (emperor's "declaration of humanity"), 44, 63–64; and MacArthur, 64
Nippon Steel Co., 165
Nippon Times. See *Japan Times*
Nishimura Kumao, 275, 280
Nishio Suehiro, 149, 171, 177, 178, 216
Nitze, Paul H., 266
Nōkyō (agricultural cooperatives), 132
Nomura Kichisaburō, 283
Norman, E. Herbert, 50, 78, 189, 190, 200, 218, 333n.11
Northcott, J. F., 154
Norway, 303
Nosaka Sanzō, 40–41, 108, 115; attacked by Cominform, 233
Nugent, Donald R., 37, 60, 168
Nuremberg trial, 76, 78, 179–180, 183

Occupation, 28; appraisal of, 315–316; costs, 37, 332n.25; end of, 311–312; "hard occupation," 123–124; planning, 28–34, 52, 331n.7; policy omissions, 28, 33; punitive policies, 44, 75; reduction of controls, 207; sources of policy, 33; turning points, 191, 241, 242

Oiso, 6
Okazaki Katsuo, 38, 217, 264, 277, 310
Okinawa, 11, 13, 204, 238, 359n. 30;
    MacArthur's views on, 202, 245–246,
    255, 274–275, 281; peace treaty and,
    271, 304. See also Ryukyu Islands
Ōkita Saburō, 39–40, 146
Ōkubo Toshimichi, 20
Oppler, Alfred C., 118, 169
Ordinance Review Committee (Seirei
    Shimon Iinkai), 295
Organization Control Law, 232, 294
Oriental Economist, 112, 128
Overseas Consultants, Inc., 198

Pacific pact, 272, 281–282
Pakenham, Compton, 256, 283
Pakistan, 225, 303, 304
Pal, Radhabinob, 179, 183, 187
Patrick, William D., 181
Pauley, Edwin W., and Pauley report, 70–
    71, 198
Pax Americana, 13, 28, 192, 269
Peace Preservation Law of 1925, 49, 50
Peace treaty: and Asia power balance,
    242, 306; China issue, 298, 303, 304,
    307–309; draft outline of 1952 treaty,
    280; early drafts by U.S., 158, 245,
    247, 251, 272–273; initialed, 282–
    283; early Japanese role, 246, 247,
    249–250, 273–274, 277–279; key
    players, 241, 242; and Korean War,
    241–242, 270; MacArthur's memo
    on, 254; MacArthur at peace confer-
    ence, 301; MacArthur's press confer-
    ence, 156–157; main provisions of,
    304–305; negotiations in 1950, 253–
    257; negotiations in 1951, 275–283,
    284, 290–291; NSC 60/1, 271; and
    Okinawa, 271, 303; Pentagon views,
    247, 251, 252, 270–271, 273; rati-
    fication of, 306–307, 309; technical
    and side issues, 280–281, 282, 283,
    290–291, 298–299; Truman deci-
    sions, 271, 272; U.K. treaty draft,
    290, 298; Yoshida-MacArthur-Dulles
    meeting, 276. See also San Francisco
    peace conference; Security Treaty
People's Cooperative Party, 108, 163,
    171, 211
People's Republic of China (PRC), 157,
    185, 192, 242, 260, 261, 262, 272,
    275, 287, 295, 306; and Japanese
    peace treaty, 273, 290, 303, 304, 306;
    Sino-Soviet treaty, 242
Perry, Matthew C., 10, 12
Philippines, 14, 15, 16, 80, 81, 92, 199,
    204, 242, 303; and peace treaty, 272,

283–284, 290–291, 304; and Pacific
    pact, 272, 282; reparations claim,
    156, 290–291, 299; and security
    treaty with U.S., 306
POLAD, 37–38, 90, 94, 153, 218, 261,
    310
Poland, 304
Police reform, 39, 165–166, 230, 294,
    313; Kennan's views on, 204–205,
    206; Police Law, 165–166; rivalry of
    G-2 and GS, 165–166
Political parties, 41–42, 91; 1946 plat-
    forms, 42; 1947 platforms, 147–148;
    two-party system, 42, 170, 217
Political prisoners, release of, 49, 50
The Political Reorientation of Japan, 33,
    92, 98
Postal Service and Communications
    Ministry, 176, 177
Postwar population shifts, 12
Potsdam Declaration, 2, 5, 6, 17, 18, 28,
    29–30, 31, 32, 66, 70, 76, 82–83, 99,
    107, 118, 121, 153, 254, 295;
    accepted by Japan, 5; "ignored" by
    Japan, 2
Press, 47; censorship, 47; criticisms of
    SCAP, 47–48; MacArthur's press con-
    ference, 156; "production control"
    and Japanese press, 53; SCAP press
    policy, 47
Priority production, 146–147, 268
Prisoners of war, 11, 152–153, 184–185,
    228, 351n. 7
Production control, 53
Progressive Party, 42, 91, 108, 110, 121,
    143, 148
Pu Yi, Henry, 181
Public Health and Welfare Section, SCAP,
    51
Purges, 30, 34, 75, 82–86, 161; and ACJ,
    152; of communists, 233–235; de-
    purges, 296; education purge, 60, 177,
    237; and emperor's alleged views,
    256–257; Kennan's views on, 203,
    206; and Korean War, 267; 1946
    directives, 83–85, 86; 1947 extension
    of, 125–128; and public opinion, 125;
    Ridgway policy, 296; U.S. policy, 82–
    83, 206; U.S. zone of Germany, 83;
    Yoshida's views on, 126, 235, 296

Quirino, Elpidio, 284

Rearmament, 170–171, 242, 257, 272–
    273, 281; Article 9, 115–117, 281;
    Dulles and, 242, 256–257, 272–273,
    279–280, 297; Japan's initial pro-
    gram, 279–280; Kennan's views, 208,

Rearmament (*continued*)
242; MacArthur's views, 170–171,
242; MacArthur-Yoshida-Dulles
meeting, 276; and Ridgway, 296–
297; U.S. policy, 116–117; Vandenburg resolution, 276–277; Yoshida-
Dulles meetings, 256, 275. *See also*
NPR; Security Treaty
Red Purge. *See* Purges
Reischauer, Edwin O., 218–219; and
Japanese writing, 347n. 32
Religion, 30, 62–64, 167–169; emperor
and Christianity, 62–63, 189; emper-
or's "declaration of humanity," 63–
64; *kami* (god), 64; MacArthur and
Christianity, 62–63; Truman's view
of, 62; and U.S. policy, 62–63
Reminiscences (Douglas MacArthur),
180, 188, 209, 315
Reparations, 30, 67, 70–71; advance
transfers, 155–156; and Draper, 197–
199; and FEC, 155–156, 197, 198,
199; Johnston report, 198; NSC 13/3,
198; MacArthur's views, 71; Pauley
report, 70–71; and peace treaty, 290–
291, 299; resentment of Allies, 199;
Strike report, 198; U.S. policy, 70–71,
198–199; "war booty," 155, 198
Repatriation of Japanese prisoners of war,
152–153, 229; and peace treaty, 298;
SCAP-Soviet agreement, 153; Soviet
data, 350n. 7
Republic of China (ROC): and FEC/ACJ,
28, 151, 153, 199; role in East Asia,
28, 71, 155, 193, 242; and sending
forces to Korea, 261, 287; and treaty
with Japan, 308, 309–310; and war
crimes, 154, 184, 187
Republican Party (U.S.), 157–160, 288
Resistance: by Japanese during war, 13;
during occupation, 34–35, 123–124,
147; by Ishibashi, 127–128; by
Japanese diplomat, 328n. 9
Reverse course, 105–106, 142–143, 199,
207–208, 235, 242–243, 316, 348–
349n. 17
Rhee, Syngman, 253
Ridgway, Matthew B., 286, 287, 288,
289, 290, 291; agenda, 296; and
emperor, 295; and NPR, 296–297;
and end of occupation, 311; and re-
view of occupation laws, 295; and
Yoshida, 293, 295, 296, 297, 311
Rizzo, Frank, 294
Rockefeller, John D., III, 272
Röling, Bert V. A., 182, 187
Romaji (Roman alphabet), 62, 133

Roosevelt, Franklin D.: and MacArthur,
12, 15, 160, 174, 306; and Okinawa,
359n. 27
Roxas, Manuel, 168
Royall, Kenneth C., 164, 183, 197, 247
Rusk, Dean, 310
Rutledge, Wiley, 81
Ryukyu Islands, 12, 107, 271, 277, 280,
303, 343–344n. 2. *See also* Okinawa

Saionji Kimmochi, 26
San Francisco peace conference, 300–
306; attendance, 302; Japanese delegation, 300–301; and MacArthur,
301; proceedings and signatories,
302–304; and San Francisco system,
306; security treaty, 305–306
Sansom, George, 27, 31, 90, 132; and
emperor, 27, 73
Sasakawa Ryōichi, 184
Satō Eisaku, 217
Satō Tatsuō, 101
SCAP, 19, 35–38, 87–88; control of
leftist organizations, 232; and non-
use of formal directives, 88, 153; and
Japanese noncooperation, 123–124;
and Koreans in Japan, 238–239; and
labor movement, 236; leftists in, 124–
125, 203; military units, 35–37; organization, 35–37; SCAPINs, 35, 83–
84, 109; staff sections, 35. *See also*
MacArthur, Douglas
Schacht, Hjalmar, 56, 180
School Education Law, 133–134
Sebald, William J., 37, 153, 209, 218,
261, 277, 301, 303; and MacArthur's
dismissal, 286–287, 290; on Yoshida-
Dulles meetings, 256, 275; on Yoshida
and MacArthur, 293, 294, 295,
329n. 21
Security treaty: administrative agreement,
310–311; Ashida memo, 250; clause
on internal disturbances in Japan,
300; confusion of military with police,
263–264; Dulles's redraft, 281; early
Japanese views, 248; Far East clause,
299–300; Ikeda-Dodge meeting in
Washington, 249–250; Ikeda memo,
249–250; Japan's "initial rearmament program" of 1951, 279–280;
MacArthur on need for U.S. bases in
Japan, 254–255; negotiating break-
through, 277–280; ratification, 306–
307, 309; secrecy of agreement, 300;
security as key issue, 247; significance of, 306; signing ceremony, 305;
title, 299; Yoshida staff security plans,